Echoes of the Past, Epi

Stone Tile Cruz Stone
Fireplaces
909 335-6060
St Orlando
1033 Orlando
Goodyear
93374

밤을 지키는 집의- '92 가을 전현

Echoes of the Past, Epics of Dissent

A South Korean Social Movement

Nancy Abelmann

UNIVERSITY OF CALIFORNIA PRESS
Berkeley   Los Angeles   London

University of California Press
Berkeley and Los Angeles, California

University of California Press
London, England

Copyright © 1996 by The Regents of the University of California

Library of Congress Cataloging-in-Publication Data

Abelmann, Nancy.
  Echoes of the past, epics of dissent : a South Korean social
movement / Nancy Abelmann.
    p.   cm.
  Includes bibliographical references (p.   ) and index.
    ISBN 0-520-08590-6 (cloth : alk. paper).—ISBN 0-520-20418-2
(pbk. : alk. paper)
    1. Social movements—Korea (South)—Case studies.   2. Tenant
farmers—Korea (south)—Political activity.   3. Land tenure—Korea
(South)   4. Social movements.   I. Title.
HN730.5.A8A24   1996
303.48'4—dc20   95-35055
                                                                        CIP

Printed in the United States of America

1 2 3 4 5 6 7 8 9

In Memory of Murakami Tamotsu

Scenes which make vital changes in our neighbors' lot are but the background of our own, yes, like a particular aspect of the field and the trees, they become associated for us with the epochs of our own history, and make part of that unity which lies in the selection of our keenest consciousness.

GEORGE ELIOT, *MIDDLEMARCH*

CONTENTS

ILLUSTRATIONS

Frontispiece: Painting by Kim Chŏng-hŏn, "Pap ŭl chik'inŭn Kim-ssi" (Mr. Kim Who Protects the Rice)

MAPS

FIGURES

PLATES following page 138

ACKNOWLEDGMENTS

I was told several times during my fieldwork that I was blessed with *saram-bok*, or human luck. As I think back on this book's path, which spans my graduate school and early professional years, it is one of faithful friends; encouraging teachers, colleagues, and students; and thousands of small and large kindnesses that I met in the field—a path of immense sarambok. It is a pleasure to name some of the many who contributed to this good fortune.

During graduate school, the community of South Korean immigrants and graduate students in Berkeley, California, and beyond brought me several friends who introduced their homeland to me with enormous care. They include Soon-kyoung *Cho,* Chungmoo *Choi,* Keun *Lee,* Heh-Rahn *Park,* Jung-sun *Park,* Sun Joo *Yoon,* and Taek-Lim *Yoon.* I remain awed at how patiently each one of them bore my ignorance. Over the years, the community of scholars of South Korea with whom I have enjoyed wonderful dialogue has expanded to include other friends: Yunshik *Chang,* Byung-Ho *Chung,* Richard Grinker, Do Hyun *Han,* Roger Janelli, Laurel Kendall, Seung-Kyung *Kim,* Choong Soon *Kim,* Eun-Shil *Kim,* Jim Kim, Seong Nae *Kim,* Laura Nelson, Pak Myŏng-gyu, Pak Pu-jin, John Seel, Jim Thomas, and Eunhee Kim *Yi.*

My work in South Korea was enriched by assistants who painstakingly engaged in the near-impossible task of aiding in the "translation" of worlds. I am indebted to them for their patience, honesty, and hard work. I can only search for words to thank Jinhon *Oh,* with whom I look forward to lifelong friendship. Yi So-yŏng and Kim Sun-hŭi were also challenging and helpful colleagues in the field. I was assisted in conducting household surveys by a number of scholars and students whose passionate engagement was inspiring: An Ŭn-suk, Chŏng Ŭn-hŭi, Han Do Hyun, Kim Chŏng-ch'ae, Pae Ŭn-gyŏng, Sŏ Suk-hyŏn, Yi Che-hun, and Yu Hŭi. In the United States I benefited from the kind assistance of several people in working with Korean texts: Ha Sŏk-ku, June Lee, Soo-Jung *Lee,* Seungsook *Mun,* Jackie Park, Mrs. Suh, Jae-Jung *Suh,* Yi Sang-ryong and Chong-Ae *Yun.*

I am grateful for the generous help of several academics in South Korea. Professor Pak Myŏng-gyu was an unfailing supporter of this research and welcomed my questions during a number of breaks from the field; I was particularly fortunate that he was living in Cambridge, Massachusetts, when I was writing my dissertation there. I would also like to thank Professors Chang Sang-hwan, Cho Uhn, Cho Haejoang, Choi Chun-sŏk, Kim Kwang-ŏk, Yi Mun-ung, and Yi U-jae. Professor Cho Haejoang's active mind and warm spirit have been extremely important in my encounter with South Korea.

A number of households in South Korea have welcomed and cared for me over the years. These include the homes of Cho Yŏng-ja and Pak Mu-sŏng, Kim Yŏng-ae and Yi Chu-sŏp, Chŏng To-yŏng and Yi Ki-sŏp (and my dear friend Yi So-yŏn), Kim Yŏng-ja and Yun Hyŏn-ok, the father and late mother of Taek-Lim *Yoon,* Choi Ch'un-ja and Kim In-guk (and their son Kim Tong-sŏp, one of the most joyous people I have ever known), Kwŏn Tu-ri and Pak Su-ho, Ch'a Sun-i and Kim Pong-du, and Sin Hyo-ch'ŏl and O Se-yŏng. The generosity and empathy of the mothers of these households will inspire me throughout my life.

I am grateful to many farmers, students, and activists I met in the field. I will only name a few whose companionship is the heart of this book: Kang Ki-jŏng, Kilmaji-*taek,* Kim Ik-sŏng, the Mun family, Pak Pae-gu, Pak Sang-gyu, Pak Sŏng-ja, Yi Hae-sam, Yi Sang-ch'ŏl and family, Yi Yong-sŏk and Yu Kap-sang. Let me also extend my gratitude to all of the residents of Kung-san and Kŭmp'yŏng villages. I am also thankful to family and friends who visited me in the field: Arthur Abelmann and Rena Abelmann, Barbara Brown, and Dori Dominis.

I would like to extend deep appreciation to the members of my dissertation committee, Robert Bellah, Laurel Kendall, Paul Rabinow, and my adviser, Nelson Graburn. Nelson's open-minded, kind directorship is a model I continue to aspire to. Laurel Kendall's kindness and expertise guided me throughout fieldwork and dissertation writing. At Harvard University, I was fortunate to receive the excellent advice of Professors Carter Eckert, Ezra Vogel, and Edward Wagner.

I am grateful for a group of friends from the anthropology department at the University of California, Berkeley, whose letters and phone calls were the staple of my graduate school years. They include Joe Alter, Jeanne

Bergman, Nicole Constable, Cecilia Demello, Charlene Hunter, Christopher Keener, Ondina Fachel Leal, Molly Lee, Sarah Murray, Linda-Anne Rebhun, and Lesley Sharp. Above all, I thank them for their wonderful correspondence in the field and their enduring friendships. Charlene, Christopher, Lesley, Nicole, and Molly ministered to many of the logistics of my dissertation and degree. I am also grateful to several students ahead of me in graduate school who served as mentors: Nancy Lutz, Richard Parker, and Jackie Urla. Beyond the anthropology department a number of people enriched those years: Ann-Catherine Åquist, Barbara Brown, Judson Feder, Susan Kim, Jack Lee, Saul Perlmutter, and Farshid Zarbakhsh.

I completed the dissertation among childhood friends and family and among new friends. I am grateful to Chris Astondoa, Doyung *Choi*, Tina Choi, Paul Craig, Eve Epstein, Lisa Faber, Doug Gallager, Brant Helf, Jayasinhji Bhopa Jhala, Jim Kim, Andy Mapel, Miho Matsugu, Raquel Pinderhughes, Suketu Sanghvi, Ann Saphir, Chikako Sasaki, Cara Seiderman, John Seel, Philip Setel, Susan Shoobe, Kerry Smith, Frank Tortorella, Alan Wachman, Vince Yotsukura, and Min-su *Yun*. Many thanks to Cara, Dori, Doug, and Kerry for keeping me laughing and swimming.

The Departments of Anthropology and East Asian Languages and Cultures at the University of Illinois at Urbana-Champaign have provided a congenial intellectual home for me. The university has been extremely generous in providing release time, research assistance, and a wonderful scholarly community. I would also like to acknowledge the support I received from the Fulbright Commission.

In Urbana-Champaign, Illinois, I am grateful for the friendship and intellectual stimulus of many wonderful colleagues and students, among them, Bill Kelleher, Ramona Curry, Moshe and Rodi Farjoun, Alma Gottlieb, JaHyun Haboush, Tom Havens, Hu Ying, Kathleen McHugh, Cynthia Peterson, Diego Quiroga, Patricia Sandler, Ron Toby, Karen Winter-Nelson, Yi Sang-ryong, and Yi Sang-suk.

Many people have been kind enough to read, comment on, and edit the manuscript in full. How does one begin to thank them? They are Walter Abelmann, Marsha Brofka, Bruce Cumings, Ann Dean, Richard Grinker, Do Hyun *Han*, Judith Hopping, Roger Janelli, Eunhee Kim *Yi*, Soo-Jung *Lee*, John Lie, Kathy Litherland, Rebecca Matthews, Laura Nelson, Pak Myŏng-gyu, Sang Ah *Park*, Ann Saphir, Cara Seiderman, Laura Smith, and Jesook *Song*. So-Min *Chong*, Eun Hui *Ryo*, Carlo Spindel, and Nan Volinsky lent their kind attention to parts of the manuscript. I am particularly grateful to Eun Hui, Jesook, Kathy, Laura S., Marsha, and Soo-Jung for their technical and research assistance. I am also indebted to the assistance of Chris Astondoa, Shari Eide, Bernardo Feliciano, Lisa Faber, Amanda Grunden, Jim Kim, Paek Uk-in, Philip Setel, and Kwang-kyoon *Yeo*. Richard

Freeman was helpful in the preparation of the photographs. The charts
and maps for this book were meticulously prepared by Jane Domier. I am
very appreciative of Kim Chŏng-hŏn's permission to reproduce his artwork
in this book.

In the often painful final stage of this book several friends have been
emotional mainstays: Ruth Abelmann, Nicole Constable, Eve Epstein, Judith Hopping, Hu Ying, Bill Kelleher, Jack Lee, Soo-Jung *Lee,* John Lie,
Kathleen McHugh, Eun Hui *Ryo,* Patricia Sandler, Cara Seiderman, and
Jesook *Song.*

At the University of California Press, I am grateful for the kind guidance
of Stan Holwitz from beginning to end. I would also like to thank Michelle
Nordon for her careful management of the manuscript and Sheila Berg
for her painstaking copyediting.

My parents, Rena and Walter Abelmann, have long "read" this book and
its daily inscriptions on me. Their selfless and seamless empathy is awe-
some; they are the core of my sarambok. Ruth Abelmann and Woody
Phelps and their children, Graham and Molly, have often provided a retreat for writing and always a warm respite. I would also like to thank members of the Abelmann family, Amanda, Arthur, Minky, Ronald and Jeryl,
and Karen Gross, Steven and Zachary Cooper, Julie and Henry Landau,
Stanley White, and Barbara Wreschner. I am especially grateful to a family
that has cared for me lovingly throughout my post-teenage life—the Mura-
kamis, Tamie, Junko, Mutsumi, and Noboru. As I think back on this book's
story, I mourn the untimely deaths of four people whose love of humanity
and passion for learning inspired me: Moriya Takeshi, Murakami Tamotsu,
Bernard Seiderman, and Yi Ch'an-u.

Finally, I would not have finished this book without the nudging, nour-
ishment, and nurturing of John Lie.

CHAPTER ONE

Ethnography and Social Movements

No story is like a wheeled vehicle whose contact with the road is continuous. Stories walk, like animals or men. And their steps are not only between narrated events but between each sentence, sometimes each word. Every step is a stride over something not said.

JOHN BERGER (1982: 284–285)

This book is an ethnography of a South Korean social movement. The Koch'ang Tenant Farmers Movement was formed in the mid-1980s and peaked from August 12 to September 13, 1987, when over two hundred tenant farmers from sixteen villages in Koch'ang, a county in southwestern North Chŏlla Province, occupied the Seoul headquarters of their landlord company, the Samyang Corporation. The protesters demanded that the corporation distribute its 291-hectare Haeri Estate to its tenants. The Haeri Estate dates to the Japanese colonial period, when the Kim family of Koch'ang (the founders and owners of Samyang)—considered by some to be Japanese collaborators—undertook a large-scale land reclamation project. Despite the 1949 land reform, the farmlands of the Haeri Estate remained in the hands of the Kim family.

The movement began with local rumblings: demonstrations on the banks of an irrigation reservoir and at the gates of Samyang's local land management office, refusals to remit rent, struggles with local officials and police, and court hearings. In the weeks before the Seoul protest, two hundred university students from Seoul dispersed throughout the tenant farmer villages to politicize farmers and to experience the countryside. On their arrival in Seoul, these farmers established a daily routine of protest that included street demonstrations, negotiation sessions with the corporation, and appeals to various institutions. As the movement escalated, protest activities were suppressed by military and police units. Finally, eight negotiation sessions between farmers and corporate representatives in Seoul resulted in a purchase agreement in August 1987, and by January 1988, most farmers had purchased their tenant plots. The purchase settlement was, however, a radical departure from the original goal of the movement: a remittance of the land with no payment. Although most farmers agreed to these final arrangements, the course of the movement was marked by considerable internal dissension.

This chapter begins with a brief journey through the contemporary theories of social movements. I explore what sort of ethnography emerges from a consideration of social movements in their discursive and dialogic contexts, beyond "things" with clear-cut causes and effects. Because social movements are always processes, neither bounded nor easily defined, my ethnography considers the Koch'ang Tenant Farmers Movement's larger discursive contexts, including contemporary historical consciousness and nationalism. After a brief theoretical foray, I begin the larger project of ethnographically, temporally, and narratively contextualizing a social movement.

THEORIZING SOCIAL MOVEMENTS, NEW AND OLD

Where, in the long-standing and dense engagement with social movements, shall I begin my discussion of local rumblings in a South Korean hinterland? The contemporary debate on the "new social movements" (NSMs) provides a helpful point of departure. Commentators across the disciplines, from sociology and political science to anthropology and philosophy, have set out to characterize and to clarify new social movements. Broadly, they refer to activism that is particular to contemporary capitalist democracy. Most notably, NSMs do not arise from long-standing class struggles that pit capital and labor against each other. Rather, such activism extends beyond the "privileged revolutionary subject" that Stuart Hall (1988: 169) portrays and parodies.

> Socialist Man, with one mind, one set of interests, one project, is dead. And good riddance. Who needs "him" now, with his investment in a particular historical period, with "his" particular sense of masculinity, shoring "his" identity up in a particular set of familial relations, a particular kind of sexual identity? Who needs "him" as the singular identity through which the great diversity of human beings and ethnic cultures in our world must enter the twenty-first century? This "he" is dead: finished.

For the Italian social movement theorist Alberto Melucci (1985: 809), it is precisely such "epic representation" of social movements as "tragic figures" that is out of step with the contemporary order and its activisms. In the wake of this "socialist man" new activisms are born with an expanded sense of politics and power (Hall 1988: 167). They take place in new political spaces, employ new political tactics, and mobilize previously unheard-of networks. Arturo Escobar and Sonia E. Alvarez (1992b: 2, 3) summarize these dynamics: "The catchall concept of NSMs lumped ecclesiastical base communities and urban protest of various kinds together with ethnic movements and primarily middle-class ecology, feminist, and gay liberation movements. . . . In the new situation, a multiplicity of social actors establish their presence and spheres of autonomy in a fragmented social and political space."

The scholarship on NSMs proceeds from fundamental reconceptualizations of power. Following Michel Foucault (1982), "power" operates not only by obvious repression or through visible institutions but also and even more effectively through the production of human subjectivities through the spaces and grammar of everyday life (see also Mitchell 1988). New social movements, then, contest the exercise of power through new sites and subjectivities that are particular to postindustrial capitalism (Melucci 1985: 791). In short, new social movement theory both situates activism in its larger political and economic contexts and examines, on the ground, its networks and strategies.

How are these discussions relevant to the story of farmers' land struggle in South Korea, a movement that is in many senses "old" for its historically recognizable actors, tenant peasants,[1] landlords, capitalists, and the state? Quite simply, the relevance lies in appreciating the salience of this theory for movements that do not wholly qualify as "new." In this vein, some have even asked, "What is so new about the new social movements?" either to trivialize the new social movement literature or to suggest the relevance of its theoretical innovations for "old" social movements (Epstein 1990; Plotke 1990). In the spirit of the latter motivation, we can query whether this theory can make sense of movements produced and documented in other moments, through other social scientific imaginations. It is possible to recognize new forms of activism and to take up the theorizing in their very name as we consider both new and old activisms.

After discussing several new social movement theorists, I will, by way of ethnographic and analytical strategy, introduce how this ethnography "defines" social movements. Best understood as processes rather than as things, social movements are emergent phenomena that are never entirely prefigured or scripted by their agendas, and consequently, they are constituted in particular historical moments and on particular discursive terrains. Thus social movement theorizing is nothing short of theorizing society itself. As discursive phenomena, social movements are always "cultural" in their contests. The understanding of discourse that undergirds these perspectives follows Foucault's (1972: 49) explication that discourses are "practices that systematically form the objects of which they speak." For Chantal Mouffe (1988: 104), "discursive" refers not only to "speech and writing, but also to a series of social practices" such that "discourse is not just a question of ideas." Mouffe (1988: 90) writes against a "conception of economy as a world of objects and relations that exist prior to any ideological and political conditions of existence."[2]

Melucci has articulated a processual, emergent approach to social movements. Against the theatrical imaginary in which social movements are characters or "subjects endowed with an essence and a purpose within a *pièce* whose finale is knowable," he argues that social movements operate as signs "in the sense that they translate their action into symbolic challenges that upset the dominant cultural codes" (1988: 245, 249). He asserts that we must challenge the "ontological assumption that the actor [the social movement] exists" and hence that we must explain "how that empirical unit which can be observed and called a 'movement' comes to be formed" (1988: 246–247). In this theoretical intervention, he challenges definitional tendencies to sketch the contours of social movements as phenomena that are already constituted and scripted. In challenging ontological assumptions, however, he never loses the empirical reality of social movements and their "sets of relationships." Movements do not have "deep minds," but rather *"movement networks* or *movement areas"* (Melucci 1985: 793)—"the network of groups and individuals sharing a conflictual culture and collective identity" (1985: 798–799).

In a similar vein, Escobar writes of the "autopoetic character of social movements" (1992*b:* 44). "[Social movements] produce themselves and the larger social order through their own organizing processes (sets of relations or articulations among key elements)" (1992*b:* 45). He suggests a dialogic relationship between social movements and the "larger social order." He explains that observers of social movements "characterize these interactions between movements and environment in terms of 'politics,' 'economic conditions,' and the like" (1992*b:* 45), such that we can mistakenly think that such categories produce the movement. The notion of autopoesis, however, challenges a naturalized "field of categories" (1992*b:* 45).

Escobar demands that we historicize this field of categories through which social movements have been examined and that we consider social movements' self-producing or self-organizing features. Thus he questions the ontological contours of social movements. This is not to say that they do not comprise real organizations and mobilize real struggles, but that received categories have prefigured phenomena that are, in fact, processual and dialogic. Building on Melucci's discussion of the "submerged reality" of social movements, Escobar explains that theorizing which does not take up a processual approach "make[s] analytically invisible a crucial network of relationships that underlie collective action before, during and after the events" (1992*a:* 73). This "latent aspect of movements," he continues, is "no less real because it is less readily observable empirically" (1992*a:* 73). Escobar and Melucci are mindful that social movements have been ontologically, historically, and socially constructed from particular theoretical venues.

The French social theorist Alain Touraine, whose writings have been central to the understanding of contemporary social movements, takes up the third point—the historical and discursive particularity of social movements. Touraine's definition of social movements turns on his conception of historicity: "A social movement is the action, both culturally oriented and socially conflictual, of a social class defined by its position of domination or dependency in the mode of appropriation of historicity, of the cultural models of investment, knowledge, and morality, toward which the social movement is itself oriented" (1988: 68). Like Escobar, Touraine considers historicity as the social capacity to produce the models by which society operates and as "the set of cultural, cognitive, economic, and ethical models by means of which a collectivity sets up relations with its environment" (1988: 40). Like Melucci, Touraine believes that a social movement does not exist independent of its "environment" or "society" but is itself part of the ongoing cultural struggles that *are* the fabric of society: "Social life is not ordered by natural or historical laws but by the action of those who fight and negotiate in order to endow the cultural orientations they valorize with a firm social form" (1988: 18). "Society" and "social movements" are thus dialectically produced. Touraine (1988: 66) employs "social movement" to describe *particular* activisms with *particular* levels of historicity or "cultural orientations." They occur "only if actors are capable of rising above mere claims and even above political negotiations in order to acknowledge, and to assert, themselves as producers rather than consumers of social situations, as capable of questioning social situations rather than merely responding to them" (1988: 11). He thus reserves social movements for particular moments of historical "development" and consciousness.

Escobar, however, offers an insightful criticism of Touraine's historicity as one in which "only post-industrial society has achieved the 'highest level of historicity,' namely that of self-production" (1992b: 37). He charges that this formulation is Eurocentric because "the Third World is represented as lacking historical agency" and argues that we need to consider the non-Western metaphors, myths, and resistances that comprise other historicities (Escobar 1992b: 37). We can respond to this critique by expanding Touraine's notion of struggles over historicity. Blurring the epistemic shifts on which Touraine's social movement theory is grounded allows us to query the consciousness through which societies produce themselves beyond North American and European postindustrial society.

It is tempting to turn to the "real movement" that one finds in the field: the stream of real actions and strategies apart from such theorizing. To follow this path, however, is to assume that in their own historical and geographic settings, social movements can somehow be isolated from their discursive production, and to render them again as discrete "things." I take up Touraine's perspective that abstractions of social movements are already part of their production, rather than after-the-fact reconstructions of already constituted wholes. In this sense I am drawn to Touraine's notion of social movements as struggles over historicity, but I am also in agreement with Escobar's corrective that historicities are multiple and that they emerge in heterogeneous idioms and metaphors in different historical moments and cultural milieus. I also concur with Orin Starn's (1992: 93) warning that in taking up such a constructivist position, there is no need to jettison "traditional" concerns with the origins and causes of movements or with the "quite elemental matters of scarcity and survival that drive people to act."

The sociologist Pierre Bourdieu's (1990: 130) notion of "spontaneous sociology" as "the spontaneous visions of the social world" is also helpful for conceptualizing social movements. Such sociologies are in no way incidental; rather, Bourdieu (1990: 130) argues that they are not only "part of social reality," but can also "acquire an altogether real constructive power." If we pay attention to the moments and metaphors of the construction of social movements, and to their spontaneous sociology, how are we to write their ethnographies? As we reconceptualize our analyses, we transform the contents and contours of our fieldwork ventures and of our ethnographies (Clifford and Marcus 1986).[3]

These framings of social movements have implications for the nature of the tasks and the horizons of the contexts that ethnographers should embrace. For example, the photo essays of John Berger and Jean Mohr (1982) narrate lives beyond the strictly autobiographical or narrowly contextual. Berger and Mohr introduce a photo sequence on a French peasant woman's life with the following statement: "The photographs of this sequence are not intended to be a documentary. That is to say they do not *document* the woman's life—not even her subjective life. There are photographs included of moments and scenes which she could never have witnessed" (1982: 134).[4] These photos trace beyond the face-to-face and even to cities she would never have seen; they evoke the reaches to which a movement, or a life, can extend. If we are to historicize the social movements we study, we need to first situate them discursively—to understand the reigning social imaginaries on social movements and activisms, their vocabularies, their grammars, their aesthetics, and their historical consciousnesses.

In examining the Koch'ang Tenant Farmers Movement, we need to ask how this movement has been imagined and to pay attention to the constitutive processes that comprise it, even as it often resembles a finished product. We must explore the submerged social networks from which the movement emerged and take up the political contexts that have produced the subjectivities—the actors of the movement. Although social movements need not be subsumed by fixed social parameters that explain their "why," or by any limited sense of resources to explain their "how" (Alvarez and Escobar 1992: 319), we should not abandon the "why" and "how" of movements in their more material senses. This ethnography takes up these tasks and turns on these contexts.

THE CONTEXTS AT HAND: BOOK GEOGRAPHY

In the spirit of new social movement theory, I consider this book an ethnography of a South Korean social movement and an exploration of popular narratives on Korean history, South Korean nationalisms, and postcolonial discourse. The movement was produced across multiple sites and subjectivities and in concert with heterogeneous social discourses and narrative practices. The reader should be mindful that although I call this an ethnography of a social movement and implicitly sketch a number of boundaries that objectify it, in the final analysis this work is but a path across the movement's terrain, bounded or limited as is all ethnography. This movement is difficult to reproduce; consequently, the book geography is jagged and unruly, as it jumps among vistas near and far and touches on an array of social discourses. I know, however, that my readers will look for "the story"—some constellation of events that follow one after the other and seem to mark a beginning and an end: Appendix 1 answers this call. I hope that the shifts and turns of this book and the discoveries made while reading along will juggle the reader's understandings of the movement, and in so doing shed light on both the apperception and the production of social movements generally.

Let me outline how this book's chapters meander along the ethnographic path of the Koch'ang Tenant Farmers Movement. From the vantage point of the mid-1990s, the movement was a *minjung* movement—literally, a "people's" movement. *Minjung,* however, is much more than a simple adjective or noun; over the 1970s and through the 1980s in South Korea, minjung was both a political prism and the regnant narrative of dissent. In chapter 2, I examine this minjung discourse, arguing that memory and mobilization are the cornerstones of its narrative. Through these discussions, I attempt to historicize the moment of my fieldwork, which has by now been framed as a watershed in post-Liberation (post-1945) South Korean history. Throughout this book, the past figures as a terrain that is variously periodized and interpreted; indeed, the movement itself was a struggle over the historical interpretation of matters both mammoth and minute.

Chapter 3 takes the reader to the protest's climax: the month of occupation in Seoul. Here I sketch the micro-workings of protest—from food preparation to demonstration antics—not to portray platforms or positions, but to illuminate the production of the movement.

Backtracking from this protest venue, chapter 4 turns to the historical contest that produced the movement in its various guises. Here I juxtapose corporate histories and farmer accounts of the history at issue in the land struggle. Through the colonial, land reform, and Korean War eras, nation and class emerge as pivotal discourses driving the dissension.

Chapter 5 builds from these discussions of class and nation by returning to the protest month in Seoul, this time to the backstage farmer–corporate negotiation sessions. These discussions turn on the postcolonial discourse of modernity, the legitimacy of the bourgeoisie, and the nature of South Korean capitalism. Here I take up political, popular, and scholarly discourses on culture and the nation to further contextualize the movement. In the course of these farmer–corporate dialogues, the farmers split, and the seeming unities of the movement's front-stage view were shattered.

Chapter 6 returns to the oppositional discourses and institutions in which the Koch'ang movement was situated. Here I introduce the movement before summer 1987 and follow it after the Seoul protest. I examine these developments amid the discussions and mediations between farmers and the so-called external forces, including organizers and students.

In chapter 7, I turn from these external forces to the local site of the movement's production: the villages in Koch'ang County. There, I introduce two villages and profile their histories, land relations, and stratifications in order to sketch patterns of movement participation. I offer these sketches, not to document autonomous variables that explain participation, but as another vital element of the movement story.

From these rural nodes, chapter 8 turns to a general analysis of farmer mobilization in post-Liberation South Korea. I survey the history of the state's intervention in the agricultural sector and the history of organized farmers' movements and daily resistance. I review farmer subjectivities through the state's institutions and its ideological programs, and I attempt to situate the Koch'ang movement in this history, amid these subjectivities.

The concluding chapter considers transformations in social activism from the 1980s to the 1990s. I examine the diverse ways in which 1980s activism is being recollected and the current climate of dissent. These discussions take up the 1990s waning of the notion of minjung.

I will now proceed with the route through which I came to the Koch'ang Tenant Farmers Movement. The paths I describe here are not the roads that wind their way from Seoul to the Koch'ang villages—I will travel those paths in subsequent chapters—but, rather, the path of inquiry, beginning in my graduate student days in Berkeley, California. I then turn to the ways in which the very moment of my fieldwork was becoming historicized in popular and activist narratives and end this chapter with a brief visit to fictional and ethnographic accounts of land. Through these narratives, I hope that the reader will realize that stories about rice paddies can reveal charged histories and passionate identities.

FINDING THE FIELD

How was I set—discursively and dialogically—to chance upon this field project? The dialogic nature of anthropological fieldwork has become commonsensical in anthropology. I underscore it here because of the many and various dialogues in which my fieldwork was suspended: the dialogues that brought me to the field site, the dialogues with locals (and in turn the metadialogues with nonlocals, as I tried to make sense of these), and, finally, the dialogues that emerged from the considerable attention my fieldwork venue attracted.

I am particularly fond of E. Valentine Daniel's (1984) formulations about dialogue in anthropology. In writing about Tamil identity, he asserts that the only Tamil identities that his pen can render are those fashioned in dialogue with him. This caveat aside, he proceeds with great industry to examine Tamil identity; his is a reflexive gaze that does not paralyze, but instead clears space. In this spirit, I will backtrack along my fieldwork path so that I can forge ahead with the ethnography.

My anthropological encounters with South Korea began at the University of California in 1983 among South Korean *yuhaksaeng*[5] (students abroad) where discussions about Korean history were highly politicized and passionate. From the outset, Korean history was presented to me as a debate, and I was introduced to the complex, spiraling web of revisionist historiography in which each revision is in turn successively refashioned. Through these discussions, I became acquainted with the pace, urgency, and passion of South Korean historical discourse and, correspondingly, of South Korean political activity in the sense that "all political activity is intrinsically a process of historical argument and definition," as the Popular Memory Group (1982: 213) has insisted:

> All political programmes involve some construction of the past as well as the future, and these processes go on every day, often outrunning, especially in terms of period, the preoccupations of historians. Political domination involves historical definition. History—in particular popular memory—is at stake in the constant struggle for hegemony. The relation between history and politics, like the relation between past and present, is, therefore, an *internal* one: it is about the politics of history and the historical dimensions of politics.

My first field site in South Korea was Seoul's P'agoda Kongwŏn (P'agoda Park),[6] a place of ongoing historical engagement. It was at P'agoda Park that the reading of the 1919 March First Movement's declaration of independence marked the start of the largest nationwide anticolonial uprising during the Japanese colonial era (1910–1945). Widely pictured in and on the cover of school textbooks, the park is an inherently ironic site because the thirty-three signers of the March First Movement declaration were absent at the reading of the declaration, having retreated to a nearby restaurant. For many South Koreans, these signers of the declaration (primarily representatives of indigenous and foreign faiths) are notorious for their later collaboration with the Japanese.

For one month I went to the park daily, spending time among elderly Koreans (mostly men) for whom the park was their daytime social world. There, surrounded by memories of the colonial period—and some of 1919—I found a cacophony of perspectives on the March First Movement amid the official commemorative signs, sculptures, and paintings. The park was circumscribed by relief sculptures representing sites of the March First Movement to highlight brilliant Korean resistance and cruel Japanese suppression. The pagoda at the park's center, a fifteenth-century fixture, is entirely covered with carvings; some parkgoers interpreted these etchings as narratives that recalled the past *and* foretold the future. One daily frequenter of the park, the so-called P'agoda paksa (Dr. P'agoda), would wind his way through the etchings, narrating to a crowd both early and modern Korean history and even the vicissitudes of the current Korean situation. The park was a site for observing what the Popular Memory Group (1982: 211) calls "the relation of dominant historical representation and subordinated private experience." Throughout the post-Liberation era, the park has been variously signified in Seoul's urban geography. In accordance with various regimes of commemorative politics, the park's walls have been both raised and razed, alternately closing it to the city and opening it to welcome urban residents. Such resignification continued into the 1990s when the park was renamed the T'apkol Kongwŏn (T'apkol Park), indigenizing the name to mean "a park with a pagoda."

I was particularly fascinated to find that people in both of these enclaves—Berkeley and P'agoda Park—evoked the notion of the Korean minjung in their self-consciously revisionist historical narratives and memories. In the 1980s in South Korea, "minjung," as a descriptive term, was attached to literary, dramatic, dance, musical, historical, and political practices. In this book, I explore this concept as a praxis and a perspective that delineated an anti-imperialist, antielite popular nationalism. During the time of my fieldwork, 1987 to 1988, a minjung aesthetic characterized the practice and culture of dissent. The community of organizers engaged in this movement—student and farmer activists—employed minjung historiography and sensibilities. This minjung trope was central to farmers' movements because farmers and farmer culture were among its most important referents. The minjung imaginary surfaced in well-publicized historical debates, popular historical novels, and even in the drama of a farmer protest.

Through my experiences in P'agoda Park, I became interested in this evocation of minjung and in the theory and practice of an oppositional or counterhegemonic nationalism. I wanted to examine a situation in which minjung was a practice. At both Berkeley and P'agoda Park, however, it was hard for me to situate the individuals and discourses I encountered. Most of all, from these age and class enclaves—in Berkeley, largely upper-middle- or upper-class men in their twenties, and in P'agoda Park, primarily educated men in their sixties, seventies, and eighties—I could not gather the more general life and implications of these historical debates and subjectivities. Beyond this expatriate community in Berkeley and this Seoul enclave, I meandered my way to tenant farmers in a peripheral region—North Chŏlla Province. On this path I encountered yet more dialogues.

I learned of the Koch'ang conflict from professors at North Chŏlla University, a provincial national university, and decided to begin a field study in one of its tenant villages. The professors who were most interested in the Koch'ang events were members of a group producing the journal *Nammin* (Southern People) that focused largely on local cultural practices including folk art, dance, drama, and storytelling. Gathered from different disciplines, provinces, and workplaces, the members were committed to a celebration of North Chŏlla's dissident history and culture. The province had particular meaning for them because the Chŏlla provinces (North and South) are known for antistate and radical pasts, though North Chŏlla is less heralded in this regard than South Chŏlla.[7] *Nammin* (vol. 3, 1989) would later devote almost an entire issue to the Koch'ang protest story. I accompanied several members of this group as they attended the revival of a folk festival in a mountainous hinterland. Many of these scholars had been exiled to South Korea's periphery by escalating academic competition. Their interest in local peoples and cultures, in some sense an accommodation to their employment destinies, was in keeping with the minjung imagination.[8]

I decided to conduct my fieldwork in the Samyang villages in Koch'ang County because the historical matters that were implicated in the land struggle there—which was then in its early stages—echoed the major historiographical debates in South Korea. They included the issues of wealth, power, and collaboration with the Japanese during the colonial period; peasant struggle and the Left in the immediate post-Liberation era; the 1949 land reform and the rule of the U.S. military government; land, ideology, and the Korean War; and landownership, retenantization, and differential development between the agricultural and industrial sectors in the post–Korean War period. I was drawn to the Koch'ang movement as an illuminating window on postcolonial discursive practice. Because its participants were easily imagined by outsiders to be quintessential min-jung, the movement evoked various national and historical images. Con-versely, its participants had vivid images of the South Korean elites. The meeting of these images was central to the course of the movement.

My fieldwork was conducted across dialogues of revisionism in another sense as well because I did most of my fieldwork with the assistance of three women who were themselves wrestling with revisionism in various ways.[9] One was an undergraduate anthropology major who took time off from school to come to the field with me. Another was an unemployed history graduate who was wavering about her relationship to social activism. The third was a recent college graduate who had been committed to social activ-ism both during and after college. She had spent a period in a rural village with the aim of organizing farmers but abandoned that course in favor of urban activism. I met her through the Koch'ang movement, and she even-tually agreed to work with me because of her own personal interest in the Koch'ang story; at the time, she contemplated writing a novel on the strug-gle. The latter two assistants had vested interests in understanding the rural dissent in Koch'ang in particular historical narratives. Thus the politics and subjectivities of representation were salient throughout my fieldwork. For these women, the farmers of Koch'ang were Others fabricated by rapid urbanization and industrialization. Speaking in Korean, I reviewed each interview encounter with these assistants, comparing our understandings of the interview texts and subtexts. In the English versions that became the field notes that I cite in this work, I often added parenthetical comments on the divergences of our readings and reactions.[10] As I reviewed my field notes, these parenthetical jottings allowed me to recall most vividly the spiral of dialogues upon dialogues that comprise my fieldwork and the analyses I present here. These parenthetical remarks also brought to mind moments of exasperation when the rites of translation upon translation seemed never-ending.

In addition to the three assistants, I was aided by two teams of students and several independent researcher-activists—all together, ten people—in conducting household surveys. One group of students was composed of sociology undergraduates from North Chŏlla University. The second group was composed of Seoul National University students who had been part of an undergraduate research group that published a highly praised report on the agricultural sector and farmers' movements. The researcher-activ-ists, most of them social science graduate students or professors, were affil-iates of the Research Association on the Problems of Korean Farming and Fishing Villages (Han'guk Nong-Ŏch'on Munje Yŏn'guso). They arrived in the countryside with particular intellectual and activist agendas. We met often to discuss the findings of these surveys, including both what was ex-plicitly recorded and what was revealed in their silences.

From the outset, then, this ethnography was conducted and produced in dialogue with many people who cared deeply about coming to terms with the Koch'ang movement in the interest of far-reaching historiographical and political goals.

WHERE I FIT

Keeping in mind that all social observers are, as Renato Rosaldo (1989: 207) observes, "positioned subjects" who emerge as "complicit actor[s] in human events rather than as . . . innocent onlooker[s]" (see also Touraine 1981), I wish to comment briefly on my position during this field research.

The field research from which this book emerges involved considerable geographic and social travel—to and from Seoul and rural villages, in and out of class and generational enclaves, between politically divided sites of protest, from the protest site to the homes of middle-class friends in Seoul, and from home to home of farmers with different takes on the movement. In the countryside, I was positioned as instigator by the local government and company employees. Local police visited my residences regularly, sending each and every one of their employees to "greet" me. On a visit to the Samyang land management office, I was told by company officials that I was feigning ignorance to ask "such questions" since they had watched me "traveling among the villages." Like many other outsiders who visited the villages, I was viewed by farmers sympathetic to the movement as a supporter of their cause. In this capacity, I was asked to help publicize their story, to "let the world know." For other farmers, my presence was jarring or enigmatic: on the one hand, I was an imagined instigator; on the other, I was an American residing in an obviously off-the-beaten-path place.

In Seoul, I met activists (particularly students) with anti-American politics, who were at first skeptical about my aims and concerned about my role at the protest scene. I was asked many searching questions that deeply affected my fieldwork. For onlooking company employees and citizens, I was no doubt a protest anomaly. Many months after the protest, a middle-aged man approached me at an outdoor market in a middle-class enclave in Seoul to chide me for having been among "those boisterous, troublemaking farmers." I also visited the homes of middle-class and middle-aged friends in Seoul where I discovered considerable antipathy to the farmers' struggle.

In the later stages of the Seoul protest, I was asked by external activists to lead several meetings. They once asked me to take the microphone and to shout movement slogans and messages. At that time, several farmers suggested that I translate some of the slogans into English for greater appeal—something I did with great discomfort. This book in no way aims to document transformations in my positioning, but I offer these comments so that the reader can imagine more fully the locations from which this ethnography emerged, and that, as Berger put it, "every step is a stride over something not said."

RECKONING THE ERA

Like its site, the historical moment of my fieldwork was also charged. June 1987 was South Korea's moment in the international media; worldwide press looked on as millions of South Koreans participated in nationwide protests against the military dictatorship of Chun Doo Hwan. This massive civil disobedience erupted after Chun attempted to suspend debate over constitutional reforms concerning the election of his successor. The culmination of citizen protest was the June 29 Declaration to implement democratic measures—a declaration that was widely understood as a state response to citizens' successful dissent (see Ogle 1990; West and Baker 1988).[11] In South Korea, the marking or naming of eras is highly contested. In 1987, well before its final gasps, the decade was already being historically reckoned. In June 1987, I remember riding a bus to Seoul with a friend and reviewing the escalation of events that had led up to that month's tumultuous political events. As we spoke in a code of numbers that referred to dates—2-7, 3-1, 3-3, 4-1-3, 4-1-9, 5-1-6, 6-10, and so on— several people joined in the recitation to add dates they felt should be included. This was a moment not only of increased political participation but also of collective mobilization. These numerical codes signaled collective narratives of politicization, changes in public consciousness, and popular revisionist histories.

In this atmosphere of politicized history and historicized politics, the calendar was a symbolically loaded roulette wheel. Calendar dates had increasingly come to mark crimes of the South Korean state, and in some cases of the United States, against the Korean minjung, as well as the heroism of the Korean people against the state. Thus to the long-standing dates 3-1 (the aforementioned March First Movement), 4-1-9 (the April 19, 1960, Student Revolution), 5-1-6 (the May 16, 1961, military coup d'etat), and so on, people added dates commemorating the spiral of dissent in 1987. These included February 7—the memorial service for Pak Chong-ch'ŏl, the dissident who was tortured to death at the offices of the Agency for National Security Planning (Kukka Anjŏn Kihoekpu, or Angibu); March 3—the Buddhist commemorative ceremony of his death; April 13— the presidential measure closing the door on constitutional revision; June 10—nationwide democratic rallies; and June 29—the declaration to implement democratic measures. Additionally, at this juncture many of the events were renamed in popular discourse to proclaim particular lineages of struggle in minjung history: history textbooks' "movements" were spo-

ken of as "revolutions," their "revolutions" were rendered as "military take-
overs," and "restorations of order" were exposed as "government massa-
cres." At work here was what Ana Maria Alonso (1988: 39) describes in her
discussion of the popular reading of a rural Mexican protest and suppression: "The name is a mnemonic sign which condenses an interpretation of
events and gives the day a historical saliency, but a saliency which is selec-
tive, which highlights some aspects and obscures others." Most of these
dates named and recalled the dead; indeed, the largest rallies were funer-
ary processions led by people carrying enormous photographs of the deceased and accompanied by the mourning behaviors of a village funeral.
In 1987, the mothers of students and activists tortured or killed by the state
were important in mobilizing broad-based protest participation. Describing a similar public mobilization around death and memory in Colombia,
Michael Taussig (1989: 15–16) writes,

> What the Mothers of the Disappeared do is to collectively harness the magical
> power of the lost souls of purgatory and relocate memory in this contested
> public sphere, away from the fear-numbing and crazy-making fastness of the
> individual mind where paramilitary death squads and the State machinery of
> concealment would fix it. In so courageously naming the names and holding
> the photographic image of the dead and disappeared, the mothers create
> the specific image necessary to reverse public and State memory. As women,
> giving birth to life, they collectively hold the political and ritual lifeline to
> death and memory as well.

Indeed, popular memories and unofficial histories seemed to triumph
in 1987. Many people reckoned the 1980s, and indeed the entire post-
Liberation era, as an ebb and flow of popular quiescence, punctuated by
outbursts of popular outcry or protest. I think of this depiction of the Korean historical landscape as a particular historical gaze, by which I mean
the aesthetics and narratives that produce and mobilize the past. The decade is sketched in terms of periods of action and retreat: the Kwangju
Uprising[12] and the retreat following this 1980 democracy spring, the
storming of the American Cultural Ministry in 1985 and retreats in mid-
decade, the climax in 1987 and retreat again in the final years of the decade. Farmer organizations and vanguard activists considered post-Liberation activism in similar terms. They talked about revolutionary activism in
the immediate postcolonial era, silence in the 1950s and 1960s, renewed
activity in the late 1970s, and finally activism taking off in the early 1980s.
They saw lost ground in the middle of the 1980s, broken silences later in
the decade, and, again, retreat into the 1990s.

Whereas external activists talked about epochs of activism, farmers
placed *land*—making it, farming it, obtaining it, maintaining it, losing it—
at the heart of their histories. Below I turn to three rice paddy stories,

spanning decades and generations, to begin to sketch this book's narrative frames. The minutiae of rice paddies reveal the sensibilities of the historical accounts that meander through this book.

THREE RICE PADDY STORIES

During fieldwork, I came upon novelist Ch'ae Man-sik's 1946 story, "Non iyagi," or "The Rice Paddy Story," set in North Chŏlla Province. In its few pages, the story touched on many aspects of the 1980s land struggle unfolding in my midst, including Japanese colonialism, the South Korean state, and land reform.

Written and set immediately after the Korean liberation from Japanese colonialism—when people cried *manse* (Long Live Korea!)—"The Rice Paddy Story" seems to lament that national dramas make their way to local arenas in profoundly transformed ways. The protagonist, Han, a farmer heavily in debt, sold his land at an inflated price to the Japanese during the colonial period. He thought that he would be able to buy another plot, but this never came to pass. He later hoped that after the Japanese left, the land would return to him. In his village, however, the notion that "things would change when the Japanese left" had become a joke, an aphorism for impossible fancies. After Liberation, when Han learned that the land could only become his if he bought it back at a price that he couldn't afford, he reckoned that he had been wise not to cry manse at Liberation. He decided that for *paeksŏng* (the Korean common people) "it doesn't matter if the *nara* [country] is ours or foreign, there is nothing good for us" (Im 1985: 197). The story closes as his land is sold away. Han mutters, "Again I am a paeksŏng without a country" (Im 1985: 197).

* * * *

Day after day in the North Chŏlla countryside, I filled my notebooks with stories about landownership, and I learned that life stories there only made sense "from the ground up." One of the farming women who came to play a very important role in the Koch'ang Tenant Farmers Movement sat down with me after months of daily chatting to tell me her "rice paddy story." Hers is an eloquent account of a battle against landlessness, a personal struggle that went public through the course of the movement. She documented her life from marriage to the time of the Koch'ang land struggle to explain "why I am fighting for my land."

> I came as a bride twenty years ago. The matchmaker said that the man was a farming man, but when I came I saw that he was a *koji*,[13] someone who farms for other people—bringing them all the produce and plants, weeds, cuts, and harvests, and getting only one sŏm for 600 p'yŏng (.07 hectare). I was embarrassed that he was a koji.

Until ten years ago we villagers used to make straw sacks for salt to sell to Samyang. . . . Things were very difficult so in the winter we had to go into debt to other houses. . . . We became more and more indebted and I kept having more children, our debts continued to get bigger, and my husband never ceased drinking all day long and hitting me. . . . My mother-in-law was lying ill with a stroke and for two years the only thing she could do was go to the bathroom. We were always saddled by debts that we couldn't repay. . . . From time to time he would secure a koji; but we couldn't live at all—it was such a struggle— so I escaped.

I was pregnant then, but I had an abortion and became a maid for two years. Until then I used to think that going to the city to become a maid was a really embarrassing thing, but after that—since it is for making money—I didn't think so. I received 80,000 wŏn [14] per month. . . . I didn't contact my house for two years, but I would cry when I ate, and when I threw away food that they didn't eat I would think of my children, hungry. . . . In Seoul [during the protest] we sang a song asking for rice [during the demonstration], and when I sang that song I thought of the times I cried in Pusan [where she was a maid]. I would eat after everyone had finished, and I would think about the struggle that went into getting this rice. . . . When they bought a color television and were going to sell the black-and-white one, I asked for it so that I could send it to my family. I sent it to my mother's house and told them to send it to my house so that I wouldn't reveal my whereabouts. . . .

They found out my address and a relative who is a fisherman in the village came to me, telling me to return to the village, and that "there are no bad people in the village now" . . . I told him "I will never go. . . . I will get a divorce, and I will save money to educate my children." My younger sibling contacted me to tell me that my mother-in-law had died. When I heard that I was so sad—I had wanted to make money and buy land and to be able to show her [what I had accomplished]. But since I still hadn't saved much money I didn't go. Finally I saved about 2,000,000 wŏn. The whole time I was working I used no money—my employer just put it in the bank and showed me the bank statement. . . . I sent the money to my house and told them to buy [the tenant rights for] 1,200 p'yŏng of land and that I would return after that. I told them to plant barley there.

I went down in September and began to farm. . . . If my husband would have only worked for another house for a year we could have purchased [the tenant rights for] another 600 p'yŏng of land, but he refused. Now he tells everyone that he bought the paddy. After I returned, gathering money through the *kye* [cooperative lending associations], I bought [the tenant rights for] another 600 p'yŏng of land. We lived for two years without debts, but now on account of sending my daughter to high school, we are in debt again. After we eat and pay the rent there is nothing left. . . . No matter how much I struggle there is nothing left over, and that is why I am fighting for my land.

The day we spoke, she had just been to her mother's house, and she told me, "I fought with a guy who swore at me, and I swore back at him. In the past I would have just passed things over, not saying what I wanted, but now I have the confidence to say what I need to say."

* * * *

My fieldwork took me far from the Koch'ang rice paddy to Seoul as I followed the farmers' protest. The project carried me from farmers to students and other urban activists and to the contemporary histories and novels that were making waves in the community of dissent—these, too, were sites of struggle. In their pages I discovered yet other rice paddy stories that echoed the concerns of my research, in particular, Cho Chŏng-nae's novel *T'aebaek sanmaek* (The T'aebaek Mountain Range).

T'aebaek sanmaek was one of the most popular serial historical novels of the late 1980s and exerted considerable influence on many student activists.[15] The ten-volume work wrests the history of the famous Yŏsu Sunch'ŏn Incident, a ten-day leftist takeover in 1946, from the grips of military history and returns it to tenant–landlord conflict, seeking to recover murky lives from an ideologically crafted narrative. The incident is rewritten to focus on the grassroots efforts of those hungry for land and political justice. Above all, the work privileges the land and shows how the protest is rooted in landed narratives.

In *T'aebaek sanmaek,* Sŏ, the Communist son of a landlord, gives a minjung history lecture that begins with the late nineteenth-century Tonghak Peasant Revolution (or Tonghak Revolution), which he proclaims to be "the base of the peasant spirit" (Cho 1986, 3:159). He launches into a detailed review of colonial period land history, reviewing the impoverishment, tenantization, and struggles of the peasantry.

> Even though the March First Movement failed, the peasantry got national self-recognition through the movement. . . . The tenant movements, which happened all over the country from the twenties through Liberation were struggles for *saengjonkwŏn* [the right to live] and an anti-Japanese movement for self-recognition. The first organized tenant conflict arose at Sunch'ŏn in 1920. . . . We should notice that thirteen years later there were 1,351 peasant movement groups. The increase in the number of peasant groups, in spite of the legal restrictions of the Japanese, is a tribute to the will of national self-determination which they learned through the March First Movement. . . . In the 1930s the tenant conflict became stronger, aiming to make the land the farmer's land and topple the Japanese regime. . . . Taking up those issues they assaulted the district offices, police stations . . . [and] the economic struggle of the peasants turned into a political struggle. . . . There were three kinds of peasant revolts—Communist (206), nationalist and socialist (1,096), and moderate (149)—but the Japanese considered all of them Communist and oppressed them. (Cho 1986, 3:160)

Cho (1987) says that the main point of his novels is to challenge those who think that the cause of the Korean division was only fighting among the superpowers and to reveal how "the ideology that was introduced by the superpowers was imposed on and worked itself out in the life of the min-jung." Yŏm, the novel's local Communist leader, explains that "our problem isn't political choice between the 'isms'; the thing that we need most is the discovery of our nation" (Cho 1986, 3:176). In this vein, Kim, a radical reformer who does not join the Communist party, says that if, as in the past, "the people on behalf of ideology" is chosen over "ideology for the people," national division will be inevitable.

These stories help sketch the enormity and intensity of land as a signifier: land mediates anticolonial struggle, postcolonial political legitimacy, and contemporary economic and political dispossession. *Landless,* Han in "The Rice Paddy Story" cries out that the country is entirely removed from "the people." The Koch'ang farming woman's story turns on the deception of her *landless* marriage, on the struggle of rice cultivation unknown to the urban rich, and on her rights to own land without debt. In *T'aebaek sanmaek* the landlord's son, Sŏ, lectures that land struggles are struggles for national self-determination. These fictional and life-historical narratives thus render nothing short of national struggle and identity and the reckoning of social justice. Indeed, in considering the Koch'ang Tenant Farmers Movement, this book touches on anticolonial struggle, national identity, political legitimacy, and social justice.

We can think of land narratives as they relate to what the anthropologist Kamala Visweswaren (1994: 104–105) calls the "sign-chain of possible nationalist subject-positions," that is, the identities that people are allowed or "slotted into" by ideologies, nationalist or otherwise. Indeed, chapter 2 will proceed with the nationalist sign-chains in which the Koch'ang Tenant Farmers Movement was suspended—those of the minjung imaginary. This initiates our travels in the spontaneous sociology from whence 1980s movements emerged.

CHAPTER TWO

The Minjung Imaginary:
Memory and Mobilization

It is not too much to say that today's struggle for human rights hears the outcry and the protest of persons who participated in the March First Movement [1919] and the April 1960 Revolution. For it is evident that those who participate in the human rights struggle see their genealogy beginning with the Tonghak Movement and coming down through the Independence Association Movement, the March First Movement, and the April 1960 Movement.

SUH NAM-DONG (1981A: 171)

The Funeral of Yi Han-yŏl [a 1987 protest venue] should not be seen as an isolated event. . . . It comes from the colonial period, through 6-25 [the Korean War] and through [the 1980] Kwangju Uprising also. . . . It is much more than merely a struggle on the Right or on the Left.

CHO CHŎNG-NAE (1987)

This chapter considers the *minjung undong* (people's movement)—its various guises and texts—as a particular postcolonial engagement with history. This engagement is by no means singular; here I consider those aspects of a larger but fragmented imaginary that animated the narratives and praxis of 1980s farmers' movements. I will explore aspects of the minjung discursive practice through several histories, popular artworks, and novels that depict the history of peasant movements. In particular, the 1894 Tonghak Peasant Revolution [1] has been widely imagined as a turning point—or even the birth of a minjung or minjung consciousness. I will also begin to situate these practices and politics in the popular discourse on the Koch'ang Tenant Farmers Movement.

In the South Korean community of dissent, memory was imagined as a personal resource or collective repository that could mobilize people. Easily naturalized as an objective, neutral repository of the past, memory was posed against official histories that were edited by the hands of those with interests. Of course, memory resides at the intersection of many discourses and interests. As Foucault (1975: 25) notes, "Memory is actually a very important factor in struggle. . . . If one controls people's memories, one controls their dynamism. And one also controls their experience, their knowledge of previous struggles." The French historian Pierre Nora takes up the relation of memory and history in ways I find helpful for understanding the 1980s minjung imaginary and the internal workings of the Koch'ang Tenant Farmers Movement. He considers France's epistemological engagement with the "history of history" as a historiographical consciousness in which "anxiety arises when history assigns itself the task of tracing alien impulses within itself and discovers that it is the victim of memories which it sought to master" (Nora 1989: 10). In this way memories take revenge. In moments of national historiographical contention—as I found in South Korea—we find "the eradication of memory by history" (Nora 1989: 18). It is in such "historical" moments that memory attaches itself to sites (Nora 1989: 22); *lieu de memoire* (sites of memory) are "forever open to the full range of possible significations" (Nora 1989: 24). The minjung imaginary offers precisely such a "site," open to the "full range of possible significations."

By mobilization or "models of mobilization," I refer to South Korean narratives that took up collective and individual transformations—both toward and away from action. I pair these two terms as cornerstones of my analysis because they operate in tandem: memory posits a repository from which mobilization draws, and mobilization comprises the repository of memory.

Narratives of 1980s silences and outbursts capture the dialectic of the institutions, practices, and personnel of the state with the organization, practices, and personnel of dissent. In this elaborate dance between state institutions and antistate activisms, the decade's shifts and turns are also narrated in terms of the appearance and retreat of memory. Thus outbursts and silences conjure up repression in the past and the present and the liberation or release of memories. It is helpful, then, to think about 1980s activism as the crossroads of competing narratives or models of mobilization and of competing memories. The activist is situated within multiple discourses and fashions an identity out of these; thus her activism cannot be theorized, periodized, or understood without attention to these discourses. In this vein, June Nash (1979: 7) writes that "mythic and memorized history shapes the view of current events and gives people the rationale for action in their own life." Such attention to "mythic and memorized history" challenges ethnography to contend with historical consciousness.

Historical consciousness—long understood in the social sciences as the exclusive province of Western literate societies—demands ethnographic attention to the cultural sensibilities and political frames for perceiving the past, the historical gaze that was discussed in chapter 1. Ethnography of historical consciousness is distinct from people's history, which writes "the people" into history without considering their aesthetics and apperceptions of the past. Increasingly, though, anthropologists have made efforts to document historical consciousness across space and time. We can now explore the historical consciousness of the Saramaka in Surinam (Price 1983), eighteenth-century Hawaiians (Sahlins 1985), the Ilongot of the Philippines (Rosaldo 1980), and the miners of Bolivia (Nash 1979). These works challenge us to think against the assertions of the Popular Memory Group (1982: 226) that "the study of popular memory can begin only where the empiricist and positivist norms break down." What the Popular Memory Group calls "subordinated private experience" is always already fashioned by the empiricist and positivist politics of history, and although ethnographers look for subordinated experiences, such experiences are always in process—never divorced from dominant representations and epistemological frames. Historical revelation and construction, then, are limited by the discursive boundaries of particular times and places, and dissent is framed by its targets of protest. As Raymond Williams (1977: 114) suggests, "The dominant culture, so to say, at once produces and limits its own forms of counter-culture." Narratives of silence and outburst are thus culturally and politically constituted within a dominant discourse.

In this way, narratives of memory and mobilization have been central to both South Korean discourses about and practices of social movements. Competing models of mobilization have reflected and affected movement visions and practices in both the short and the long run. Activists and activisms in 1980s South Korea were imagined in terms of particular lineages of activism; actions or activisms were variously "read" according to competing senses of past activism.[2] In this sense, these lineages were thus literally biographical or generational; they evoked real genealogies of persons or groups. Alternatively, lineages can suggest the unconscious transmission of identities, loyalties, or politics. In the community of dissent I found in South Korea, this sense of unconscious transmission was itself a powerful cultural and discursive frame. Michael Fischer's (1986: 231) description of the reproduction of ethnicity as a "dream and transference-like process" that works alongside "cognitive language" offers an idiom that begins to capture such transmission. Here we can also find resonances in Victor Turner's (1974: 110) concept of "primary process": "A primary process does not develop from a cognitive, conscious model; it erupts from the cumulative experience of whole peoples whose deepest material and spiritual needs and wants have long been denied any legitimate expression by power-holding elites who operate in a manner analogous to that of Freud's 'censorship' in psychological systems."

I suggest that the idiom of memory and mobilization has had currency because of South Korea's postcoloniality and the cold war politics engendered by the national division. South Korean postcoloniality and anticommunism are identities and ideologies of nationhood. Indeed, imagining the nation is a central trope of the minjung discourse. Nationalism—in both its hegemonic and counterhegemonic forms—is a historical construct often framed as a cultural argument (Anderson 1983; Fox 1990; Gellner 1983; Hobsbawm and Ranger 1983). We need to pay attention to its rhetorics and constructions, its historicity. In its various guises, nation-narration was animated in the Koch'ang movement's platforms and processes.

The tropes and technologies of the cold war constituted and were constituted by the north–south division. The specter of communism has loomed large and was often mobilized to defend autocratic and repressive social and political controls. The *kukka poanpŏp* (national security law) has swept literary, cultural, and political dissidents into its vortex. Because political legitimacies in the two Koreas have been mobilized according to the histories and narratives of competing nationalisms and because extensive technologies have been geared to silence the histories and legacies of unrequited nationalisms,[3] it is not surprising to find historical narratives in which silences speak and activisms that draw on these silences.

CHARACTERIZING THE MINJUNG DISCOURSE

Discussions of the minjung in the 1980s oscillated between championing a minjung as the "subject" of—and at the center of—politics and history and identifying a counterhegemonic minjung culture that was not entirely coterminous with political activism.[4] On the one hand, minjung as political subjects exalted minjung political activity and drew on this legacy for continued revolutionary activity. Minjung as a cultural practice, on the other hand, fashioned a utopian vision of an alternative social arrangement, and at once demanded action and explained minjung silence. As a cultural practice, minjung apprehended silence by identifying a resistant culture beyond the sort of resistance that makes its way into formal historical chronicles and chronologies (see Scott 1985). These competing minjung imaginaries delineated self-conscious political historical actors and practitioners of an oppositional culture. There was, however, no clear division in the practice of these two senses of minjung, just as there is also no clear distinction between politics and culture: politics are cultural, and culture is political.

Observations by the minjung theologian Suh Nam-dong and a fictional Communist activist in the Yŏsu Sunch'ŏn Rebellion (in the South Chŏlla Province) in the popular minjung historical novel *T'aebaek sanmaek* highlight such tension in minjung conceptualizing.

> When we say that the *minjung* are the subjects of history, we are not exalting them in political terms but are affirming as authentic their identification of themselves as the masters of their own history which is told in their sociopolitical biography. (Suh Nam-dong 1981 *a*: 186)

> [In *T'aebaek sanmaek*, Yŏm, the head of the local Communists, recalls the words of his high school teacher] All men want to be at the center of history,

that is the desire to govern, but nobody can be at the center of history because history does not accept that; history's nature is cold, objective criticism.
(Cho Chŏng-nae 1986, 2:82)

Here tension exists between minjung in "political terms" (Suh) at "the center of history" (Cho) and minjung not "exalted in political terms" (Suh)
and unable to be at the center of history (Cho). In the former sense, minjung refers to a recognizable Enlightenment subject—*he* who "makes history"—while the latter sense of minjung transcends this sort of subjectivity,
championing instead a radical communitarianism.

With this tension in mind, we can identify various minjung attributes. In
delineating subject actors, minjung distinguishes collectivities or groups
that have engaged in particular *sahoe undong* or *minjok undong* (social or
national movements). As the minjung poet Ko Ŭn put it, the minjung is
not an abstract unit but "a creative unit of national struggle" (Kim 1989:
42). In South Korea, consideration of social movements goes to the heart
of debates over national legitimacy and political struggles. Because the
1945 Liberation was externally imposed, it configured a space for ever-
contending nationalisms. Indeed, successive regimes and antiregime movements have argued their legitimacies from late nineteenth-century and colonial period activisms: anti-imperial and anticolonial struggles.[5] Only a
particular path of social and national movements, however, constitutes a
lineage or legacy of minjung movements. In this sense, the minjung discussion was an ongoing debate as to which movements—or which strata within
a particular movement—have had minjung as their "subject." Once delineated, this lineage was in turn evoked by minjung thinkers and activists to
legitimize successive movements. In this lineage of minjung struggle, the
Tonghak Peasant Revolution was widely evoked by the community of
farmer activists. In the minjung-as-subject lineage, social actors who carry
the torch of Tonghak are the legitimate national subjects.

Minjung activists fashioned themselves against state-centered activisms:
the elitist, collaborating line of nationalist movements. These nationalisms
were co-narrated when minjung nationalists challenged the dominant representation of movements to suggest that, both in practice and in historical
reflection, elites have co-opted minjung dissent and subjectivities. Implied,
then, are the elite's efforts to efface minjung actors and activism from public memory. Further, some argue that because minjung participation was
subordinated or co-opted in the course of these social movements, they
failed to achieve their full potential.[6]

In briefly mentioning P'agoda Park and the 1919 March First Movement in chapter 1, I noted that the thirty-three signers of the declaration
of independence comprise the empty center of that movement. In another
minjung historical gaze, however, the park and the declaration of independence itself are yet another empty center. Although the official movement

called for peaceful demonstrations and diplomacy, violent outbursts of peasants and laborers took place all over Korea. Some South Korean scholars have argued that there are thus two March First movements; its minjung rendition refers to the struggles of peasants and laborers that extend from a legacy of late nineteenth-century Tonghak Peasant Revolution and from *ŭibyŏng* (righteous armies) [7] struggles, tenant wars, guerrilla independence armies in Manchuria, and so on. Although the government evokes the thirty-three signers, the park, the declaration, and the pagoda to symbolize the movement, many revisionists consider these symbols to have eclipsed minjung subjectivity both at the time of the movement and in the present.

Divergent readings of historical movements and events also characterize competing nationalisms of the North and South Korean states. Both states claim to be the legitimate offspring of colonial period national movements; each presents itself as the legitimate state for the entire Korean nation. Related to the minjung concept was the impossibility of separating minjung collectivities from the agenda of national subjectivity: the call for an independent state in the global state system. Korean unification was a necessary corollary of such subjectivity.[8] The notion of a state as *chuch'e* (subject) is also the central concept of Kim Il Sung's North Korean state ideology: *chuch'e sasang* (subject ideology). Social movements devoted to a South Korean state based on minjung subjects were thus also struggles for a minjung-based national unification. A legitimate South Korean state, a legitimate unified Korean state, and minjung collectivities of dissent were thus mutually constituted with the minjung as the desired subjects of struggle. Thus minjung was an inherently national and political category, which referred to people as subjects in national struggle. Minjung could not be reduced to a class category.

Whereas this sense of minjung is based on notions of historical subjectivity—persons and states *making* history—attention was called to cultural practices and resources by another conceptualization that focused, not on brilliant participation in "making history," but on the quotidian resistance of its cultures and communities. This conceptualization rendered Korean peasant culture and rural village life subversive to the colonial, post-Liberation imperialist, and capitalist projects. This subversive cultural element comprised a latent dissenting force.

Endowed with these meanings, minjung was not merely a stratum in a divided society or a legacy of oppositional activity but also a cultural characterization that imagined a horizontal community or an indigenous cultural socialism—the grist of a particular historical gaze. Although the political formulation posited minjung actors in political struggles, this cultural perspective imagined an alternative national community based on a vision of indigenous village socialism. In this cultural characterization, then, minjung nationalists are interested not only in political activism but also in a culture that embodies counterhegemonic oppositional practices of daily life in order to account for the long durations in history when minjung have remained silent and their political practices have gone unrecorded. Cultural expression—songs, dance, oral traditions, and the like—was taken as the repository of such minjung consciousness and practice. In the oppositional community in general, and among student activists in particular, peasant culture symbolized dissent.

These two minjung practices—political historical minjung and oppositional culture minjung—thus broadly referred to two socialisms: a political socialism of the national and international Left and a cultural or indigenous socialism. The political socialism described a minjung-centered lineage of political action and placed the minjung at the heart of the history of Korean socialist nationalist struggles. Conversely, the cultural socialism posited the minjung as practitioners of an alternative politics and social formation; here, the genealogies of minjung-as-subject activity were not as important as the memory and practice of village socialisms.

Both of these minjung conceptions mobilized the past in order to achieve alternative social and political arrangements in the present. The notion of *ŭisikhwa* (conscientization or "consciousness raising") became a central fixture in the idiom of dissent, suggesting historical legacies or genealogies and a sense of interactive historical consciousnesses.

In an oversimplified formulation, the political historical minjung posits a "genealogical" relation to the past, whereas the oppositional culture formulation puts minjung in an "analogous" relation to the past. The former constructs lineages; the latter evokes a sketchier metaphor.[9] They were blurred both in discourse and in practice. Indeed, both were narratives of resistance: minjung political actors emerged from, and acted in accordance with, minjung quotidian cultural practice. In this way, village socialism called to, and represented a lineage of, minjung political activity. History was a patchwork of minjung "silence" and minjung "outburst" reflecting both political and cultural socialisms. Here, Jean Baudrillard's consideration of the relationship between silence and passivity and the masses is enlightening. He queries how the "silence of the masses" is apprehended as silencing and apathy is apprehended as the imposition of power: "In any case, this indifference *ought* not to be, hence it has nothing to tell us. In other words, the 'silent majority' is even stripped of its indifference, it has no right even that this be recognized and imputed to it, even this apathy must have been imposed on it by power" (Baudrillard 1983: 12–13). The silent majority live then as a potential: "According to their imaginary representation, the masses drift somewhere between passivity and wild spontaneity, but always as a potential energy, a reservoir of the social and social energy; today a mute referent, tomorrow, when they speak up and cease to be the 'silent majority,' a protagonist of history" (Baudrillard 1983: 4).

I will now take these discussions to the Tonghak Revolution, a central event in minjung imagining. An examination of the literature on the Tonghak Revolution reveals the various articulators of minjung historical lineages and nationalisms.

MINJUNG AND THE 1894 TONGHAK PEASANT REVOLUTION

In minjung histories, historical novels, and works of art, the 1894 revolution marks an important historical juncture. It began in Kobu County in North Chŏlla Province in response to exploitation by a *yangban* (elite) magistrate[10] and coalesced under an antioligarchy, anti-Japanese program. As Carter Eckert et al. (1990: 217–218) summarize,

> The peasants occupied the county office, seized weapons, distributed illegally collected tax rice to the poor, and then destroyed a new reservoir built with their own forced labor. When news of the incident reached the government, a special investigator was dispatched to Kobu, but he arbitrarily charged the Tonghak with responsibility for the uprising, imprisoning some Tonghak members and summarily executing others. Furious at this added injustice, the peasants rallied around Chŏn Pong-jun and other local Tonghak leaders, and launched an armed insurrection.
>
>   Peasants from all surrounding areas joined with the Tonghak forces, swelling its ranks to some several thousands. They tied multicolored cloths around their heads and waists, and armed themselves with the few rifles, swords and lances they had seized, but mostly with bamboo spears and cudgels.[11]

The Tonghak discourse has been strikingly present oriented: although the revolution occurred in another century, it is easily discussed as a contemporary historical and cultural repository. It has been represented as a legacy that continues to incite minjung consciousness and action. Minjung discursive treatments of the Tonghak Peasant Revolution revealed both Korean peasant cultural patterns and political genealogies of state and minjung subjectivity. While the state commemorated the Tonghak Revolution for its anti-Japanese legacy, the community of dissent celebrated its protest tactics, slogans, and culture, as well as its struggles against elites.[12]

A look at two late 1980s minjung artistic images will aid the discussion of the nature of historical gaze in Tonghak reflection in particular and in postcolonial South Korea in general. The most frequently depicted personage in the offices, pamphlets, publications, and art of the farmers' movements is Chŏn Pong-jun, the leader of the Tonghak Peasant Revolution. In fact, images of Chŏn and of the Tonghak Revolution exist even beyond farmers' movements. The June 1989 issue of *Hamkke hanŭn nongmin*

Figure 1. Woodblock print by Ch'oe Pyŏng-su, *Harabŏji rŭl ch'assŭmnida* [We are looking for Grandfather]

(Farmers Working Together) includes works from the minjung art movement that commemorate a poem on the revolution by Sin Tong-yŏp entitled "Kŭmgang" (The Kŭm River), which is described by the literary critic Kim Uchang (1989: 28) as "the first imaginative work definitely committed to a populist reading of modern Korean history." I analyze two of the eight reproductions in this issue, both with obvious depictions of Chŏn and suggestive of the relationship between past and present struggles. Taken together, the two works demonstrate the flexibility of this relationship.

In Ch'oe Pyŏng-su's woodblock on cloth, *Harabŏji rŭl ch'assŭmnida* (We Are Looking for Grandfather) [13] (fig. 1), Chŏn is carved out of an imposing sky and centered in an expansive halo that at once transcends and cuts away the jagged lines of successive horizons of mountains. The image of Chŏn looms over a host of laboring men in jackets and blue jeans marching forward with clenched fists and heavy steps. Presumably, they represent

Figure 2. Acrylic by Yi Myŏng-bok, *Kŭmgang* [Kŭm River]

farmers, but they could also easily pass for industrial laborers. In his stance
and in his oblique and angry gaze, Chŏn's canonized form is easily recognizable. The deeply cracked wasteland of the expansive foreground awaits
the shadow of the angry onslaught. Read with an empty center—without
Chŏn—the farmers outline a new dawn, an awakening. The image of the
brooding revolutionary eclipses the light, capturing the accumulated anger
of past struggle.

In Yi Myŏng-bok's acrylic, *Kŭmgang* (The Kŭm River) (fig. 2), Chŏn's
upper body is foregrounded, overlaid on a landscape of corpses. Unlike
Ch'oe, Yi does not portray Chŏn as a clear center of focus; instead, Yi forces
the viewer's eye to jump from Chŏn to the image of a farmer who appears
in the lower right-hand corner, almost outside of the painting but also
burdened by the weight of the history depicted in it. The viewer's gaze
then shifts between several small scenes detailing a dark but reddened
landscape. In Ch'oe's work, Chŏn is propelled forward; in Yi's work,
Chŏn's image drifts back into a narrowing landscape. The quiet, undra-
matic, blue-gray visage of the obviously contemporary farmer in Yi's foreground contrasts sharply with the pocked relief and red tones of Chŏn's

face. With a weary and time-worn face, the farmer stands to one side of a wheel painted with anti-Communist slogans. The wheel refers to the structures that posted government propaganda in villages as part of the state-initiated Saemaŭl Undong (New Village Movement) campaigns that began in the early 1970s. On the other side of the wheel opposite the farmers is the line of South Korea's post-Liberation presidents (Rhee, Park, and Chun) and their wives. This genealogy of authoritarian regimes thus sets in place a literal ideological boundary that acts as a wedge between the farmers and Chŏn and thwarts conversation between them. The farmer's body is silhouettelike, in contrast to the miniature but vividly detailed South Korean autocratic rulers. In this collage, the farmer's relationship to both the state and Chŏn is not clearly inscribed; rather, his glance suggests a negotiation with or against these pasts—a negotiation that characterized the flux of rural realities in 1989 when the image was produced. Yi's acrylic montage includes two other scenes in which dark, even-colored, shadowy figures disappear into history's terrain. In the first, a row of claylike bodies marches toward a hill with heads bowed; their suggested martyrdom is highlighted by the image of a brightly lit woman folded in mourning below them. Taken together, these signs suggest a massacre. In the second vignette, the earthen silhouettes are pushing a memorial tower upright, aiming to stand it on a hill, again a scene of struggle and martyrdom.

In Ch'oe's piece, the laboring men lunge forward directly from Chŏn as if driven by great conviction and a guiding force; in Yi's montage, in spite of the suggestion of a rich legacy, the foreground is effaced by the farmer's hesitant gaze and the weight of receding corpses. The contemporary farmer is portrayed differently in the two pieces, as is the dialogue of the farmers, history, and the terrain or land. In academic and literary discourses, we also find such dialogues between the past and the present that take up the Tonghak Revolution.

A late 1980s article by the South Korean historian An Pyŏng-ok (1987: 11) distinguished three periods of Tonghak Peasant Revolution historiography. In the 1950s, the focus was on the Tonghak Revolution as a farmers' movement to overcome imperial Japan. The 1960s and 1970s highlighted "national subjectivity" by championing it as a farmers' war and stressed its revolutionary logic. In the 1980s, scholars attempted to overcome a "false subjectivity," the exaggerated attribution of a revolutionary consciousness to the farmers. The historical and literary texts of the 1980s, however, reveal a less easily compartmentalized progression. Here we find that the dialogue between political subjectivity and resistant culture shapes the contours of the minjung discourse. I do not intend to offer a review of the proliferating secondary literature on the Tonghak Revolution, but through a juxtaposition of several texts, I consider the politics and aesthetics of particular historical gazes—models of mobilization. I begin with two late 1980s historical treatments of the Tonghak Revolution that are both minjung identified and then extend the discussion to other genres.

Kim Chong-gyu's *Han'guk kŭn-hyŏndaesa ŭi ideollogi* (The Ideology of Modern and Contemporary Korean History, 1988) exalts the minjung as the subject of the Tonghak and recuperates it from all *ijŭmdŭl* (isms) or ideologies. Kim advocates a populist nationalism that decries elitist nationalist legacies on both "the Left" and "the Right." I will contrast Kim's work with a widely read 1986 minjung history, *Han'guk minjungsa* (The History of the Korean Minjung) (collectively written by the Han'guk Minjungsa Yŏn'guhoe). This book became well known when it was censored and the publisher was put on trial in 1987 (Chŏng, Kang, and Kim 1987). In keeping with the 1980s reaction against false subjectivity, the latter work outlines the limits and failings of the Tonghak Revolution. I juxtapose these texts not "to get to the bottom" of Tonghak but to begin a journey in postcolonial historical apperception.

The "national subject perspective" is Kim's historical and interpretive template (Kim C. 1988: 162). He advocates moving away from ideologically inspired historiographical practice and turning toward national development in the present in which the Korean *taejung* (mass) is the subject. It is only Tonghak and violent tenant movements during the colonial period that withstand the scrutiny of his national subject perspective. Kim claims that the Tonghak "Farmers Revolution," a "minjung national liberation movement," is free of the ideological dogmatism of the Right and the Left. Kim (1988: 164) argues that Tonghak's land slogans, which some historians suggest were calls for a land reform (this is a point of controversy in the Tonghak historiography),[14] attracted and originated from the minjung. He thus places Tonghak and its legacy in a "national-mass-subject lineage" untainted by foreign ideological dogma and intellectualism.

Kim challenges Koreans to overcome "dogmatism," which is responsible for thwarting "historical progress." Dogmatism, he proclaims, is antiminjung and antinational: it is precisely movements that are "correct" or legitimate from the minjung perspective that have been trivialized by dogmatic ideological positions (Kim C. 1988: 166). "Correct" movements that are well suited to propel Korean history are those that achieve mass-based national subjectivity. Kim's (1988: 64) legitimate national and mass subjects are delicately balanced between the Western-admiring opportunists, who, he argues, led the country to colonialism, and the leftists, who acted beyond the reach of the masses and obeyed global Communist interests. The Right is epitomized by the Kaehwap'a (Enlightenment Faction)[15] and the Tongnip Hyŏphoe (Independence Club);[16] the Left is represented by the socialists during the colonial period and the Namnodang (Southern Labor party) after the Liberation (Kim C. 1988: 162). Thus Kim characterizes both the Right and the Left as foreign oriented, guilty of intellectual elitism, and therefore unable to win mass base support. He notes that the Taewŏn'gun faction,[17] although mass oriented in its anti-imperial line, ignored land issues and thus precluded a real mass base (Kim C. 1988: 163).

Han'guk minjungsa differs in its reading of the Tonghak Revolution by considering it a turning point in modern Korean history and a landmark in national movements' efforts to achieve *chajujŏk* (autonomous) modernization. The Tonghak Revolution represents Korea's most vigorous attack against feudalism; "world historically," it figures as nothing short of an attack of the Asian minjung against world powers. Nevertheless, *Han'guk minjungsa* introduces several weaknesses of the Tonghak Revolution. The authors argue that it was thwarted by the absence of a bourgeoisie, a class that could have achieved indigenous modernization. They also argue that the so-called Chŏnju Agreement, when peasants succumbed to government pressure and dispersed in Chŏnju, was a tactical error that attenuated the spirit of the movement. They point again to the failure to achieve a compromise between the government-initiated Kabo reforms in 1894[18] and the minjung-initiated Tonghak Revolution—a failure that revealed the inability to transcend the monarchical system and feudal consciousness (HMY 1986: 86–88).

Kim challenges these arguments from his national subject perspective by criticizing the claim that the Tonghak Revolution failed because of an absence of a bourgeoisie: in his opinion, such a claim denies the historical precedent and potential of Third World countries to sustain national liberation movements. The Chŏnju conciliation, Kim explains, was a technically effective ploy for reorganizing the masses, not a cause of the failure of the revolution. He insists that to evaluate the Chŏnju Agreement that way is to "deny historical fact, to be antihistorical" (Kim C. 1988: 47). Instead he charges that the potential of the peasant militia was underestimated and that, as with Mao's peasant army, they should have fought in guerrilla fashion, relying on the ultimate strength of the broad-based popular support of the Tonghak Revolution (Kim C. 1988: 47). He also notes that the Chipkangso—local offices in the Tonghak Revolution hierarchy—grew much stronger after the Chŏnju Agreement, as their numbers increased fifteenfold (Kim C. 1988: 40). The breadth of participation was expanded as the *ch'ŏnmin*, the lowest class, joined the army in great numbers. Concerning the compromise between the Kabo reforms and the Tonghak Revolution, Kim explains that because they were fundamentally at odds (one pro-Japanese and the other anti-imperialist), they shared no legitimate grounds for compromise. In answer to the charge of the Tonghak Revolution's monarchical or feudal character, he writes that some of its rhetoric endorsed such perspectives in a merely tactical move to win the support of the masses and that had the revolutionaries achieved power, they would have abandoned such positions.

Kim's strategical history of minjung struggle is both nationalized—divorced from foreign ideologies of democracy and communism—and popularized—removed from elite politics that are similarly oriented toward foreign ideologies. He thus recuperates minjung "experience" or "culture" beyond elite politics and foreign ideologies. Championing the idea that the Korean past be read apart from ideology, as closer to the earth and closer to the issues of the earth, Kim makes an appeal for a distinctly Korean national and minjung subjectivity. Although both the *Han'guk min-jungsa* and Kim's work describe the Tonghak Revolution as a minjung watershed, Kim argues that a national subject perspective explains all limitations and failings and also provides a blueprint for current politics. These models of mobilization for the Tonghak Revolution are not merely historical explanation, but barometers of the very production of historical discourse. Because history writing is so political, and history is often that which is to be rescued or resuscitated from these charged accounts, fiction has played a critical role in the South Korean historical imagination.

The most outspoken minjung historical reflection has taken place in novels, particularly in multivolume historical novels that offer microsociological accounts over time, often of a single village or family, to demonstrate the imposition of ideological and political projects. The prominent economic historian Kang Man-gil (1985: 329) asserts that while historical studies are "restricted by historical data," novels can better attain "historical truth and a historical present." He writes, for example, of a "people's perspective" in Pak Kyŏng-ni's *T'oji* (The Land), one of the earliest and most important serial historical novels because of its attention to the "historical consciousness of fighting leaders" and the extent of the subject-consciousness of its protagonists. Kang praises *T'oji* for putting the peasantry at the center of history and for its plot development in which the Tonghak revolutionary fighters become righteous army activists. Through a description of a righteous army uprising, Pak portrays the shift from yangban (elite) to *sang-min*[19] (freeborn commoner) peasant leadership and, correspondingly, from a "protect the Dynasty" to an "antifeudal" platform. Kang (1985: 341) praises *T'oji* for showing that "even if the Tonghak failed, our true national movement must progress on a peasant base—and that without peasant power history cannot develop."

Kim Chi-ha—poet, novelist, activist, and perhaps the most important articulator of the minjung concept in the 1970s—was deeply affected by the Tonghak legacy. In his "Declaration of Conscience," written on toilet paper in his prison cell, he declared, "I have never defined myself as an adherent to any 'ism' " (1977: 9); he discussed instead his Tonghak inspiration for "Chang Il Tam," a ballad about a thief who, having escaped from prison, preaches to farmers and workers:

> I heard something then about the Tonghak teaching that "Man is Heaven." At first it was a pianissimo idea that made only a slight impression. Later I learned more about the Tonghak Revolution, and an image took shape in my mind. I could see that awesome band of starving peasants, their proud banner proclaiming "An end to violence, save the people," as they marched off to fight. Suddenly the Tonghak teaching became fortissimo, as thunderous as the battle cries of those marching peasants. I have been grappling with that image for ten years. At some point I gave it a name, "The unity of God and revolution." I also changed the [Tonghak] phrase "Man is Heaven" into "Rice is Heaven" and used it in my poetry. (Kim 1977: 11–12)

A treatment of the Tonghak Revolution in which its politics, its personages, and its symbols are mobilized in a contemporary vein persists into the 1980s. A striking, if remarkably literal, evocation of this lineage is Chŏng Kyŏng-mo's *Tchijŏjin sanha* (Torn Mountains and Rivers) (1984), a fictional dialogue in which historical personages—leftist nationalists Yŏ Unhyong and Chang Chun-ha, who had vied for political legitimacy and national unification after the Liberation, and nationalist Kim Ku—engage in a contemporary political discussion set in heaven in 1983.[20] Yŏ suggests, "We should find the spirit to solve all our problems in Tonghak" (Chŏng 1984: 138), and argues that the democratic movement today is a second peasant movement in which "the dispossessed and weak have the power to change human history" (Chŏng 1984: 143).

For the theologian Suh Nam-dong, the Tonghak Revolution similarly inspires a minjung historical trajectory. He suggests that Tonghak cannot be understood by "socioeconomic analysis" alone. Chŏn Pong-jun, the chief leader of the Tonghak revolution, did not "resort to the method of socioeconomic analysis to understand the reality of the *minjung*" (Suh 1981*a*: 167). Drawing on this interesting analogy, Suh thus renders the minjung legacy simultaneously empirical and analytical, such that historiographical and minjung practice converge.

The minjung theologian Kim Yong-bock characterizes the Tonghak Revolution as a popular messianism (in contrast to political messianism). Kim explains that political messianism includes "Japanese ultranationalism in its colonial form; the North Korean Communist movement; and the emerging modern technocracy in Korea" (1981: 189). He writes of political messianism as the language of elite political ideologies on the Right and the Left and of minjung who "experience political messianism as a contradiction" (1981: 191). The move away from the so-called false subjectivity of traditional Tonghak historiography can be seen precisely as a rejection of political messianism. Kim (1981: 192) explains that the roots of popular messianism are in the "traditions inherent in Maitreya Messianic Buddhism and Tonghak religion." Here, the minjung is recognizable as a cultural practice.

Many historical novels and much of the discourse on the Tonghak Revolution portray genealogical connections with the past. In a number of historical novels, some personages participate in key minjung movements as Tonghak army members or March First Movement fighters, finally appearing as Korean War victims. From struggle to struggle within lives, and again from struggle to struggle over generations, these works carefully consider both the experience of political or national struggle and the effects of state suppression. They draw bloodlines of activism.[21]

Such a lineage exists in *T'aebaek sanmaek.* Ha, one of the Communists, is the grandson of a Tonghak fighter. His grandfather, a slave to a Japanese landlord, was killed by the landlord for having participated in the Tonghak Revolution. Ha's father then escaped to the mountains for ten years and came out because he heard of a Japanese land reclamation project and was hopeful of the possibility of wages and land. Above all, the father wanted to educate Ha, but the son, a tenant activist imprisoned several times during the colonial period, continued in the political struggle after Liberation. Finally, after the leftist murder of local landlords, Ha's father was killed by a gang of landlords' sons because his son was a Communist. In this lineage, then, the legacy of the Tonghak Revolution limits the son, liberates the grandson, and finally brings the death of the father.

MINJUNG AND THE KOCH'ANG TENANT FARMERS MOVEMENT

These genealogical discussions offer cultural and discursive repositories that figure prominently in contemporary activisms. The reckoning of outbursts and silences are genealogical and analytical lineages. These minjung trajectories have shaped the discursive context of movements such as the Koch'ang Tenant Farmers Movement.

I will briefly examine how Tonghak Revolution legacies and genealogies surfaced in the Koch'ang movement. The Revolution figured easily in contemporary Koch'ang County in part because the district is not far from where it is purported to have begun. Minjung and the Tonghak Revolution were particularly relevant for students and other outside organizers as they struggled to understand, explain, and conscientize farmers. Indeed, both farmers and nonfarmers were quick to draw lineages and legacies to explain the movement. A prominent literary critic interested in farmers movements warned me that without a "key informant," the history of the Koch'ang Tenant Farmers Movement would never surface because "people don't necessarily tell you that their ancestors were Tonghak fighters."

Other references to the Tonghak Revolution sketched more fragmented lineages—looser renderings of literal or fictive linkages of pasts and presents.

The founder of a regional culture center in Koch'ang,[22] himself a former village enlightenment activist in the 1960s and a son of a once-prosperous landlord, insisted that contrary to received wisdom, not only did the Tonghak Revolution begin in the Koch'ang region, but that the greatest colonial period independence fighters *all* hail from Koch'ang. He spoke about the "hundred-year-old roots of the Koch'ang Tenant Farmers Movement," proclaiming, "It is just that the tenants don't know the roots themselves, although they have been passed down in their hearts." When talking about the transformation of farmer consciousness that had been accomplished through the movement, one of the Samyang employees in Koch'ang similarly explained, "They [farmers] have acquired a 'dormant subconsciousness' [activated in spite of the fact that] in capitalist society, it doesn't work to just try and take away others' property."

Many students who were involved in the movement also stressed that the Koch'ang Tenant Farmers Movement followed the hidden history of dissent in general and in this region in particular. One history major who was himself raised in rural North Chŏlla wanted to situate the Koch'ang Tenant Farmers Movement both in its "Korean context" and in terms of the "flow of world history." He spoke of the movement's place in the "unswerving flow of the history of peasant movements." In high school he had come to understand the coincidence of the suppression of peasant movements, the growth of capitalism, and the combined force of foreign and feudal power in the late Chosŏn period—that "the rule of landlords over the lower class had settled like layers of rock in history." A self-declared believer in "the inevitability of class struggle in human history," he underscored the power of the Left and class consciousness in the Tonghak Revolution.

In the course of the Koch'ang Tenant Farmers Movement, however, the evocation of the Tonghak Revolution was not only to explain activity but also to take stock of inactivity or even passivity. Several activists explained that in Tonghak regions farmers had learned the extraordinarily high costs of political activity. These lessons, however, signaled a productive potential: *han* (pent-up resentment, in this case due to brutal suppression) can lead to action. Here, *han* refers obliquely and variously to anger and resentment that build over time and under the weight of hardship.[23] The following comments of an outside organizer, in discussing the Koch'ang region, reveal both senses of the Tonghak legacy:

> Koch'ang in particular had a strong Left. There are lots of spiritual hardships and wounds. . . . On the other hand, this experience has become a wall to action today. . . . So if you look at Koch'ang, you find that although it has no concrete farmers' organization, the opposition

party is strong. . . . But the [farmers'] defeatism and slave mentality must be obliterated.

Minjung thus also allows for a history of compromise, collaboration, acquiescence, and weakness. The minjung theologian Suh Kwang-sun (1981: 24) points out that han, for example, has a "negative element": "It does not change anything. It might arouse a sense of revenge at most. But mostly it would be submission or resignation to fate." We will see that submission or resignation also figures in the drama and idioms of the Koch'ang Tenant Farmers Movement.

The idiom of han, a historical poesis, sketches some of the aesthetics of the minjung historical gaze. I am interested in han not as an essential element of "Korean culture" but rather as an idiomatic convention employed in particular narratives of mobilization. It makes room for a concept of memory that is not defined by temporally bounded straight lines and the drawing of historical or political lineages but, rather, by a fragmented pastiche. In conjunction, then, han also allows for corresponding notions of conscientization whereby both the genealogical "real" memory of individual biographies and the "fragmentary memory" of the past can politicize. In a single word, "han" connotes both the collective and the individual genealogical senses of the hardship of historical experience. In implying the accumulated anger of resentment born of such experience, it relaxes the temporal and geographic patchwork of passive and active, resistance and nonresistance—by not forcing the distinction. It furthermore assumes that historical experience does not need to be individually or consciously part of the rationale by which people explain their actions or motivations, particularly when protest or struggle is involved. Han's latency renders it powerful: when the collective or individual experience is not the source of self-conscious action, han accumulates, gradually becoming a greater force to fuel an eventual "blow-up." Indeed, people speak about han as something that eventually explodes. Pak Kyŏng-ni, the author of the aforementioned serial novel T'oji, referred at length to han at the October 1994 "First T'oji Seminar" (Che 1-hoe T'oji semina). Although the work is widely appreciated as a historical novel, she directed readers to focus on the work as an exploration of han: "If one wants to find the subject of T'oji, one would first need to begin with an exploration of han. What is han? It is a word that refers to the spirit that is forced out [like blood]. . . . T'oji's primary intrinsic form is the accumulation of han [han-maech'im] and the solving of han [haehan], and its primary subject is the severe homeland of those lives that face this haehan" (Chŏng 1994: 209).

Ŭisikhwa (conscientization), a central trope in the Koch'ang movement, is precisely a narrative of such explosion. Ŭisikhwa imagines a dialectical process instead of a unidirectional imposition. It is not merely the awakening of dormant minjung histories, but a meeting between models of political awakening itself, between variant understandings of the relation of the present and the past. In the very moment of evocation, historical conscious-ness is already a dialogue. For some in the community of dissent, the pro-cess of conscientization was understood as a natural process of revelation or awakening of the radical historical experience that had been silenced by state hegemonic processes. For people invested against conscientization and the changes it augured, the farmers protest was understood as the result of artifices produced by activists and activism. Revelation and con-struction, however, make for an artificial dichotomy. Rather, the stasis shat-tered by historical revelation and the potential for historical construction are both historically contingent on and circumscribed by hegemonic pro-cesses. Conscientization was predominantly an awakening of farmers to the strategic value of subjectifying historical practice of minjung culture and history, *rather than* the alerting of farmers to some "natural" or "historical" essence. An examination of such dialogues and dialectics is integral to the analysis of a social movement.

I am intrigued by a distinction that Benedict Anderson draws in *Imagined Communities* when he notes that "the difference between the inventions of 'official nationalism' and that of other types is usually that between *lies and myth*" (1983: 146; emphasis mine). Both official lies and dissenting myths exist in the discourses and practices of the Koch'ang Tenant Farmers Movement. Both are real historical strategies and real politics: the farmers stand in the discursive space of both state lies of official nationalism and activist myths of other nationalisms. A consideration of both the mobiliza-tion and the silence of farmers must take place in the context of these dialectics.

Drawn from the literature on the Tonghak Revolution and from discus-sions of conscientization in the Koch'ang Tenant Farmers Movement, this chapter's narratives constitute models of memory and mobilization. Min-jung emerges as a creative idiom for imagining a past that offers legacies—conscious and unconscious—of broad-based anticolonial, anti-imperial, and antiauthoritarian action. The next chapter introduces the Koch'ang Tenant Farmers Movement during the month of protest in Seoul, replete with the narratives and practices of mobilization.

CHAPTER THREE

The Practices of Protest: A Month in Seoul

As social movements develop a struggle around a particular program, meanings which appear to have been fixed in place forever begin to lose their moorings.
—STUART HALL (1985: 112)

When three million slept, we awoke—
The day that the Korean farmer brothers and sisters screamed out—
Biting at our fingers, we are brothers and sisters vowing to shout out the truth—
Our new history springs forth from the bright sun—
Three thousand ri,[1] all over the country, it is the banner of the farmers—
Yearning for a day of brilliant victory—
We are dancing, fighting brothers and sisters.
—*NONGMIN' GA* (FARMER SONG)

From August 12 to September 12, 1987, two hundred tenant farmers from sixteen villages in Koch'ang in North Chŏlla Province staged a monthlong sit-in demonstration—characterized by communal living, protest, violent confrontation, and formal negotiation—at the headquarters of their corporate landlord, Samyang Corporation, in Seoul.[2] At that time, a protest of this sort was unprecedented. This chapter presents an interpretive narrative of that month, documenting both its routines and ruptures. The month of protest was not simply a confrontation between fixed sides, with set platforms and goals, but involved actions and agendas that were continually restructured and reconstituted on both sides.[3] Alongside the more public and obviously political aspects of the protest, the mundane aspects of daily protest life, including the food preparation and the sleeping arrangements, were also significant. Setting up house in Seoul was an effort at livelihood, an integral part of the struggle—part of the business of "living and eating" that farmers so often told me was their province.

Although the numbers of protesters largely remained constant, the membership shifted. In many cases, husband and wife, or father and son, traded off one or more times. Invisible in Seoul was the enormous effort required in the countryside to tend to the duties of household management, including the care of children, crops, and animals, in the absence of critical family members. In one of the villages with extensive participation

39

of both adult males and females, the son of one farmer single-handedly tended to the fields of some five families.

Before I continue, I will briefly visit a mediated protest, a late 1980s South Korean film (and play), *Ch'il-su wa Man-su* (Ch'il-su and Man-su). The film is an ironic parable in which protest is quite literally fabricated by the forces that suppress it. Although I do not intend to suggest that the struggle of these farmers was in any way fictional or imaginary, from *Ch'il-su wa Man-su* I came to appreciate aspects of the escalation of dissent under repressive regimes. In the film, Ch'il-su and Man-su are comrades in the South Korean underclass. Their marginality is easily ascertained. Man-su passed his childhood in a brothel with an alcoholic father who now lives off of a prostitute who once catered to American GIs; Ch'il-su's father is a wartime leftist sentenced by the cold war to lifetime imprisonment.

Ch'il-su and Man-su are billboard painters, and the movie's plot literally balances precariously on the scaffolding of a large billboard. After a long day of work, Man-su follows Ch'il-su to the ledge on the top of the scaffolding where they stand peering at the bird's-eye view cityscape and drinking liquor. They begin, spontaneously, to call out vague critiques of class privilege; the calls escalate to outright denunciations of the urban upper classes. Their voices mount, and their screams become cathartic. Slowly a crowd of passersby coalesces at the base of the building, and before long state agents are drawn to this apparent "labor strike." What follows is the rapid succession of the mobilization of the ranks of the billboard painting company, police units, city officials, and even the army.

Ch'il-su and Man-su continue to yell as the authorities respond to their "demonstration." "What are your demands?" "Is it wages? Are you staging a labor strike?" "Will you commit protest suicides?" "Isn't that a Molotov cocktail you are gripping [actually a bottle]?" Met only with silence—for Ch'il-su and Man-su cannot make out a word and are entirely perplexed by the goings-on—the authorities' queries turn to pleas: "Don't throw the Molotov cocktail!" "We will meet your demands." "Don't commit suicide!" Ch'il-su and Man-su are truly baffled; they are not holding a labor strike, staging a demonstration, or threatening a suicide protest, but simply taking a break after a long day of work. As the authorities begin to amplify their messages, Ch'il-su and Man-su communicate their bewilderment. Their voices still do not carry; they are mere objects propelled by mechanisms of repression against social protest. As members of the riot police begin to climb the scaffolding, Ch'il-su and Man-su beg to be left alone. After a futile attempt to escape the authorities, Ch'il-su ends up taking a suicide leap.

At first, Ch'il-su and Man-su are an empty center—the activism imagined by state mobilization. This silent/silenced core, however, is inscribed by the effects of marginalization that can *in fact* be mobilized. As they come to see themselves being seen, the target of their anger shifts from urban privilege—"You down there, you urban elites"—to the tactics and mechanisms of state apparatuses. The suicide completes, or cuts, the spiral of politicization and repression.

I turn now to the projects and projections that comprise the dialectics and spirals that escalated the Koch'ang movement at the acme of its activity.

TO SEOUL: THE PERIPHERY MEETS THE "CITIZENRY"[4]

The largest number of farmers traveling to Seoul went via Chŏngŭp, a regional city in North Chŏlla, where the last trial of farmers taken to court for failing to pay their 1986 tenant rents had been scheduled.[5] The suit had been filed by the company in order to cancel the tenancy contracts and to retrieve the land. Although the decision to boycott the rents had been an organizational one, in the end it was only the farmers who had held out who were being tried. The court cases had become spectator events. Many farmers set out to Chŏngŭp to witness the trial that they hoped would resolve the land issue; most had no idea that they would travel to Seoul. Those who knew of the Seoul plan were not interested in waiting for the unfavorable decision they anticipated. The decision to travel to Seoul on August 12 was an abandonment of the legal process. Some farmers traveled via the courthouse at Chŏngŭp—two hours closer to Seoul than their villages—for an indirect but discreet route to Seoul. Two busloads of farmers left for Seoul at dawn, stealing away from their villages in the dark and quiet of early morning. This group was a testimony to the movement's organizational abilities; representatives in each village had been sworn to secrecy for days about the plan. (In chapter 7, I will explore the internal workings of the villages, which illuminate the need for such stealth.) The two buses, however, never made it out of the district; the police stopped them and the farmers were bused home again. It was commonly understood that news always broke to the police with ease because there were spies among the farmers.

Leaving the courthouse in small groups or traveling directly from their villages, the farmers took various roads to Seoul. Those who chose the always-crowded and infrequent local buses waited for hours and hours. Others went by train. Traveling from Koch'ang to Seoul was always a daylong affair, not because of the distances, but because of the infrequency of public transportation to the underdeveloped pockets of the South Korean countryside. The villages from which these farmers came were quite different from the clusters of "modern" farmhouses that flanked the highway bus routes, built to face those whizzing by. The network of roads that extended to these villages was the final reach of the system: they were unpaved, unkempt, and inconvenient and led to Seoul inefficiently and expensively.

Already on the first night of the tenants' arrival in Seoul, the storytelling had begun—competing tales of how they had come to Seoul and of the trouble they had met on the way. The farmers were gathered at the front of the large grassy expanse at Koryŏ University, whose students had already taken an active part in the pre-Seoul struggle. Koryŏ University grew out of the middle school operated at Posŏng College that Kim Sŏng-su, the deceased founder of Samyang, established during the colonial period for teaching a Korean curriculum. Kim Sang-hyŏp, the son of Kim Yŏn-su who was co-founder of the University and one of the Haeri landlords involved in this struggle, had earlier served as the president of the university. In the final days of the Seoul protest, his emeritus office at the university became a second protest locale for the farmers. On arriving in Seoul, the farmers who had traveled there in their separate ways seemed to be amazed at the strength of their numbers. En route that day, it had been impossible to know the extent and resolve of the Samyang tenants. The farmers were seated by village, a count was taken, and the delight of those from well-represented villages was sounded with cheers. Well past 10:00 P.M., the farmers were growing tired, hungry, and excited. The protest reprise, the *Farmer Song*, pierced the evening silence of this otherwise deserted college campus.

Koryŏ University, one of South Korea's most prestigious private universities, is known for its student activism. The small but attractive campus, with Gothic buildings, inclines upward from a busy throughway. At this university, as at others, there is a small space at the front of the campus, a narrow half of a hexagon between a small building for the university guards and street traffic. It is there that students demonstrated.[6] It is almost as if university planners had anticipated the need for a "protest strip." The grassy hill on which the farmers were assembled stretched out just behind this televised protest spot. In the geography of student protest, the drama unfolds at university gates, and the zone between the campus and the city becomes the border between illegal public space for the students and off-limits private space for the police units assigned to suppress the students. In the thick of student protests, these borders blurred in the clouds of tear gas, the confusion of army green, and piercing protest cries. That night, though, there was no confrontation and the university guards stood by quietly. One wonders what response the farmers would have received had they arrived in Seoul even a year earlier, before the events of June 1987. That evening, though, the Koryŏ University yard was merely a reunion spot, not a protest milieu.

Traveling to Seoul, most farmers had absolutely no idea, and the members of the leadership committee little more, of where they would spend the night. This decision—where to house the sit-in—was crucial, for it more than anything else defined the enemy both for the protesters and for onlookers. Weeks later, well settled in the Samyang headquarters, farmers began to laugh about residing there permanently if they did not retrieve their land. They joked about having *ch'ulse* (risen in the world). By the time the farmers were established at the Samyang headquarters, it was hard to imagine that initially there was no consensus as to where the protest should be staged. Many of the farmers themselves were not aware that their final destination was still being debated that first night on the Koryŏ University campus. The Samyang corporate headquarters was but one of several sleeping arrangements that students, *oebuseryŏk* (external forces),[7] and farmer leaders had debated by moonlight.

Considerations of economy, history, politics, law, and logistics contended for center stage in the determination of a protest site. The ruling party's political headquarters, the opposition party's political headquarters, the Christian Hall, and Koryŏ University were among the locales considered. Outside organizers—nonfarmers or at least nonlocal farmers—reasoned that farmers' energy could be best concentrated with the experientially "nearest" enemy close at hand. In this case, the Samyang headquarters, the most prominent symbol of their economic oppressor, made the most sense. In 1987, these farmers' relationship to Samyang Corporation, however, was a distant one because Samyang Salt, the company managing the tenant land, had split from Samyang Corporation in June 1956. The situation was even more complicated because the land title was in the name of four individuals[8] who held positions at both Samyang Corporation and Samyang Salt but did not represent either company. In contemporary terms it would only have made sense to go to Samyang Salt, which directly administered the farmers' tenancy. Although Samyang Corporation criticized the farmers for not appealing to Samyang Salt, farmers countered that Samyang Corporation was built with money accrued from their tenant rents.

If the organizers considered the farmers' struggle in its political and historical contexts, it was clear that the government, the "ruling powers," and their American backing had condoned, if not engineered, the history that had left these farmers tenants in the 1980s. In this vein, some proposed a struggle with the ruling party (*yŏdang*), the Minju Chŏngŭidang. Others suggested that as protesters, ready to join the larger community of dissent in South Korea, it would make sense to work under the wing of one of the opposition political parties (*yadang*) or oppositional Christian organizations. Thus some proposed settling at one of the opposition party headquarters or at the Christian Center. Distinguished for its regional identification with the Chŏllas, the opposition party headed by Kim Dae Jung, a South Chŏlla Province native and long-term political dissident, seemed a reasonable option. Organizers, though, also had practical concerns—the logistics of lodging and feeding two hundred farmers. Ultimately, it was these logistical considerations, and a consensus that the economic relations to the landlord were most central for the farmers, that guided the group to the corporation headquarters. Nevertheless, the question of state and corporate complicity in the Koch'ang land matter, and thus the particular nature of state-supported capitalist development, loomed large, as it would throughout the month of protest.

It was near midnight that first day when the farmers ventured to the Samyang headquarters at Chongno 5-ga, a neighborhood on one of Seoul's main arteries, next to the Christian Broadcasting Station (CBS) in the Yŏnji-dong section of the city. Running parallel to Chongno, one of Seoul's east–west arteries, are a primary subway line and fleets of crowded buses. The sidewalks of Chongno 5-ga, stretching between 6-ga and 4-ga, were lined, storefront after storefront, with drugstores whose counters seemed to abut the picture frame windows. The line of white-coated personnel framed against ceiling-high drug mosaics seemed to stretch uninterrupted from store to store and block to block. In this city of specialized commercial zones, the Western-style drugstores of Chongno 5-ga dwindled into electronic outlets approaching Chongno 6-ga, and again into Chinese medicine, prosthetics, and finally shamanic paraphernalia in the opposite direction of Chongno 4-ga. This restorative stretch spanned nation and class with "Western" pharmaceuticals, exorbitantly priced Chinese medicines, and "traditionally Korean" shamanic rituals. Stepping south from this city way, paralleling the stretch from prosthetics to electronic parts, was the East Gate Market (Tongdaemun Sijang). Considered together with the South Gate Market (Namdaemun Sijang) as one of Seoul's major traditional commercial centers, this market was a sea of small booths, market cries, and haggling crowds. Diagonally northeast from Chongno, a small side street led to Samyang's well-manicured eleven-story building, a corporate edifice in an otherwise petty commercial neighborhood. Next door, where the diagonal side street met Taehangno, a much larger road perpendicular to Chongno, stood the Christian Hall, home to CBS and the headquarters of many of South Korea's national Christian organizations. It was a well-known Christian landmark in a city where the Christian cross—"sipcha" (the Chinese character or ideogram for "ten"),[9] so called for its resemblance to the Chinese character—is a green neon mark on every hilltop in the evening landscape. The first floor of the Christian Hall housed a small variety store, a store containing Christian paraphernalia and books, and a small cake shop. Down the street was an alcohol-free gospel restaurant with Christian maxims posted on the walls and a continuous stream of gospel music to accompany standard Korean fare.[10] Although some of the hall's office space was given to the politically conservative Christian organizations, it was also home to many more political groups that had maintained firm oppositional politics throughout the succession of authoritarian regimes in postwar South Korea. Because CBS was allowed to broadcast news during various interludes, it often tested the limits of South Korea's firmly controlled press. In the summer of 1987, however, political news was off-limits. At some distance down the road from CBS, Taehangno (University Street), so called because it once housed Seoul National University (SNU), was a popular center for youth and the arts. Its bourgeois exteriors, however, did not entirely silence the street's historical significance in the history of student protest. In the 1970s, SNU had been relocated—exiled to Seoul's periphery—in the face of mounting student unrest.

Neither the drugstore stretch nor the Christian Center, though, were familiar landmarks for the almost two hundred farmers who had traveled to Seoul on August 12. Samyang, however, was a household name—not only for the plastic pouches of sugar, salt, and animal feed that they purchased at the local agricultural cooperatives at a slight discount[11] but as the landlord corporation for the 291 hectares of land on which they cultivated rice as tenant farmers.

The farmers' decision to protest in Seoul was radical. They sought a dialogue with the Seoul *simin* (citizenry). They had traveled "up" to Seoul, South Korea's political, economic, and cultural core, to transform their peripheral relationship to South Korea's center. They were peripheral on several counts: as *chibang saram* (people of the regions, not Seoul); as *sigol saram* (also *ch'onnom*, men and women of the countryside); and as those who hailed from the Chŏlla provinces on the economically least developed southwestern coast, a region also known for its oppositional politics.[12] During my fieldwork, farmers often asked me, Why did you think to spend your time outside of Seoul? Why in the Chŏlla provinces?[13] Why in agricultural villages? Why in these poorest of all villages? And I would often reply, "Would a Seoul National University professor be able to tell me about your lives?" To this query the answer was usually a resounding "No."[14]

In the months before ascending to Seoul, many farmers had grown fond of an aphorism that underscored the marginalization of this periphery: "A single duck dies in the Han River [Seoul's main river] making newspaper headlines, while thousands in the countryside protest unnoticed, unreported." The river made headlines at this time because of a pre-Olympics beautification measure. Although these farmers' protest chants began in 1985, they had echoed only "between mountain and sea in our villages." Their protest activities earlier that summer in Koch'ang, the primary city in Koch'ang County, had garnered scarcely more attention. Hence traveling up to the capital made perfect sense. In the countryside, farmers knew that Seoul was in flux, and they carefully monitored the changing winds of Seoul's political climate as an index of the country's future.

It was the summer, in a time of political heat, when the farmers set out. They hoped to be noticed not only by the corporate landlords who could relinquish their tenant land, and the political and legal institutions that could wield direct power over the corporation, but also by those who could exert pressure from below, Seoul's simin. The farmers wanted to be reported, to make headlines, and to have newspapers and television carry their struggle back to the periphery. Such reports would send an important message to those who had decided not to participate. On the eve of a return trip to the countryside during the protest, countless demonstrators in Seoul asked me to find out what Koch'ang had "seen" of the demonstration. Indeed, the eyes of cameras and onlookers became vital protest participants.

In the early days of the protest, many farmers, particularly the women, practiced reciting the story of why they had come. The *chidobu* (leadership committee) [15] instructed that such accounts should represent a united movement voice, a single story. Most women, however, were concerned with appealing—emotionally—to the Seoul simin, particularly women. The fourth-floor windows of the room the farmers occupied were picture frames from which to watch—and be watched by—the public; the farmers often peered out to catch people responding to the stream of their announcements broadcast from a loudspeaker. Many women, reflecting later on their time in Seoul, recalled how empowering it had been to recite their story to Seoul citizens. In the countryside, farmers often said to me, "To talk I must have words," meaning, What would a person like me have to say? In Seoul, however, they had sung out in public. Daily visits to the East Gate Market for food shopping, fund-raising outings, and rallies among city dwellers provided opportunities for passionate appeals as they bartered for reduced produce prices, donations, political support, and above all sympathetic indignation over a story that they could tell again and again.

The women, particularly those in their twenties and thirties, tried to appear presentable, to dispel a stereotype of which they were well aware: that rural women were ugly, unkempt, and ignorant. In fact, in the countryside when villagers went out, even to the market, they dressed up, leaving behind the clothes that bespoke physical labor in the fields. I was often chided by village women for wearing my regular village attire to the market. But in Seoul the women's efforts backfired. Several middle-class housewife spectators commented to me that although the old farmers had the faces of poor men—with some sort of legitimate claim to such a movement—the women appeared well fed, prosperous, and not deserving of making such a spectacle of their hardship. The farming women's image of attire befitting an urban audience was not convincing for middle-class women, who expected the drab attire of their stereotype. Although they did not always change their dress, the women did come to comprehend this sensibility.

Back in the countryside, some women criticized each other and the women of other villages for having worn jewelry or applied makeup in Seoul—for having appeared too citified.

Many middle-class onlookers were clearly not sympathetic to the farmers' cause. My own relations with middle-aged middle-class friends became strained when they learned of my activities. In these discussions, prejudices against farmers surfaced in ways they never had when I had previously spoken of farmers as my neighbors and friends in the countryside. One younger friend in Seoul told me that her mother-in-law had said of the Koch'ang farmers, "It will only end if ignorance dies," meaning that the ignorance of these protesting farmers would only disappear with the death of "their sort" of people. In Seoul there was a cultural discourse about backward, lazy, and superstitious villagers. Such rhetoric had particular salience because of the fantastic speed with which a class of those spun from urban success stories has been able to differentiate itself from those they left behind in the countryside. In understanding the response of middle-class onlookers, it is important to remember that many Seoul residents left the countryside during their own lifetimes and continue to own and rent land there. Their reactions to these farmers' cries for landownership were necessarily complex.

THE MESSAGE AND THE MEDIA

When the farmers finally entered the Samyang headquarters on that first evening in Seoul, it had already been a long day. As they left Koryŏ University, they stayed together in groups with student and organizer navigators. On this first day, and many to come, they would joke about the ways in which the vast city eluded them. Most could literally count the times they had been to Seoul, usually under the careful guidance of urban relatives. It is often said that farmers arriving in Seoul use taxis—a luxury well beyond their means—because the intricacies of the bus routes and the city-wide subway system are hard to maneuver and because some of them have difficulty reading.

It was just before 11:00 P.M. when most of these smaller groups began calmly walking through the opening in the iron gate next to the guard house, then through the glass doors into the first floor of the building, past another group of uniformed guards who were always seated toward the back of the first-floor foyer, past the elevator to the stairway, and up to the company's main meeting hall on the fourth floor. The farmers' smooth entrance suggested that the company officials were aware of their plans and had decided to let them enter unopposed.

The enormous meeting hall stretched almost the entire length and much of the width of the building. The base of the building was made up of four stories, and some seven floors stretched from a section of it, making for an L-shaped building; part of the fourth floor was thus a large veranda that extended off of the meeting hall. The veranda was closed in by hand-rails and was furnished with potted plants and concrete benches. The meeting room had little in the way of furniture or decoration: rectangular tables, office chairs, a standing blackboard, and several framed photographs and documents—items of company pride—that were quickly, albeit modestly, defaced. Some farmers spoke of this discreet defacement to demonstrate their good manners, the decorum of their protest. The room opened out to the stairwell and elevator area. After some weeks the banisters had collapsed and protest slogans had been spray-painted in red and black on the stairs and the steel doors at the top of the stairs. Beyond the elevator were the women's and men's bathrooms. Off both sides of a broad hallway running alongside most of the length of the meeting hall were small offices and electrical rooms. The occupiers set up house in this large room and its appendages for thirty days. The props were minimal, and the makeshift pattern of living that the farmers established was as ingenious as their protest was spirited. Urban onlookers commented to me that only farmers could sustain day-to-day life under such circumstances. The farmers complained most that their bodies cricked with discomfort for having done no physical labor for so long.

In clusters organized by village, the occupiers went about claiming spots on the cold floor where scattered bits of clothing doubled as bedding. Many of the older men claimed the tabletops that had already been pushed together in two corners of the room to clear floor space for the expanse of bodies. Stretched from head to toe, the approximately two hundred farmers left little room in the meeting hall for anything else. On warmer nights many of the young farmers and organizers sang and danced on the veranda until the early morning, often sleeping outside.

At 1:00 A.M. that first night, the slumbering few were awakened for the first meeting. At the center were the two men who would most often stand in front of the group over the month to come: Min and Yun. During this time they often stood side by side, competing, although not explicitly, for leadership and followers. Min, short and sturdy and in his late thirties, was a professional organizer, a charismatic officer of the Catholic Farmers Union (CFU; K'at'ollik Nongminhoe) in the North Chŏlla region. His voice was loud, though his words were garbled, and his tone was aggressive yet mocking and sometimes playful. His every movement and utterance were spirited and robust. He laughed heartily, spoke in bursts, and exuded an arrogant confidence. Min often presented himself as a local because he was residing in and hailed from North Chŏlla Province and because he had tilled the earth. Although he was not an active farmer at this time, he had farmed for several years in North Chŏlla. He had a seemingly never-ending store of irreverent tales and anecdotes drawn from his own years of protest, imprisonment, and hardship. He often spoke of his Vietnam War[16] days when the "eyes" of the enemy cried out to him as a "fellow Asian," of the crimes of the United States, and of his exodus during the Kwangju Uprising. Again and again, he pointed to injustices of the U.S. and South Korean states. The farmers also came to know that he met and fell in love with his wife while in hiding after the Kwangju Uprising and that he had broken with Korean kinship norms by adopting a child.[17] The details of his personal and political life were of great interest to the farmers. One woman told me and a small group of women that she would die happy if she could spend even a single day married to a man like him; Min's warmth, humor, and conviction were indeed captivating.

Yun, a tall, wiry, handsome fisherman/farmer with well-chiseled features, was the self-proclaimed and widely recognized founder of the movement and head of the Relinquish Committee. He was soft-spoken and businesslike, and commanded leadership in a very different way than Min; he exuded a quieter confidence, a shy charisma. Yun also had protest stories, but none that predated this movement. Yun, like Min, spoke well and marshaled authority with ease. He secured attention with silence, saying that he was tired and that struggles are long and difficult. Min, in contrast, called for attention with his unyielding verve and subversive spirit, appealing to the true fighters of the crowd.

Yun, lifelong local resident, and Min, astute organizer, were both savvy about their audience—how to quiet, appeal to, and persuade them. Later it became clear that Min aspired to mentor a vanguard but Yun saw himself as the founder of the movement and the mouthpiece for "all" the protesters. Both Min and Yun were successful leaders, but by the end of the month, they came to openly oppose each other, having divided the farmers' allegiances.

That first night, Min—an outsider himself and often an interpreter of outside events—reported on the August 12 court trial where he had served as the farmers' spokesman, explaining that it was unlikely that anything would be decided before winter because of the Land Leasing Protection Law that was proposed for October 1987.[18] He proclaimed that regardless of the trial and court decision, "we" should fight to make the land "our" own. Then Yun instructed the group on five rules of protest and occupation: they were to act in an orderly fashion precluding "individual action" (action not in accordance with the group); they were, if asked, to tell the police or people from the corporation that "we have already long paid [in rents] more than the price of the land, that it should have become ours over thirty years ago, and that this building was constructed with rents we should never have paid"; they should, however, never engage in detailed discussion with company people or the police; they should, by village, compile a list of those present; and finally, they should select people to be put in charge of directing the protest, announcing the slogans and songs, and guarding the doors of the large meeting room. The farmers were explicitly warned that if they talked too much, if they indulged in personal stories or renditions, they might undermine the group's official position. The safest plan, the leaders figured, was a memorized pitch; the consensus, though, was never as solid as these directives mandated.

That first night the farmers were mainly concerned about their meeting with the public the following day when the movement's declaration of purpose would be presented to the press. By 2:00 A.M., the lights were off and the farmers were sleeping, clustered in village enclaves segregated by sex. I slept near the door close to the elevator with the women from Kungsan, the village where I had been living.

The next morning, activity began when one of the organizers proclaimed "Farmers are nothing unless they have strength and power. Otherwise, they are like wild apricots with a delicious-looking skin but no taste, no content. To embark on this struggle as subjects and to be victorious, we must cooperate and mobilize all methods." The crowd bellowed "Right, right" and applauded, but the mood that morning was anxious. Although there was not yet a pattern that could predict the day's routine, in keeping with village life everyone was up early. Announcements began at 8:00 A.M., and by 9:30 everyone had gathered on the veranda to sing songs and chant slogans. They nervously anticipated the media that was due to arrive sometime in the morning.

Demonstrating was a learned art. In the farmers' minds it was the special province of students and young urban types, so when it came to the techniques of protest, they stood ready to learn. A caller stood in front, and in antiphonic unison they repeated the final words of each slogan line; the effect was not unlike that of cheerleading in the United States. The songs were written on both sides of a large blackboard that was placed in plain view of the crowd, though many of the farmers could not read the letters.

> The farmers of Koch'ang have united!
> Samyang, be ready to meet our demands!
> Samyang, who robbed farmers' land, are thieves!
> The current government—to which Samyang gives thanks—retreat!
> Samyang—after fifty years of bleeding [farmers]—stand up!

The organizers instructed the farmers on the voice, tone, and body movements of slogan chanting.

> When you yell out the slogans, don't hold your hands just any way. We must be strong so that when others look they think, "Ah, those people are strong." Do it like this: first extend your fist to the sky and in the

final thrust let your fingers fly open; this is how to do it when you sing the *Farmer Song*. Follow us at the front and it will be fine.

And the farmers were led in another chorus of slogans.

Samyang—evil landlord—leave this land!
Fifty years of unjust exploitation—down with Samyang!
Relinquish the tenant fields immediately!
We farmers who cried as tenants—let's find our land and laugh!
We farmers want to live—return the land!
Samyang that sucks farmers' blood—self-destruct!
Retrieve our land—pass it down to our descendants!
The Koch'ang farmers have united—let's retrieve the land taken from us!
The current government that protects Samyang—repent!
Fifty years of flowing blood—now you pay the price!
Human leach Kim Sang-hyŏp—return our blood!
Let's drive out the evil landlord Samyang!
We have banded together—we will win!
Koch'ang farmers united—Samyang apologize!

The protest culture of students and urbanites had for a long time borrowed explicitly from the repertoire of resistance in rural daily life and from the history of peasant protest. Instructing farmers in protest technique and song was thus a cultural and historical sleight of hand. The students, those who had dispersed in the Koch'ang villages before Seoul and those who helped out in Seoul, were merely enlightening farmers on what was already understood as the farmer's own province. Over and over, farmers expressed their appreciation of student demonstrators. One farmer spoke of students' "beauty and power" when they extended their fists and fingers for the demonstration chants. This awe, however, was not entirely uniform; for most farmers it was newfound. The controlled media to which the farmers had long been subject had brandished students as extremists, North Korean sympathizers, and Communists—a lexicon of fear and loathing for most farmers at that time. Furthermore, for farmers, demonstrating students symbolized missed opportunity; it was unthinkable that the lucky few who attended Seoul's finest universities would give up their chances to succeed. After all, for many farmers hope hung on the dream of a university education for a son (and less often a daughter). Thus, through the experience of protest in the countryside and in Seoul, powerful transformations occurred: social protest generated hope, and demonstrating students became "beautiful." If farmers, however, were sure that students were the modern-day protesters, the ones from whom to learn the code of protest, students were certain that the heart of protest was to be found in the popular culture of poor peasants who, if not actual protesters in the past, danced and sang an oppositional culture.

Protest reports often implied that the angry mob had spontaneously authored the movement's slogans, declarations, and songs. The brilliance, though, of this often tutored authorship was precisely this appearance: the words befitted the sentiment of the crowd and were voiced as if their source was spontaneously collective. This is not to suggest that the farmer crowd had no spontaneity or veto power; it had both. Over time some songs and slogans became the standard ones, while others, although carefully instructed, never took root. In some cases, the repertoire was extended by farmers' contributions and innovations. There was also the veto power of memory: farmers chose to memorize some songs and not others. Some farmers resisted slogans that strayed from the immediate issue into more general political and social ills. A slogan calling for the "retreat" of the government, for example, was spontaneously mollified and settled into the protest routine as "reform." The songs, slogans, and protest were aimed at public audiences, but they also played a vital part in the "private" life on the fourth floor of the building. Organizers, farmer leaders, and farmers themselves quickly realized that singing and slogan chanting brought people together and enlivened the spirit of the crowd. The *Farmer Song* was the most repeated refrain when the demonstrators faced crowds of onlookers and during the residential life of the protest. It was not uncommon to hear the song ten or twenty times daily. Some farmers performed the song with powerful hand motions they had learned from participating students. Its tempo was always guarded by thrusts of clenched fists, the standard gesture to accompany protest songs. The "new history" that "springs forth from the bright sun" resonated with this movement's claims. "Awakening," "screaming out," "shouting out the truth," the song was determined and dramatic, and farmers sang it to shatter calm and to announce that calm had been shattered.

Nonfarmer organizers and citizens' groups validated the significance of the farmers' drama, celebrating the movement both for its historical representativeness and its historical particularity. They affirmed the claim that the tenant land should have been distributed to the farmers long ago by establishing that the farmers' story reflected deep historical structures—the laws of victors and losers in South Korea's postwar era. In turn, they noted the movement's particularity as a novel protest that took up dangerous issues in a very public forum.

On that first morning of protest, immediately after the reading of the declaration, five organizations joined in presenting a declaration of support. It told the farmers that by coming to Seoul to this meeting room, they had "exposed history," revealing a very "embarrassing affair." Their declaration referred to history's "universal conscience" and "natural principles" and trumpeted the Enlightenment path of human history: "What you have insisted on until now is only the most natural thing. The first principle of farming is that 'land goes to the tiller'; this is not only the path that our country must take, but also the public opinion of the world. If those in politics would only relinquish their political power, everything would be fine." The declaration addressed the farmers not only as Samyang's brave tenants but also as members of a farming class in a particular historic relationship to industrial capitalist production: "Your struggle exposes how farmers—the subject of life, our basic industry and production—have been long ridiculed but will no longer be overlooked. So, as the head of the farmers' division of the Kungmin Undong Ponbu [National Movement Headquarters],[19] we present this declaration."

This declaration called for the government to create a "basic policy for the land problem" and to suspend the "import of foreign agricultural goods" so as to secure the "key points of a self-sufficient economy." It addressed farmers as those who "amid hardship had struggled under the banner of farmer liberation and national unification." It referred to the landlords as supporters of the country's academic, business, and current dictatorial political community. In this way the farmers were told that their movement was at the center of both national and international economic and political struggle. Farmers were also told that land issues like theirs were widespread in South Korea and that if they were successful, many people would fight against corporate ownership and nonresident landlords.

Many visitors stressed the economic and even moral value of farmers, speaking of their fundamental social role as providing the staple food product for every Korean. One women's group addressed the farmers on the question of police violence: "How can police be violent to farmers? . . . We must tell everyone in Seoul that without farmers there would be no police. . . . We can live without Samyang sugar [one of Samyang's products], but can we live without rice?" Fishermen from nearby Kyŏnggi Province offered: "Our people's minjung movement hasn't been victorious since the time of Tan'gun [the mythical founder of Korea], including Tonghak. So, the achievement of your goal has great meaning for the farmers and fishermen of the Republic of Korea. You should be ready to die for your victory and become ancestors that your descendants can be proud of." The chairman of the Christian Farmers League (CFL) said, "The government, under the banner of constitutional revision, is ignoring the issue of human rights. . . . Insist on the 'truth' that the land should belong to the farmers and continue the movement until that truth is realized." A minister from Chŏnju, the capital city of North Chŏlla, cheered the farmers on—"Korean democracy will be achieved if the Koch'ang farmers unite"—and praised them by adding, "You will be the standard for all farmers."

On that first morning, the songs and slogans quieted to make way for the farmers' formal declaration. Choi, the vice president of the Relinquish

Committee, a heavy-set farmer whose city suit could not conceal a complex-ion ruddy from field work, presented it. This was all a rehearsal for a later performance in front of the television cameras. By 9:40 A.M., MBC, South Korea's public broadcasting company, and CBS, the Christian station, had arrived. Cheers, multiple declarations, and songs were repeated for televi-sion, the eye of the public. The protesters knew not only that these televi-sion cameras would report their news but also that the reports themselves would help produce their movement. It was with this understanding that the farmers had come to Seoul. When it turned out that the response of the press was indifference, the farmers were angered by this more deeply than by any other external response to the movement.

But that morning, having addressed the media, the farmers next faced Kim Sang-don, one of four landlords who had arrived at 11:15 A.M. Within moments a confrontation ensued. Although no clear consensus had been reached about the movement's agenda, farmers were easily united as to how they wanted to be treated: as social equals of the landlords. When Kim Sang-don appeared, he seemed to perform a caricature of himself: the generic landlord whom the farming women had hilariously parodied in village improvisational dramas that organizers had led them in—a man who struts like a peacock, chirps in a piqued voice, and frowns on the "plebes," the farmer riffraff.[20] Although Kim Sang-don did not strut, his son-in-law, Kim Sŏn-hwi, vice president of Samyang Salt, did. Both had en-tered the large room and rushed to a lectern on a slightly raised dais at the far end. Moments after Kim Sang-don began his address,[21] the farmers demanded that he come down from the platform and stand on the same ground with them. His limbs were shaking when he finally stepped down, and he stood petrified in front of the seated farmers. Having stepped down, it was as if he understood that his logic, the rules of his world, would not be accepted here. The farmers' wrath at the landlord's inclination to "stand above" them was spontaneous, not an outcome of teachings in pro-test technique. On several occasions over the course of the protest month, Korean language usage became a bone of contention because it marked social hierarchy and distance.[22]

Just the day before, when many farmers had been furtively stealing to-ward Seoul, a language skirmish had broken the formal, if nervous, deco-rum of the courthouse in Chŏngŭp. One spry farming woman in her forties complained bitterly of the haughty manner in which the judge, in his late thirties or early forties, had addressed an elder from the village. Up in arms, she stood and repeated her objection, to which the judge replied in a harsh tone and informal language that if she spoke further she would have to leave the courtroom. Her behavior was a transgression of standard comportment in a formal or bureaucratic setting. The skirmish occurred over the terms that the elderly farmer had employed to refer to a unit of farmland. Because the judge wanted to understand the productivity of the land, it was essential to understand the farmer's land measurement terms. However, the witness, who had worked as a laborer during the land reclamation, narrated the history of the land in his local dialect and measured the land by local terms. Land measurement terms are decentralized, varying even within districts. The judge had asked the witness to translate the local terms into a more "standard idiom" and was eventually discourteous as he pressured the elderly farmer to translate. Several village women who had traveled to observe the trial arduously defended his terms, and with them the authority of local narratives. When the judge finally told these women to leave the courtroom, he used *panmal* (half-language) reserved for younger or familiar people and thus further incurred the farmers' wrath. When the crowd burst into an uproar at the judge's impolite address, he apologized.

After having made Kim Sang-don "step down," and having successfully addressed the media and the landlords, the farmers awaited their television appearance. They watched each news hour, afternoon, evening, and night, but it soon became clear that except for a brief radio report, the August 13 footage had not made the news. This lack of coverage shocked the farmers; it was as if nobody had taken notice that they had turned the(ir) world on its head. Visitors to the headquarters were barraged with questions as to whether they had seen anything on television. In fact, it was not until August 15 that the story was covered in the *Dong-A Daily*,[23] one of the most prominent national newspapers, which farmers would later refer to as the "eyes and ears of the nation." The August 15 article, however, was not only scanty and marginally placed but also contained blatant distortions, denying the legitimacy of the farmers' protest by entirely negating their historical claim.

> Farmers from North Chŏlla Province, Koch'ang County, Haeri and Simwŏn districts, have come to Seoul and are on the fourth day of occupying the fourth floor of the Samyang building in Chongno-gu, Yŏnji-dong, and are demanding a relinquishment of the Samyang Salt land that they cultivate. The farmers claim that "since 1955 we have farmed 291 hectares of land in the Koch'ang region, the land must be returned to those who are currently cultivating it." In answer to these assertions and demands, Samyang, for its part, clarified that "the Haeri reclamation land is legitimately owned property and the call for relinquishment by the Relinquish Committee is unjust."

The *Dong-A Daily* appeared to have colluded with the company in negating the farmers' central charge, by indicating that the farmers had only been farming since 1955 and by further reporting that this was the farmers' own claim. The movement turned on whether the farmers had been cultivating the reclamation land at the time of the South Korean land reform in 1949.

It would have been an absurdity if the farmers had professed to have only begun farming the land in 1955.

Both farmers and nonfarmers responded angrily to the *Dong-A Daily* article. Their responses, however, were founded on somewhat different grounds, depending on how each group understood the particular history on trial and, more generally, the authority of history in contemporary South Korea. Nonfarmer activists were concerned with the historical connection between the Samyang and Dong-A corporations. Samyang's Kim Sŏng-su was also one of the 1920 founders of the *Dong-A Daily*. They saw this relationship as symbolizing the collusion of Korea's power elite with successive authoritarian regimes. From this view, the newspaper distortion revealed above all the *Dong-A Daily* Samyang connection, a meticulously embroidered web of oppressors. Movement publications, largely authored by external forces, correspondingly denounced the *Dong-A Daily* for its "antinational character."

Farmers, however, were most bitter that their protest had been ignored, their history distorted, and their words twisted. The power relationship between farmers like themselves and institutions like the *Dong-A Daily* was obvious even without knowing about the particulars of the historical relations between the elites implicated in their struggle, connections they largely learned about for the first time through the movement.

On the morning of August 15, the day the article appeared, the farmers began to cover the walls outside with posters proclaiming the unjust coverage and calling for Seoul citizens to phone the *Dong-A Daily* and complain. The farmers themselves became relentless phone protesters. Among the farmers it became known that a reporter at another newspaper company had said, "If the *Dong-A Daily* does not report it [the story], we can't either. It is customary practice among the newspaper companies to refrain from reporting incidents about other newspaper companies." Collusion among the various presses was a fact of this protest, and by the end of the month, some farmers had become quite articulate on the historical relations of the corporate elite, the landowning class, and the state.

By August 19, a week into the protest, farmers and organizers alike had become furious at the lack of media attention—by then only a flash on television, distorted newspaper tidbits, and mediocre radio coverage. Because the *Dong-A Daily* had made no print concessions despite the farmers' written demands, the farmers thus decided to venture directly to the *Dong-A Daily* headquarters and make their demands known. One *Dong-A Daily* writer reportedly said that never before in the sixty-two-year history of the newspaper had a group of farmers staged a protest there. Most memorable about the protest was that the farmers arrived at the newspaper offices with the feces and urine that Min had encouraged the women to save. *Ttong* (shit) is but a slight variation of the *tong* (east) of *Dong-A* (*Tonga* in standard

romanization) *Daily*. *Ttonga Ilbo* thus became a wordplay for "Shit Daily."
Months later, back in the countryside, farmers still referred laughingly to
the newspaper as the *Ttonga Ilbo*.

Early on August 19, about twenty farmers—armed with their own shit—
set out for the newspaper company. The group included old men, chosen
for their impressive presence as witnesses of history, and the most adamant
demonstrators among the younger women, included for their verve. Because the newspaper happened to be conducting a fund-raising campaign,
the farmers managed to enter four and five at a time under false pretenses.
They proceeded directly to the editor's office, and there they smeared their
cargo on the desks and phones and against the wall, on which they wrote,
"Hey, you bastards from *Dong-A Daily* who deceive farmers, why don't you
eat shit." Having overturned desks and bookshelves and ripped up newspaper drafts, they proceeded to make four demands: first, that the distortions
from the August 15 article be corrected; second, that there be fair reporting of the tenant relinquishment demonstration activities; third, that
the incident of Tongdaemun police officers (to be discussed later) against
the farmers at Taehangno be reported; and finally, that the chief editor
make a public apology directly to the farmers. The assistant editor appeared and promised to correct the errors in the article. He apologized
that the Taehangno incident had been "omitted" and promised to cover it
fairly. The farmers were eventually pushed out of the company by some
two hundred policemen.

Two days later, on August 21, a second article appeared in the *Dong-A
Daily:*

> On the fourth floor of the headquarters of the Samyang company approxi-
> mately 200 demonstrators from Koch'ang have proclaimed that the land they
> are farming has been continuously cultivated since 1939. And furthermore,
> they insist on an unconditional relinquishment given that the tenant rents
> [they have paid over the years] add up to eight times the price of the paddy.

The farmers were still dissatisfied with this second article, for it spoke of
the continuous cultivation as only the farmers' *contention*. They responded
with a pamphlet in which they described their grievance. In it they listed
the phone numbers for Samyang, the *Dong-A Daily,* and Koryŏ University
and appealed that citizens make phone calls to protest the "antinational
character" of these institutions. They asked that people not read the *Dong-
A Daily,* boycott Samyang products, and drive Kim Sang-hyŏp out of the
university. They also printed a bank account number for donations to the
movement.[24]

Samyang reprimanded the farmers for the *Dong-A* incident at the third
of eight formal negotiation sessions. Although the Samyang chairman
acknowledged that the *Dong-A Daily* had misreported the incident, he

defended the newspaper, saying that it was not alone in making such reports. The chairman went on at great length about the opprobrium the farmers had incurred from the corporation and from Seoul citizens because of their behavior. He called the *Dong-A Daily* a "national mouthpiece" and chided the farmers for throwing excrement on "this sacred mass media institution of our history and tradition." For the company elite, the incident had been a vulgar public display, an insult not only to a kindred corporation but also to a national symbol. Throughout the month, the company feared "group action"—anything out of control. The farmers explained that what the company called "offensive" was what they "couldn't help but do" given the circumstances. They proclaimed that "in spite of their phone requests," the newspaper had the audacity to "speak as if it [the distortion] was a proud thing." Yun explained the *Dong-A* incident, saying, "In Seoul, we feel that in our society the common people have been completely forgotten. If people don't listen to our just demands it is inevitable that we proceed to such action." Beyond media machinations and scatological scenes, the farmers established a daily life of protest, to which I now turn.

THE DAILY LIFE OF PROTEST

Daily midmorning and midafternoon protest sessions made meals and slumber seem like preparation, like lag periods between protest. By the second day, a geography of protest had already been mapped. The demonstrations were staged on the corporation's cement driveway behind the iron gates, which were open during the day. This was the ideal place for performance since the driveway sloped down to meet the street. The farmers would walk down the four flights of stairs, past the guards, and out to the cement stretch where they lined up in rows. They squatted, the standard pose in rural areas for field work and spontaneous conversation, and sometimes sat directly on the pavement. It was warm, sometimes hot and humid. The side street on which the corporation stood was not a busy one, and it was easy for onlookers to cluster there, to gawk at the farmers or sympathize with the chants, cries, and song. Some of the elderly male farmers (some in their eighties) who were dressed in Korean white garb—a long-standing national symbol—lined up at the front. In addition to being a sign of respect for their senior positions in village hierarchies, their position at the front of the protest was designed to highlight their role as "real witnesses" in this fight over history. From the very early days the older men took to propping up body-sized placards with detailed messages for onlookers to focus on. Headbands of torn white cloth emblazoned with red slogans—in the image of premodern peasant rebels, like those in the Tonghak Peasant Revolution—were features of the protest garb. Facing this front line of "grandfathers" stood slogan chanters, younger men and women who had been appointed at a general assembly, whose job it was to call out slogans for choruslike repetition. The songs and chants of the farmers were punctuated by the thrusting fists and outstretched fingers that the student protesters had taught them. Some farmers became known for their particularly passionate facial expressions while singing and chanting. Several women were identified with particular songs, songs that they sang out best and loudest, and some were even given nicknames for the songs, chants, or postures that they had somehow personalized. Farmers often praised one another for "sincere" and "dramatic" facial expressions and for effective poses.

The songs presented the basic aims of the movement. Most of them were reworked student movement protest songs, which were in turn adaptations of folk songs or political songs from the 1970s and 1980s. Other than the *Farmer Song*, the one that settled most easily into the routine was one with straightforward claims and demands:

North Chŏlla Province, Koch'ang County, Haeri District, Simwŏn District
   2,850,000 p'yŏng is our land
No matter how much Samyang demands it is theirs—the tenant fields are
   our land
The farmers of Koch'ang have united—Samyang resign yourselves
The fifty years of flowing blood are truly unfair
Now we have found our land
Samyang—leave
Kim Sŏng-su, Kim Yŏn-su—collaborators of the Japanese, no matter how
   much you defend yourselves
Brothers whose life work was clearly collaborating with the Japanese—you
   are national betrayers
What is this talk of unfinished land? [25]
What is this change to salt fields? [26]
It [the reclamation land] was excluded from land distribution—Samyang
   that despised the farmers, you are thieves.

In addition to such informative songs, the movement also communicated with posters that were affixed daily on a brick wall in front of the corporation that veered toward Chongno 3-ga. They were carefully lettered and quite often lengthy declarations for the public eye. Initially it was largely the official declarations of the movement organization and of other supporting organizations that were posted, but this changed over time. Historical accounts were added which documented the background of the movement, and eventually the posters reported primarily on the farmers' residence in Seoul, focusing on the various injustices they suffered. These posters were composed and lettered by the support staff of students and organizers well into the early hours of each morning. As was common practice on university campuses, the posters were removed regularly, and day after day they had to be rewritten because each morning only tatters remained.

From the fourth floor, farmers peered with great interest at the men in business suits who stopped to read these signs. Some farmers took to standing by the posters, ready to launch into spirited discussion with interested passersby. I observed how carefully some onlookers read the posters, scanning one after another for well over thirty minutes. This was in part a reflection of how out of the ordinary it was to find at a corporation protesting farmers who looked like the *kohyang* (hometown) relatives of so many Seoulites. The interest of passersby also reflected the times: August 1987, suspended between the June 1987 declaration and the December 1987 elections, was a time of increased freedom for dissent and of the restructuring of public discourse. This made for city residents who were not afraid to stop and observe the protest and to learn about the events. The onlookers could hardly have missed the August 14 (Day 3) message spray-painted on the protest ground: "National betrayers Kim Sŏng-su, Kim Yŏn-su, Samyang—blow yourselves up!" They were surprised at this defamation of historical personages heralded by the state as great nationalists.

The street in front of the building was bordered on the other side by a makeshift wall that enclosed an empty lot occasionally used for parking. Beyond the lot was a busy throughway well traveled by cars, taxis, and buses. There were times when a second crowd of onlookers would gather behind the wall, another layer away from the core. But onlookers of another sort, various Seoul officials, hovered on both sides of the company building. At times farmers noticed the policemen perched in the second- and third-story windows of a building across the street. Farmers asked me again and again to photograph the policemen in the windows, to document those particular spectators. At the most violent and tumultuous moments of the demonstration, the vacant lot behind the wall transmogrified into the parking zone for buses of combat police units in military green who "hid" well noticed behind the wall.

Also among the onlookers were the uniformed women and the men in business suits, the employees of Samyang, who stared, perplexed, down on the veranda from behind curtains on the upper floors of the Samyang building. In some of the windows the curtains were pushed far to the side and the employees gawked; in others an employee or two stole careful glances. The farmers were not antagonistic; these were workers with whom many farmers assumed their cause would strike an empathetic chord. Over time, though, it became clear that the chord of empathy was unresounding, as day and night the curtains remained fully drawn. As relations between white-collar workers and farmers became increasingly strained, it was only an occasional early-morning maid who would, a corner of curtain clutched in hand, glance down at the daily spectacle of breakfast preparation on the veranda.

On August 20, one of the guards called the farmers "reds," querying facetiously, "Who, in today's society, talks of [no-compensation] relinquishment?" and then hit one farmer on the head and chest. Talk of "no-compensation relinquishment" was emotionally charged because it was understood to be a Communist land reform practice, like the one promulgated in North Korea. Farm women went to attack this guard, but the other guards locked shoulders to protect him. Although the farmers reported this incident to the police, who sent a detective, it was never resolved. Farmers and guards on many occasions were mutually offended and angered by undeferential tones or crass language. That the building guards, those lowest on Samyang's urban totem pole, would be the ones to confront their rural counterparts most violently was an irony noticed both by farmers and organizers. That a few elites would not lend sympathy did not offend their common sense, but that the regular folk of Seoul—the daughters and sons of farmers or low company employees—did not was harder to accept.

Over time, the protest spaces were extended. On the third day of protest, the farmers had demonstrated in the first-floor elevator foyer where one or two guards were always seated. Protest in this space, although less public and hardly visible from the street, was more disruptive to internal company workings since it blocked the elevators and was noisy. The first assembly in this space initiated a different sort of demonstration as farmers formed a circle and village elders adept at *nongak* (farmers' music) led the group round and round to the strong, steady beats of the music.[27] In nongak, an array of percussion instruments are played at first in slow, melodious beats, and then as the beat escalates, faster and faster, louder and louder. After the music climaxes, it usually stops abruptly, and this makes for a piercing silence. And, after some pause for recuperation, it all begins again. The circle and line dancing to the beat of this music is still much a part of village life and was nothing that farmers had to learn in Seoul. The feet shuffle to the beat in a rather understated fashion, while the focus of the dancing appears to be the arms, extending out to the side, that shift back and forth as the shoulders roll in tandem. Similarly, the palms and fingers turn from side to side in a vigorous sway. When the music is slow, body movements follow almost in slow motion, but as the music picks up, tiny steps become forward lunges that chase after the rapid shoulder rolls. The speed, volume, and vigorous movements make for an almost frenzied atmosphere. The circle or snake draws everyone in; there is no place for spectators. The poker-faced guards remained motionless in the midst of all this movement.

From that day forward, every Monday, Wednesday, and Friday the protest sessions included dance. Later in the month, farmers took this dance, music, and drama to the nearby public streets. Many farmers and students took the time to remind me not to misunderstand the seeming gaiety of song and dance. These dances were expressions of sadness and pain, they would tell me. Farmers' music and dance were perhaps the main elements of the countryside cultural repository that students and the minjung culture movement employed in their urban protests. In fact, many universities had nongak clubs that were considered politically oppositional, a sort of school band for the student movement.

Yet another protest locale was the veranda, visible only to company employees from higher floors. This space developed its own identity as the daily place of food preparation and at night, as a spot for younger farmers and organizers to talk, sing, and dance. As the summer days grew ever hotter and muggier, some farmers sought refuge on the veranda in the evening for a cool breeze and to escape the confines of group living, which was unfamiliar to most of them. Clothes that had been hand-laundered in the bathroom, almost exclusively by women, were draped over the veranda's plants. Most of the farmers had arrived in Seoul with few clothes and made do sharing whatever people could gather from relatives in Seoul and visits to the countryside. On the veranda, students, organizers, and farmers would dance simply choreographed steps with hand motions keyed to particular protest songs. Particularly popular were the *haebang ch'um* (Liberation dance) and the *t'ongil ch'um* (national reunification dance). Several such dances were high-contact pair dances, in which the couple link arms and legs and finally bump bodies with full force. Many of the farming women learned these dances on the veranda. These were dances for laughter in the private evening time away from official audiences.

The successful management of the logistics of protest life against all odds made farmers as proud as the more standard protest activities. Although they continued to sleep grouped by village and sex in the large room on pieces of foam that had been donated, by day the room became organized along lines other than strictly village ones. The deepest inside corner of the room, for example, became a private space for the leadership committee. This section of the room was informally marked off by a blackboard used for song lyrics, directions, and schedules. Here, the leadership committee members were joined by those who had been playing informal leadership roles—village leaders, students, and organizers. There were two tables, one steadily encircled by students and organizers who were busy writing the text for announcements and posters and another where key organizers and leaders talked day and night over strategy, organization, logistics, and finances. It was clear that these protesters, mostly men, comprised the movement's elite. This area was also home to the public announcement system, which bellowed slogans and speeches out to the streets below. Because these corner discussions were private, it was hard for many farmers to later reconstruct what had happened and how and why things had occurred in one way or another.

The protest's greatest ingenuity was in food provision. From the earliest days, dissension over the food problem reflected broader controversy regarding how to structure the movement's agenda and protest. In a struggle over rice, years and years of rice that had been "stolen away," food was more than just a matter of sustenance. In the early excitement, farmer leaders and organizers bought bread, which in South Korea includes all cakes, pastries, and breads, often wrapped singly in plastic. For Koreans, bread does not constitute a meal and is hardly understood as sustenance: indeed, one of the words for meal is *pap* (cooked rice). With only a bread apiece at each of the first three meals, the farmers had already "fasted" for the first twenty-four hours. Initially, some farmers figured that as "guests," or country cousins, Samyang owed them sustenance. Others, however, calculated that in calling for the termination of a relationship, feeding themselves would be a more effective protest tactic. Eventually, farmers devised an impressive self-sufficient, efficient food production system. On the first day, though, the farmers' demand for food was spontaneous and spirited. The first morning the company had arranged for a nearby restaurant to provide rice with tofu and a side dish of seasoned bean sprouts. On learning that food would be provided, some farmers said, "Now they are talking," but because the food did not come until late in the morning and there was not enough, they complained bitterly. At the meeting with Kim Sang-don, various farmers yelled, "How will we eat from now on?" Yun put it directly, "Give us an offer of a meal," and the chairman replied, "Fine." In the early days many of the women sang a song about rice, which was their way of demanding it. The women chanted the song's chorus, a medley of pap, "*pabarabababap*," with aggressive enthusiasm.

The women prepared and served the food on the veranda. After several days, they decided to make a schedule, putting villages in charge of different meals. Local activist churches interested in social struggles supplied several enormous gas burners, and several men became their constant caretakers, struggling in all sorts of weather to light them and setting enormous pots of rice to boil. A man known as a "good-for-nothing" in the village where I had been living distinguished himself in this service, impressing village women who had thought little of him. Over most of the month, only one rice meal was cooked each day, and farmers made do with *ramyŏn* (ramen, or instant noodles)—known in South Korea as cheap student food—for the other meals. The side dishes, *panch'an* (dishes served with rice), were meager and uninteresting; for one long stretch, raw onions in a red pepper sauce—an unpopular fare—was the only rice supplement. Some meals were augmented with fresh vegetables purchased at local markets or with prepared pickled vegetables donated by external groups or provided from visits back to the countryside. Although on occasion the farmers' relatives in Seoul brought special foodstuffs, particularly the much longed for pickled cabbage *kimch'i* (the primary Korean nonrice staple), hoarding of individual foodstuffs was collectively shunned by the farmers. Gossip censored selfish behaviors or "individual actions." Exceptions were made, however, for the elderly men, who were allowed to receive some extras, were always given rice first, and were assured rice even when the supply was limited, as would also have been the case back home.

The life of protest was in all ways sustained by women; they were the cooks as well as fearless protesters. Although there were individual men who participated in some of the cooking and cleanup, these efforts were largely undertaken by women. It was common knowledge that women were more indispensable than men in this movement, in keeping with their countryside roles as farm laborers, wage laborers, and household managers. In every confrontation women were at the front line, and it was understood—by both women and men—that while women were relatively fearless, men were more attentive to the repercussions of their protest activities both in Seoul and back in the countryside.

In considering women's prominence, several points are noteworthy. As the women's rice paddy stories often reflect, landlessness and the humiliation of tenancy are conditions of marriage and in some cases visceral signs of downward mobility and of unfulfilled hopes. It is also relevant that women's considerable social and geographic mobility through marriage makes for sibling groups that are far-flung across the class spectrum; women are often keenly aware of their own mobility and of avenues for affecting their children's futures. This is not to say that class reproduction is entirely the province of women but to underscore that many of its elements, from education to the nurturing of social and kinship ties, are more prominently assigned to women (see Moon 1990). Some of the behaviors of protest— including occasional near-ecstatic states and sustained self-sacrifice—were easily engendered in the context of both the more secular and religious routines of village life. Finally, the protest venue liberated women from their labor-intensive routines of family nurturing. They spent the better part of most days with women from their own and other villages. In this sense, the transgressions of daily village life were greater and possibly more energizing for women than they were for men.

EXTERNAL FORCES

Nonfarmers and nonlocal farmers played an important role during the month of protest and affected the Koch'ang farmers' notions of settlements. These groups and individuals were known, both by farmers and among themselves, as oebuseryŏk (external forces). One of their primary contributions was to legitimate the movement, contributing to the strength and conviction of the farmers. Their presence and their words, both informal addresses and formal declarations, also boosted the Koch'ang farmers' morale.

Who were the external forces? They were students, farmers' urban relatives, general oppositional groups, farmers' movement organization members, scholars, and, finally, independent supporters.[28] At the Samyang headquarters, they never accounted for more than about twenty people. Seldom were more than ten present on any day, and the numbers dwindled over the month. In the final stages of the protest, organizers became disenchanted and felt there was little role left for them.

Under which category did I fall? I was perhaps most similar to the individuals who participated as supporters and resided in the building. On many occasions, I would overhear farmers from Kungsan explaining to farmers from other villages that I had been residing in their village. My initial interaction with organizers and students, however, was problematic. Nightly, various students and organizers asked to speak with me on the veranda, often interviewing me for two or three hours. I was asked about my historical perspectives on a range of Korea–U.S. issues and about my own background and rationale for being there; they often inquired about my *munje ŭisik* (problem consciousness). I tried to be honest and patient through each of these often painful interactions. I explained my political socialization in the United States and compared the cultural and political hegemonies in South Korea and the United States. In this way I pondered over the critique of ethnography from "home" in the midst of my field research. Several organizers suggested that my presence and affective relationship with farmers personalized the United States in a way that was counterproductive to the anti-American education that was a part of this movement. The discussions with Min were particularly lengthy and soul-searching. As I mentioned in chapter 1, I was at one point asked to address the farmers on my understanding of the chapters of American history implicated in this movement, and I did make such a public presentation. I did not pass these exams and become an insider. Just as my relations with outside activists would ease, a new one would arrive and demand to know my position. The process was thus never-ending, but I was often told that my labor—I was considered a tireless dishwasher—convinced people of my sincerity. In the months following the Seoul protest, I kept in contact with many students and organizers, who were eager to learn about the developments in the village. Similarly, many villagers were curious about the well-being of the individuals who had been part of their protest life.

The affiliates of various farmers' movement organizations were crucial figures throughout the entire month. The most important was the Catholic Farmers Union.[29] The CFU was a national organization with branches in all provinces and in some counties, districts, and villages. In 1986, a branch of the CFU had been established in Koch'ang. Some affiliates of the CFU from other regions joined in the activities, but most CFU organizers were from other villages in Koch'ang County, joining as interested individuals for brief periods of the occupation. The Christian Farmers League, with branches in several districts near the Haeri and Simwŏn districts, was also involved in this movement. The branch of the CFL that played the largest role in the Seoul protests, however, was the Koch'ang Nongminhoe (Koch'ang Farmers Association), which had started as a branch organization of the CFL but later declared itself independent of any national or umbrella organization. This group represented a newly burgeoning commitment to the localization of farmers' movements, a phenomenon that will be discussed in chapters 6 and 8. One of the leaders of the independent Koch'ang Farmers Association, a particularly prominent and charismatic figure, was quite different from Yun and Min. He was not a professional organizer, but a full-time farmer and a family man committed to organizing the people of his own village and district. He not only had fields to tend, but his energy was also pledged to other local struggles.

There were also farmers' movement organization affiliates and independent organizers who participated as individuals during the protest. They included young farming men, typically unmarried, who had joined local or regional farmers' organizations and who in some cases held office. There were also organizers who had settled in farming villages, a small but rapidly growing class of activists who were typically college-educated, politically radical, and ready to devote many years of their lives to rural political organizing. Typically, they farmed for experience, to become working members of the communities they sought to "organize," and to make a living to sustain their political organizing work. A handful of such organizers from areas in the Chŏlla provinces far from Koch'ang came to Seoul to lend their support. Because many aspects of this protest and occupation were perceived by the protest community to be unprecedented, activists throughout the country took an interest and ventured to observe the events firsthand. In some cases, they offered their own time and energy. For many, this was made possible by the timing of the protest. The events of the first half of the month coincided with the summer agricultural slack season when organizers who were active farmers could be absent from their fields for short periods.

Organizers were expert demonstrators. They were skilled tacticians, ideologically informed and motivated actors, resourceful individuals with contacts for money, goods, and services, and astute articulators of political currents. Outside organizers frequently stayed with the farmers in the fourth-floor room or in the various offices in the Christian Hall next door. By the end of the month, two groups of farmers had been distinguished:

those largely allied with outsiders, particularly the CFU, and those who stayed with the original leadership committee. The CFU affiliates and believers embraced a stronger agenda and pursued more aggressive action. They believed in its ability to protect individuals and in its vision of an alternative future for Korea.

Notable among the outsiders were Koryŏ University students, many of whom had spent time in the villages engaged in *nonghwal* (agricultural action). In nonghwal, students go to the countryside to radicalize farmers and educate themselves through manual labor. (Their role in the Koch'ang Tenant Farmers Movement will be discussed in chapter 6.) Although over two hundred Koryŏ University students had descended on the Samyang tenant villages for several weeks in July 1987, their numbers in the Samyang headquarters were limited. Some visited for a morning, afternoon, or evening at a time, but only a handful joined in residence for round-the-clock protest activity. These students held high leadership positions in nonghwal and, correspondingly, in the *haksaenghoe* (student association), the primary umbrella organization for student movement activity. Some of these students had been particularly moved by their first-time rural experiences. Other nonghwal participants, however, were from farming areas themselves; some were even from the same province. The paucity of their numbers at the headquarters can be explained by seasonal factors and by the directives of the leadership committee. School was out of session by then and students had dispersed either into their private lives or into the storm of August 1987 protests; it was a political climate in which university, labor, and political party issues contended for their time and attention in an unending stream of campaigns, rallies, and *temo* (demonstrations). Although Yun appealed to the students of various universities in Seoul, he was also careful to ensure that this protest would not become a student demonstration. On August 15, for example, he visited Seoul National University to appeal for the help and backing of students but asked them to stay on the sidelines as supporters rather than as co-demonstrators.

Also joining on the fourth floor were students or recent graduates who appeared to be unaffiliated. They were drawn to the struggle for highly personal reasons, such as hailing from the same region, having particular sympathy for the plight of these farmers, or through happenstance—having been in the neighborhood and hearing the commotion, or having a good high school chum already involved. Many of them were by no means student activists; indeed, for some, this was their first experience with activism. Some of them, however, proved the most steadfast supporters of the movement's activities. For them, the movement did not, in its various shifts and turns, stray from a particular agenda or ideology they espoused as it did for many of the more professional organizers and activists. Rather, they focused on the movement's concrete objectives. One such student in particular became the round-the-clock microphone voice of the movement; his words, phrases, and passionate speeches sounded throughout the neighborhood.

The Seoul relatives of the farmers—largely sons, daughters, and siblings of those who had left their villages for Seoul—were another essential support group. It was their presence that swelled the fourth-floor room and protest grounds during the day. Some families became almost permanent fixtures at the building; others came intermittently, working around their own busy schedules. Young women factory workers, typically the daughters of the poorer farmers, often visited on Sundays.[30]

These relatives needed to be continually informed of the latest events, words, and violence of the protest story. Women, in particular, would gather in large groups to report on the latest events. The relatives spanned Seoul's class diversity; some were laborers, eking out the most marginal of employed lifestyles in Seoul, while others were long-term residents, secure members of the middle class. Many were independent entrepreneurs, and fewer were employees of large companies. The daily scene at the headquarters offered a rare panorama of rural exodus and urban settlement in which family and village social biographies of class mobility were exposed. At one point the relatives formed an official committee, but because of scheduling and other difficulties, they were largely unable to act as a unified group. The Relinquish Committee was determined to maintain contact with tenants' Seoul families so as to strengthen the appeal to Seoul residents and to mobilize them to make protest calls to Koryŏ University, the Red Cross (headed by Kim Sang-hyŏp), the Tongdaemun police, and the *Dong-A Daily*. One of their primary contributions was economic: they donated food, money, time, and their personal contacts for securing necessary goods.

Frequently, the fourth floor became the stage of personal dramas—long overdue family reunions, doting over infirm parents, and cuddling of newborn babies—as much as of public drama and protest. Sometimes relatives or close family friends had stumbled on news of the goings-on and appeared unexpectedly. Overall, the warmth, financial contributions, and political sympathy of those who chose to visit and concern themselves with the struggle was impressive.

Some nonstudent Seoul residents sought out the fourth floor simply because they were from North Chŏlla Province or from Koch'ang (although not from the particular villages involved) and were longing for their homelands. People from the Chŏllas know discrimination in Seoul—in housing, employment, and even marriage. A recently hired bus driver originally from Chŏlla addressed the farmers, saying that before he came to Seoul he had been jealous of relatives who had made it there. He had come to realize, however, that "in Seoul, farmers and laborers are the same."[31]

The supporting declarations and participation of other oppositional groups, many of them not exclusively focused on the problems of the rural sector (i.e., groups working for labor, constitutional reform, women's rights, human rights, etc.), persisted throughout the month. Farmers became accustomed to their visits and monetary contributions—typically ₩50,000 to ₩100,000 (approximately $70–$140) donations. The proximity of the Christian Hall made for many visitors from various Christian organizations. Clergy, particularly those who long had played roles as human rights spokesmen for the opposition, joined and lent moral authority to the movement, even though only a handful of the farmers were Christians or churchgoers.

Finally, scholars with interests in social reform and protest generally and in the issues of farmers in particular appeared off and on and were largely revered as a cadre of intellectual elites from the nation's finest universities. In the hierarchy of knowledge, most farmers placed themselves at the low extreme of a scale and scholars at the other extreme.[32] Newspaper and magazine reporters, mostly from small activist-oriented publications, were similarly welcomed. They would often spend entire days in the fourth-floor room interviewing and discussing. Their presence was carefully noted and, for the most part, appreciated. Although little reporting found its way to the mainstream press, many of these newspapers and magazines did print stories about the Koch'ang farmers.

Although the diversity of support was important to the movement's growth, it was the politics and positions of the external forces that would eventually divide the farmers' positions, sympathies, and protest inclinations.

PROTEST VIOLENCE, ESCALATING CONFRONTATION

As the protest intensified and spiraled into violence, some farmers were swept into the spirit and politics of confrontation, while others chose to retreat. As one man, decrying the escalation of violence put it, "This is a *sojak chaengŭi* [tenant war], right? But it is becoming a sahoe undong [social movement] and that isn't good." With this comment he implied that social movements are broad-based, ongoing forces, whereas the aims and duration of tenant struggles are limited. Two protests in particular served to intensify the character of the farmers' confrontation with Samyang: the Taehangno incident and the Attempted Murder incident. These events expanded the object of the farmers' protest beyond Samyang to include the police and the military. The violence farmers experienced dealing with police units and company forces affected their understanding of the student movement and other social protest. In the countryside the violence that student protesters met with was never fully shown on television; as one farming woman screamed to the police, "You murdering bastards—you try to kill the students and now us."

As farmers began to talk about the violence they encountered in Seoul, other silences were shattered. In their villages, stories of post-Liberation leftists, of contemporary farmer suicides, and of the student movement–related deaths or imprisonments of local sons or daughters had generally been muffled, told in a hush-hush fashion. Through the demonstration experience, however, these accounts and talk of other protests surfaced. In particular, many farmers began to talk about the 1980 Kwangju Uprising. A number of farmers had stories to tell about friends and family who had been in nearby Kwangju—just over the mountains—during the massacre. These were stories of locals who had been there either as citizens or as army or police officials.

The Taehangno Incident began on August 16 with a small confrontation in which the police set out to block farmers who had taken to the streets to appeal for citizens' support. Fifteen farmers were injured and one hospitalized when they clashed with, according to some reports, up to two hundred *chŏnt'u kyŏngch'al or chŏn'gyŏng* (combat police). On this particular Sunday, approximately forty farmers, primarily women, demonstrated on the street demanding absolute protection for their fund-raising activities. The farmers proceeded to Taehangno, which on Sundays was closed off as a pedestrian street where young people and shoppers strolled. At Taehangno, however, they were confronted by armed police holding shields and with their faces hidden behind grates. Dressed in fatigues, they resembled a military combat line. A front line of the most active farming women threw themselves against the combat police, who tried to stop their advance. A number of women flailed against the shields, screaming and moaning, and several women even lunged against the troops. I stood holding the hand of the youngest protester, a sixth-grader, who was horrified as she watched her parents disappear into the throng of farmers confronting the police. The troops retreated, and in a frenzy of anger, fear, and profound exhaustion, some twenty women fell to the pavement, wailing and chanting as if mourning at a village funeral. They refused to move, attracting much attention from Sunday strollers and from local merchants who rushed out with water and materials for bandaging. Eventually, members of the leadership committee encouraged them to return to the headquarters. The farmers had extended their protest activities beyond the bounds of the protest practice set in the earlier days of their Seoul stay. Many women were badly cut and bruised and traumatized by their first confrontation with violence. The hallway abutting the large room at the headquarters was designated as an infirmary, where ill or injured farmers could sleep in a quieter, more secluded area. In the din of the incident's aftermath, some farmers had become erroneously convinced that several farmers had died in the confrontation.

The day (August 16) that had begun with police confrontation over peaceful fund-raising had ended with the sort of violence that many farming women and men had heretofore only known in television reporting of student and other political demonstrations. It challenged the farmers to question the validity of the state's claims about the groups and movements it suppressed with violence. If a cause as just and peaceful as theirs had met with state violence, what about the charges they had so often heard in the media about "Communists" and "threats to national security"? The mood at the headquarters was irreversibly changed; some farmers thought the situation was out of hand, moving too quickly into the maelstrom of nationwide summer protest, while others rode the currents of this escalation with ease and conviction. By the end of the day of the Taehangno Incident, the farmers had secured a promise from the chief information officer of the Tongdaemun Police Office that their fund-raising activities would be protected.

In the aftermath, many farmers wanted to appeal for damages and to demand an official apology from the police. With this in mind, a group of farmers went to the ruling party headquarters on August 18. At the entrance they again met with combat police. They asked to speak to the chief of human rights but were told that he was absent. They proceeded to the office for civil petitions, where they were told the government did not recognize the events they were reporting. Their trip to the T'ongil Minjudang (oppositional party) headquarters was more successful. They were greeted warmly and offered tea (which the farmers refused), and the chief of human rights and fishing and farming agreed to investigate the matter. Neither that day nor in days to come, however, did they receive the formal apology that they had demanded from the police.

The climax of the month was what farmers named the "Attempted Murder Incident," the most violent confrontation of the protest. On August 24 at 3:00 P.M., the company's iron gates were firmly shut and reinforced with extra wiring, locking out one group of farmers. The neighborhood came to resemble the entrance of a university during a demonstration, with combat police units, tear gas, and protest frenzy. There were both combat police in green fatigues and white helmets and undercover policemen in blue jeans. Inside the building, the farmers barricaded the elevators, thrusting tables, chairs, and all available debris against the shaft. As always, the younger male farmers guarded the stairwell door, but now the farmers were also concerned about the security of the veranda. Anticipating attack from the floors above, they gathered the potted plants and threw them against the side of the building beneath the windows. Material and bodies, all had become barricades.

Outside the company gates, the farmers who had been shut out protested. Inside, the leadership and the crowd of farmers were convinced that the impressive military-green police display aimed to do more than merely keep the small group of farmers outside. They surmised that the company was determined to end the occupation with force. They knew that just a day before, at the fourth negotiation session with the corporation, the company had gone so far as to offer buses to transport the farmers back to the countryside. They suspected that their protest sanctuary, until then never once invaded by legal, company, or military officers, would be under imminent attack.

The farmers in the building were lined shoulder-to-shoulder down the whole length of the veranda and along the window space of the fourth-floor room, looking down on their fellow villagers, friends, and relatives who were by then yanking at the bars of the gate as if they were imprisoned outside; for those inside, the bars came to symbolize their forced confinement. Many farmers were peering down at the ongoing drama when—after seconds of confusion—two bodies went up in flames. For some, the flames, which severely injured two university students, signaled even more strongly that things had gone too far, that the costs had become too great, that it was time to settle, and that it was time to concede in any way that would bring things to a close. Many spoke of the "enormous responsibility" for having injured "others' children." For others, this was the final straw in a different sense: they concluded that this land struggle was no longer a matter to be settled in a compromise fashion across a conference table.

It is necessary to backtrack to understand how the farmers had come to be divided by the barricades. On August 24, after the fourth negotiation session with the corporation in which little progress had been made, the farmers decided on more aggressive tactics and agreed to send a group to the home of the most public and prominent of the landlords, Kim Sang-hyŏp. When they arrived, they posted many copies of their second "urgent report" on the walls outside his home. The farmers were impressed by the walls, and they continued to talk about this fortress of wealth and privilege for days. Some thirty-five farmers stood outside, yelling "Kim Sang-hyŏp come out—return the land to us," and one of the farmers made a long speech. The police came immediately and detained thirty-two of them, taking them to the central police station. In turn, some sixty-two farmers from the headquarters, having heard what had happened, traveled to the police station to protest the detainment. Some of this group were also then locked up. Finally, six were retained in the station and forty-three were sent home to Koch'ang by bus. It was the farmers from this latter group, having again made the large financial investment to return to Seoul, who were locked out of their own occupation on the day of the Attempted Murder Incident.

The onlooking citizenry, including many who had come out from their offices at the Christian Hall, had swelled to a crowd of well over two hundred. The company guards had been throwing water at two students, one a senior in sociology at Koryŏ University and the chairman of the Proselytization Committee of the Presbyterian Youth Committee and the other a sophomore at Hanyang University and member of the Han'guk Kidok Haksaenghoe Ch'ong Yŏnmaeng (Korean Student Christian Federation) who had been spray-painting the company wall: "Samyang *kusadae* (goons, company protection units)—go ahead," "Punish the Japanese collaborator Kim Sang-hyŏp," "Return my land." One student approached the guards to tell them to stop throwing water, but when the guards persisted, they attacked them with spray paint. The combat police then joined the action, throwing kerosene at the two students. The farmers at the window and on the veranda watched incredulously as the kerosene ignited and the bodies went up in flames and as a young woman ripped off her shirt to help quell the flames. In the evening pandemonium, the police blocked the gates, keeping the outraged citizens and farmers from entering. This was the first time that members of the Seoul citizenry had been drawn into the struggle in a sustained fashion. This was also the first time that the farmers began to throw things off the veranda at the adversaries below; the mood and reality had become violent. This was a very difficult moment for me; I was experiencing what some South Korean students had identified in themselves as "bourgeois fear"—that is, a fear of violent action that they spoke of as something they needed to "overcome" in order to become a student activist. The police took five students to the police station, and to the outrage of the farmers and citizen crowd, none of the guards or combat police were detained. Fistfights between students and policemen followed.

Meanwhile, the farmers and strategists inside were communicating with those outside by means of a string, pulley, and basket hookup strung from the fourth-floor women's bathroom to the Christian Hall. The headquarters were charged with alarm. After witnessing the flaming bodies, many farmers assumed that the students were dead. Rumor about the life and death of the students ignited the farmer crowd. The students had been rushed to the hospital. One would remain in critical condition for months to follow, and the other would be transferred to the regular wards after several weeks. From the microphone the farmers announced their four demands between cries of "Violent police, leave!" "Samyang repent," and reprises from the *Farmer Song*.[33] The farmers demanded, first, that the police withdraw; second, that the combat units that had thrown the kerosene be arrested; third, that the company take complete financial responsibility for the burn victims; and finally, that the gates be opened. On August 25, the third farmers' bulletin announced, "The land thefts go so far as a murder scene; the kusadae of Samyang pour flames on the sons of farmers."

Finally, at 3:00 P.M. on August 25, thirty hours later, the company opened the gates. The reunion, largely village by village, was teary and emotional. As had so often been the case, the enormous room bustled with the exchange of stories, tales from both inside and outside. Even within the confines of this single room, people gathered for yet another account, and for gossip and rumor, much in the same way farmers did back in the villages at the well, by the field, or at a bend in the path. For every incident, every police encounter, every dramatic moment, one or two farmers' accounts would become authoritative. In the countryside, the accounts from people who had been in the eye of one or another storm would be told again and again on demand.

The farmers and organizers held a prayer service on August 27 and a reenactment on September 1. To the demands made on August 25, the August 27 session added a call for a nationwide boycott of Samyang products. The prayer service took place in the main auditorium of the Christian Center. They also demanded that Samyang take full financial responsibility for the injured students and that all six major South Korean newspapers apologize to them. The events of the Attempted Murder Incident were reenacted in front of the corporation, culminating in the burning of an effigy of landlord Kim Sang-hyŏp, direct descendant of Kim Yŏn-su. A crowd of some five hundred Seoul residents joined in the commemorative activities. The farmers closed the gates, to which they had attached a white cross, and reenacted the confrontation from several days before in a tense and emotional protest.

Perhaps the most influential experience for some farmers, however, was not their struggle with Samyang but their participation in the larger ongoing labor, democracy, and anti-American struggles in the city at that time. On August 28, a group of the more fearless and politicized farmers, many of whom had by then developed CFU sympathies, set out for Yŏngdŭngp'o, an area in Seoul with many factories that had become a center of labor protests. A large demonstration was planned, drawing many people nationwide to protest the murder of a laborer, Yi Sŏk-kyu. The farmers were shocked at the police violence they found there and talked for days of police who "walked on people." They wondered why the city residents were so passive and uninterested. One farmer, who broke stones for demonstrators to hurl, said, "What students do in Seoul, farmers must do in the countryside." I will break from the protest narrative at this point; chapters 5 and 6 take up the end of this story.

FALTERING HEGEMONY

As Stuart Hall suggests, the month of protest made for realignments in the farmers' sense of the moorings of social reality, of meanings. In *Weapons of the Weak*, a study of rural stratification and counterhegemonic acts of daily life in Malaysia, James C. Scott suggests that we should look for hegemony not only in unconscious consent to mystifications of social reality but also in the way in which people mark off domains of social life where they can or cannot effect change. Scott's (1985: 326) working definition of hegemony, "a system of domination . . . defining what is realistic and what is not realistic and driving certain goals and aspirations into the realm of the impossible, the realm of idle dreams, of wishful thinking," renders historical consciousness integral to the counterhegemony of political participation.[34]

Farmers did not discuss those things about which "there is nothing to be done." In speaking of national reunification, for example, one farmer explained "I know about the Korean War and the problems of unification but even if I were president, I could not solve the problem; since there is no solution, it is better not to talk about it." For some, the experiences of the Korean War and the repressive apparatus of post–Korean War society had effectively silenced dissent, leaving farmers to their problems with "no solution." In the Koch'ang case, however, the political climate of the late 1980s and the farmers' experience of dissent combined to challenge this inaction. What was mobilized through the Koch'ang movement was not a radically new sense of social justice in a capitalist democratic state—this was, as will be seen in chapter 5, in many ways already present—but rather the conviction that local experience could legitimately challenge the status quo. In the Korean idiom, aspects of farmers' lives were at least partially transformed from arenas where *ŏttŏk'e hal su ŏpta* (there is nothing one can do about it) to matters of *issŭl su ŏpta* (it cannot be this way). "*Issŭl su ŏpta*" could refer to ethics of a particular system and thus imply a call for a change. Through the negotiation with the corporation, however, farmers discovered that, 1987 "democratization" aside, an idiom of justice had no place in the corporate elite discourse on capitalism, development, and even democracy.

For many tenant farmers, the protest experience changed their ideas about themselves in relation to history and the national community— about their making of national history. These thoughts on history and the national community were located in a moment of discursive liberalization and an increasingly public space of dissent in the name of democracy and social justice. The movement experience can be seen as a dialectic of the localization of history and the historicization of local experience. As history was localized, national historical and political structures became clearer to farmers as realities they could think to change according to their sense of justice. In the historicization of local experience, their stories were validated as part of national history. As the local past and the protest experience were historicized, farmers came to understand themselves as people with public knowledge and thus the right and responsibility to protest.

As history was reformulated through protest experience, so too was the sense of national community. For the Koch'ang tenant farmers, the national community—the citizenry—was increasingly understood to include the rural sector and the community of dissent; in turn, they became convinced that the state should respond to the needs of the rural sector and to the demands of the community of dissent. Farmers came to understand activists—from student demonstrators to opposition party candidates and professional farmer organizers—as neither antinational nor remote from their lives.

Farmer interactions with elites—the government, the corporation and the media—revealed elite, ideological, historical, and political constructions of farmers in South Korea. Farmers observed that these institutions resisted the historicizing of local experience and thus denied their legitimacy. In this way, as farmers became keenly aware of the discord between their reality and the forced harmony of public presentations of history in South Korea, the irony of the dominant discourses became clear. The farmers remarked on the irony, for example, of ruling party presidential candidate Roh Tae Woo's rhetoric about *pot'ong saram* (ordinary people) [35] in the "age of the Western coast," as they remained largely impoverished tenant farmers in South Korea's underdeveloped Chŏlla provinces. As one farmer put it, "You call people living like this 'ordinary people'?" Others, alluding to Roh's role in the suppression of the Kwangju Uprising, pointed to the atrocities one must commit to become an "ordinary person like Roh Tae Woo."

Clearly, the Koch'ang Tenant Farmers Movement's Seoul protest unfolded not as the enacting of a script, the exercise of platforms and agendas, but rather at the intersection of multiple discourses and actors. Even the most basic movement props—the setting, the protest narratives, and so on— were negotiated and contested over the course of the month. As in *Ch'il-su wa Man-su,* the month of protest was also fabricated by the forces that suppressed the movement—their actions and imaginaries.

CHAPTER FOUR

Historical Tribulations and Trials

We pragmatists think that the reality-appearance distinction is an awkward and misleading tool of analysis, one that needs to be replaced with a distinction between the oppressors' descriptions of what is going on and the oppressed's descriptions, unsupplemented by the claim that the oppressed are on the side of the really real. . . . The oppressed have different purposes and wants from their oppressors, but they do not have deeper insight into reality. They just want to relieve suffering to change things for the better.

RICHARD RORTY (1991: 73)

On the one hand, the reclamation project was really good; if Samyang did something wrong, it was to register the land "unfinished land" such that it was excluded from distribution, but you can think well of that too. . . .

But they [Samyang] didn't reflect on what they had done, and did nothing to assure that the land would go to the farmers, but even that, well. . . .

But after 1955 when it was decided by the American military government that rents should be 3:7 [30 percent to the landlord, 70 percent to the farmer], they didn't register it; still we can forgive. . .

We can even understand that they continued to receive 3:7 after the 5–16 Revolution [1961]. If, in the end, they hadn't walked up and down the paddy [to determine the production of the plants and the rent], this struggle with Samyang would have never happened.

KOCH'ANG TENANT FARMER

The farmer above chronicles Samyang's transgressions. After every one but the last, he backs off from the accusation and excuses the violation. The final breach, that Samyang employees, like colonial period agricultural bureaucrats, had paced the length of the rice paddy paths in order to check their productivity and set the rents, was inexcusable. This farmer, who would have been a boy in the days of Japanese rule, was referring obliquely to the colonial era, as did much of the debate over the Samyang story. On my first day in Koch'ang I was surrounded by farmers eager to relate the Samyang story, and I was struck by one farmer who said matter-of-factly, "The colonial era still has not ended here."

This chapter juxtaposes the histories produced by the corporation and spoken by the farmers, not as texts to corroborate a single reality—the "*really* real" that Richard Rorty describes above—but as texts that sketch the political contours of an arena of historical debate. The company history

77

is explored through its own texts, primarily its fiftieth- and sixtieth-anniversary volumes. The historian Carter Eckert counts such texts as "capitalist hagiography" in which "Korean capitalists have sought to embellish their image as nationalists" (1986: 463). He notes that to this end the landlord Kims "have invariably been able to convince, cajole, or simply hire the very best writers available" (Eckert 1986: 463). Below, I review the initial stages of the Haeri land reclamation and estate management and then turn to divergent understandings of the Samyang Corporation in the post-Liberation/Korean War era. I conclude with farmers' senses of land as they emerged in the interstices of personal memories, dominant historical narratives, and the sensibilities of the heterogeneous activists introduced in chapter 3.

SAMYANG NATIONALISM: THE "MODEL" ESTATES

During the era of Japanese rule, the Samyang estates were lonely, isolated islands. It is not an exaggeration to say that for our healthy farmers these isolated islands were a paradise where there was no agony to be found.

SY60 1985: 79

Samyang's vision of the history of its *nongjang* (agricultural estates), a particular version of the Korean colonial past, highlights its contribution to Korean national development. Although revisionist understandings have marred the legacy of the Koch'ang Kims, they are still widely celebrated for their nationalist achievements during the colonial period. Indeed, Kim Sŏng-su and Kim Yŏn-su are household names in South Korea. Samyang is one of the most prominent national capital corporations—a category that distinguishes Korean from non-Korean concerns.

In its histories, the corporation distinguishes national from antinational behavior and, correspondingly, historical from antihistorical acts. They portray nongjang like the one in Koch'ang as nationalistic efforts and equate national, corporate, and peasant interests with one another. Eckert (1986: 76–77) characterizes their nationalism as "an unconscious identification of class with country that would eventually [after the Liberation] be put to the test and shattered." Samyang official histories herald the Haeri reclamation project—the project that literally put the Koch'ang paddy on the map—as nationalistic efforts to extend the Korean landmass and to develop rational farm management. They celebrate the agricultural estates as modern, rational capitalist oases in the late colonial period *ponggŏnjŏk* ("feudalistic") [1] landscape.[2] According to company history, Samyang (then Samsusa)[3] was founded to "modernize our [Korean] agricultural villages" and to introduce "modern capitalist management" (SY60 1985: 72). Thus not only were the estates "modern" and "capitalist," they were also Korean, not Japanese: "Compared to Japanese estates, conditions were vastly more benevolent, and were praised for being rational" (SY60 1985: 100). The histories refer to the estate management system as the "model village movement" effort and portray farmers as content with the new, rational agricultural technology. Obscured is evidence of farmers' protests against the company.

According to the company history, Kim Yŏn-su decided on the estate form of agricultural management to protest Japanese exploitation of Korean farmers—particularly those in North Chŏlla—who were left to eat inferior grains while the choicest rice was carried to Japan.

> When he [Kim Yŏn-su] saw the farmers of Namwŏn (one of the estates in North Chŏlla Province) at the time, he decided to begin his work of Changang [the first of his estates, 1924]. He was at once surprised and felt great pain. . . . [A long discussion ensues of the various productivity increase programs for export rice] Meanwhile they were only given [for consumption] bad rice strains from abroad, such as Manchuria. (SY60 1985: 72–73)

Agricultural estate practices are heralded as the antidote to evil Japanese landlord management. However, the organization and management practices of the estates, particularly their disciplinary tactics and methods of extraction, mimicked Japanese landlord practices at home and in the colonial territories. Samyang farmers often said that Samyang had "learned from the Japanese." They established the first estate, Changang, in 1924 and designated it a "model" estate with "model" management techniques, including "modern management concepts," "reformed agricultural technology," and a "rational management structure" (SY60 1985: 75). Kim Yŏn-su, having made the rounds of villages in Namwŏn, established the following regulations for the "farmers' benefit": "(1) no liquor, (2) no gambling, (3) weave five hundred straw bags, (4) clean around one's house, (5) make many composts, (6) help each other with farm work, (7) men do not marry before twenty" (SY60 1985: 73).

Farmers were assured tenant rights semipermanently "if they restrained themselves in daily life." The histories boast that such semipermanency was a "condition that one could not find anywhere at that time" (SY60 1985: 79). Farming households were ensured substantial plots, set at two hectares, which by rural standards both then and today are relatively large. Consequently, many farmers in the area likely lost their farmland, although the details of the redistribution are not included. The histories, however, document that because of such losses, three thousand farmers were relocated as laborers for Samyang reclamation projects in other areas: "[Kim Yŏn-su] found them a new place to live" (SY60 1985: 76). And in later discussions of reclamation efforts at Sŏnbul District in Hamp'yŏng County in South Chŏlla Province in 1931 and 1933, Samyang's first large-scale project, relocated laborers are described as difficult to manage and reported to have been harshly treated.

> The most difficult thing of all was managing the labor. . . . The 4,000 participating in the construction, most all of whom had lost land, were strugglers behind the times who knew the sadness of earning wages as daily laborers. . . . In rain or snow the labor heads would make them [the laborers] get up at dawn. . . . One such person [labor head] was called "Sŏnbul tiger." (SY60 1985: 88)

These workers presumably suffered both for having lost tenant rights when farmers' plots were extended and for serving under the likes of "Sŏnbul tiger."

Crews of *nonggujang*[4] (agricultural managers), who were purported to be very different from *marŭm* (landlord assistants residing locally among tenants), administered "rational management techniques." They were to "break out of the hold" of traditional marŭm–tenant arrangements (SY60 1985: 72). These "talented men chosen from among the highest-ranking graduates of agricultural schools" were to promote the "spirit of revival of [farmers'] *charyŏk kaengsaeng* [self-effort]" and to record the rice payments of the Kim household (SY60 1985: 74). The histories contend that with marŭm eliminated, farmers would no longer suffer under the landlord–tenant system: "Since there is no one to be an exploiter, there are no servile people, and no place for force, pressure, or unjust demands to emerge" (SY60 1985: 79). The histories argue circuitously that the new relations were modern and thus a priori not exploitative. According to a long-term nonggujang in Haeri District, nonggujang were assigned an area of land close to their village and farmers were randomly assigned one, two, or three 600-p'yŏng plots: "It was luck as to whether you received good or bad plots." An older farmer from the Kungsan village, however, remembers things differently: in the first "distribution"[5] Samyang "just said farm what you want, but when the nonggujang system began, people in the nonggujang's favor were given good land and those out of favor were given bad land." This account of nonggujang partiality and power contrasts with the company and nonggujang insistence on the system's impartiality and rationality.

The contract for the settlers of Sŏnbul reveals the "modern" agricultural management on the reclamation estates. The conditions governed the terms of the move, their tenancy, and their farming techniques.

1. House, tools, and moving costs will be supplied.
2. The land to be cultivated will be determined in consultation between the tenant and the estate. The location of the land will be determined according to the tenant's convenience. Each cultivator will get two

hectares of paddy [for rice farming] and 0.7 hectare of field [for nonrice farming].

3. In the first year seeds and seedlings will be provided, but thereafter the tenant will supply them.

4. In the first year rent is exempt on both paddy and field; in the second year ⅓ of the paddy rent will be exempted.

5. Farmers will obey directions and orders so as to improve farming technique and to ensure abundant production.

6. The farmers who move here will work the already arable land until their land becomes arable so that they can receive wages. (SY60 1985: 100)

In the settlement of Sŏnbul, families were given priority because Samyang calculated that in this way at least two people would be able to work (SY60 1985: 100). Sŏnbul farmers were required to work at the so-called *chigyŏngdap*, the land directly managed by the company, farmed by wage labor, and used as experimental fields. The productivity of this paddy became a standard against which the performance of farmers at other estates was gauged. In fact, Sŏnbul's technology and technical personnel were later transferred to the Haeri Estate.

Into the 1980s, Samyang collected rents on a portion of the Sŏnbul land—forty hectares that had literally surfaced in the early 1960s when a reservoir was drained. Because the Sŏnbul Estate had closed during the land reform period when the land was distributed, this land was managed from Haeri by Samyang Salt. Most tenants of these reservoir plots were poor. As one Sŏnbul farmer explained to me, "Rich farmers don't like having to pay rents." When the stirrings began in Koch'ang, the CFU sent representatives to Sŏnbul, and consequently several younger farmers traveled to meet Koch'ang activists.

Although Sŏnbul farmers were eventually only peripherally involved in the struggles in Koch'ang and Seoul, their sympathies were divided along the same lines as those of the Koch'ang farmers: a number of younger farmers wanted to follow the CFU agenda, while a larger group of farmers united behind the Relinquish Committee leadership and hoped to purchase the land. Finally, Sŏnbul farmers, although largely absent from the Seoul protest, were awarded purchase options. Younger farmers sympathetic with the CFU criticized both their seniors who "reaped rewards with no work" and what many took to be the compromising terms of the final settlement.

COLONIAL AGRICULTURE: CLASS AND NATION

Samyang's claim that the estate system contributed to Korean nationalism—as a rational and modern management system that outstripped

Japanese management and development—in part mimics Japanese colonial rhetoric in which Korea is portrayed as backward, irrational, fraught with factionalism, and unsuited for self-rule. For the Koch'ang Kims, the peasants were backward and irrational—class Others. Class, however, is effaced in Samyang's rhetoric. They insist that by virtue of being Korean, their agricultural estates were just.

This vexed relation between class and nation is at the heart of contentious and far-reaching debates on peasants in the colonial period. These debates reveal the historiographical weight of details that might otherwise seem trivial: whether tenancy rates increased in the early or later years of the colonial period, whether tenancy rights could be easily renewed year after year, and whether agriculture became part of a capitalist nexus in the late Chosŏn Dynasty. These queries all hinge on the reckoning of similarity and difference across precolonial, colonial, and postcolonial practices and eras, recalling the symbolic genealogies discussed in chapter 2. Amid this larger debate we can examine how Samyang aims to set itself in the sweep of precolonial, colonial, and postcolonial history.

Although some assert that agriculture was in fact modernized during the colonial period, others retort that it met a terrible fate and that Korean farmers suffered disproportionately (Grajdanzev 1944; Suh 1978: 83, 145). The latter position maintains emphatically that the colonial period did not lead to modern economic growth (Suh 1978: 156) but, rather, reversed or ruined precolonial dynamism that would have spurred modern economic growth. Hypothetical historical queries—what if Korea had not been colonized, divided, etc.—are widespread in South Korean scholarship and fiction. For example, Kim Yong-sŏp, an authority on precolonial land tenure, argues that had the Chosŏn Dynasty continued, a bourgeois class would have eventually developed and overturned the old order. He thus turns his attention to protocapitalist developments in the precolonial era (Shin 1978: 188). Susan S. Shin (1978: 195) asserts, however, that Kim Yong-sŏp's Chosŏn Dynasty agricultural entrepreneur is a "shadowy figure" and that his conclusions about the protocapitalist trajectory of Chosŏn Dynasty agricultural innovation are unfounded.

Transformations in the nature and extent of land tenure in the early period of Japanese colonialism are also a vexed matter. These transformations include both the nationality of the landowner and the form of landownership: landlord, owner-farmer, owner-tenant (those who farm more owner than tenant land), and tenant-owner (those who farm more tenant than owner land). Anticolonialist history (historical writing posed against colonial perspectives) argues that the land survey the Japanese conducted facilitated significant transfer of land title to the Japanese and that the colonial tax structure engineered the impoverishment of many Korean owner-farmers who were forced to sell to Japanese landowners (Myers and Saburō 1984: 429–430).

In recent years scholars have challenged anticolonialist history that is excessively nationalistic and assumes a priori the ill effects of colonialism.[6] Instead of proclaiming the profound rupture of the colonial arrangement, they point to the continuity of its structures—including oppressive ones— with the Chosŏn Dynasty. In this vein, Edwin Gragert argues that a "contin- uation of past traditions and patterns was the rule" (1982: 6; see also Shin 1975: 74) and stresses that the modes of production and labor remained the same (1982: 127). The early cadastral surveys rationalized and system- atized late Chosŏn Dynasty practices: "The survey, by creating accurate and legally binding land registers, facilitated capitalist development of Korea's land" (1982: 328). Similarly, Sang-chul *Suh* (1978: 81) argues that the "land tenure system of the colonial period did not change the old system, but had the effect of legalizing it." The dramatic tenantization of Korea over the colonial period occurs not on account of the Japanese cadastral surveys but because of the dramatic impact of the later economic depres- sion on the colony (Gragert 1982: 297–299). In this revision of the antico- lonial position, detrimental shifts are attributed to increased capitalist inte- gration of the economy—albeit a colonial program—rather than to the machinations of Japanese legal codes or land surveys. Gragert (1982: 327) suggests that the extent of suffering and hardship and the widespread ten- ancy later in the colonial period have undergirded the erroneous historical sense that socioeconomic change occurred in the beginning of the colonial period.

Scholars also argue whether customary tenancy rights, or *t'ojikwŏn* (re- ferred to as *sojakkwŏn* for the Samyang tenancy in Koch'ang), that allowed the same tenant to continue farming the same plots year after year were a feature of Chosŏn Dynasty social arrangements. Many suggest that the capitalization of land relations gradually eroded these rights. Others in- stead underscore the destruction of tenancy rights as the result of Japanese colonial practice. Sin (1978: 26) argues that the protection of tenant rights or "precapitalist rents" developed over the Chosŏn Dynasty. He maintains that widespread permanent tenure in the nineteenth century virtually dis- appeared after Japanese formal colonization in 1910 (Shin 1975: 68). Al- though Susan Shin similarly understands t'ojikwŏn as a "response to spe- cific economic conditions" (1975: 61–69), she argues that the violation of tenants' customary rights predate the Japanese incursion (1975: 72–73). Gragert (1982: 124) concurs with Shin that tenancy rights became vulnera- ble in cities in the late Chosŏn Dynasty: "Economic forces were already at work creating tenancy patterns similar to those found more generally later in the colonial period" (see also Gragert 1982: 299; Lee 1936: 165, 175).

Determining the "national" and "progressive" or "antinational" and "conservative" nature of colonial period agricultural arrangements involves complex calculations that turn both on contested facts of the era and on broader understandings of the nature of nationalist and progressive histor-ical trajectories. Although Samyang considered national agricultural man-agement virtuous and rationalization progressive, farmers took issue with the very meanings of "progressive" and "nationalist."

BLOCKING THE SEA: THE EARLY HAERI ESTATE

It is through the minutiae of the land story that Samyang and the various activists took on these larger historiographical struggles. I will begin to fol-low this contest in a July 1987 Samyang document, "Samyangsa sojaktap yangdo ch'ujin undong e kwanhan chilûi e taehan hoesin" (The Answer to Questions Concerning the Samyang Tenant Relinquish Promotion Com-mittee), in which Samyang criticizes a 1987 CFU document, "Samyangsa kanch'ŏkchi yangdo undong chosa pogosŏ" (A Look at a Survey of the Movement to Relinquish Samyang Reclamation Land).

The CFU document begins with the land reclamation, asserting that the Kims were awarded rights to reclaim the land because they had bargained with the colonial government. Samyang retorts that they were "forced" to take on the contract and that it was only their competitors who had pur-sued the contract with mercenary aims. Scattered throughout the discus-sion below, in the left-hand column are passages from the movement pam-phlet and in the right-hand column are the corporate responses.

Koch'ang Tenant Farmers Movement
In April 1936 [Kim] Yŏn-su re-ceived construction rights from the colonial government Department of Agriculture and Forestry before Pak Yŏng-ch'ŏl [another con-tender] could take it over.

Samyang
At that time, Pak Yŏng-chŏl who was the president of the Chŏnju Com-mercial Bank figured that there would be huge benefits from the reclamation project and hoped for the construction contract from the Japanese colonial government, but the colonial government forced Kim Yŏn-su, who knew well the dif-ficulty and accompanying damages [of reclamation work], to take on the project. He refused several times, but having financial power and experience, he was forced to take on the project (SYY 1987: 3).

The Samyang efforts in Haeri followed the earlier reclamation attempts of a Japanese company, Haewŏn (from Hae[ri] and [Sim]wŏn districts) Agriculture, Inc., which began in 1930 and were abandoned five years later. A farmer explained that the owner, Mori, also ran a distillery where he made a fortune because Koreans were prohibited from the liquor business. The Samyang histories claim that Haewŏn acted only because they "wanted to receive government aid" and that after their failure the Japanese colonial government decided to "help them [the Japanese] out by selling to Samyang" (SY60 1985: 88). They also claim that the reclamation project began in 1936[7] and that it served society because it coincided with a drought that had destroyed the rice and barley crop. Farmers instead focused their accounts on Samyang's monetary interests and connections with the colonial government. The volumes explain that Haeri tenant farmers "hurried diligently with the labor of taking out the salt [from the fields], and meanwhile raised fertilizer plants on public land, and in the slack season they wove straw bags at machines for the estate . . . so each house had a significant additional income. . . . In this way after about four years those who began with will and diligence had quite a bit of financial flexibility in their lives" (SY60 1985: 103). Recalling the various capacities in which she had worked for Samyang over the years, one older farming woman did not stress "financial flexibility." She explained instead that she and her village neighbors had been " 'Samyang boys,' weaving salt bags to send to the company, working at the salt fields, and remitting rents."

The reclamation brought many laborers to the area for extremely dangerous work. An older farmer who remembers the period explained that Kim Yŏn-su was the "protagonist [*chuin'gong*] of blocking the sea" and that he brought laborers from all eight (Korean) provinces and unemployed workers from China as well. The project reportedly employed 2,000 to 3,000 workers on any given workday, and up to 4,000 at times. The construction was difficult. When it was almost completed, the dam was destroyed and the seawater washed everything away. Although two hundred chŏngbo larger than the Sŏnbul reclamation land, the project was eventually finished in fourteen months, one-third the time taken by the Sŏnbul project. The 188 Haeri settler families "moved people with the provision that they would work as reclamation laborers," and Samyang asserts that "rather than people from this [Haeri] region, they came based on rumors they heard in Sŏnbul" (SY60 1985: 102).

The biography of Kim Yŏn-su mentions a local prophecy that had foretold the dangers of reclamation: "If they [Samyang] block the sea a war will break out. . . . At the time of the sixteenth-century Japanese invasion, they tried to block this sea and a war broke out, . . . and also at the time of the Manchurian Incident. . . . Someone started this same rumor to block construction immediately before the Japanese [Haewŏn Agriculture, Inc.]

tried to block it and trouble did ensue" (Kim 1971: 143). This prophecy reveals Korean geomantic sensibilities that the contours of natural formations affect the fate and fortune of men and women. Changing the coastline, and thus the relationship of the settled and cultivated land to the central axes in geomancy (water and mountains), thus prophesied disaster. An older farmer laughed thinking that in this region the expression "simnyŏn imyŏn kangsan do pyŏnhanda" (in ten years the rivers and mountains change) was literally the case. It is, as farmers said over and over again, an impressive amount of land, "so broad that you can't even see the end of it, and the salt fields are even more extensive." Of the reclamation land, one farmer said, "The sea of the past—not owned by anyone—is now mine or yours."

In the movement's reckoning of Kim Yŏn-su, collaboration with the Japanese came up again and again. The continued land management and capitalist successes of the company were similarly scrutinized. The movement used an expression for the landlord–tenant relationship, *nanwŏ mŏkta* (dividing [crops]), to depict the Samyang–colonial government relationship. The company, in turn, countered that the corporate financial legacy had deeper family roots.

Koch'ang Tenant Farmers Movement	*Samyang*
Samyang became one of the largest land *chaebŏl* [business conglomerates] by increasing its property by dividing [crops] [*nanwŏ mŏkko*] with the Japanese colonial government.[8]	Kim Yo-hyŏp [grandfather] gave land that produced 1,000 sŏm to Kim Ki-chung and land that produced 1,200 sŏm to Kim Kyŏng-chung (second son). Kim Kyŏng-chung was good at making money and was frugal, so he increased his wealth and his son, Kim Yŏn-su, expanded the business and developed Kyŏngsŏng Spinning and Samyang. So it makes no sense to call this "dividing with the colonial government" (SYY 1987: 2).

About the relation to the Japanese, one farmer said, "Kim Sŏng-su ran errands for the Japanese. . . . He was completely a robber. . . . How good for Samyang—they would sit and we brought the washed, dried rice." Another farmer remarked, "Sometimes I wonder about how he [Sŏng-su] was able to build a school [one of the "nationalist" activities he is known for] and all of that [under Japanese rule], but I still see him as a patriot. The question is how Yŏn-su [in contrast with his brother] could have been a collaborator, but I know that professors in universities are researching this now." Another farmer offered, "Why did the Japanese give him this money?—to be able to exploit farmers—but now Samyang insists that they improved this land to provide a means of sustenance for our poor farmers, calling it a patriotic activity." Although the movement rhetoric on the colonial period collaboration of the Kims with the Japanese was convincing to many farmers, some refused to dismiss the image of the Kim brothers as the great nationalists they had learned about in school. One former village head, for example, was offended that movement people swore against "great nationalists": "This is an insult to our country's people." One farmer, however, explained that the collaborator allegation goes way back: "In the past people used to routinely say 'collaborator,' but now—after Sŏng-su's term as vice president—you don't hear that so often."

In the post-Liberation era in 1949, Kim Yŏn-su was brought before the Committee to Punish Anti-National Violators. Not surprisingly, the movement and the company have different interpretations of what transpired. I heard the following version frequently: "Under Japanese imperialism [Kim] Yŏn-su—who was something like let's say the president today—saved [Kim] Sŏng-su [i.e., by being a collaborator], and after the Liberation Sŏng-su saved Yŏn-su [by having a 'clean' record and political clout]."[9] The company, in contrast, answers that Kim Yŏn-su was innocent because his "national deeds for development were recognized . . . by every sector and class."

Koch'ang Tenant Farmers Movement
Using Kim Sŏng-su's incredibly strong power and *ppaek* [backing or connections; he was the vice president of the Hanmidang political party, noted for its many collaborators], he [Kim Yŏn-su] managed to escape being punished according to the terms of antinational laws [after the Liberation].

Samyang
The Committee to Punish Anti-National Violators deliberated Kim Yŏn-su's involvement on August 6, 1949. Toward the final years of the colonial period—in that difficult period—we competed with the Japanese, cultivated our economic power, raised national capital, and fostered the national economic independence spirit. Before and after Liberation—in that difficult period—we were on the vanguard of corporate industrial activity. . . . Our contributions to national development and national education under the Japanese were recognized by every sector and class; thus it was decided that he was innocent.

As with the dissension over the terms of the blocking of the sea, the early management of the land was also contested. Although the movement claimed that the company had employed a divide-and-rule tactic to contain dissent, the company denied such practices and the precedence of such protest.

Koch'ang Tenant Farmers Movement	*Samyang*
Those farmers who somehow became literate or raised their voices didn't get their farming rights and were kicked off the land, or they were apprenticed as nonggujang. They treated the nonggujang well and thus continued these divide-and-rule tactics.	You say these are straightforward words, but your claim that we withdrew rent agreements or kicked farmers off the land is unfounded. The nonggujang are farmers chosen from among sincere renting cultivators.

Several farmers claimed that in the aftermath of an unsuccessful land struggle in 1955, some of the activists were awarded nonggujang or other positions in the company. One farmer explained that because it was troublesome for the company to claim the land of farmers who were behind in their rent, they instead reclaimed it by planting trees.

Samyang's official account of the "early marriage problem" at the Haeri Estate demonstrates how the company explains away the incidence of farmer dissent. The history notes that early marriage, which increased as the area became prosperous, threatened the productivity of the state. The biography of Kim Yŏn-su explains the problem of "unenlightened" farmers: "The farmers who came here [to Haeri] were lazy and it took some time to enlighten them. . . . Because of the economic boom of wartime the Haeri area was prosperous, so much so that after three or four years farmers from other villagers wanted to marry their daughters to Haeri men" (Kim 1971: 144–145). Farmers' early marriages were described as "unrivaled evil practices," and those who disobeyed marriage regulations were sent off the estate. The employees, in turn, were prohibited from marrying before the age of twenty-five so as to ensure their community involvement with the farmers. The only tenant protest that appears in the official histories is that of a man who was driven off the estate for allowing his sixteen-year-old son to marry. The volume reports that this incident was "unique" because it was not a tenant dispute tied to the national liberation movement: "From the 1920s to the 1930s there were about five thousand tenant wars in our country, but at Samyang it was only this one over early marriage" (SY60 1985: 103, 104). This disclaimer asserts that Samyang was in no way the object of attack in any real social struggle. At the same time, the disclaimer acknowledges that tenant struggles are nationalist struggles; they thus suggest that "real" tenant struggles did not occur against Korean landlords (of course this is not true) and certainly not against Samyang. In the name of the nation, class is denied. In the immediate aftermath of the Liberation, tenants joined in widespread social and political struggles. The land reform that was eventually enacted was the critical point of contention in this movement—that the tenant plots should have been distributed.

THE LAND REFORM ERA

Why do I have no land? Thirty-seven years ago I was working at the district office. . . . I was ignorant, but I hated the Communists and so when the guerrillas came I couldn't be here . . . so I left and when I came back the guerrillas had taken away all my rice [because of my government connections through district office employment] and I couldn't pay my tenant rents. So I sold my land to pay the rents. After 1945 Rhee Syngman, who had by then become an American, came back [to Korea], but his land distribution didn't work.

KOCH'ANG TENANT FARMER

In the immediate post-Liberation era, widespread farmer protest was dramatically silenced by the United States and Korean states. People's Committees and unions had mobilized farmers for self-determination in preparation for a unified Korean state. In *The Origins of the Korean War*, Bruce Cumings refers to the post-Liberation period as one of "rural participation unmatched in Korean history before or since" (1981: 267). Consideration of the hearts and minds of farmers challenges diplomatic, military, and great-men theories of state building. People's Committees' programs reveal the extent of the farmers' political and economic agenda, including demands for an end to grain collections, better terms of tenancy, and—most dramatically—a major land reform; the agenda for changed terms of tenancy demanded that 3:7 arrangement ($\frac{3}{10}$ of the produce to the landlord, $\frac{7}{10}$ for the tenant) replace the 5:5 status quo ($\frac{1}{2}$ of the produce to the landlord, $\frac{1}{2}$ for the tenant). Farmers' political and economic struggles took up the colonial period legacy of anti-imperialist (Japanese) and anti-landlord struggles (see Shin n.d.). Political forces that suppressed farmer dissent in the post-Liberation period resemble the colonial control of the countryside.[10]

By the late colonial period, 68 percent of Korean rice paddy was tenant land, 70.1 percent of the farmers were tenant farmers, and of those, 53.6 percent were tenants who only farmed tenant plots (Chang 1988: 127), a situation of "land conditions and relationships" that "augured revolution" (Cumings 1981: xii). Shortly after Liberation, tenant struggles were organized under the Chŏn'guk Nongmin Chohap Ch'ong Yŏnmaeng (Chŏn-nong, National League of Farmers Unions), which was affiliated with the Communist party. By November 1945, there were 188 city or county branches, 1,745 district branches, 25,288 village branches, and 3,323,197 members (Scalapino and Lee 1972: 260).[11] They protested not just rural social injustices and state economic policies but also the ruling coalition of the U.S. Army military government in Korea and conservative Korean collaborationist landlords.

Chŏnnong took up tenancy reform for the short run and land reform as a more long-term measure. The initial 3:7 demand, for example, did not compromise the demands for land reform but was considered an interim step. Chŏnnong hoped that through the 3:7 campaigns farmers would build the necessary confidence and courage with which to wage the struggle for a comprehensive noncompensatory land reform. With these measures Chŏnnong also hoped to gather the support of medium and small landlords (Lee and Scalapino 1972: 39; Yi 1989: 223). One leadership group in Chŏnnong, however, called for immediate confiscation and distribution of land by Chŏnnong branches or People's Committees. Incidences of tenant unrest reported to the Supreme Court escalated after Liberation: 136 in 1945 and 1946, 62 in the first four months of 1947 (Yi 1989: 226). The U.S. military government reduced tenant rent to one-third of production in kind, slightly greater than the Chŏnnong 3:7 demand. In practice, however, landlords did not comply with this rate, and there were no provisions for punishing offenders (Mitchell 1952: 7).

Farmer resistance was directed not only against land arrangements but also against a state structure of control reminiscent of the colonial period. The ethnographer Cornelius Osgood reported on just such a mobilization.

> When a group of [Chŏnnong] leaders went to the police to ask for permission to hold a meeting, they were arrested. The reaction to this renewal of the old Japanese methods of dominance swept through the countryside like a violent windstorm, blowing bitterness up and down the valleys. Membership in the Farmers' Committee shot up like a star shell and burst into a white light over the pine-topped hills. (Osgood 1951: 309; see also Gayn 1981)

A farmer's account from 1946 details this bitterness.

> Our life at that time was miserable. Commodity prices were rising daily. "Liberation," moreover, was empty talk. The rascal who had been *myŏn* [district] office clerk under the Japanese was still there, behaving as arrogantly as ever. If a farmer fell into arrears in paying his taxes, he would make that farmer kneel on the ground, even if it was a rainy day. He himself was a farmer who had gotten rich under the Japanese.[12]

The U.S. military government declared on October 30, 1945, that it would turn over Japanese-owned land to its tenants, but subsequently reneged. In late 1945, it took over the colonial Oriental Development Company and renamed it the New Korea Company, thus becoming the postcolonial state landlord. Tenants of the New Korea Company were required to pay all of their farming costs and to remit one-third of the crop and the straw. With 212 subbranches and 3,300 employees, the New Korea Company established a palpable presence in village life. However, it met with enormous resistance over payments, particularly the requirement to remit rents from both the rice and early spring barley harvests, and eventually decided to collect on only one of the crops, to be determined in consultation with the farmers (Yi 1989: 225).

Not surprisingly, with the widely reported land distribution in the north in March 1946, farmers' attention turned to land matters. Farmers' dissatisfaction escalated in the south, where the U.S. military government and Korean statesmen realized that they would need to effect some sort of land reform. In fact, these stirrings ushered in an informal land reform in which many landlords, fearing what was to come, sold their land. By May 1946, Chŏnnong was determined to win a no-compensation land distribution; in October 1946, it changed its name to the Nongmin Wiwŏnhoe (Farmers' Committee) and crafted a land reform that was announced in February 1947.

However, on August 30, 1947, the Nongch'ong or Taehan Tongnip Nongmin Ch'ong Yŏnmaeng (Korean Independent Farmer Federation) displaced Chŏnnong and its radical agenda (Yi 1989: 264–265). The U.S. military government was actively involved in this state co-optation of farmers' dissent. In March 1948, the government finally decided to sell the Japanese land (245,554 chŏngbo), which represented one-fourth of the South Korean farmland, and the New Korea Company became the National Land Administration (Chang 1988: 132). The farmers' demand for land reform in the south was a call for radical social reformation, and the belated implementation revealed South Korea's political colors. The Land Reform Act was promulgated in June 1949 and finalized in March 1950. The payment price was set at one and a half times the average annual produce to be paid over five years.

Although there is broad consensus that the land reform succeeded in destroying the premodern and colonial period landlord class, the land reform record is marred by several factors: the foot-dragging approach of the U.S. military government and the South Korean landlord class in the immediate post-Liberation era; the fact that land reform over the long run did not effect productivity increases or real changes in income distribution; and gradual retenantization in the aftermath of the reform and particularly during the 1980s. Although the land reform destroyed semifeudal land relations, it was not farmer centered and did not represent a significant commitment to the small farmers it produced (Chang 1988: 137; see also Pak C. 1988). The state's post–land reform neglect of agriculture, grain extraction, and land taxes diminished the achievements of the land transfer.[13]

The land reform, then, did effect a significant distribution, but the post-war agricultural policy thwarted its full potential (Burmeister 1988; Wade 1982:5, 1983). Some land was omitted by changing the land usage to orchards or mulberry fields, or by registering it as unfinished reclamation land in accordance with special provisions for exemptions in the land law.[14] Pak Chin-do (1988: 230) asserts that state policy through 1960 can be considered a reactionary response to land reform and that "if developments had continued in that direction, there would have been a return to the pre–land reform parasitic system."[15] I turn now to Samyang and farmer perspectives on the land reform and the fate of the Samyang plots.

LAND REFORM AND THE SAMYANG PLOTS

Samyang's report on the land reform era is carefully crafted: it acquiesces to the reform's inevitability, criticizes aspects of its promulgation, and laments its demands. Interestingly, in its criticism of the land reform, the company partially echoes the claims of activists. Although the company history does not offer a sustained critique of how the Korean power structure or U.S. intervention thwarted the principles and promulgation of the land reform, it maintains that the intended land reform principles were perverted by a Communist orientation and that its promulgation was not fully exercised. The South Korean land reform is described as the unfortunate overflow of Northern practices and the result of anger against Japanese practices that was misdirected against Korean landlords. Samyang also reports problems with the promulgation, such as the independent sale and purchase of land. And the history maintains that post–land reform policies mediated against the maintenance of small plot ownership—one of the reform's principles. Finally, it declares that the "root aims of the land reform"—"productivity increases and development"—were not achieved. And it was "a national tragedy" that its own lands, lands of those with "national [Korean] interests" in mind, were subjected to the awkward vagaries of the land reform. Its logic figures that because the corporation worked for "national interests," its landholdings should not have been subject to land reform. Although the history does report on employees who protested that they wanted to "run the estate themselves," it presents both employees and farmers as victims of the unfortunate "flow of the times." Finally, it was "international trends" that compelled its (disgruntled) compliance with land reform.

The company highlights that little changed for farmers immediately following Liberation. In keeping with critical histories that stress ways in which the Korean elite in conjunction with the American occupying forces reproduced Japanese colonial institutions and practices, the company writes that the New Korea Company was nothing other than the Japanese Oriental Development Company by another name (see Mitchell 1952: 9).

> The Oriental Development Company changed its name to the New Korea Company and was left as is with Americans collecting rents. Also because of falling rice prices, rice collections began. For farmers, the Oriental Development Company and the New Korea Company were almost identical. . . . Of course, the grain collections were no different than those of the Japanese at the end of the colonial period. (SY60 1985: 123–125)

They continue by explaining that farmers, angered by the exercise of Japanese colonial practices by the New Korea Company, unfairly berated "all landowners as exploiters." They then assert that it was only the "leftist power" Chŏnnong that began to call for a Northern-style no-compensation land reform. In this way, they suggest that widespread farmer dissatisfaction was unrelated to the calls for a land reform.

> And so farmers berated all landowners as exploiters, and demanded that they remove their hands from the land. In fact these kinds of disturbances were aimed at the New Korea Company, but for a while they even went against regular landlords. At this time a leftist power called Chŏnnong instigated the farmers, and they began to insist that in the South too, as in the North, a no-compensation land reform should be effected. (SY60 1985: 123–125)

At the Samyang estates "selfish opportunists" joined with the farmers in calling for a land reform, even traveling to the Seoul headquarters to voice their protest. They demanded, "Let's run the estate ourselves, and distribute the grains in the warehouse for free." The history reports that these employees later bowed to their "superiors," "regretted their past errors," and that, moved by the "kindness and tolerance of the company," they "became even more loving to the company and faced their duties ever more diligently." The company president, Kim Yŏn-su, however, was "terribly sad about this agitation of a small number of employees," and because he understood it as "a test of the changing times," he did not "rebuke them." Farmers and the low-level employees are again reported as "blindly following" opportunists or leftists and in the case of the farmers, as "dazzled by propaganda" (SY60 1985: 123–125).

The account reports that the North Korean land reform had made North Korean unemployed farmers and laborers "positively inclined to Communist ideology" and that this sentiment "spread to South Korea" and made it imperative to undertake land reform in the South so as to "restore political and social stability" (SY60 1985: 123–125). The report goes on to explain that the land reform principles were subverted by loopholes in the law itself, combined with landlord maneuverings to assure continued ownership. It demonstrates that owner-cultivators were unlikely to be able to hold on to their land because of "awkward policies that threatened owner cultivators" and an unreasonable repayment schedule. Instead, the reforms decreased middle-sized farmers and increased poor and tenant farmers, making "things . . . worse than they were sixty years before land reform."

> But some landlords were able to forecast the inevitability of the execution of a land reform and they made forced sales [to tenants] at a cheap price of some of their land ahead of time. And some landlords put the title of some of their land in the names of relatives or close friends . . . such that the extent of the land originally designated for purchase and distribution shrunk considerably. Also, the land reform law itself had several articles designed to exclude land from the object of purchase. . . .
>
> Although Communist forces schemed to break free from democracy by distributing land to farmers, the South Korean government failed at breaking down semifeudal tenant relations because they could not make all farmers cultivator-owners. Also, after the land reform, they did nothing to support the farmer ownership of those who had become owner cultivators. On the contrary, they extended awkward policies that threatened owner-cultivators. (SY6o 1985: 123–125)

The history documents how "painful and difficult" it was for Kim Yŏn-su to part with his estates, his "flesh and blood." It was necessary to comply with "the trends of the era and state policy," which were in step with "international trends" in the "underdeveloped countries liberated [after World War II] from imperialism."

> Parting with large plots of land in accordance with the land reform law, Samyang also had to turn over land to the government starting with Changsŏng, Sŏnbul, Koch'ang [not the Haeri Estate, but another estate in Koch'ang], Yŏnggwang, Pŏpsŏng, and Chŭlp'o.
>
> It was land that they had devoted themselves to and cared for with blood and sweat over a long period of time, land with a total annual harvest of 150,000 sŏm. Of course, parting with this large amount of land which was like their flesh and blood was painful and difficult for President Kim Yŏn-su and for all the employees, but in order to conform with the trends of the era and state policy, they had to overcome their grief. (SY6o 1985: 123–125)

In the midst of Samyang reflections on the land reform—undesirable, but inevitable—the case of the Haeri Estate was, for Samyang, a justifiable exclusion. For the movement, however, it was an ethical breach. The most central question of the tenant struggle was whether the land was indeed "finished" (agriculturally productive) and thus subject to redistribution at the time of land reform. The movement charged that the land was finished; the company remembered differently.

Koch'ang Tenant Farmers Movement

They [unfoundedly] declared that Simwŏn-Haeri reclamation land was "unfinished" in order to be able to exclude it [from land reform].

Samyang

The Simwŏn-Haeri region reclamation land was finished in 1939 with the seashore bank [about 2 km]. . . . At that point we had no modern equipment and relied on human power to make the Kungsan Reservoir, the land division, the waterways, and the facilities for salt mining. . . . It took ten years and the Kungsan Reservoir was only eighty chŏngbo. So it was impossible to make farmland as the water was insufficient for the 700 chŏngbo of reclamation land. . . . Of the remaining reclamation land [after taking 380 chŏngbo for salt fields] most of it was unfinished, but some of the land below the Kungsan Reservoir was finished since it was near to the source of water. . . . It is unfounded to distort these facts and say that the land was excluded because of pressure or power (SYY 1987: 4).

The company explains that an important difference between the Haeri and Sŏnbul projects was the water system, which had facilitated irrigation at Sŏnbul. In the Sŏnbul case, there was a mountain river that they were able to block: "Because of the sufficiently large reservoir, the land could be planted after only one year. And after two to three years it was no different from finished land [*sukchi*]." In the Haeri case, there was no comparable natural water source (SY60 1985: 101). Because of water shortages in Haeri, they extended the tenant rent collection one year longer than for Sŏnbul, setting it at three years and thus bringing it to about 1942–1943, as the Haeri project was begun in 1936 and completed in 1938.

These dates are crucial for calculating whether the farmland was or was not productive, or "finished," at the time of the reclamation. Farmers were generally interested not only in this but also in the justice of the contemporary arrangement. Many were confident that the paddy was productive before Liberation and certainly before the Korean War. They concluded that if they could remember paying rents, then the land must have been productive. In one of the regional court sessions to terminate tenants who did not pay rent, the landlord's lawyer agreed that the company assigned land numbers and designated land types on September 13, 1940, but maintained that "although the land was registered with a number and usage, this was only a registration on paper—it was in fact unfinished land" (CR July 1987). One of the farmer witnesses at that court session explained that after reclamation was finished in 1937, the farmers dug up the soil in order to flatten the ground for about two years. He added that for three years the plants burned and there was no harvest. He remembers, then, that it was after five years (ca. 1942) that the company began to collect rents (CR August 12, 1987). Some farmers told me that they owned rights to what they claimed was productive paddy that was transformed into salt fields in the late 1940s. I was also told by farmers that they had been given replacement paddy for these plots, but they complained that they had been far away and thus difficult to farm. Many shared the understanding that "Kim Yŏn-su and Kim Sŏng-su excluded their [productive] land from distribution by turning it into salt fields."[16] Some farmers, however, dissented, claiming that Samyang made the salt fields so as to decrease the land that needed irrigation and shrink the reservoir to create new paddy; the rights to this new paddy, they explained, were handed out to pacify tenants who protested against Samyang during land reform.

Samyang's later post-Liberation venture into salt production on the reclamation land is also recorded as a nationalistic contribution because of the Japanese monopoly on salt production during the colonial period. Salt production allowed them to retain employees who lost their jobs when the estates were closed: "At that time there was still some unfinished land left, and changing the use of this land was a way to solve the employees' problem" (SY60 1985: 129). On June 12, 1946, they received permission from the state to construct the salt fields, and in July 1947, the real work began (SY60 1985: 129). By 1949, the first stage of construction was completed with 527 chŏngbo producing 8,998 kama of salt (SY60 1985: 129). At this point the Haeri Estate became the Haeri *chijŏm* (branch), with separate agricultural and salt field sections.

The more I learned about the region, the less clear it became whether the land had been uniformly finished at the time of distribution. Although, in general, reclamation paddies closer to the sea are saltier than inland paddies closer to the reservoir, some of the paddies can also be salty because they are at sea level, and there can be variance even within a single paddy. Farmers were candid in talking about their land at the time of reclamation. Although some claimed that their rent receipts went back that far, or that because they remember hiding in stacks of rice stalk during the Korean War (1950–1953) the fields must have been productive, others said that at that time the fields were salty and not very productive.[17]

For those farmers convinced that the land was finished, however, the exclusion of the paddy from reform was hardly surprising given their understanding that Samyang was powerful enough to manipulate the state for its benefits. A farmer in his seventies said, "At the time of the land distribution the government was simply bribed by the company so they didn't distribute the land. President Syngman Rhee had a deep [nationalist] history and made many efforts to distribute the land, but since then there have been no attempts to distribute the land to the farmers." In a similar vein, many farmers spoke of Samyang as somehow larger than the state, "able to do as they please." Farmers claimed variously: "The government can't win against Samyang because Samyang is everywhere; they have factories here and there so the government can't touch them. The government is weak in the face of money," "The government was deceived," "Samyang is like an island with no relation to the law," "If the Samyang reclamation had been controlled by the state we would have received our land long ago." One relatively well-off farmer explained that until the 1970s "there was no capitalism here—our lives were entirely part of Samyang" and that "it was the United States' imposition of capitalism that changed our sense of Samyang." Like the question of the state of the Samyang plots at the end of the land reform, also contested was farmer dissent in the immediate post-Liberation and Korean War eras.

POST-LIBERATION DISSENT AND THE KOREAN WAR

When Liberation came[18] *I was in sixth grade. Japan was ruined and the United States came in. The administration, the police, and education all stopped. . . . It became a* mubŏp ch'ŏnji *[lawless heaven and earth]. After thirty-six years of life as slaves, we found liberty. We were really happy, and then the division problem came up. It occurred because of the policies of Western democracy and* lax-maninchuйi *[sic for Maksй-renin-chuйi or Marxism-Leninism] centered in the Soviet Union. They opposed each other on our land.*

KOCH'ANG TENANT FARMER

In the colonial period there was feudal thinking left over from the Yi Chosŏn period: yangban *and* sangnom, *and landlords and tenants. These distinctions still remained after 1945. The power of people with land was incredible, so the consciousness of sangnom and tenants exploded in 6-2-5 [the date of the beginning of the Korean War, June 25, 1950, and thus a popular reference to the war]. In 6-2-5 many landlords died.*

KOCH'ANG TENANT FARMER

It is not easy to get a clear sense of the immediate post-Liberation or Korean War period—the "lawless heaven and earth"—in this region. Varied accounts of the Sip-il sagŏn (10-1 [October 1] Incident), a 1951 Korean War struggle that took place at the Samyang salt fields, reveal conflicting corporate and farmer understandings of the place of Samyang, the salt fields, and tenancy during this period of confusion.

During the Korean War, sixteen armies were activated under U.S. and UN command to fight against North Korean and Chinese armies. It was a war in which more than three million Koreans were killed (Halliday and Cumings 1988: 11), and it was a war that divided siblings, families, lineages, and villages, through its tribunals, executions, and retreats. Villages today are marked as places to which and from which people retreated and are populated by those who retreated there. Also, southern Koreans made their way North and northern Koreans made their way South, as the 38th parallel divided the nation. This individual and national experience, the rhetorics and rationales of postwar regimes, and the continued U.S. military presence have nurtured South Korea's cold war. The dominant South Korean and U.S. historiography focuses on who started the war, while revisionist historians examine the global political economy that led to the division and the radically opposed visions of a Korean national social formation that had already bifurcated the nation. Jon Halliday and Bruce Cumings (1988: 10) describe the war as a "civil struggle" between "a revolutionary nationalist movement, which had its roots in tough anti-colonial struggle, and a conservative movement tied to the *status quo*."

Korean War ethnography poses particular challenges. Although historians and ethnographers look for sides and positions, farmers' accounts seldom conform with them. It was often difficult to determine whether farmers were referring to the South Korean forces, the northern forces, or local sympathizers within northern forces. I read this obfuscation in two ways. First, post–Korean War South Korean rhetorics and regimes have affected both the spoken discourse and the memory of wartime. Second, both at the time or on reflection, local action is not always circumscribed by or correlated with the larger dictates of the times. Through local translation, large agendas and positions can be transformed beyond obvious recognition. In the early days of fieldwork, I assumed that all problems of translation were my own, but I discovered that South Korean university students in the field with me were also unable to distinguish "sides" in Korean War narratives. They, too, frequently interjected "Are you talking about Taehan [as the South Korean forces are referred to in these villages] or about the partisans or In'gong [Korea People's Republic]?" Although farmers did address such queries, I became convinced that these answers served to distort or discipline local memories of the era. Laurel Kendall (1988: 49), in *The Life and Hard Times of a Korean Shaman,* documents these difficulties in the Korean War account of Yongsu's mother: "The people's army opened it [a warehouse]. Or, no, the National Army opened it as they retreated. They left it when they retreated so that the People's Army wouldn't gobble it up." Kendall (1988: 49–50) continues with another telling of the episode in which Yongsu's mother does not waiver in narrating that the "reds" or People's Army opened the warehouse. Kendall queries "To what degree was her account colored by the incessant anti-communism of prime-time Korean television?" And she continues, parenthetically, "To what degree are my own doubts prompted by my thorough impatience with this genre [prime-time television]" (1988: 54)?

My reading of Korean War accounts in Koch'ang was mediated by, through, and sometimes against the interpretation of my assistants—South Korean students and activists with broad revisionist sympathies who were suspicious of the editorial hand of the cold war. Where we had not explicitly asked, "Are you talking about the National Army or the People's Army?" we often later disagreed, suggesting that we had heard one or the other, or that "clearly" one or the other had been implied, or that one or the other detail betrayed the rest of the narrative. By the end of my fieldwork I wondered where I stood between my doubts about my assistants who steadfastly looked for pro-Communist sympathies and my doubts about farmers' often pro-southern accounts. Nonetheless, farmer accounts, although of course heterogeneous, challenge and even shatter dominant South Korean perspectives on the war.

To make sense of farmer discourse on the war, I had to pay attention both to silences and to idiomatic subtleties. In much farmer discussion, political positions—of any sort—were marked as "ideological," which often referred exclusively to Communism. One farmer spoke of the Korean War as the time when "people died over *sasang* [ideology]." Another farmer said, "People died right side up and upside down, but what do we ch'onnom [village guys] know about the world?" Thus for farmers, "ideology" came to loosely connote political sympathies over which people have fought and died. Ideology, then, referred to ideas, in contradistinction to "natural" thoughts and practices. As one farmer put it while talking about the Korean War, "My life is a green life; like the dew on a blade of grass, like a reed; if it goes there, I go there; if it goes here, I go here. . . . We don't have ideology. . . . Isn't that what we paeksŏng [Korean common people] are? . . . What do people like us know? Life? No one wants to die. . . . I know all about the In'gong time, but I don't want to talk about it." "In'gong" has various meanings in farmers' discourse. It can refer to the Korea People's Republic, which was set up in 1945 and dismantled by the American military government—a period shrouded in the silences of mainstream history that has effaced the post-Liberation democratic efforts. "In'gong" is also employed to refer to the brief interlude of formal rule by the Chosŏn Inmin Konghwaguk (Democratic People's Republic of Korea, i.e., North Korea). It is in this sense that the term is also a synecdoche for the Korean War era. The slippage between the two temporally distinct moments arises because of the conflation between the earlier moment and the Korean War; some people self-consciously reproduced this silence knowing the political charge of these histories.

Although "ideology" in farmer idioms blurred histories and masked personal positions, it also hinted at hidden stories and sympathies. In such idioms, ideology marks the terrain and positions of the intelligent, educated members of society. The countryside is portrayed as an entirely residual space. Many farmers explained that all the intelligent people, those "with ideology," were killed or over time propelled by state sanctions to depart for Seoul. Similarly, farmers often explained that in recent years, enterprising and intelligent people—those with a vision of a better life—have also left for the city.[19] As one man said, during the Korean War "ignorant people couldn't be reds—you had to know something. We [i.e., ignorant people] just went there if they said 'go there' and the other way if they said 'go over the other way.' " This sort of talk, of the ideological and practical intelligence dragged and drained from the countryside, was a mainstay of my discussions with farmers.

I recognized two characteristics of such discourse: adulation for local Communists and their agenda and the silence of feigned ignorance that veiled the speaker's position. These idioms suggest that the South Korean state effectively constituted and in turn distanced the entire realm of the political as "ideological." Although many farmers' versions of good and bad in appraising individuals or agendas did not accord with official histories of the Korean War, they conformed to the official casting of the war in terms of ideology. When farmers discursively recast ideology to the realm of intelligence and overt politics, it was only "eating and living"—the direct extensions of the land—that were left to them.

In the Samyang villages, farmers were quick to say that this region was among the last to be "recovered" by South Korean forces and that they lived through the schizophrenia of "South Korean rule by day and Communist rule by night" much longer than in most other regions. There is evidence of strong support for the northern Communists. The dense mountain forest at the nearby Buddhist temple grounds of Sŏnunsa was a well-known stronghold for guerrillas. In recalling the era, farmers referred not to the "10-1 Incident"—the uprising at Samyang—but to the very public mass killing of Communists by the South Korean forces, who lined them up along the beach at the end of the reclamation land and shot them. In the village of Kojŏn, an impressive tree recalls these killings; elevated on a small hill, the tree can be seen for miles around, and it looms in Korean War accounts. One farmer recalled the incident.

> The people who had been arrested were killed at Kojŏn, and the rest
> of the people were pushed to the sea. The Hwarang[20] 20 regiment of
> the 11th Army Division were all armed with M-1 revolvers. The parti-
> sans [local Communists] had among them only one 50-caliber rifle

and one 50-year-old carbine. About 200 partisans were armed with knives they had carved by hand. They were lined up five meters apart in front of the sea breaker. I was nineteen, and I figured that the only way to live was to follow close behind the people with weapons. One partisan who knew the region well figured out a way to break the line so that people could escape, and then they fired their 50-caliber. The Hwarang 20 retreated and about 200 partisans escaped. Among them were many true partisans, but many ordinary people were left there to die when the army attacked again.

But what about Samyang—landlord and salt field manager—in the local turmoil of this post-Liberation and Korean War era? The Samyang history reports on leftist activity in the immediate post-Liberation: "After Liberation the riots of leftist elements were getting worse. . . . They killed and kidnapped village heads. . . . They cut off Samyang's power [after 1947]" (SY60 1985: 130). Already before the Korean War, Samyang found it necessary to open a police station at the heart of the salt fields, close to the water pump. One farmer explained, "The Samyang police were not real police, but Samyang employees—they had the money so they could buy guns." During the war, Kim Yŏn-su took refuge in Pusan, the managers went into hiding at the headquarters, and the work of Samyang came to a halt. Another farmer said "The Samyang people got in their planes and went to Japan. . . . The Samyang people stick around [in Haeri]? You have to be kidding." Samyang built a barricade and concrete forts at strategic locations. The forts housed two small cannons, three machine guns, and one hundred M-1 rifles.

The Samyang history describes the 1951 10-1 Incident as a struggle between partisans and Samyang "employees" that took place after the employees came out of hiding when they thought that a South Korean recovery had been achieved. It appears that on October 1 the head of the Salt Division who had taken refuge in Koch'ang came to tell the Haeri employees that this area too was now recovered. An out-and-out struggle between employees and local farmers or partisans ensued. In response, Samyang "was forced to petition the police station at the Haeri quarters to cope with the barbarity of leftist elements" (SY60 1985: 132). Accounts vary considerably as to who exactly was fighting with the Samyang employees. Similarly, accounts diverge as to which strata of workers comprised "Samyang employees." From neither company nor farmer accounts can we gather clear "sides" or a clear agenda in this incident. The Samyang history describes the incident as follows:

> They [Samyang employees and farmers] went to the reservoir and fought for three hours throwing stones across the reservoir gates. Finally, since we [Samyang employees] were outnumbered, we were kicked out by the enemies, and in this process, beginning with Division Chief Chin, some twenty

division chiefs were brutally killed. Not only that, but as the family members of those killed came near [the bodies] they slaughtered them, leaving 132 victims. These were brutal acts that would enrage both the heavens and humans. Kim Yŏn-su dispatched his second son, Kim Sang-hyŏp, to the Haeri Branch where the employees had met such a pitiful end. . . . They [the owners] loved them like their own family members. (SY60 1985: 131)

The fifty- and sixty-year anniversary volumes report the incident slightly differently. In the earlier volume, "villagers" are mentioned in the descriptions of the incident. In the 1960 version, the only reference is to "leftist elements." The later version thus partly removes the 10-1 Incident from its local context.

Fiftieth-Anniversary Volume	*Sixtieth-Anniversary Volume*
On September 30 all the leftist elements suddenly disappeared so the employees who had been hiding there were wondering what happened. [Division Chief] Chin then brought the news that Seoul had been recovered, and at his order the employees came out of hiding. At 10:00 A.M. the leftist elements came back and forced the villagers to attack the branch office (SY50 1974: 192).	The eighty workers had spent three months living in the midst of fear and oppression and yearning for freedom. When they heard this announcement they followed the orders of Division Chief Chin who came to the salt fields and told them to take up bamboo spears. They cried out "Long live Taehanmin'-guk" and after occupying the People's Committee office and the Communist police office, they again entered the Haeri branch office and organized themselves into a police force. But on 8-31 [date seems mistaken] at 10:00 A.M. the leftist elements who had retreated into the mountains suddenly appeared and attacked the Haeri branch (SY60 1985: 131).

Pak Yun-do,[21] a long-term company manager in Haeri and in 1987 an employee of Samyang Salt in Seoul, explained that the struggle of workers/tenants (unclear in his discussion) against the company was a struggle—"inevitable under capitalism"—of the "haves and the have-nots." The events were founded, he explained, in poor people's misunderstanding that the rich do not just get rich for nothing but on account of diligence.

> Before and after 6-2-5 [the Korean War] there were many reds [*ppal-gaengi*] in this region. . . . Under capitalism there are many workers and workers don't like capitalism . . . since the have-nots have han

[pent-up resentment] labor unconditionally hates rich people. Rich people are diligent so they got rich, but poor people don't acknowledge this diligence and there is a bad tendency for them to merely think "it's mine." At the time of 6-2-5, the Communist party said "Let's just distribute the land," so many people followed them. The regional Communists, the *ppalch'isan* [partisans], went around at night, and the Samyang employees took up guns to protect the company.... Many employees died.... The Communist party occupied the company for several months. The land distribution wasn't carried out because the time period [of occupation] was too short. Since they [the Communists] hated the haves, they used former *mŏsŭm* [farmhands] in their police and administration.

Farmers recalled the events of what many called "the salt field rebellion" differently. One farmer explained that the onset of the rebellion had been negotiated among locals, rather than having a directive from "leftist elements." "At the salt fields there were many refugees [from the North] and returnees from [wartime] forced labor service in Japan. One such returnee from Tongho was being forced to escape with the Inmin'gun [northern forces] but ran into the South Korean forces and ran off. He returned and announced: 'Taehan [the South] is coming—I saw it with my own eyes.'" Suggesting the motives behind the bloody encounter, some farmer accounts included laborers among the Samyang "employees," pitting salt workers and farmers against each other, while others implied that "employees" were the white-collar managerial staff, thus suggesting a divide between semielite Samyang employees and laborers and farmers alike. The farmer accounts below sketch different interpretations. The first implies that farmers—less satisfied than laborers—comprised the "local Communists." The second suggests the shared consciousness of low-level laborers and the unemployed.

> The laborers who fought against local Communists all died; they were on the side of Taehanmin'guk.... They were better compensated than farmers and weren't dissatisfied.... In today's words I guess you could call it a temo [demonstration].... Although the incident wasn't over ideology, that was a time when people died over ideology.

> The guys left in the Communist police station attacked the salt fields. ... It was mostly laborers who were left.... The uppers [upper-level officers] had left [the salt fields], and the Communist police activists, who were mostly unemployed people who were neither "this" [ideology] nor "that," did much of the fighting.

Farmer accounts thus highlight the local struggle between the rich and poor rather than clearly delineated ideological sides. The farmer quoted in the first passage above insists that although the struggle was between employees with greater benefits and farmers/tenants, it was not over ideology.

The farmer quoted in the second passage similarly dismisses ideology and thus renders it acceptable in the regimen of cold war discourse. One former nonggujang was emphatic that farmers "all supported In'gong" and fought against company employees.

> There was a rebellion at the salt fields. . . . It was fought against the employees there, the people who were close to Samyang. In 6-2-5 this was one of the regions ruled latest by the Communist government. At that time the Communists [*inmin*] were governing, but the Samyang leaders were sure that Taehan would recover, so they agitated the farmers. But since all the farmers supported In'gong, they caught some of the employees and even killed them. And the Samyang employees who had escaped when the Communists came in, thinking that the area was recovered, came back in and the locals went to kill them.

Although farmers objected to the corporation's landownership, the divisions that were enlivened in those years of dramatic food shortages and confusion were those between laborers and nonlaborers, between those with a job with food disbursements, on the one hand, and farmers and the unemployed, on the other hand. Amid the confusion and violence of local struggle, failed agriculture, and the ransacking of agricultural goods by all sides, it is not surprising that Samyang would have been an object of local discontent. We can imagine, though, that primary objects of attack might have been Samyang's granaries and employees/laborers whose coveted positions partially shielded them from the era's violence and hunger. Also, it is likely that the laborer hierarchy was based on distinctions among tenant farmers, such that dutiful tenants were perhaps rewarded with labor opportunities and thus food disbursements.

One farmer suggested that the 10-1 Incident was merely a struggle over control of goods in Samyang warehouses. The Samyang histories indeed report that "all the properties of Samyang were lost or stolen" (SY60 1985: 131). This farmer explained that those who were hiding in the Samyang buildings were no more than gatekeepers of Samyang goods and foodstuffs, rather than necessarily a particular economic stratum of the population in Samyang villages.

> People from the People's Army had gone off for training in Imsil [a city in North Chŏlla Province], but they were sent back when Taehan came in, and these are the people who came and fought with the employees of Samyang. . . . They fought with bamboo sticks. . . . They weren't fighting because they hated Samyang but because they wanted the goods in Samyang's warehouses. . . . It was more because of individual emotion than ideology. . . . One of the goods they primarily fought over was tobacco.

Again "ideology" is downplayed.

Struggles did not cease with the 10-1 Incident. A Samyang employee explained that "even in 1952, the recovery here wasn't perfect—there were still many partisans. . . . The police were afraid of being attacked at night so they [Samyang] bought guns, hired guards, and built a barricade at the salt fields. Police officers died, and many Samyang people died. I'm not sure about what happened to the farmers then." Similarly, the Samyang history reports, "In early 1951 the salt field construction was resumed. And so they [Samyang employees] worked during the day, and at night they endured the hardships of fighting with Communists who were wriggling like animals in the mountains" (SY60 1985: 131). Such passages describing the continued struggles against the company through 1952 suggest that it was indeed an object of considerable local disdain. It remains difficult to determine to what extent land or tenant discontent figured in this contempt.

> The activities of the Communists did not quiet down after the October 1 Incident. On the evening of February 15, 1952, leftist attacks destroyed the branch office, killing one policeman, two employees, and eight villagers. . . . In early July 1952, at the Tongho Police Station . . . [when] five policemen and twenty employees of the branch office were on duty, eighty Communist guerrillas attacked the police office and fought for three hours. . . . They [employees and policemen] defeated them. After sunrise, the police in cooperation with the military chased the guerrillas, who retreated to Sŏnunsa where twenty-eight of them were killed. They took away their weapons and after that evening, activity decreased. Still, for a year they [Samyang] lived by Taehanmin'guk during the day and the Communists at night. (SY50 1974: 193)

Although farmer accounts did not indicate that Samyang's landholdings were a central issue of local farmer or Communist aggression during the war, many students and organizers in the Koch'ang Tenant Farmers Movement believed that the 1980s land struggle followed in the spirit of immediate post-Liberation and Korean War land-related struggles. I am inclined to think that these 1952 attacks and the 10-1 Incident were not silent on the land question. Interestingly, at the aforementioned model estate for Haeri, the Sŏnbul Estate that was also reclaimed paddy, the land reform was achieved through farmer struggle. One young Sŏnbul farmer described what happened at that time, noting that a veritable movement had been launched.

> One farmer knew that Samyang was planning to turn the paddy into salt fields. . . . Evaluating today what they did then, I think we can call it an *undong* (movement): they went to each house and collected funds. An order of arrest was issued for the chief organizer, who meanwhile went to the pastor, who in turn went to a political candidate and promised him that he would win if he could solve this problem. . . . The

activist spent all of his money on this effort, the land was distributed,
and the politician was indeed elected.

In the fiftieth-anniversary book, the Sŏnbul reclamation estate is only sin-
gled out for having been distributed "a bit later" than the other estates.
This reference, though, does not appear in the sixtieth-anniversary volume.
The eventual distribution of Samyang lands is recorded by Samyang as having been enacted smoothly in accordance with the national and international times, but not because of farmer protest.

Regardless of the character of the events in Koch'ang in 1951 and 1952,
it is certain that in 1955 there was an out-and-out struggle for the distribution of the Samyang plots. This protest fell at a time when land reform
disbursements continued to be made. With the increasing yield of the Samyang land—that is, as the plots became more "finished" or salt-free—its
exclusion from land reform could have easily been noticed by politicians
and farmers alike. Although the 1955 struggle is frequently described as
largely the political efforts of a senatorial candidate and of one or two
influential farmers in each village, many farmers remarked that even before the 1980s movement "there had already been talk in the air of the
land becoming *sanghwandap* [land purchased through a land reform pro-
gram]." The 1955 struggle employed precisely the terms of the South Korean land reform, calling for sanghwandap. Farmer accounts focused on
the harsh sanctions meted against the 1955 participants. One farmer recalled that the company reclaimed their property by attaching stickers even
to rice stalk and door padlocks and that it had been very expensive to have
them removed. Another farmer explained that one by one the leaders were
bribed, some given land and others rewarded with nonggujang positions
until only a few "stupid farmers remained whose property was all marked
up by the government." Similar allegations of bribery were made in the
final stages of the 1987 Koch'ang Tenant Farmers Movement.

For farmers engaged in the 1980s land struggle, the memory of the
1955 movement—particularly strong in villages from which its leaders
hailed—recalled the extraordinary power of Samyang in quelling the
movement, the greed and self-serving tactics of the movement leaders (who
"sold out"), and the movement's elitist orientation. Interestingly, these
themes were relevant both during and after the late 1980s land struggle
under examination here.

FARMERS FIGURE THE LAND

Land histories are often hardship stories that narrate people's fate over
time. Political turns and ideological shifts have been grounded for farmers
by their effects on land tenure. The historical experience of Koch'ang's
farmers—as reclamation construction laborers, as activists in or against left-

ist activity after Liberation and during the Korean War, and as tenants to the corporation in the postwar era—loomed large in the land calculations and demands that farmers made in this movement. For farmers and external activists alike, the land issue was much greater than simply a determination of whether the Samyang paddy was or was not "finished [arable]" at the time of land reform, the most clearly and publicly stated point of contention in the movement. The specific land reform provisions that included particular land as the legitimate object of distribution were not farmers' only concern. Rather, the memory of land reform contributed to a way of thinking about land. Thus tenant calculations of a rationale for land relinquishment did not entirely conform to the calculations of outside activists, who tended to focus on the land reform history and provisions.

The land reform memory, one that centers on principles of prosperity and equality, is not singular but a composite of distinct memories of the immediate post-Liberation South Korean and of North Korean platforms and reforms. The farmers' 1980s call for land relinquishment emerged from these individual, collective, and mediated memories of leftist land and social agendas. Over the course of the 1980s movement, these memories met with the readings of Samyang history by the various external activists. During fieldwork I heard vivid memories of the land relinquishment demands made by post-Liberation leftists and of the land reform plans of the Communist rule during the Korean War. In'gong land reforms were never fully promulgated, but farmers remembered their plans and promises. One farmer, for example, reported that "during Communist rule they took a survey of all the paddy and fields and distributed it according to the number of family members, but the period was short and it only affected the barley crop. . . . We were poor so we were given land." Farmers' talk of the principles of land and life under Communist rule was not infrequent. A thirty-nine-year-old farmer, referring to times before his birth, remarked, "Here and there people came with all sorts of propaganda. They gave us education about a world that would be good to live in [*salgi choŭn sesang*]. . . . No-compensation relinquishment and no-compensation distribution were good. . . . If you divide the land between more people, they farm more diligently." Another farmer lamented, "If In'gong had done politics for a long time we could have concluded something, but they came and just left again. . . . They needed law and administrative power in order to make it so that people could live in ease [*inmin ŭl ansim hage*]."

One of the most ardent movement participants explained that he had taken part in the pre–Korean War *pallan* (resistance) and had been a local representative to Chŏnnong where "land to the tiller" was the central issue. He said, "I thought it would be good for people to live equally," and he remembered as many as one hundred fifty people, "men and women," attending the monthly meetings in the Haeri township. Mostly men in their thirties and forties, "they all died." He recalled how his house had been surrounded, how he was taken to the nearby Tongho police station, and how he was forced to write a "self-reflection," a remorseful apology. He was sent to the coast guard as an officer, where he lived comfortably, and although "nothing of those years remains in writing [i.e., in his record]," he noted, "the things of those years are still with me." Many farmers shared memories of just social measures and reforms. One woman explained that it was only many years later that she figured out that the start of "Communist rule," or In'gong, was the *pallan'gun* (local rebel armies): "They both [In'gong and pallan'gun] talked about not having to pay taxes and everyone living the same." Some farmers referred specifically to the land reform that was promulgated in North Korea: "The farmers' hearts rest easy; they just farm and give it to the country, and the country then gives them a share." A farmer in his seventies and a committed CFU activist explained that "in North Korea because of Communism they gave land to all the people, but here they decided not to take the land from people with lots of it."

Because land reform was agreed on in principle, contemporary long-term tenancy was considered anachronistic. Farmers pointed to land reform provisions that implicitly questioned Samyang's status as a landlord. In the court case to terminate contracts that was brought against farmers who refused to pay rent, the farmers' lawyer and the farmers took the stand that because the landlords did not farm land themselves, the farmers did not recognize their ownership of the land (CR May 1987).[22] Furthermore, they asserted that the very collection of rents was a violation of the land reform law (CR July 1987). The lawyer for the landlord counterclaimed, however, that since this land was not affected by the land distribution, the provision did not apply (CR May 1987).

Farmers figured that land—whenever it becomes productive—should be distributed regardless of statutes of limitation in the land reform law. Tenancy, then, was a temporary situation; they understood that over time tenants should become owners. The number of years in which farmers calculated that the tenant land would become owner land ranged from ten to forty years. In the terms of this logic, farmers referred to sanghwandap (repayment fields), a term from the South Korean land reform, to indicate that the land reform proscribed the gradual return of tenant land to its cultivators. As one farmer said, "I assumed it would become sanghwandap." And in 1987, many farmers referred to the land they purchased as sanghwandap. One older man explained that before he met Yun, the head of the Relinquish Committee, "I just wondered when this would become my land." A young farmer who worked as a laborer for the company and had only moved to the region in 1981 put it this way: "There was a law that after receiving rents for a certain number of years they had to return it to the farmers." Another farmer similarly asserted, "It is illegal because it has been forty years since reclamation. . . . Isn't it that after ten or twenty years of collecting rents you have to turn over the ownership?" Other farmers argued in similar terms but voiced no concerns for legal prescriptions. A seventy-eight-year-old farmer, one of the oldest men in Kungsan and the self-proclaimed oldest person still around who remembers working on the reclamation project, explained matter-of-factly,

> We have been insisting that since we are the ones who farm it, the land is ours. . . . So we are telling them to subtract the land price and give us all the money they have exploited us for. . . . If they *only* give it to us for free, well then all those tenant rents we paid over the years are lost. . . . The government should take away the land from the company and give it to us, but the government is on the side of the people with lots of money, so that won't happen.

One older woman explained her right to ownership, beyond legal dictates or the idioms of dissent: "Samyang didn't give me my land. . . . I've paid rents up until now; it's my land. . . . I'm tired of paying rents. . . . They have been gnawing at farmers' things, eating well, living well, becoming rich people, buying up land here and there; I don't know about this collaborator business, but . . ."

The movement's initial demand for *musang yangdo* (no-compensation relinquishment) made good sense in the context of these widespread understandings that land reform included a permanent mechanism for undoing long-term tenancy situations, particularly those of large landlords extending back to the colonial period. I found these various senses of "musang"—as principle and as historical precedent (referring both to the immediate post-Liberation and North Korean land programs)—in contemporary farmers' calculations. The talk of one salt field laborer meandered between these meanings: "The rents are for living off of others' land, so you have to pay them. . . . Musang is an impossible demand. . . . It has been forty years since the salt fields were made and still now every year they give the tenants contracts. If they had started [asking for musang] from the beginning it would have worked. Originally if you farmed for ten years it seems there was a law to give it over." Thus although he supported musang as a historical precedent, he dismissed it in principle; in other accounts, these calculations were reversed.

Extending beyond the idea that tenancy naturally unravels over time and that a relinquishment should make up for past injustices, farmers believed that land rights belong to those who labor. For long-term tenants and for those with direct personal or genealogical links to the reclamation project, "labor" had meaning beyond the daily labor of tenancy. They claimed ownership because although Samyang "made" the land, the farmers forged the paddy: "We made something that wasn't paddy into paddy, so it became ours," or "Kim Yŏn-su may have blocked the sea, but it is our labor that made the paddy," or "Samyang just blocked the sea—we are the ones who invested and made it paddy." One farmer complained about the tombstones of Sŏng-su and Yŏn-su: "It is written that in 1939[23] they started the project. . . . They started it, but it was with our strength and labor that it became rice paddy." Other farmers extended the discussion of labor even further and asserted that in society "rewards should be commensurate with labor."

Some farmers were resolutely against the musang claims, evoking the logic of capitalist ownership. One older farmer, for example, explained that "it [the Koch'ang land] wasn't distributed at land reform because the rice stalks weren't regular yet; it was not illegal at that time, and it didn't become sanghwandap because it wasn't paddy yet. By 1955 the land was finished, and we asked for sanghwandap, not musang; we demanded musang only because of the amount of rent we had paid." The same farmer added, "Musang is an unfair Communist claim." The comments of the father of a policeman, and others with relatives with white-collar jobs at Samyang, concurred: "You can't just take others' land away," "You can't just steal others' property for free," or "It is their land, so naturally they should collect when others farm it." Relatives of a former nonggujang similarly stated their objections: "Musang has no practicality. People who ask others for their property have no shame," or "Samyang's is not a wrongdoing. Where is the person who wants to give up his land?" Thus some farmers objected to what they considered to be the movement's distortions of the history of Samyang and abrogations of capitalist logic and relations.

Farmer ideologies—of land and otherwise—are inextricable from competing and shifting historical and collective memories. Similarly, the corporate histories are not easily fixed positions but complex negotiations of the local and the national, the past and the present. In chapter 5 I return to the Seoul site of protest where these competing ideologies and memories came face-to-face with the landlords in a series of negotiation sessions that became a contest over the very nature of capitalism and democracy.

CHAPTER FIVE

Capitalism and Democracy on Trial: Corporate–Farmer Dialogues

"Private" experiences undergo nothing less than a change of state *when they recognize themselves in the* public objectivity *of an already constituted discourse, the objective sign of recognition of their right to be spoken and to be spoken publicly: "Words wreak havoc," says Sartre, "when they find a name for what had up to then been lived namelessly." Because any language that can command attention is an "authorized language," invested with the authority of a group, the things it designates are not simply expressed but also authorized and legitimated. This is true not only of establishment language but also of the heretical discourses which draw their legitimacy and authority from the very groups over which they exert their power and which they literally produce by expressing them: they derive their power from their capacity to* objectify *unformulated experiences, to make them public—a step on the road to officialization and legitimation—and, when the occasion arises, to manifest and reinforce their concordance.*

PIERRE BOURDIEU (1977: 170–171)

The dominated classes have an interest in pushing back the limits of doxa *and exposing the arbitrariness of the taken for granted; the dominant classes have an interest in defending the integrity of* doxa *or, short of this, of establishing in its place the necessarily imperfect substitute,* orthodoxy.

PIERRE BOURDIEU (1977: 169)

In this chapter, I return to the month of protest in Seoul, to examine the progression of the eight negotiation sessions between the farmers and landlords. They offer a window on competing visions of modernity in South Korea that turn on the legitimacy of democracy and capitalism. While the corporation espoused capitalist rationality and representative liberal democracy, the farmers appealed to an egalitarian and participatory arrangement. In accordance with two visions of modernity, two conflicting notions of settlement emerged through the course of the month: a contractual or price settlement versus a settlement of historical injustices. The farmers called for social democracy or socialism in keeping with the general culture of dissent in the late 1980s. Although not consciously formed in these ideological crucibles, the farmers' discourse shared similar rationales and historical referents and was directly influenced by the external activists.

These legitimacies are reckoned according to the logics of nationalism [1] and culturalism: distinguishing what is right or moral from a national perspective and determining the nature of the Korean cultural legacy. Notions of a Korean cultural legacy figure a cultural terrain on which modernity descends. Culture and tradition are not entities to be "correctly" captured or recuperated, but socially and historically constituted discourses (see Hobsbawm and Ranger 1983).[2] Capitalism and democracy are not fixed signifiers, but flexible systems of meaning that work discursively by identifying "antimodern" transgressions.

Because the national project and the cultural project are mutually constitutive, we can take them together as dialogues with the past. I use "dialogues" to stress that they are not linear formulations; modernity, for example, does not supplant a premodern state-of-being, but rather operates as a patchwork of historical legacies that both beckon and resist the modern.

Over the course of the negotiations, farmers occasionally made instrumental concessions to the capitalists, even articulating their demands in the company's idiom. At other times, though, farmers rejected corporate idioms outright. At such moments the farmers were interested, in Bourdieu's terms, in "pushing back the limits of *doxa*," whereas the corporation had "an interest in defending the integrity of *doxa*." Above and beyond any instrumental demand, it was thus the discursive frame itself that stood trial. In the earliest sessions, the company argued in historical and legal terms, and farmers became astute talkers in this language. Later, however, as the corporate representatives realized that historical arguments did not serve them well, they retreated from more subjective discussions of history and morality and persisted with legal arguments. And when the farmers insisted on legal discussions with historical dimensions, the corporate spokesmen abandoned legal argument as well. In the final sessions, the company representatives spoke of land as strictly a commodity for purchase and sale. Having groped alternatively for ethical legitimacy and failed, they turned to sheer political and economic strength in the absence of ideological or cultural hegemony. A comment made by the company chairman in the final negotiation session starkly reveals how far they had retreated from any pretensions of legitimacy. When the farmers asked whether the company did not care about recovering honor, he replied, "By now I don't care. I've become insensitive."

The farmers began the negotiations with little legal or historically grounded argument. In the third negotiation session when Samyang declared that the farmers had no legal grounds, the farmers claimed history. As the corporation increasingly argued for a realistic, financial settlement, the farmers defended their no-compensation claim in historical, moral, and legal terms. Eventually, however, one group of farmers retreated from these terms in favor of a practical settlement. Examination of the progression of farmer–landlord negotiations also reveals the nature and development of the farmers' internal dissension over the month of protest in Seoul. By the time of the settlement in September 1987, however, the discursive practices of the corporation—land as commodity—had triumphed. Although the farmers purchased the land, victory was not so easy to figure. The settlement achieved the desired change in land tenure, but it did not satisfy many farmers' and activists' yearnings for social justice.

Before turning to the farmer-corporate dialogues, I draw briefly from the scholarly discourse on and the political rhetoric in contemporary South Korea to sketch the contours of the debate on modernity and its touchstones—democracy and capitalism. The scholarly examples concern the legitimacy of the South Korean bourgeoisie; the political rhetoric considers "Korean-style democracy" and popular resistance. Both concerns— the legitimacy of the bourgeoisie and the nature of democracy—figure prominently in the corporate–farmer dialogues. In the negotiation process, these discursive contests do not operate as fixed sides or positions.

"NATIONAL" CAPITALISTS AND "KOREAN" EGALITARIANISM

Scholarly literature on the bourgeoisie in contemporary South Korea widely concurs that in spite of their economic ascendancy, increasing political autonomy, and even cultural presence as a class,[3] they have been unable to secure cultural or ideological hegemony (Eckert 1990; Janelli and Janelli 1993; Koo 1987a, 1987b).[4] In considering this phenomenon, two queries arise: Is capitalism at odds with an indigenous Korean egalitarian ethic? And is capitalism somehow at odds with the interests of "Korea" as a national entity?

The first query turns on ideas of a counterhegemonic legacy. The anthropologist Vincent Brandt (1971: 232–233) calls this "the other ideology," a powerful social imaginary in contemporary South Korea that we have already seen at work in the conceptions of minjung culture and practice. Brandt, however, examined this "other ideology" not as a discursive phenomenon but as a social organizational feature of Korean villages. The "other ideology" has "an almost automatic resistance to the exercise of direct personal authority outside the family" (Brandt 1971: 232–233). Here Brandt touches on a legacy of resistance to Confucian, lineage-oriented, hierarchical, patriarchal, and authoritarian ideologies and social organization. Nonelites have sustained horizontal ties and radical communitarian values. The "other ideology" has broad implications for thinking about resistances to capitalism and the bourgeoisie in contemporary South Korea.

In the village where Brandt did fieldwork, he found that the lineage ideal persisted in the almost exclusively yangban single surname section (*ssijok maŭl*) (a village where everybody is from the same lineage), in contrast with the village section where relatives and nonrelatives lived side by side. He describes village egalitarianism: "Although some animosity and envy is generated along kinship lines . . . social life in the village is predominantly harmonious [with] a widespread concern with cooperation and integration throughout the entire community" (1971: 235). Brandt argues that egalitarianism reflects both an "ancient tradition," referring to pre-Confucian society, and the culture of "elements of the lower class" (1971:240).[5]

The sociologist Yunshik *Chang* maintains that the egalitarian ethic ironically helps to legitimize one of South Korean capitalism's key features: favoritism. He suggests that practices at odds with strict meritocratic ascendancy are immune from public criticism because they emerge from village or hamlet solidarity or what he calls personalism or communitarianism. "In urban industrial Korea, the personalist ethic merged with utilitarianism so effectively in the public domain that the personalist ethic is not likely to be criticized as a cause of corruption and hence escapes its demise" (Chang 1991: 125). He argues that Koreans act according to anti-individualistic principles, including kinship-, family-, village-, and school-based corporate groups. Thus he maintains that a persistent rural egalitarian ethic justifies personalism in urban corporate and political institutions. While Chang's discussion is helpful for identifying the social practices of various corporate groups in contemporary South Korea, the nature and extent of dissent in South Korea over the last decades suggests that the people have not been completely satisfied by the justice of the arrangement. There is widespread sympathy for those in South Korea who cannot wield connections with high-status or high-power corporate groups. The image of the have-nots, those with neither money nor *ppaek* (backing), or connections, is portrayed in numerous literary, film, political, and social commentaries. The 1993 assets disclosure of politicians and bureaucrats became a veritable national court for the social critique of the real effects of personalism in South Korea as their consumption excesses and graft were paraded before the public (see Nelson 1994).

The second query concerning the unstable legitimacy of the bourgeoisie is taken up by Eckert, who understands the failed hegemony in terms of an abandonment of nationalism. He contrasts bourgeois ideology and management practice with a "robust egalitarian ethic" (Eckert 1990: 134) or a "moral principle of equity in the distribution of wealth" (1990: 141) in Korean popular culture. He argues that the bourgeoisie is estranged (1990: 116)—"surrounded by an aura of public disapproval and illegitimacy" (1990: 130)—and that corporate South Korea rests precariously on a "seismic fault of social disaffection" (1990: 148). Eckert stresses that before it became a socioeconomic system, capitalism in Korea emerged as a development strategy in the face of the onslaught of Western imperialism.

"Ideas of Confucianism, nationalism, and capitalism thus all fused in the late nineteenth-century Korean intellectual milieu to produce a moral vision of capitalist activity that stressed national needs and goals and denigrated the purely private pursuit of wealth" (1990: 137). Indeed, this was the logic at work in the rhetoric of Samyang's histories.

That capitalists seek to justify the pursuit of profit as ethical action is hardly surprising, but the place of nationalism in these rationalizations helps us make sense of economic rationalization in contemporary South Korea (see Janelli and Janelli 1993). It is against these logics that a broad spectrum of social dissent denounced "collaborating capitalists" during the colonial period and dependent monopoly capitalists in the 1980s (Hong 1985; Im 1991).

"KOREAN-STYLE DEMOCRACY"

In political discourse on democracy, we find similar delineations of Korean cultural and national repositories. While some proclaim a brilliant Korean historical legacy of "democratic" institutions, others refer to neo-Confucian institutions and political ideologies at odds with democratic principles. These discussions turn on the legacies of premodern kingship and kinship, benevolent sage-kings, and family/lineage political systems writ large.

The writings of President Park Chung Hee (president, 1961–1979) draw on a discourse of "traditional Korean" patterns and politics. Park's conceptions touch on persistent cultural discourses in contemporary South Korea that had considerable play in the negotiation sessions. In an ironic twist, Park's discursive foe, premodern political culture, provides the rationale for a highly centralized, tightly controlled authoritarian state. Park decries the Korean legacy of elite authoritarian rule and justifies his so-called Korean-style democracy (*Han'gukchŏk minjujuŭi*).[6] Although he rationalizes military and authoritarian control, his discourse is remarkable for its populist flavor (he was the son of a humble farmer)—not unlike that described by Brandt's "other ideology."

For Park (1970: 78), the evil vestiges of the premodern era—"the vicious heritage bequeathed to us by the Yi Dynasty"[7]—highlight the organizational and ideological features of a rigid status-stratified society. He blames Confucianism for perpetuating a hereditary ruling class: "The Confucian doctrine, when put into practice, was utilized as a means whereby the government justified discrimination according to hereditary social caste and status, and as such was the most potent means of perpetuating this peculiarly Asian system of autocracy and class differentiation" (Park 1970: 56). The modern era must thus wrestle against the "privilege consciousness" that "occup[ies] the whole of our conscious life."

The consciousness of privilege, and special position, manifests itself in various ways; e.g., wealth consciousness ("I have more money than you."); rank consciousness ("I am higher than you on the social ladder."); academic snobbery ("I am the graduate of a better school than yours."); family complex ("One of my ancestors was a royal vizier" or "My elder brother is the so-and-so bureau director of such-and-such government Minister"); and partisan factionalism ("Since you don't belong to my party, my club, my church denomination, I regard you as my archenemy"). (Park 1970: 22)

Park (1970: 85) saves his harshest criticism for clan consciousness or clannishness, which effectively creates "small states within the state" and fosters "a narrow family and caste consciousness."

In the face of this privilege consciousness, Park (1970: 53) suggests that the "people" were economically impoverished and mentally backward. The masses "were extremely lacking in originality and initiative," "timorous," "weak of resolve," and had "a sense of futility and of living for the moment" (Park 1970: 59–60). Thus "the spirit of popular resistance to authoritarianism was totally nonexistent" (Park 1970: 60). He (1970: 92–93) accedes, however, that there were healthy democratic legacies that, "suppressed by Confucian narrowness," did not "blossom beautifully," but are still deserving of study.[8]

For Park (1970: 62), the modern era thus suffers from legacies that thwarted the development of democratic institutions and ideologies: privilege consciousness and "the stunted growth of the masses as a political force." He bemoans the absence of "local autonomy," "the fundamental basis of modern democracy," and of patriotism or "nationalistic feeling," a "sense of social solidarity or of consciousness of a common national destiny" (1970: 59). He (1970: 89) also finds no "responsible 'I' " with its commensurate "healthy spirit of judgment" in Korea. The "I," he argues, must be at the heart of a national consciousness: "With an established ego, one will get the firm self-consciousness of belonging to the national entity and will realize how much vassalism and kowtowing defile oneself and harm one's people" (Park 1970: 29). Against this reading of the past, Park (1970: 121) calls for a particular Korean-style democracy and justifies his "military revolution" as a response to the failed democracy of the first sixteen post-Liberation years under the "all-powerful dictatorship of Syngman Rhee." Rhee, he asserts, retained "semifeudal and colonial leading forces (nobles created by the Liberation, landlords, Yangban, etc., who formed the Liberal and Democratic parties)" (1970: 121).

Park's democratic revolution thus requires leaders who can inspire a "human spiritual revolution."

> It is insane to apply the classic democracy of the West to a Korean society dominated by the historical traditions of Oriental autocracy and feudalism. To believe that democratic freedom does not require leaders is to say a spin-

ning top has no pivot. The accomplishment of the modernization of Korean society and a social revolution, therefore, first requires a human spiritual revolution. A human revolution, allow me to emphasize, must be effected by healthy training in leadership. (Park 1970: 185)

It is in this context that Park (1970: 189) turns to medical analogy, asserting that the military revolution is a surgical operation to save democracy: "The revolution was staged with the compassion of a benevolent surgeon who sometimes must cause pain in order to preserve life and restore health." Explaining that "we cannot, as a matter of fact, enjoy complete political freedom in this revolutionary period," his was an "administrative democracy" (1970: 198–199). Park (1970: 125) called for a developmentalist state with an aggressive economic program and argued that economic equality must precede political democracy—that first the mass of the people must be raised to the middle class: "The gem without luster called democracy was meaningless to people suffering from starvation and despair" (Park 1970: 196). Park's modernity thus both conjures up and dismisses the past, simultaneously locating the antimodern in the past and recuperating its structures and tactics of control.

We can recognize Park's perspectives on the past and the logic of rule in the rhetoric of dissenting groups and ideologies coeval with his rule, including the writings of Kim Dae Jung, a long-term dissident activist/politician who after losing to Park in obviously rigged elections in 1971 became a key oppositional figure and symbol. Kim Dae Jung's *Prison Writings* (1987: 123) decries the moral crisis in South Korea and takes as one of its primary sources the "conflict and confusion" of "the polarization between a tendency to hold our native morals in absolute contempt and the tendency to overemphasize traditional morals."[9] Indeed, in Park's rhetoric, there is a strategic combination of both tendencies. Like Park, Kim (1987: 234) also denounces the history and legacy of the yangban class, suggesting that a survey of the "origins of the Yangban . . . is indispensable . . . to grasping the reasons for our nation's collapse." He explains that yangban culture is but the legacy of a particular class and historical period, not the true character of Korea. In a lengthy discussion of the reasons for Japanese colonialism, he cautions, "We have to realize that these bad habits [factionalism, regionalism, and intense vengefulness] are not a unique characteristic of our nation, as some argue, but the products of the Yangban politics since the middle period of the Yi Dynasty. We must recognize that the vestiges of evil still persist to a large extent among us, and we must strive boldly to be rid of them" (Kim 1987: 238–239). In short, Kim highlights the antinational character of the yangban class. He diverges from Park, however, in sketching yangban practices and politics as superstructural, rather than essential cultural proclivities according to which democracy must be tailored or curtailed.

CORPORATE–FARMER DIALOGUES, AN OVERVIEW

This internal cultural debate over "traditional legacies" appears, if quietly, in the interstices of the dialogue between Samyang and the farmers. The capitalists talked about what well-born, elite Koreans ought to do when they evoked Korea, "the country of manners," in contrast to the unruly, mob behavior of village ruffians. The "other" Korea, with its resistant egalitarian impulse, was precisely the object of their bourgeois indignation. They considered this other Korea to be antimodern and regressive. Farmers made no explicit claim to a dissenting cultural "tradition," but their vision of modernity called for radical social and economic reordering that rendered bourgeois excesses antimodern. On my first day of fieldwork in the village, one farmer's words implied that the expanse of Samyang tenant plots was spatially and temporally anachronistic. Spatially, these were not "South Korean" paddies because the state had nothing to do with this Samyang-controlled region ("We grow up knowing nothing but Samyang"). Temporally, these lands evaded the present because "in this region the colonial period never ended" ("We live not knowing Liberation"). Although farmers' resistance did not necessarily conform to an imagined counterhegemonic democratic tradition, their calls for popular assembly and equal land distribution were demands pitched in dialogue with "modernity."

The capitalists championed the morality of paternalism, articulated here as the landlord–tenant ties between "people sharing the same hometown." They exploited the notion of "hometown" in terms of the political and economic marginalization of the Chŏlla provinces. Although the capitalists made no claims to having shared their wealth, they boasted about exercising social responsibility and caring for the farmers as parents would for children. Farmers wrestled with this paternalism, at times dismissing it and at other times manipulating it to their own ends. They queried, for example, "Why, then, would you treat your next of kin in this fashion?" While company representatives attempted to frame the negotiations in conciliatory terms, the farmers often proclaimed outright conflict, calling a demonstration a demonstration.

The capitalists referred to democracy as a rational system of order and control. They proclaimed legal order to be democratic, while they denounced mass assembly as anarchic. Throughout the negotiations, the farmers championed public meetings, and the capitalists retorted that these assemblies would defy the law. The "masses" were thus pitted against the "experts." Although farmers did not refer explicitly to egalitarian or democratic cultural legacies, their arguments were concertedly antielitist. In conflict were the competing senses of "democracy" that Raymond Williams (1976: 96) outlines in *Keywords:* the socialist tradition of popular power versus the liberal tradition of elections. The capitalists' response to the farmers' concept of democracy echoed the "strongly unfavorable" sense of the term as it was used before the nineteenth century: "popular power, where the ordinary people, by force of numbers, governed—oppressed—the rich; the whole people acting like a tyrant" (Williams 1976: 94).

At the heart of this contest over tenant plots was an argument over ethics and economic distribution. The farmers took up the land question through historical and ethical consideration, whereas the capitalists went to great lengths to isolate it in its contemporary capitalist context. Farmers, as we saw in chapter 4, claimed that collaboration with the Japanese literally fashioned the land and that the elite collusion excluded the Koch'ang paddies from land reform. Similarly, as we saw in chapter 3, it was colluding institutions and practices, the company in concert with the military and the police, that suppressed the 1980s movement. The farmers' call for the end of tenancy appealed to egalitarian principles even beyond consideration of the historical exclusion of the plots from land reform. The capitalists wrestled to liberate the land from these historical referents. When the capitalists engaged in historical discussion, they argued that inequality and victimization were sacrifices for the nation—necessary features of development and modernity. In the following vignettes from the August–September corporate–farmer dialogues, the shifting contours of these broad discussions will be apparent.

SETTING THE TONE

From the very first full day of protest (August 13, 1987) farmers' slogans and declarations were far-reaching. Their opening declaration denounced contemporary South Korea, its history, government, bureaucracy, elite, military, judiciary, ideology, and morality. The August 13 opening speech of the landlords, their first response to the sit-in and this declaration, was a stroke-by-stroke denial of the declaration's claims. In this confrontation divergent nationalisms came head-to-head. The exchange that ensued, the first negotiation session, was one of three in which all the demonstrating farmers participated. Beginning with the fourth session (August 23), only a few members of the leadership committee participated. The negotiation results were reported in brief general assemblies, and few farmers had a clear idea of how these sessions were conducted or of how the dialogue progressed. These assemblies were often conflict-ridden, and seldom was a consensus of farmer opinion concluded; rather, they faded into song, or attention waned and they simply died out.

The farmers' declaration identified many enemies: Samyang's founders and current officers, the Japanese colonial government; the *Dong-A Daily;*

the military dictatorship; the bureaucracy; the judiciary; chaebŏl; and the police. Thus it set its heights far beyond the relinquishment of 291 hectares of paddy in "a corner" of the "national land." The farmers charged the company with antinational roots, parodying its self-proclaimed status as a "national capital corporation." They described Samyang as a "borrower of colonial money" and claimed that in the post-Liberation period it thrived on support from military dictatorships.

> Let's clean up the remnants of the colonial period and let's brilliantly carry out the principles of the people. . . . Kim Yŏn-su, the father of Kim Sang-hyŏp, who stood on the side of the colonial government enjoying government posts and splendor, carried out a two-million-p'yŏng land reclamation in Haeri, Koch'ang, in 1939 with the help and patronage of the colonial government. And in each following year, he collected—again and again—huge tenant rents. And after the Liberation, just as the signs of land reform were in sight, in collusion with his older brother the vice president, he changed the "land use" on the registration [from paddy] to salt fields and lied that the rest of it was not productive as farmland. In this way he excluded it from the land reform, and ate our tenant blood; in today's figures he gathered two hundred million wŏn over forty years of exploitation and thus built up a big company.
>
> In the name of farmers, we strongly condemn Kim Yŏn-su's sons, especially Kim Sang-hyŏp, Red Cross president, former Koryŏ University president, and famous historian, and Kim Sang-jun, Kim Sang-hong, Kim Sang-don, and Kim Sang-ha who brag about their national capital corporation and say that they have lived without shame. . . . And over the last two years the *Dong-A Daily* has never once reported our struggles against our adverse situation. We send our warning with hatred. We are no longer going to tolerate Samyang's—those borrowers [of colonial money]—misdemeanor in one corner of our national land [Koch'ang].
>
> We are [also] addressing our military dictatorship government. Turning its face away from the responsibility of correct government, authorities, and supervisory offices, particularly those in charge of important departments, it supported Samyang and the crimes of its brothers. Today, when the government talks about democratization, it is democratization without a kernel of the voice of Korea's paeksŏng [common people].
>
> We insist on the immediate relinquishment of the land that is owned illegally by Samyang to the tenants.
>
> [The crowd yells, "Relinquish! Relinquish! Relinquish!"]
>
> The government must distribute the chaebŏl-owned land and government-owned land to the farmers and restore our sound national economy.
>
> [The crowd yells, "Restore! Restore! Restore!"]
>
> Violent Police—do not suppress our peaceful relinquishment movement any longer.
>
> [The crowd yells, "Don't suppress! Don't suppress! Don't suppress!"]

Dong-A Daily that supports the evil corporation Samyang—apologize in front of the *kungmin* [the people] and employ all your strength to report the facts.

[The crowd yells, "Use your strength! Use your strength! Use your strength!"]

As farmers declared the self-proclaimed national capitalists "shameless," they contested the legitimacy of the bourgeoisie. At his first appearance, Kim Sang-don, speaking for the landlords, attempted to negate the legitimacy of the movement. He noted their common bonds as North Chŏlla compatriots, but the farmers stressed difference. While Kim talked about quiet conciliation, the farmers celebrated conflict. Fearing the power of the crowd, or the farmer "masses," as Kim referred to them, he called for a quiet, civil meeting in a "calm environment." Yun, the head of the Relinquish Committee, complied, promising that he would tame the crowd. He turned to the farmers, saying, "Even if the Chairman [Kim Sang-don] says incorrect things, bad behavior and harsh language won't do. . . . Can you keep that promise?" "Yes" resounded, but some farmers called out, "Hold the meetings in front of us." One farmer yelled, "That is fine, but if the problem isn't solved, I will go to the house of the landlord and commit suicide!"[10]

Kim Sang-don distinguished between contractual and historical relationships and declared accordingly that the occupation was inappropriate because the farmers had no formal contractual relationship with the company. He proceeded to call for an orderly meeting with a "mild atmosphere" in which farmers would "open their hearts" to him.

I sympathize with the hardship you have endured to come so far to Seoul, but I must tell all of you that this building has no relationship to us landlords. This is the stock company of Samyang; it is inappropriate for you to be demonstrating here. This office has no relationship to you, no *capital* [financial] relationship. It is a separate company; there is no relationship. . . . As your landlord let me ask that you disband your protest, return to your houses, and designate several representatives to remain behind who, without pointing blame, will have an honest meeting with the landlords in a calm atmosphere. Only in that way will it work.

If you carry on this way, trying to show your power through the assembly of many, there will be no solution. It is better for a few representatives to open their hearts to me. This group activity is no start toward a solution. In any case, I address you as a landlord, and I tell you that we are all from the same Koch'ang region and share an attachment to our homeland. As we are all brothers and sisters of the same homeland, I want to listen to the conditions of your demands with a big heart, and in a mild atmosphere with only a few representatives.

One of the farmers responded by screaming, "All farmers are representatives." Kim answered, "You are too unyielding, you will break. Don't rush so. Act with an open heart. As it is said, 'The more quickly a path goes, the more it goes astray.' " To this, another farmer screamed, "Speak simply"; this abstract metaphor was not the order of the farmers' day. Yun and Kim Sang-don proceeded to a debate over the kinship between the building, Kim Yŏn-su, and the farmers. Yun conceded that if it was truly the case that there was really no relation between the building and Kim Yŏn-su, they would leave.

> *Kim Sang-don:* Kim Yŏn-su is dead. The largest stockholders are Kim Sang-hong, Sang-ha, and Sang-hyŏp. The other stockholders are common stockholders, and after that there are several thousand small and medium shareholders. This building is that corporation's building. Legally speaking, your demonstration here is wrong. It's an encroachment, and an interruption of business.
>
> *Yun:* That's what I'm saying. It is widely known that Kim Yŏn-su built this building and that because of him we have come here today as tenant farmers. So, is this building related to Sudan [*ho* (epitaph) for Kim Yŏn-su]—or isn't it?
>
> *Kim Sang-don:* There is no relation. This building was built by the Samyang Corporation . . .
>
> *Yun:* [interrupting him] Are you saying there is absolutely no relation?
>
> *Kim Sang-don:* No relation, no relation to our deceased father.
>
> *Yun:* So, we farmers are to depart immediately, leaving representatives. You, Mr. Chairman, have come here from the neighborhood, while we have traveled the thousand-ri road.[11] What do you think of these tenant farmers who until today have been living in these tenant villages? Isn't our relationship the same as a family?

Yun went on to promise that if the chairman complied sufficiently, he would incur no inconvenience. The chairman interrupted, "What are these shouts of anger from here and there?" Yun replied, "If you comply with our representatives, I will take responsibility for them, the taejung [masses], as the chairman referred to them earlier." The chairman, however, persisted, saying that as long as the discussion was out in the open, it would be a "power struggle." One farmer interjected, "If you do not use your authority and financial power, we will not use our 'power of the masses.' " The chairman then said, "With something [a dialogue] so one-sided we will be pushed by the farmers, and in the final analysis we will be able to claim legally that we were forced." Although the chairman feared the power of the masses, he rested easy with his overriding legal power.

At this point in the protest (August 13) both the chairman and his corporate men and the farmers were not quite sure what the power of the crowd was or could become. At various junctures, conflicting assessments—of the extent to which the South Korean authoritarian regime had really been cracked and of the extent to which corporate giants had really become vulnerable—determined the courses of action of the corporation and of the farmers. More radical farmers strongly believed that a new order would arrive in South Korea. Many were confident that in the upcoming election of December 1987—brought about by popular protest—the opposition, embodied in Kim Dae Jung of the Chŏlla provinces, would surely win. It did not.

Kim Sang-don tried to deny the "mass" power of the farmers by repeatedly referring to them as "hometown people." Yun finally asked the chairman what he thought of his "family" members living "this way" (i.e., in poverty). The slogans spoke of Samyang sucking their blood, of fifty years of bloodshed, and of their rights to occupy the building—not as family but as its human mortar and cement. Over the course of the negotiations, the landlords continued to demand, as they had in this first session, that the farmers send only a few representatives to negotiate.

The farmers' understanding of their relationship to the building they had occupied differed. Some considered it to be their patron's quarters where they could appeal to family solidarity and paternal responsibility; others took the building to be enemy quarters under siege. One farmer's words straddled these sensibilities; he seemed to acquiesce to a continuous relationship with Samyang when he yelled spontaneously, "We are the guests, and we won't go down [to the countryside] before this affair is settled."

From the beginning, Yun appeared to be searching for a mode of protest that both sides could agree on, so as to domesticate the protest. Much of the discussion turned on family metaphors in which the landlords defended themselves as responsible patriarchs and the farmers charged that they had not fulfilled their duties. Over time, some farmers resisted the patriarchal family metaphor itself.[12]

CONTESTING DEMOCRACY AND DABBLING IN THE "PAST"

The corporate vision of democracy denied local participation in the name of "order" and "development." The following dialogue occurred in the fifth negotiation session (August 26) following the Attempted Murder Incident (August 24), in response to the farmers' request to hold open meetings in the countryside to gather facts about the history of the land in question.

Vice President: In the Republic of Korea if you only talk about having public
      meetings, then there would be no use in having judiciary or

legislative bodies, and even trials wouldn't be necessary. . . .
Public meetings can't solve problems. . . . So [are you sug-
gesting] it is useless to have trials; so the bar exam wouldn't
be necessary and the people studying for the bar exam
would be crazy? . . . A public meeting is, well . . .

Farmer: [interrupting] . . . something that people make.

The vice president's response to this farmer's comment revealed his real
fear that public meetings would lead to anarchy.

Vice President: Of course, people make them [public meetings] and they also
make organizations, and people make everything, but . . .
public meetings are in fact used in both developed and
underdeveloped countries. But . . . when the people discussed constitutional revision [in June 1987], statesmen
and elders gathered from various fields and discussed the
problem on the basis of their special fields of knowledge.
. . . That is a [desirable or legitimate] public meeting. . . .
*So you want to have a public meeting about every paddy, every field,
every orchard?* Then what is the use of law in this country?

The dialogue continued in the same vein:

Farmer: But what I'm talking about is whether it [our land claim] is
legitimate or illegitimate.

Vice President: Public meetings are only for determining who is right and
wrong, but what *you* want is land, so let's talk about land. If
they had to have public meetings over everything, countries
like the United States—its administration and various social
fields—would dissolve. Just take a look at the history of the
United States, at how the white people took the land where
the Indians lived.

The farmers argued that the "open meeting" would allow nontenant
farmers, who would be disinterested and thus impartial, to report on the
land distribution era. The company retorted, however, that public meetings would preclude just legal procedures. The chairman turned the tables
on them: "So you want to show your legitimacy, so you ignore the law and
thus [abandon] the taejung." The company's assertion that whites were
able to ravage Native American territory precisely because they refrained
from public meetings was a defense of the inevitability of "development's"
victims. This defense is similar to the rhetoric of state development, particularly of the kind meted out to South Korea's rural sector (which I explore
in chapter 8). By calling for an open meeting, farmers asserted the authority of their local experience in establishing the facts of history.

The farmers and capitalists contested the very meaning of the negotiation process. Although the farmers set out to weigh historical matters, the

capitalists aimed to set a purchase price. In the course of the fifth negotiation session (August 26) discussions, the capitalists were forced to grapple with the history of nationalist struggles. Finally they retreated by proclaiming that "attachment to the past deters solution of present-day problems."

> *Vice President:* In any case let's not talk about this occupation of the company and the protest. These only break up our negotiation. Let's really get down to the negotiation.
> *Farmer:* That is our purpose, our first purpose.
> *Vice President:* Have you come to buy the land or to demonstrate and occupy?
> *Farmer:* It isn't for buying the land that we have come.
> *Vice President:* That *isn't* your purpose? Then is demonstrating your purpose?

The vice president summed up the company's reaction to the farmers' extensive discussion of the past during the first five negotiation sessions, sung out in their chants and songs and dramatized in their protest: "Yes, well, everyone has a position—*where is the person without a story?* . . . The thing I find doubtful . . . is whether you intend to complete this thing [negotiation process] or to smash it." "Having a story" was the protest tactic of farmers, but for the vice president these stories blocked a conciliatory solution to the company's embarrassing situation. The vice president continued that in Korea, "the country of manners," it is "wrong" to even refer to the past.

> Countries with hostile relations must do everything through conversation. When Japan and [South] Korea had no diplomatic relations [pre-1965] many people demonstrated [when these relations were established], and people also demonstrated over the problems with the Japanese textbooks [during the early 1980s].[13] And many died in the March First Movement [1919] and in the independence movements. . . . *There are many such people who died for no reason.* In all international and modern societies, internally and externally, the most important thing is to figure out solutions to the current situation. If we are attached to the past, everything will be difficult to solve.

To this speech, which moved back and forth in time, a farmer replied, "Isn't it true that because there is a past, there's history; so, in history, we must go on correcting history. Always the most current generation is promoting history." The vice president argued that the failure of mass political participation in Korea's past should instruct that only through conciliatory diplomacy and an orientation toward the present can anything be accomplished. Asserting that people died in independence movements "for no reason," the vice president elevated his family, and others like it, as nationalist resisters against Japan, while denigrating the myriad who really did resist. Particularly telling was his assertion that modern society demands a focus on the present. This allowed him to dismiss arguments that focused on the past and to denigrate a particular nationalist legacy as antimodern.

While the capitalists portrayed a patrician Korean culture in which the past is silenced, the farmers insisted that the contest was, in fact, a struggle over history. As the discussion continued, the vice president expounded: "As human beings we should respect each other. For example, one cannot speak up about a former lover at a young man's wedding. It is morals and manners that keep us from doing such things. So one should not use people's pasts to manipulate a compromise. *Even if we know* [about this past], *morals and manners should keep us from talking.*" It was at this point that he went so far as to call the farmers' knowledge of history a "weapon" and proceeded to ask rhetorically, "And why would we want to give you that power?" Precisely, history had become the farmers' weapon, and the corporate representatives aimed to disarm. It was at this fifth negotiation that both sides concurred that the talks were going nowhere, and the vice president said, "A fight is a fight, a meeting is a meeting. You have just been firing cannon balls." A farmer, however, used almost the same words to disagree: "The struggle and the negotiation meetings are different," meaning that the discussions of price that were central in the negotiations could never settle the historical and moral issues involved.

PAYING THE PRICE: LEGALITY VERSUS LEGITIMACY

What began in the countryside as a call for a no-compensation relinquishment of land would eventually become minute negotiations over a settlement price. The price became the subject of endless debate that strayed far beyond narrow calculations of value. These sessions struggled over meanings. A price was first attached to the land at the third negotiation session (August 21). This session, the first after the *Dong-A* Incident (August 19; see chap. 3), began on a tense note when farmers demanded that Kim Sang-don stand because they could not hear him. It was in the midst of heated discussion over the police and corporate responses at Tae-hangno (August 16; see chap. 3) that the farmers challenged the company: "Do you hit people gathering money for food? Why do you pay employees [referring to kusadae] ₩10,000 a day to watch us? Do you think we are spies?" One farmer proposed a land purchase price of one wŏn per majigi (200 p'yŏng), an amount that would mock even a nominal fee. Kim Sang-don misheard and said that one wŏn per p'ilchi (600 p'yŏng) was absurd, and he began to elaborate the repair costs for the building and offices that the company had incurred because of the demonstration alone.

Kim Sang-don surprised the farmers by interrupting these arguments to suggest that they break for a lunch together, adding, "Since you have suf-

fered for fifty years we will present you with liquor when you go home."
Although these offers angered some farmers, other indulged such pa-
tronizing conciliation. When soon thereafter the chairman announced
that their senses were by now dull to any criticism that the farmers could
lodge, Yun suggested, "Why don't we talk about the fundamental issues?
And as for the things that haven't gone well in the past, as long as we solve
this problem—well—I will fall on my knees and make apologies to you, Mr.
Chairman." Over time, though, price tags beyond nominal fees became a
centerpiece of the negotiation sessions. It was over the question of price
that the farmers eventually split into two camps.

By the sixth negotiation session (August 27), both the company and
farmer positions and the divisions among the farmers had become clearer.
While one group of farmers was comfortably talking about a price, another
emerged above all committed to settling historical questions of legitimacy
beyond a price tag. For this latter group, any talk of contracts or price was
a denial of history. While the company argued that legitimacy was a moot
concern and demanded that they only talk about the land and its price,
this dissenting group of farmers appealed to the life stories of locals and
the collective memory of the region. While these farmers considered their
collective memories to be legitimate testimony, the corporation dismissed
their memories as disorderly and called their machinations a "mob affair."
While the farmers claimed the legitimacy of a people's history, a nonelite
province, the capitalists claimed a patrician, orderly culture. By the end of
the session, the farmers acceded to the company's manner of circumscrib-
ing history and agreed to examine "historical documents" at a closed meeting. Thus they consented to silence the cacophony and mitigate the power
of memory. Farmers also adopted "legal" arguments in concert with the
idiom of the landlords, but they understood "legal" in a different sense
from the corporation: the farmers argued that legally sanctioning immoral
or "illegal" historical developments was the greatest breach of morality,
while the corporation answered only with a discussion about contemporary
"laws" and purchase contracts.

> *Chairman:* There is no illegality . . .
>   *Farmer:* But you don't feel bad for having legalized the illegal transfer of
>   land?
> *Chairman:* Your words are already mistaken.
>   *Farmer:* So are you saying that our broadcasts and pamphlets aren't based
>   on fact, that they are groundless?
> *Chairman:* Yes, [they have] no legal basis.
>   *Farmer:* Well, then, this problem [the land struggle] cannot but continue.
> *Chairman:* We need to discuss the land, not the legitimacy.
>   *Farmer:* Legitimacy—because of our past history we have been demanding
>   a no-compensation relinquishment and talking about ₩100.

Chairman: If you want to talk legitimacy, we can't talk now. . . . We need to talk about the land. Aren't you the ones who were talking about a land price before?

By the end of the meeting, the vice president concluded, "You are saying you don't want to talk about price but about the principle of things?" And in one of his final statements, the chairman made his stance on principles very clear: "We can take the government-set price [set by the Ministry of Internal Affairs at approximately one-fourth of the market price, ₩1,881] from a blank sheet situation." Most of the farmers would not tolerate a tabula rasa that negated the legitimacy of their entire movement. One farmer described the stalemate: "We say *we have no illegality because of the past;* the chairman also says he has no illegality. So how can we have a meeting? How can we talk about anything else but each other's arguments?"

The company was adamant about the legal grounds of their defense, and they went to great lengths to establish that any concessions they made to the farmers were not admissions of legal impropriety—that a sale would be nothing more than a contractual arrangement. At the third negotiation session, the Samyang chairman had stressed, "This is not a legally related affair." Self-conscious about the 1985 rent concessions that Samyang had made in the early stages of the Koch'ang Tenant Farmers Movement in 1985 (from 3:7 to 2:8), he explained that they had been effected only because the farmers were "people of the same homeland": "You have misunderstood this as our admission of some legal problem over the landlord's earnings." The chairman expanded that the farmers mistook the rent concession as an admission of legal guilt because the farmers' "base spirit is mistaken."

As the corporation retreated from legal argument and historical facts, the farmers increasingly stressed the legal and historical legitimacy of their movement's claims. They argued, as they had in their initial declarations, that in calculations of their composite rents they had by now purchased the tenant land eight times over. It was in this spirit that the farmers had come to talking about ₩100 per p'yŏng, an absurd token sum in relation to market values, while the landlords began talking about a rate slightly below the market price. At the fifth negotiation session, the farmers said, "You will not be mistaken if you interpret this agreement as a no-compensation relinquishment" and that ₩100 was merely a measure for the company to "save face" and to avoid setting a dangerous precedent for other corporations. The farmers mentioned "other corporations" because the company had explained that they could not begin to go lower than this price because struggling small-scale landlords would be furious. They elaborated that in Kyŏnggi Province, on the outskirts of Seoul, many landlords are not rich at all and among them are even civil servants who painstakingly saved their rents to purchase the land. The farmers did not think much of this argument, and as one farmer put it, "You spoke of the fact that 26.8 percent of farmers rent to tenants; we also know about that, but we are the only ones talking about 52 years [of tenancy]." The farmers kept repeating that they would buy at a price so as to help the corporation save face, to make it look as if the land was not snatched away by their moral prerogative. Yun closed this fifth negotiation (August 26) by conceding, perhaps ironically, "We know that for you this is not a matter of money greed. . . . It is only so as to not set precedent for other corporate or state property." In this spirit the farmers said that, ₩100 or ₩500, the price mattered little to them.

It was at this fifth meeting that the company proposed ₩1,881 per p'yŏng, the government-set price and the price at which the farmers eventually purchased the land some two weeks later. The chairman announced that it was "the price recommended by media institutions, virtuous citizens, and company officials." This was the first meeting in which some of the farmer representatives began to discuss the land transfer in terms of a negotiable sale according to economic estimates of the farmers' ability to pay. In this way, the farmers' discursive frame or strategy had shifted—from a historical settlement to a capitalist bargain. Yun explained that although at an earlier negotiation the farmers had spoken about ₩1,000 per p'ilchi, a nominal amount, it "will no longer do" to talk in such terms. Thus he implied that such no-compensation plans were no longer possible and acquiesced to a real purchase of the land. The company, though, was furious at "the tone of the farmers' voices," at their continued presumption of a noncompensatory arrangement. Yun explained that the company was upset because they had misunderstood the farmers' proposal for ₩100 per p'yŏng as a no-compensation measure, but that "we figured it at that level so that no burden would fall on our *sŏmin* (common folk) farmers." In this way, Yun retreated from the earlier articulation that the nominal fee was, in fact, a sign of the legitimacy of the farmers' land story, symbolically a no-compensation land relinquishment.

Yun's retreat marked a concession to the landlords. It reversed the movement's central logic by suggesting that a low price was not a symbolic no-compensation measure but rather a price settlement. He thus assuaged the company fear that a non-compensation agreement would imply guilt. For other farmers, however, the ₩100 purchase proposal was not simply a reasonable price within the reaches of farmer incomes but a negation of the historical, moral, and legal legitimacy of their claims. The turn of events at this fifth negotiation session thus sketched the lines of dissension that would later tear the movement apart: a group that was willing to barter for a price and a group that insisted on a no-compensation arrangement. As was discussed in the last chapter, the no-compensation call was symbolic:

it referred to land struggles and to a more egalitarian arrangement. The fifth negotiation session was also a turning point because the corporation spoke openly of the breakdown of farmers' solidarity and thus challenged their consensus on local history. The vice president claimed that he knew from "information gathered on the fourth floor that quite a number of people agree with the government-set price." He added, "Even my children have different ideas, so how can all you farmers agree on the same price?"

At a general assembly following this fifth negotiation session, farmers discussed their views on the ₩1,881 proposal. Four different opinions surfaced: first, farmers should set a price and not waver from it; second, they should continue to bargain with the corporation; third, the leadership group, in conjunction with village representatives, should decide on a settlement price; and fourth, a vote should be taken as to whether the price should be ₩100, ₩500, or determined by a committee of village representatives. Onlooking citizens seemed to feel that to do justice to the injured students, they should continue to fight. No conclusions were reached at this meeting.

In the sixth session the following day (August 27), there was again an interesting discursive shift. For the first time, farmers calculated the land price in terms of *sanghwan'gok,* the rice payments for the title transfer of tenant land during the South Korean land reform. Although they discussed price and abandoned their demand for a noncompensatory settlement, they reasserted the movement's historical legitimacy by employing the vocabulary of the land reform. Farmers talked about bales of rice rather than currency. In the chairman's response to the sanghwan'gok discussion— "You have misunderstood. . . . The payments were legally determined by the government"—he tried to divorce the land reform payments from the *principles* of land reform. He referred to the land reform law as merely politics—as "legally determined payments." Eventually, however, Yun conceded (as he had on the issue of a no-compensation relinquishment the day before) that it was no longer appropriate to think in terms of sanghwan'gok, thus retreating from this subtle historical calculation to a merely economic one—disengaging the price entirely from its contexts.

At the August 31 general assembly, Yun organized a straw vote to determine how much the farmers were willing to pay. The leadership committee was shocked at the broad range of opinion. Just a week later, however, Yun was emphatic that, on the issue of price, a vote made no sense—that farmers must simply follow the will of the majority, the will of the leadership committee. Kang, one of the farmers strongly identified with CFU, however, took a strong stance against this directive. At this point, one organizer noted that the farmers had begun to take sides according to the district from which they hailed: "The farmers from the Simwŏn District objected to Kang's protests, while farmers from the Haeri District supported him."

This organizer expanded, distinguishing Simwŏn's "Samyang spies" and Haeri's small-scale farmers. At this assembly, farmers seeking a more comprehensive historical and moral solution became an identifiable minority; the clear majority favored a price settlement.

THE FARMERS DIVIDE[14]

After the August 31 general assembly, some farmers ventured to a new location, the Koryŏ University office of retired president Kim Sang-hyŏp. It later became the headquarters for the minority group that would not concede to a price settlement. On August 31, the farmers had gone to the campus only to distribute leaflets and thus fortify their appeal, but three days later, on September 2 at 11:00 A.M., a group began an occupation of the emeritus president's office. Over the next few days farmers and students held daily demonstrations together on the campus. The farmers slept in the plush office and ate their meals at the inexpensive student union. Very quickly it became apparent that it was a particular group that had clustered at Koryŏ University; there was no formal split, however, until September 7, when at a general meeting at the Samyang headquarters the leaders declared separate groups, each with a different price tag. Finally, Yun called for those who "believed" the leadership committee to stay and for those who did not to leave. Kang asked those who wanted a no-compensation settlement to follow him to Koryŏ University. He explained that he felt comfortable when he arrived at Koryŏ University, as the mood there was similar to the culture of Chŏnju's CFU center: "I was happy to see that there were lots of posters against the government and I felt, 'Aha, indeed the students are on our side.'" On this same day (September 7) a few members of the Koryŏ University group dug up the grave of Kim Sŏng-su at the university, thus committing perhaps the greatest symbolic offense or defamation possible in Korea.[15]

Long before the dramatic split on September 7, however, the leadership committee and the farmers at large had addressed the diminishing protest spirit. The farmer crowd had visibly dwindled, and at a general meeting they resolved to continue the fight and to begin new methods of protest. Their proposals were far-reaching: one person per family should participate; families that could not send a representative to Seoul should send ₩10,000; the financial report should be clarified; discussions must be open; leaders should set an example; the leadership committee should unite; in honor of the injured students, everyone should get along well; and people should not wander off, but stay together.

On September 3, one day after the minority group had begun to camp out at Koryŏ University, attempts were made to mediate between the two locales, prices, and philosophies. Several village elders traveled between the locales hoping to reach some agreement. On September 2, the farmers at Koryŏ University were busy phoning their home villages to gather more support. Similarly, at the corporation on September 3, the farmers discussed what to do because so many people were returning to the countryside. The following day, a group of farmers from Koryŏ University went to the headquarters of the Red Cross, where Kim Sang-hyŏp was president, to request a meeting with him. They occupied his office for eight hours. The same day, Kang addressed the Koryŏ University students and employees. He went so far as to say that they were equipped with gas and would commit suicide by self-immolation if they were forced to disperse and that five of the elderly men were actually carrying their wills. He vowed to fight until victory and assured them that time was not an issue.

On September 4, the vice president of the corporation went to the Red Cross office himself to call for a seventh negotiation session, contingent on the farmers' dispersal. The farmers accepted. In the seventh negotiation (September 5), the landlords told Yun to persuade "his" farmers to leave quickly and to stop defaming their ancestors, Kim Yŏn-su and Kim Sŏng-su. Later, at a group meeting about this negotiation, Yun reviewed the events as if there had been a clear consensus among farmers: "Instead of just insisting on ₩100, we figured that we could be the first to retreat from our position, and this seems to be what we think, so we suggested ₩500; we will see what happens tomorrow [at the eighth negotiation session]. . . . If we offer only ₩100 or ₩200, there are limits and the situation might get worse." There had, however, been no such agreement among the farmers.

At this group meeting following the seventh negotiation session, a lengthy discussion revealed the competing movement logics. Some farmers advocated getting support from external groups. Yun, in contrast, stressed the importance of farmer strength and would not straightforwardly address the matter of external support. He argued that since it was impossible to achieve a consensus, they should rely on the leadership committee. Although one farmer clearly advocated a speedy settlement because of the student injuries and the political dangers of the increased participation of external actors, the discussion neared its end with a student's aggressive call to "squeeze the neck of [the] poisonous snake" Samyang. The final comment by the moderator feigned a consensus: "Let's leave it up to the leadership committee."

> *Woman:* We have come 200 ri. Why is the leadership committee split? Let's not do this!
> *Man:* We paid rents till yesterday, so we have to buy it.
> *Moderator:* How should we fight? It seems like ₩1,500 is a possibility. They [Samyang] mentioned it [this price] at the Red Cross.

Yun: The problem is that if we discuss it, there will
be rumors, but if we don't discuss it, then
there will be no basis to work from. Please
believe the leadership committee—we will
follow the majority,

Woman: How long will you persist with ₩500?

Leadership Committee Member: Leave it up to us. . . . We can't say.

Old Man: Don't split. We came up believing Yun, so let's
go down the same way.

Old Man: We are so hungry we can't sleep. Hungry people always have difficulties. . . . Those people
[the corporation] eat well and are full. . . .
Let's leave it to the leadership group.

Old Man: [said very strongly] We can't do it with our own
power so let's get other organizations be-
cause the company doesn't take us seriously
[applause].

Leadership Committee Member: Let's cooperate with as many organizations as
possible.

Yun: It is not that I am against that, but without the
farmers, other groups can't do anything.
Our farmers should come up [to Seoul].

Man: The village representatives should go to Koryŏ
University and phone from there.

Yun: Six hundred farmers cannot agree on a price,
so the leadership committee should do it.

Man: If we don't have people, we can't work. Let's get
people from farmers' organizations and be
really active.

Yun: First of all, we need more farmers.

Man: There has been a dramatic drop in the numbers
since we first started. Our will and the will of
the leaders has weakened. We should figure
out how many people there were and bring
the numbers back up to that level.

Young Activist: It is important to ask youth groups, such as
religious youth groups, to participate. . . .
They don't have private desire [self-inter-
est]. And let's get help from the students
also.

Man: Actually two students have been injured; if we
get more support, there will be more [injur-
ies] so let's quickly settle.

Student: Let's squeeze the neck of the poisonous snake;
if we let it be, we will never be victorious.
Let's strengthen our ability at internal solidarity and internal unification. Let's develop

> better struggle methods. The demonstration
> at Koryŏ University is very effective.
> *Moderator:* There is the Red Cross protest and various
> other methods; so let's leave it up to the
> leadership committee.

THE SETTLEMENT

At the final negotiation session on September 6, the company announced that it could not go any lower than the government-set price. Yun became openly conciliatory, willing to consider various prices and also offering to put an end to farmers' denouncement of the company. Other farmers, however, presented the most comprehensive land history so far. It was a formal presentation of what by then had become the day-to-day appeals of the movement beyond the company walls. For the first time in a negotiation session, they formally detailed and documented their calculations that the land in question must have been paddy long before the land reform programs. In this final negotiation meeting, pushed to its limits, Samyang talked about history for a brief moment, suggesting that in the process of modernization somebody is bound to suffer. They asked how farmers could even make so much of their story; after all, "It isn't that we gave [you] no money, food, or freedom; it wasn't slavery." "It isn't as if it was just you cultivators who suffered, it was true of the whole nation."

Exasperated with the farmer appeals, the vice president repeated throughout the session, "What kind of a country is this?" At one point a farmer answered him, "A nation with a law against tenancy." The vice president then shifted the course of his discussion, asking the farmers to think about "law that, although not enacted, can be established between humans based on common sense." Legally, the company's stand had grown weak; their historical ground had faltered, and here in this final meeting they appealed to common sense—naturalized manners that would entirely preclude protest. Here, then, two nations emerged: one with a law against tenancy as a symbol of egalitarianism and the triumph of popular struggle and the other embodying a naturalized patrician culture that could even supersede legal statutes.

By the end of this final meeting, there were three clear articulations: the company spoke only of contracts and of instrumental calculations; a more conciliatory group of farmers was willing to settle on a price but still wanted some symbolic concessions; and finally, a more radical group of farmers held their ground, willing only to settle according to the terms of their histories. In the last moment of the final negotiation, representatives of the conciliatory group called out, "We haven't gained anything financially coming to Seoul. We should put out the seed of fire on both sides."

Yun bargained to have at least ₩200 or ₩300 shaved off of the ₩1,881 price to reward "the efforts of their struggle": "We are not saying ₩1,881 is unfair for us, but just that you should consider that it is too expensive for us." Nevertheless, the final settlement was ₩1,881 per p'yŏng. The contract read as follows:

1. The farmland which can be bought or sold (according to the terms of this agreement) is limited to reclaimed paddy which is being contractually leased [i.e., tenant lands].
2. The price of the farmland is to be set at today's current price—September 11, 1987—according to the grade of each unit of farmland designated by the [South Korean] Ministry of Interior.
3. Payment for this transaction must be made on a onetime basis.
4. Transactions of the applicable units of land will be carried out individually.
5. The payment for land purchase and lease must be made before December 10, 1987.
6. In order to register the transfer of property rights, the transfer must occur through an exchange of proper documents only when the tenant has completed (past) payments for the tilling rights on the land (i.e., rent). (The transfer cannot occur after December 25, 1989.)
7. If a tenant farmer cannot make the payment for the purchase and tilling of the land by the aforementioned date, December 10, 1987, the tenant will be deprived of the right to purchase the land and, accordingly, will be required to transfer the possession of the land to the owner. However, the deadline can be postponed in the case of a delay in the government agricultural property loans to aid tenant farmers in their land purchase.
8. After signing this agreement form, the representative of the tenants must publish a letter of apology the content of which will be designated by a representative for the landlords in *Dong-A Ilbo, Chosŏn Ilbo, Chungang Ilbo*, and *Chŏnbuk Ilbo* [South Korea's major newspapers] in the very near future.
9. As part of this agreement, the land tillers expressly concur that if they defame the honor or reputation of the ancestors of the landlords or if any of their words and actions cause the slightest damage to the profit of the four landlords, the landlords have the right to formally bring criminal charges against them with variously collected material evidence such as videotapes, broadcast recording tapes, and other disseminated publications.

September 11, 1989

Landlords: Kim Sang-yun
            Kim Sang-hyŏp
            Kim Sang-don
            Kim Byŏng-hwi

The corporation had triumphed: its discursive practices—whereby land was stripped of its signification—had won. Although the farmers purchased the land, there was little consensus that this signaled a victory. By the time of settlement, however, the dissenting group of farmers had retreated both from the place and platforms of the majority protest.

DOXA DEFENDED: MINJUNG IDENTITY VERSUS "RISING IN THE WORLD"

As rural pasts and personal narratives went public, many farmers literally claimed their homeland as national space. The rural areas left behind by both history and the state were, in their minds, national space rather than "residual space." However, farmers' notions of residual space where they were "left behind" had never celebrated the justice of the arrangement but instead were practical arguments for a harmonious situation in which to eat and live. In the early stages of the Koch'ang tenant farmers' protest, many farmers' appeal was not a call for better national agricultural policy but for a struggle for citizenship. Landownership promised to render their relationship to state agricultural policies a direct one, while as tenants it was only indirect. Finally, as one South Korean social scientist put it to me, "with the skins of feudalism peeled away," the realities of the farmers' relation to the state in both the present and in the past were made clear.

The movement experience challenged many farmers' long-standing ideas about the polarization of the urban and rural sectors and their own reproduction as an underclass. They came to understand the situation less as the result of inevitable economic imperatives of development and more as the result of the state's political and economic proclivities. Farmers explained how the landownership that they had achieved at such great cost was not really such a victory after all.

> Since it is my land now the taxes will increase. . . . I'm worried. . . . It is like telling an already well trotting horse to trot better and then hitting the horse so it falls, gets hurt, and can't go any farther. Government aid should fix this situation. If they really cared about farmers, the government would either buy it all for us or it should just tell us to continue living as tenant farmers. . . . They only help us partially. . . . That isn't anything at all. They are just killing farmers.

Farmers reordered their conceptions of the inevitable in their understandings of themselves, corporate elites, and the state. These conceptions, however, were always in flux, and in this particular countryside several factors contributed in the short run to a more cautious realignment of reality. The 1987 election results in which the ruling party was victorious suggested to farmers that a minjung era was not so imminent, that the structures of power were not so easy to dismantle, and that local experience would seldom be long validated as historical fact. Some farmers' resistance to protest, the decision of some farmers to abandon the protest, and the eventual dramatic falloff of protest activity in this region revealed farmers' frustration. One farmer who had been quite active told me, "We [farmers] hate education or 'history-talk,' " venting his feeling that all the talk had achieved little. As it became evident that the land settlement had not purchased symbolic justice, many farmers realized that in South Korea, landownership does not represent the social justice befitting a democratic society. In accordance with the stipulations of the settlement contract, shortly after the farmers returned to the countryside a full-page apology from the farmers appeared in every major newspaper. The apology stated that the farmers' historical claims had been false and offered an apology to Seoul residents for the confusion they had caused (see chap. 6).

The reflections and idioms through which the Seoul protest was recalled were both vexed and varied—a subtle story with no clear ending. One urban professional with rural Chŏlla roots, relatives in the Koch'ang region, and a progressive political orientation explained that both students and farmers hover between a passive line and a revolutionary line, which he illustrated for me (on a scrap of paper) as the coordinates of a grid. He told me that the minjung are like a "spring—sometimes they follow the revolutionary trajectory, but eventually they get pushed back to the stagnant trajectory again. . . . The minjung send a minority to the middle class, a select few to the [society's] leadership, and the rest of them all just aspire to those same achievements."

The experiences of protest, including both the day-to-day activities and the more explicit education programs, gave many farmers the sense that they had learned a great deal. As farmers decided that they commanded certain knowledge and that their history was in part authoritative, their participation in politics became legitimate. One activist explained that he had long been an opposition supporter but that before the movement he "couldn't openly participate [politically] as he wanted to": "[Before] I could only vote for the opposition in my heart, but now I can do it openly in front of others."

The politicization of rural life, however, is always delicately balanced between the promises of a new social order, the reality of things as they are, and the fear that things might not change so easily. Protests are always in conflict with another kind of learning: knowledge that allows individuals to ch'ulse, to climb up the social ladder. For many farmers, the experience privileged protest over "rising in the world." The movement experience emphasized the experience and plight of farmers as a group and underscored that rising in the world was no more than an individual and largely implausible strategy or solution. In addition, the farmers' experience in

Seoul amid incredible labor protest, and on the eve of a promising election, made it seem as if everything was in flux in South Korea, as if it were possible to think of a day when farmers could educate their sons and daughters to rise in the world among the educated or, even more remarkably, of a time when they could prosper as farmers.

After the settlement, however, many farmers returned to individual strategies for upward mobility. The divisive and often ugly events at the closing and in its aftermath (see chap. 6) frightened many farmers. It seemed to them that the countryside had once again become ravaged by ideological differences, and many preferred the harmony of an apolitical or at least quiet local province. In the end students and farmer organization activists were not satisfied with farmers' level of self-initiation in the movement, or with their seeming complacency with petit bourgeois ownership in the face of a continuously repressive state. The external forces backed away from the region, and repealed their valorization of farmers' political participation and of local history.

Through these negotiations we have glimpsed the discursive contours and historical contexts of competing social visions in late 1980s South Korea. Although the negotiation sessions focused closely on the details of the Samyang paddy, they stretched to broader reckonings of modernity, cultural identity, and the nation. And although not entirely a negotiation between the "other ideology" and "Korean-style democracy," the contours of far-reaching political debate are apparent in these negotiations. In the next chapter, I look back to before the month of protest in Seoul and forward to the protest's aftermath, to situate the movement in yet other dialogues and negotiations—those between the farmers and the external forces.

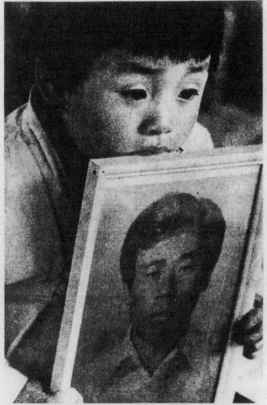

격동의 80년대
민족민주운동의 대장정
-「말」지 선정 80년대 10대 사건-

광주민중항쟁 (1980년)

80년대 민족민주운동의 출발점이자 종착점인 광주민중항쟁
더이상 무엇으로 '80년 5월 광주'를 얘기할 수 있겠는가.
전두환의 국회증언과 정호용의 공직사퇴로 '우리의 광주'를
잠재우려는 자, 그들은 이미 우리의 적이다.

Plate 1.

The 1980s are mentally sketched in rough strokes of political outcry and quiescence.

Text: "The tumultuous 1980s—the great distance of the national democratic movement."

Plate 2.

"Kim Yŏn-su may have blocked the sea, but it is our labor that made it paddy."

Plate 3.

"No matter how much we struggle, there is nothing left over, and that is why I am fighting for my land."

Plate 4.

The broken bow and the straight path.

Plate 5.

"You call people living like this 'ordinary people.' "

Plate 6.

The farmers' protest chants echoed no further, as they had taken to saying, than "between mountain and sea in our villages."

Plate 7.

"I fought with a guy who swore at me, and I swore back at him. In the past I would have just passed things over, not saying what I wanted, but now I have the confidence to say what I need to say."

Plate 8.

Moments after Kim Sang-don began his address, the farmers demanded that he come down from the platform and stand on the same ground with them.

Plate 9.

"When you yell out slogans, don't hold your hands just any way. We must be strong so that when others look they think, 'Ah, those people are strong.' First extend your fist to the sky, and in the final thrust let your fingers fly open."

Plate 10.

"We are dancing, fighting brothers and sisters."

Plate 11.

"Biting at our fingers, we are brothers and sisters vowing to shout out the truth."

Text on placards: "Punish the gangster police who harass women." "Is Samyang paying you [police] a salary?"

Plate 12.

The eyes of onlookers became vital protest participants.

Plate 13.

"How can police be violent to farmers? We must tell everyone in Seoul that without farmers there would be no police. . . .We can live without Samyang sugar, but can we live without rice?"

Plate 14.

"You murdering bastards—you try and kill the students, and now us."

7 · 8월 노동자 대투쟁(1987년)

7, 8월 노동자투쟁은 한국전쟁 이후 노동자들의 모든 투쟁을 합친 것보다 위력적인 규모였다.
7월 이후 3개월에 걸쳐 전국적으로 전 산업·업종에서 발발한 이 투쟁에는 연 인원 3백여
만명의 노동자가 참가했으며 이를 통해 1천여개에 달하는 자주적인 노동조합을 결성했다.
이 투쟁은 무엇보다도 노동운동의 대중운동시대를 열었다는 점에서 그 의의가 크다. 전국적
인 차원에서 진행된 노동자의 대투쟁은 노동자들이야말로 한국사회변혁의 중심임을 실감나게
해준 것이었다.

Plate 15.

The calendar was a symbolically loaded roulette wheel.

Text: "These demonstrations were larger scale than all the post–Korean War labor
struggles added together. . . .These struggles opened the era of mass labor movements."

CHAPTER SIX

Practicing the Minjung Ideology: Organizers in the Fields

The majority of mankind are philosophers in so far as they engage in practical activity and in their practical activity (or in their guiding lines of conduct) there is implicitly contained a conception of the world, a philosophy.

ANTONIO GRAMSCI (1971: 344)

This chapter examines the interactions between farmers and oebuseryŏk (external forces) in the Koch'ang movement from 1985 to 1987. The divisions among the farmers and the divisions between the farmers and the external forces both had roots predating the turn of events in Seoul. Much of this background, however, was not the province of shared knowledge in the day-to-day course of the movement. At critical junctures the apparent accord between the farmer and organizer communities was shattered. Disagreements were not only over movement tactics or goals but also over the meanings imparted to action. Indeed, incidences of out-and-out confrontation are often best explored and explained by probing divergences in such constructions of meaning. The contours of dissent between the communities were replicated within each community. This discord must also be considered amid changing dialectics of tumultuous political times and remarkable social flux.

Although neither the agriculturists nor the external forces constituted undifferentiated or cohesive communities, I will draw some broad contrasts between these two communities. The relation between them was not, however, primarily one of discord. In the late 1980s, there was an increased understanding between the community of opposition and the minjung. This convergence was facilitated by a discursive shift among rural organizers away from "ideology" and toward "experience"—a shift that was evident in the historiography of the Tonghak Revolution (see chap. 2). It is also helpful to recall the competing claims for the "authentic national experiences of the Korean people." The community of opposition moved closer to the farmers' agendas as it embraced "subject-oriented" activism that affirmed "experience" unaffected by dominant ideologies. Considerations over which experience to affirm, or which farmers to claim as "subjects," were central not only in theoretical discussions but also in the day-to-day decisions over the course of this movement.

ORIGIN STORIES: FARMERS MEET ORGANIZERS

In the early stages of the movement, various external forces supported divergent movement agendas. The tensions that surfaced in Seoul over the price settlement can be traced back to these competing calculations of legitimacy in the early organization of the movement. Judgments concerning this legitimacy were based on considerations of how, and by whom, history should be propelled. While some focused on *chuch'esŏng* (subjectivity), arguing that those most directly victimized should lead the movement, others opted for leaders who were most likely to be effective in the land struggle.

Although there were several renditions of the movement's beginnings, they were neither mutually exclusive nor self-consciously figured as "versions." In one view, farmers' han (accumulated resentment) eventually exploded. such a view sketched the movement as a natural development emerging from the land. A second explanation focused on the familial vendettas of particular movement leaders against Samyang. In both of these scenarios, it would have been plausible for the primary actors to be willing to work through the political system to accomplish their task. Samyang, not the system, was the enemy, and the task, not broad-based participation, was the object. There was, then, no consensus that the movement's agenda should necessarily be mobilized by a broad-based or far-reaching effort. A third explanation suggested that the information bureau of the regional police agency had promoted the movement. A CFU official called it the "internal friction and the 'eating quarrel' of the ruling class." In this account, the power struggles among business and government elites over their relations with the landlord corporation led to the movement. Specifically, these officials expected payoffs from Samyang for their favors to the company. In such a narrative, farmers were pawns in a struggle between the public and private sectors, between local political elites and national corporate elites. Finally, several accounts underscored the central role played by the external forces: some suggested that the external forces had "planted" the necessary consciousness; others argued that by revealing the hidden historical continuities of the Samyang story, they had "sparked a latent consciousness." Thus the various interpretations of the movement's beginnings—stories told throughout the movement—portrayed qualitatively different movements. I turn now in greater detail to these origin stories.

The Samyang Tenant Relinquish Committee was formed in 1986 by Yun, a fisherman who also earned income by farming his older brother's tenant plots. Yun told me that for years he had harbored a grudge about the rents they paid, which left nothing for them: "If we hadn't had to pay tenant fees, I would have been able to go to middle and upper school." In the late 1970s, he began to send appeals to the Ministry of Agriculture, and in 1980, he sent a letter to the head of a newly established government office, Chun Doo Hwan, who would later become president. Chun answered that distribution of the land was impossible and advised Yun—a farmer—to "continue to devote himself to agricultural life and development." Yun explained that in 1987 when there was talk about democratizing the military government, then ruling party officer Roh Tae Woo, in preparation for his presidential candidacy, made a public promise to "listen to and try to solve the problems of workers and farmers." Encouraged by this, Yun sent dozens of letters to President Chun, as well as various government party and ministry officials.

Farmers, farmer organizations, and students all agreed initially that the Relinquish Committee was farmer-initiated, or in the language of students and organizers, "self-initiated" or "subject-oriented." Although its self (farmer)-initiation made it legitimate, organizers asked not only the obvious question "What is a farmer?" but also "Who are the farmers? Who are the legitimate agents of change?" In addition, they queried, "Who are the farmers most likely to successfully accomplish the desirable tasks?" "What kinds of historical experience have conditioned farmers to call for the 'correct' social transformations?"

One CFU official, however, cautioned that the movement had not been farmer-initiated at all. Tracing the start of the movement to the information officer of the North Chŏlla Province police department, he asserted that Yun began activities prodded by such encouragement. He explained that the information officer provided Yun with printed material, promised protection, and even warned him that at some point he might have to feign taking Yun away. In short, he provided him with a careful script of how things were to proceed. The CFU official postulated that Yun was selected for this police plan because "he was smart, but not talkative." He elaborated on the "eating quarrel": Samyang treated local government and police personnel, such as information officers, "like the dirt at the end of one's toenail." Specifically, he alleged that the police were unhappy that routine bribe payments from the company had stopped. The officer thus planned a protest that would threaten the company just enough so that by quelling the activities he could demand a considerable payoff.

The comments of this fifty-five-year-old information officer,[1] whose parents had been tenant farmers until the land reform, revealed that he had supported the farmers' struggles, but only on his own terms: "Although on the ground we [police] have to do what we have to do—uphold the law even if it is a bad law—we can be thinking that the farmers are in the right and control the course of events from above." He emphasized that Samyang had ignored the flow of the times. "Their mistake was that they did not react quickly to society's changing social relations." Samyang, he continued, "had ignored the human being, seeing farmers only as people with no value." He emphasized that South Korea should have a "fundamental policy for farmers," and he hinted at his sympathies for one of the opposition party's 1988 presidential candidates. Remarkably, his allegiance to his post and to law enforcement did not preclude his sympathies for, and direct involvement in, this movement.

Although the information officer claimed that farmers should be treated better by Samyang and the state, he also expected farmers to be "pure and rustic"—dutiful country bumpkins. He praised Yun because, unlike other farmers, he was "very clever, always looking for possibilities." He complained that Kang, the CFU-aligned local leader, had taken up antigovernment activities because he bore a grudge about his own poverty and ignorance. He elaborated by explaining that such farmers were "educated" by external activists to stand up to the police: "Because they are ignorant, they just scream and scream at the police. If police appear, they block their ears and shout, and they scream even if you merely brush their hand. They purposely place women [who are more difficult for the police to deal with] up in the front line. They shriek vicious and radical phrases and announce 'We come from CFU.' " He referred to the region as a "problem region" where "antiadministration and antiofficialdom consciousness has been on the rise." Indeed, at the point that the movement transgressed his limited protest plans, he repealed his support. Because the officer was transferred beyond easy reach from Koch'ang—likely by design—his story never became part of the movement's official transcript but figured quietly backstage, particularly in the CFU's take on some local activists.

The initial interactions of the original movement leadership with opposition groups reveal the seeds of later tensions. Yun, for example, was skeptical about the external forces from the beginning because of their "Left orientation." In particular, he did not like the CFU because they "criticize the government." Chang, an officer of the independent Koch'ang Farmers Union, which one year before had broken away from the Christian Farmers League, heard about the tenant matter and visited Yun, whom he described as "focused on the eyes and ears of the *kwan* [bureaucracy] with no mind to talk to them [organizers]." In other words, Chang saw Yun as catering to the authorities. Chang did, however, give Yun pamphlets to show him how groups of organized farmers were prospering in South Korea.

A representative from the CFU transcribed his conversation with Yun on the first day they met.[2] The CFU representative was resolute that the CFU should aid, but not overtake, farmers' struggles. He voiced the CFU's preference for struggles waged at great risk. Yun admitted other tastes.

CFU: We are not a group to solve problems.

Yun: What do you mean?

CFU: In the past, we have wielded the power of our organization to help farmers in trouble solve things, but [we know now that] if people make efforts to solve problems themselves, they will become the *chuin* [masters] of the *nara* [country]. If you become great farmers—regardless of whether you succeed or fail in this struggle—the next time difficult things come up, in this or other regions, you will be people who can lead the fight in unison. But to become a member is a difficult decision; it is necessary to receive education and to learn how to resist suppression. You, sir, head of the Relinquish Committee, have appeared in a big gambling house. Put down your stakes!

Yun: Stakes!?

CFU: In gambling you put down your stakes. You are the person in charge of a unit—a unit attempting to capture a vast field [the land] now in another's name [Samyang]. Are you ready for the danger and oppression? Are you ready to risk your life—to victimize yourself to terror? Can you do this?

Yun: I can't do that at all.

CFU: Why can't you risk?

Yun: I'm afraid, what should I do?

CFU: Then go home. If you can't decide to sacrifice, it is impossible.

Yun: But we need to get the land. Ever since the rents were lowered [to 2:8] the residents have become much more courageous. So let's get the land. It seems that I have become the region's hero. They say that Yun [self-reference] did what even a senator [referring to the 1955 struggle] couldn't do.

The CFU, a national group, was confident in its political power and the backing of the Catholic church; it was also proud of the fearlessness of its members, who were ready to risk their lives for the movement. Stressing education, it was less concerned with winning large numbers than with raising a vanguard: "membership is serious and the stakes are high." For the CFU, the tenancy issue was but one campaign in a larger struggle; its primary goal was to train activists who would continue to struggle—to forge a new society.

Yun was not the vanguard sort, but he was willing to send other men: Cho and Kang, members of the Relinquish Committee.

CFU: If you hate to sacrifice even the slightest bit, and you have to find a way to definitely make this succeed, I have a proposal for you: why don't you go back and send a few other people? I'll give *them* education and make *them* part of the organization so that the project can succeed. *But* you must not disturb what I do. Also, you must not inform security institutions. Let's remember that government institutions and district heads are on Samyang's side.

Yun: Instead why don't you give three hundred people education and then together we can stage a hunger strike at Samyang? That should solve it. I'll take responsibility for bringing them.

CFU: That is not so wise. You must try all other ways of fighting first; at the most advanced level—with a well-trained organization—you can stage an organizational hunger strike. For farmers who live with physical labor, it's extremely unwise to have a hunger strike.

Yun: Well, then, let's have a lecture at the Koch'ang Cathedral or somewhere in our district.

CFU: That too would push things ahead, but first we must train. Send some lower-level people [in your organization] for training. It would be best if you also got some education, but if you are afraid of that, what can we do!?

Yun: So, what kinds of people shall I send?

CFU: First of all, they should be bold people. Second, they should be people who are recognized in their villages. And third, they should be people who aren't unintelligent—their level of education is of no importance.

Many months later, Yun praised the CFU to Kang, one of the farmers sent to train with the organization, and Kang asked him why he did not join if he thought it was such a good organization. Yun answered that he did not want to live *ttokttok hage* (intelligently). Kang challenged him again: "Then why are you doing this work?" Eventually, women's and men's CFU branches were founded, and the CFU representative was satisfied that the joiners were "real leaders with an ability to struggle." Cho, the other farmer sent to train with the CFU, recalled that at first he thought that if he became a member, he would die. Kang, who had never even heard of the CFU, explained that Yun introduced it to him as an organization that "criticized Chun Doo Hwan." As one young farmer who was serving as one of the youngest village heads in the region put it, "When people hear CFU they think of *undongkwŏn* [movement people] who have nothing to do with farmers." The first woman who sought out the CFU and who eventually became the head of the CFU Haeri Women's Division, went initially to "find out why the government hates the CFU." She concluded, "They tell only good things to farmers and speak about government problems, so I figured that's it [why the government hates the CFU]. . . . I didn't join, but I agreed in my heart; [I didn't join because] the police and the local government officials make it so that you can't live." One of the farmers who became closely affiliated with the CFU was a fan of late-night television seminars on South Korea's agricultural problems. He admired those "great" *paksa* (Ph.D.'s) on television: "Even if I had to die of starvation, if I could die having received a Ph.D., I would have no han [resentment]." He was also impressed with the lifestyle of the professional CFU activists; he was amazed at how Min's activism extended even to his personal or daily habits. He noted, for example, that Min did not drink coffee and Coca-Cola because they are foreign products.

Over time, the Samyang villages became divided by their CFU or anti-CFU orientation. It was widely understood—at least by those in the CFU villages—that police and local officials shied away from villages even partly organized by the CFU. This is not surprising, given the tenor of the CFU's education programs, which were antigovernment. The CFU was optimistic about the power of the opposition and the potential for a new world. Farmers, however, were not as confident. When confidence waned, the CFU and the farmers were worlds apart. A farmer in his late thirties, firmly committed to the opposition party but residing in one of the non-CFU villages, said, "When I am at the CFU education programs it seems to me that American imports are wrong, but when we farmers come home, we forget the education and again think of only eating and living." Months later on the eve of the December 1987 presidential election, this same farmer—whose passionate movement participation and antigovernment activities I had witnessed in Seoul—told me that he was afraid to join the CFU, worrying "what will happen if Kim Dae Jung doesn't become president."

Kang fulfilled the CFU's idea of a vanguard and became its steadiest and most fearless member. This confidence derived not from his membership alone but rather from his day-in, day-out contact with the CFU. Kang said that since becoming a member, he had probably traveled to the Chŏnju (the capital city of North Chŏlla Province) regional office at least one hundred times. At the slightest news of the police he had taken to calling Chŏnju: in one month alone, his phone bill tallied ₩40,000 (approximately U.S.$65).

At that time most people with incomes similar to Kang's either had no telephones or used them only for incoming and local calls. They traveled to the market town by bus to make long-distance calls at the bus station's pay phone. Private telephones in the region were always locked because farmers were keenly aware of the dire consequences of unauthorized use. Telephones were frightening, if marvelous, gadgets. In the case of one couple I knew, the husband would not even give his wife the key to the telephone, which was a source of constant arguments. Cho was fond of repeating that it had been because of the CFU and the movement that he, a welfare recipient (stressing his poverty), had installed a telephone. This anecdote served to prove the extent of his commitment to the movement. Calls from external activists were special events; to receive such a call was to be chosen to pick up the first message in what would then spiral into a rapid-fire "game-of-[personally transmitted] telephone." The excitement of those widely reported calls refers us to the political, material, and technological climate of a particular time and place.

Kang's world, however, was distant from CFU education programs: "The professors are so smart, and their *ttŭt* [thoughts] are so deep." Here "ttŭt" refers not only to thoughts but "to having a perspective on the world." Those "without ttŭt" either take up a residual space or occupy a "natural" province where there is no ideology or politics. He was particularly impressed by a university professor and newspaper columnist who had traveled to China twelve times. From this professor's lecture, "Peasant Liberation and National Unification," he learned that solving farmers' problems in South Korea was a necessary precondition to achieving unification. He summed up what he had learned from this lecture on global and political trends, particularly those in the Communist and socialist world, with the Maoist dictum that "white or black, all cats are mice eaters," meaning, "democratic or communist, all countries need to live well." In spite of his enthusiastic report of the meeting, however, he finally concluded that "people like Pak [another participant in the meeting who had been silently standing by during our discussion] and I can't know what they [scholars] are truly about."

Farmers never ceased to express their respect for those with intellectual or scholarly credentials. CFU education programs encouraged farmers to place their lived experience in the realm of broader structures and processes. Although some farmers embraced this project, others were more skeptical. Farmers tended to notice a gap between their "eating and living" and their politics, however conceived.

The CFU's activism appealed to some farmers and repelled others. In the fall of 1986, following the initial spring contact with the CFU, some two hundred farmers signed an agreement to withhold their rents. Those who signed delivered the amount of their rent-in-kind to village reserves. On January 31, 1987—already months after the rent was due—they gathered in front of Samyang's buildings in Haeri to protest. The Samyang buildings, including offices and dwellings for the high-ranking officers, enclosed a courtyard. The occasional visitor or tenant bringing her rent-in-kind would enter the complex through an imposing iron gate.

A short digression on this Samyang presence in Koch'ang will communicate something about the meanings assembled that winter day. An odd assortment of buildings and a half-heartedly manicured courtyard expanse hardly seemed an arrangement fit to inspire a treatise on the geography of power or spatial hegemony. Somehow, though, even my body learned to inscribe a particular reaction to the place. The buildings emerged from a lonely and rather unpicturesque bend in an otherwise scenic stretch. I remember that although I would circle wide to avoid the place, I never looked away from the usually closed gates. The occasional activity one

caught passing by—the gates cracked open, or the exit or entrance of uniformed personnel—commanded attention from anyone in the vicinity.
Above all, the place seemed deserted. The nearest village thinned toward
an impressive church entirely out of keeping with the built and religious
landscape of its surroundings. The church, an odd village footnote, was
really a detached piece of the Samyang complex (personnel attended on
Sundays); it too looked deserted. Also deserted was a small sundries shop
catty-corner from the company gates. I sensed that over time my body was
learning how to read the mysterious din of the headquarters to which farmers had been carrying their rents-in-kind for over a half-century.

That day, Min found the protest the farmers were staging at this regional
headquarters to be singularly unspirited. He said that the farmers were
fearful. The farmers asked him not to leave, "otherwise the police will
break it up." He described the scene:

> The *level* of the demonstration was not so good. There were no slogans, no
> songs, and no leaders. In no particular form, the farmers just stood staring
> blankly. We told them to bring drums so that they would warm up and get
> courage. They nodded "yes," but did nothing. Yun and Choi [a Relinquish
> Committee member] stood there as if to say, "Their being gathered like this
> is no fault of ours."

With nightfall, the group made a bonfire and sat around on rice stalk.
They remained silent when the police put out the fire and pulled the stalks
out from under them. Min was confident that his example had challenged
their "passivity." When the police pushed him, Min began to scream, "Why
are you pushing me?" This shocked the farmers and "gave them courage."
When a policeman demanded, "We are trying to disperse the farmers.
Leave!" Min answered, "I won't leave; I have to watch how you police treat
the farmers. I can't leave." Eventually, Yun arranged a settlement with the
chief of Koch'ang County: if the farmers paid their rents, a meeting with
the landlords would be arranged. Yun thus encouraged the farmers to sub-
mit their rents. Kang, Cho, and all those who by then were already tightly
rallied around the CFU only learned after the fact that the rents that had
been withheld in the Simwŏn District (Yun's district) had already been
remitted.

External activists were divided on farmers' potential to resist authority.
In the CFU there were tactical disagreements over the relation of the movement leaders and the farmer taejung (mass). Min judged that only a small
minority would be willing to hold out in the land struggle, and he concluded that because the movement's infrastructure was not well formed
and because the farmers were by then polarized, local officials and even
Samyang itself would end up directing the course of—or containing—the
movement in most of the villages. He suggested that the region's farmers

should be ŭisikhwa, (conscientized) for another year and that only then would he be able to lead them to forge a "mass movement": "It is a bit of a problem if the members [of the CFU] are entirely different from the tae-jung." A higher officer in the North Chŏlla CFU, however, appraised the situation differently. He figured that because of pending revisions of the farmland tenancy act (scheduled for October 1987), now was the time to fight, and he encouraged the farmers to hold out and not to remit the rents. Nine households, mostly from the Haeri villages where women's and men's CFU branches had been founded, withheld their rents. The company began to claim the property of those who had not remitted rents by affixing notices on the farmers' assets, including cows and television sets. Farmers spoke to me at great length about the humiliation of this experience which recalled the 1955 struggle. The CFU counseled the farmers to ignore the stickers and instead to focus on their education—their "resolve" and "consciousness." In April, four CFU members received a court order for negligence in their rent payments; the CFU members had, in a sense, become the central actors—or at least the central action—of the movement.

Aiming to turn the world on its head, the CFU set out to both shock and empower the farmers. In March 1987, about twenty farmers participated in a CFU education program at the Koch'ang Cathedral. When they gathered in Haeri, the local officials and police intervened and warned the farmers that they were being led astray. Min reported having said to the officials, "You bastard slaves—how is it that you ask your masters [the farmers] where they are going?" One farmer in turn chided the police chief: "Is this the achievement of 'justice-society' [a play on one of Chun's government slogans]? Who told you to do that? Did Chun [Doo Hwan]?"

The CFU figured that the court proceedings against the nonremitters would unify the farmers. They also hoped that the proceedings would win public sympathy for the farmers. One external activist from the CFL was strongly opposed to focusing resources on the court case because "court struggles lead nowhere." He stated,

> I would see this trial as a great success *even* if it goes on for twenty years. If they don't pay rents for twenty years . . . that is fine [sufficient]—*even* if they lose. Over those years there would be sufficient time for the farmers to organize [politically] as they farmed. How good that would be. . . . You can't compare a court case for people who have lost their land with one for people who still have their land [i.e., like this one]; they are entirely different matters.

Few farmers would have agreed that a twenty-year trial would be a success. With such a comment, he distanced himself from the sense of time and strategy of many of the farmers. The CFU focused on the long term, but for many farmers, this horizon stretched too far beyond the day-to-day demands of life. For the CFU activists, such farmer reserve was taken to be the effect of "barriers of consciousness."

We can recognize the gap between farmers and external activists in one event toward the end of the month in Seoul. One day, on a blackboard usually reserved for lecture notes and song lyrics that were being taught to farmers, the message "No More Education" was scrawled in enormous letters. It was unclear who had written this denunciation, but Yun later explained that he and Choi had come to share such a position: "I didn't like farmer education—the undongkwŏn indulged their desire to make farmers become 'movement people' . . . so we decided to have no more education." The final straw for Yun was when he heard a CFU leader say at one of the meetings, "If we just fight for one or two months—even if there are no results—we will be able to take the salt fields when we return to the countryside." "When I heard that," said Yun, "I didn't want anything of it. . . . I couldn't put up with it any longer. . . . I thought, 'We don't need any particular education. As long as we eat, sleep, and stay united, we will win.' " Finally it was the impulse to return home quickly to tend to their paddies, and perhaps extricate themselves from the course of spiraling politics, that appealed to the majority of farmers.

I will now return to the students, whose involvement throughout the movement had everything to do with the "education" that had been anonymously denounced.

NONGHWAL NOTES[3]

On the July eve of the August 1987 Seoul demonstration, over two hundred students from Seoul's Koryŏ University dispersed throughout twelve tenant farmer villages in Koch'ang's Haeri and Simwŏn districts for nonghwal (agricultural action), rural programs for students during their summer vacation. These visits facilitated the August escalation prior to the protest in Seoul. As previously noted, farmers associated Seoul protests with the student movement, and students were portrayed variously as the protagonists or villains in the narratives of dissent.

Students' nonghwal stories were tied to larger narratives about coming of age in the particular political milieu of universities in the 1980s. Although these stories can be appreciated beyond their place and time for their life-cycle niche—as can many narratives of spirited activism—they reveal the profound feelings of betrayal and anger that student movement learning and unlearning engendered. Joining the student movement was for many a painful process that dismantled personal and national pasts. I listened to many students' initiation stories—about the deep anger they felt as they learned that their education and common sense had deceived them, about their fears of unraveling their past, and about their hopes and dreams. Students refashioned their histories beginning with the powerful idea that, as one student put it, "everything we learned before college was a lie." The process of participating in student political activity and of eventually joining the ranks of the student movement was often painful and accompanied by family estrangement. One student told me, for example, that her mother thought of nonghwal students as "reds" who wanted to make "reds" out of other students and farmers.

Unlearning history through nonghwal was particularly dramatic for many Koryŏ University students because of the connection between campus issues and the tenant farmers' movement. In 1987, this connection took on particular meaning because the student movement had decided to work on national and international issues via local struggles for campus democratization. One student who had been "awakened" through her studies of history after entering college was particularly shocked to learn about university founder Kim Sŏng-su's collaboration activities in a book on the Liberation era that she read in an underground social science club. She explained that she first learned about the Koch'ang problem in her sophomore year when students were busy protesting the "irrationality" of the teaching of the national security law[4] in a graduate political science department at Koryŏ University. Another student was shocked in his freshman year to see a poster denouncing Kim Sŏng-su as a "man who sold the country."

One first-year student explained that only in the late 1980s could she have possibly joined the student movement: "I don't believe in *hananim* [God], but if there are *sin* [gods] I am grateful that I began university in this period rather than ten years earlier in Park's Yusin Period [1972–1979]." For this student, the Koch'ang freshman nonghwal was the climax of her spring[5] and summer initiation into the student movement. "You can't believe the world," she exclaimed after she shared a nonghwal anecdote. "A junior high school student asked me how a man who made it impossible for farmers to live and did bad things was able to become the president of a party [referring to Kim Sŏng-su and the Hanmindang]. . . . I didn't know what to say." Her experiences in Koch'ang seemed to strengthen her conviction about the new world she had learned about in just a few months of university life. The modern history she had learned in high school buckled under the weight of her new understanding of Samyang's Kim Sŏng-su. Also, she came to question the state's representation of North Korea and expressed her regrets at having discriminated against her "own people" in North Korea.

> How could an enlightened smart person [Kim Sŏng-su] tell people
> to go and fight for the voluntary Japanese military units? . . . Ignorant

citizens believed this. . . . And now [1988] Roh Tae Woo who participated in the coup d'etat [by Chun] and [the suppression of the] Kwangju [Uprising] still runs for president, calling himself a pot'ong saram
[ordinary person]; is it so easy to become a great person? If *he* is a great
person, *who* will try to become a great person? . . . When I hear male
students who study [in the student movement] say that the people in
North Korea live well and fully, I doubt them . . . but since I have seen
the distortion and hidden facts [in South Korea] I'm not really so surprised. In junior high we were asked to write down what we knew about
North Korea; I wrote "corn meal soup [i.e., in lieu of white rice],
forced labor, and reds catching flies and killing them." . . . How deplor-
able that I wrote that about people of the same nation.

She told me that before college she had been "completely unaware,"
that "things just passed me by." Her first weeks of college coincided with
the aftermath of the Pak Chong-ch'ŏl torture incident, and some students
encouraged her to go to the demonstrations, telling her, "Of course students participate." In early March, the Koch'ang farmers distributed flyers
to students and she was shocked to learn that Kim Sŏng-su had extracted
tenant rents in Koch'ang backed by the political power of the Hanmin-
dang. Until then she had only known of Kim as a nationalist and textile
industrialist who had—in a brave gesture—prevented porcelain from being
smuggled out of Korea. In April and May, the commemorations for the
April 19, 1960, Student Revolution and the May 17, 1980, Kwangju uprising proved to be further opportunities to learn "what really happened [in
history]." She wished that she had gone to the streets for the June 6, 1987,
democratization rallies—"I should have"—but admitted that she had been
"petrified" that day. She wished her friends a safe return and went home.

The protests over the arrest of Yi In-yŏng, the Seoul University student
council president, were the first in which she actively participated. The
university's front gate was locked and students ran around the athletic field
just behind the campus gates in so-called *sŭk'ŭrŏm* (from scrimmage) form,
linked shoulder to shoulder with arms interlocked around each other's
necks and shoulders. She was amazed at how the television misreported
the protest. Students, reported as "reds," were depicted as if they were hurl-
ing rocks with no reason, while no mention of the tear gas bombs was
made. Her first participation in a student demonstration beyond the campus gates was in a rally against tear gas. She trembled as she went, but
"students were calling to get rid of a bad thing—how could I not participate?" "Losing her senses" on account of military police and trails of tear
gas at every corner, she was amazed and thrilled by the warm welcome of
mothers and grandmothers who came out into the streets with water hoses
and edibles for the students. Students surrounded the riot forces but
agreed to disband when the police promised that they would not use tear

gas. The students dispersed but were nevertheless immediately fired upon. As she escaped, crying, she saw that a riot policeman had hit a girl a few paces behind her with a small tear gas bomb. She heard him scream, "Have a taste of this." As a "powerless female student in that state of not-yet-having-my-consciousness-awakened," she explained, "I was furious."

Through the rest of June she demonstrated, often returning home late and ill, lying to her parents that she had waited at school to "hear the news of the demonstrators." At one demonstration, students ran out of weapons so she joined those who were breaking stones; she said, "I had no theoretical basis, but I felt something [an awakening] at the very thought of the image of myself breaking stones." At another demonstration, she recalled riot police using tear gas as the students sang the national anthem. But perhaps her most vivid memory was of being called a "radical leftist, extreme student movement demonstrator." She wondered who they were talking about: "first-year students like me and the neatly dressed students all around me."

Although not a Christian, she joined a conservative Christian retreat during summer vacation. In our discussions, she rendered this experience as another turning point in her coming of political age. She returned from the retreat on July 10 to the news that one million people had gathered at Seoul's City Hall for the tear gas victim Yi Han-yŏl. She chided herself for having been "eating watermelon and drinking cola," for having been "oblivious to the power of Seoul citizens, only looking for God." Critical of her own indulgence, and of religion's silence on political matters, she decided to participate in nonghwal.

Thinking back on her earliest nonghwal initiation, she recalled her own surprising passivity. At a nonghwal seminar that addressed agricultural debt, the problems of the import of agricultural goods, and the methods of farmer movements, her response had been indifference: "Precisely . . . sure, sure." In the Samyang villages, she heard the "objective talk" of a former Samyang tenant who explained that he had sold his tenant plots because it was so disgusting and dirty to be treated that way. She asked him about the colonial period: "Had it been that bad?" The farmer asked her sarcastically, "Did you think farmers ate white rice?" She reflected, "I hadn't been well educated. I had lived unknowing in this fashion." She cried and cried over her own ignorance and concluded, "Such a thing as tenancy shouldn't exist." Over and over she told me that she had lived knowing nothing. She taught this man the *Farmer Song,* and he later brought chicken and liquor to the greenhouse where the nonghwal students were camping. She explained that students were unable to satisfy the farmers' request that they fight on their behalf "because students occupy a neutral position." At nonghwal's final meeting for self- and collective reflection/criticism she was asked to comment in her capacity as a freshman;

she remembered having said, "Indeed, you really need to know many things. Reading books isn't enough to understand the inside of problems; you have to come [to the countryside] and experience farmers' lives directly."

One student was similarly amazed by his own naïveté before he had begun to study history. He "had even" celebrated the suppression of Kwangju protesters by yelling "Long live Korea," and had earlier thought that South Korea would fall apart when President Park was assassinated. He had learned about peasant skirmishes against Kim Sŏng-su's family in Bruce Cumings's *The Origins of the Korean War* (1981) and was thus optimistic about protest potential in the nonghwal region. On his nonghwal trip he was not surprised to find that in the more stratified villages, the poorer farmers were unified. This was the case in his nonghwal village where people still used panmal (informal language) to address former mŏsŭm (farmhands). Class, he felt, was behind the tenants' solidarity in the land movement in Koch'ang. A history major, he had decided that one can only really know the "root cause" of activism by "feeling people's actual pain and understanding their ideological commitments." He explained that he studied history to find those roots.

Nonghwal provided a similar turning point for another student, a senior who had deliberately stayed away from student movement activities throughout his college years. Many months later, after graduation, this student moved to a farming village to engage in farming and organizing. He explained that during his freshman year it would have been impossible for him to contemplate moving to a farming village because in "accordance with the Confucian tradition [which stresses filial piety], I couldn't think of separating myself from my parents." He referred here not only to the geographic distance from Seoul but also to the metaphorical distance he would travel away from his parents by engaging in dissident activities. He had earlier interrupted his college years with compulsory military service and returned—as is most often the case—even more conservative. He explained that during his sophomore year he continued to be preoccupied with "individual desire [selfish concerns]." Although he had participated in nonghwal thinking "What is this [thing called] *nonghwal* anyway?" it was this experience that "awakened" him. A student of German literature, he had planned for a legal career and was initially interested in the Koch'ang case because of its legal aspects. Through nonghwal, he learned not only about the "contradictions of law in theory and in practice" but also about the poor farmers who "*live* like duck eggs in the Nakdong River" and "*die* without a name—they touched my heart." "Like duck eggs in the Nakdong River" was a reference to the many farmers who were killed there during the Korean War. Extraordinarily tall, witty, and spirited, this student was a favorite of village women. He visited the region many times following the protest and always arrived with humorous stories. Shortly after he had decided to devote himself to rural organizing and had settled into a village in the same province but at some distance from Haeri, he died trying to save a drowning woman. Although the outing had been recreational and the death accidental, some farmers placed it in their annals of violence and social struggle; such reckoning makes little sense in terms of the proximate causes of his death, but somehow it is how I too came to understand and mourn his death.

One French major described his rather ambivalent relation to the student movement and nonghwal. During high school, he had thought that student activists—"who sided with the North and incited confusion"—should be killed. In his freshman year he had no interest in the social sciences and professed that the only thing he cared about was dating. One of his department's seniors[6] told him to "study"—to read social scientific and historical materials under the guidance of student movement leaders. Although he had not liked the strong tone of the suggestion, he did begin to "study." He and the student movement were like a "Western pot and *ondol* [the traditional Korean water-heated, paper-covered floor]"—like oil and water. When an upperclassman who abhorred his attitude told him, "Get out of here—go away!" he became determined to continue his studies. As he studied, he developed "emotional wrath [against the state and status quo]" and a "desire for a logical movement." At that point, he was criticized again, this time by younger students who charged that he was not sufficiently active in the movement. He then realized his "responsibility as a youth of the Korean peninsula, became more certain of what [he] should study," and joined in movement activities more frequently. When I spoke with him, he had backed off from the student movement but continued to study in "undercircles"—student movement study groups. He reflected on the ways in which students in the movement hurt each other, something he really did not like.

The nonghwal experience was quite different for students who were themselves *nongch'on ch'ulsin* (born and raised in villages). Both Koryŏ University and nonghwal in general are known for their concentration of students with rural origins. Several such students told me that their "awakening" through historical studies was very different from that of city students because, in the discussions of the past, they recognized the contemporary lifestyle of their own families and villages. One student told me how strange it had been to feel that he had been living in "others' pasts." He explained sadly that the temporally distant childhood described by a teacher at the regional high school he had attended was not unlike his own rural childhood in the village he had left behind to attend the school. Although set in ostensibly familiar villages, nonghwal was nonetheless new for some of these students. As one student put it, "I grew up in an agricultural village, but nonghwal was like being born again." For rural students, nonghwal and the possibility of more long term farmer organizing presented unique challenges. Their nonghwal participation often strained their family relations because, if these students were to go to the countryside to labor, it was expected that they should return to their own villages. Furthermore, among the filial requirements for all South Korean students—particularly those from poor families—was academic success and social mobility; laboring in other people's fields ran counter to these expectations. One history major, the ninth of ten children from a North Chŏlla tenant farming village more rural, mountainous, and impoverished than those in Koch'ang, explained this vexed position: "I am very happy to have continued my studies at college. I like history, but after graduation I will go to my countryside. In the countryside they hope that I will rise in the world [and not return]." Those who were determined not to return to the countryside were also in an awkward position when they attempted to educate farmers about the vitality of the rural sector. One student reported that this irony was brought home to him when a junior high school student approached him: "Isn't it a contradiction that you tell us to stay in the countryside, but you yourself left?" Such soul-searching reflected the challenges posed by rapidly changing nonghwal practice and philosophy.

NONGHWAL TRANSFORMATIONS

The practice of nonghwal changed considerably since its origins in the first part of this century. Student trips to the countryside in the 1960s and the early 1970s were service-oriented summer vacation visits reminiscent of similar activities in the 1920s and 1930s. The female protagonist in Sim Hun's novel *Sangnoksu* (1986) has become the quintessential portrait of such colonial period enlightenment activity. From the vantage point of 1980s nonghwal, they were romantic, sentimental, and charity-oriented sojourns (HKHY 1985: 9). University "circles"—clubs devoted to hobbies, areas of study, religion, sports, and the arts—organized the visits to single villages; there was no overarching organization or particular agenda. From the 1960s to the 1970s nonghwal students were devoted to direct service; they labored and promoted increased productivity in the villages. A 1985 Han'guk Kidok Haksaenghoe Yŏnmaeng (Korean Christian Student League; KCSL) pamphlet (1985: 10) criticized such efforts for maintaining and bolstering the existing state agricultural system and obscuring the structural contradictions of the agricultural sector. The pamphlet also criticized summer holiday village retreats sponsored by religious groups that were active from the 1960s to the late 1980s. Typically organized by rural churches, they supported the Saemaŭl Movement's efforts to control farmers' political identity and cultural practice. They sought, for example, to eliminate superstitious non-Christian activity in the villages.

In the early 1970s, there was a shift toward a more political "team nonghwal," mirroring the growing minjung orientation of the student movement. While the circle and religious group nonghwal continued, team nonghwal was organized universitywide and worked in conjunction with the student movement. The team nonghwal, however, forged no relation with the escalating organization and activities of farmers' movements. The KCSL pamphlet asserted that nonghwal had an adverse effect on farmers' movements since it was often not in step with village life and made disjointed, unreasonable plans that led to nothing but distrust and frustration.

In the 1980s, the student movement became interested in mass movements. The KCSL criticized that nonghwal did not sufficiently reflect on and learn from the experience of previous team nonghwal (HKHY 1985: 11–12). Nonghwal became linked to the student movement with its branches and underground structures in academic departments.[7] The student movement made efforts to bridge the gap between activist and nonactivist students, employing nonghwal as a way to politicize the nonactivists. With its long history of state-sanctioned village service activity, nonghwal appealed broadly to students. Nevertheless, even the new minjung-oriented nonghwal promoted very little contact with farmers' movements.

This distance from farmers' movements, however, was consciously reversed in the second half of the 1980s. Coinciding with the events in Koch'ang, the very character of nonghwal was under scrutiny. By 1987, students had become interested in farmer's subjectivity or subject consciousness. Their activities were suspended in extensive reflection both on others' historical subjectivity and on their own, such that introspection and dialogue became integral to nonghwal. The nonghwal schedule included daily discussion sessions with farmers aimed at raising their consciousness and, in turn, daily self-reflection sessions to discuss the progress of this meeting of consciousnesses. Committed to considering farmers as subjects of history, just as they celebrated farmers' oppositional activity or culture, students also sought to explain farmers' passivity and inaction.

Students were self-conscious that their call for a farmer(-as-subject)-centered nonghwal heralded a new era for the student movement. Slogans on posters that appealed to students to participate in nonghwal in 1985 and 1986 revealed competing nonghwal aesthetics. Several slogans celebrated the essence of farming and agricultural life: "Ttang ŭl tikko sŏya handa" (We must stand squarely on the earth) (Foreign Language University); "Kaja! nongch'on ŭro t'anŭn hŭk kasŭm ŭro" (Let's go! to agricultural villages—all to the heart of the earth) (Kyŏnghŭi University). Other slogans referred not to organic rural essentials but to an exploited, barren, pathetic, and ungiving land crying for help. At Koryŏ University, posters read, "Let's go, to the barren red earth where dawn hasn't come yet" (Kaja! ajik to tong t'ŭji anŭn kŏch'in hwangt'o ro!); "Beads of sweat to the barren land" (Ttampangul ŭl ch'ŏkpakhan nongt'o e), or "The earth calls you" (Hŭk purŭnda) (Foreign Language University). Others appealed more directly to the imperative of labor: "Let's go—let's find the meaning of sweat and earth" (Uri kapsida. Hŭk kwa ttam ŭimi rŭl ch'ajŭrŏ), or "Let's work with my land, my sweat, my hands" (Nae ttang, nae hŭk, nae son ŭro ilgumyŏ). Finally there were more straightforward political appeals: "To agricultural villages where the price of cows is becoming the price of dogs" (Kyŏnghŭi University), or "Farming village economics—oppressed by U.S. and Japanese capital. Let's go" (Koryŏ University) (TNH 1986: 411).

The new farmer-as-subject nonghwal was to transcend farmer-as-object nonghwal. Farmers were no longer to be objectified as the recipients of student service or subordinated to the needs of the student movement. One senior forthrightly said that when he began college he saw no reason for nonghwal but that in 1985, he came to realize its meaning for the student movement. Here the consciousness of the farmers is absent; the only consciousness that matters is the students'. Nonghwal was thus a useful "experience" for student movement activists—a chance to learn about the material conditions of Korean history. Particularly important, then, was students' (often first) attempts at hard physical labor and, for some students, their first direct encounters with poverty. In contrast, the new nonghwal demanded an active dialectic between the student movement and farmers' movements and between students and farmers. A conscientization in dialogue, however, proved extremely difficult in practice. The new nonghwal challenged their own consciousness and their view of farmer consciousness. This nonghwal veered away from "serving," unidirectionally conscientizing farmers, or merely training student movement activists. As was stressed in nonghwal literature, a farmer-as-subject nonghwal must be long term, interactive, and experience centered. "Long term" referred to relationships between students and farmers, which were longer than one-shot summer vacation encounters. "Interactive and experience centered" pointed to a conscientization based on an understanding of, and an intimate interaction with, farmers' pasts and dreams. The primary goal of such a conscientization was to "awaken farmers to a realization of their own subjectivity": "Students, through a comprehension of the realities of farming villages, will personally experience the reality of their colonial territory-homeland and build an emotional link with farmers. . . . Farmers, through [their contact with] the students, will plant a consciousness to become the masters of society and get connections with students." Students had high hopes for this meeting with the farmers and students: "It should solve the contradictions of history" (KTNHCW 1987: 1, 4). This "new" equation was tricky because students were still deeply committed to providing service, training student activists, and "raising the consciousness" of farmers.

Students' "new" commitment raises a query: Did nonghwal experiences and outcomes affect the agenda or actions of the student movement? Indeed, the students' call for a transformation of their own consciousness affected—albeit slowly and in small increments—the very contours of their discourse on South Korean realities. A central issue in the Koch'ang farmers movement was the extent to which students were willing to fashion their own agenda or their vision for farmers according to minjung proclivities and priorities.

The year 1987 was a watershed for nonghwal. At many universities, including Koryŏ University, nonghwal teams decided in 1987 to venture to regions where movements were already raging. In 1985, nonghwal had reached a low point at Seoul University when local officials kicked students out of villages in South Ch'ungch'ŏng Province. The following year, however, students worked with the CFU to protect themselves from the anti-nonghwal individuals and officials in the villages (TNH 1986: 48). Such strategies were very different from those of previous nonghwal, which had established little contact with nonstudent organizers. While some university nonghwal were busily forging ties with local movements, other universities decided to forgo nonghwal in 1987, calculating that farmers were not and would not become central subjects of social movements to achieve reunification. Some schools opted instead for a different rural campaign in which they sent "conscientization letters" to junior high school students all over the country. These letters reported South Korea's social and political ills and the projects and aims of social movements. Yonsei University students spearheaded this effort (TNH 1986: 408).

In the midst of nonghwal refashioning, how did students understand and historicize the realities of farmers' consciousness? An unwritten and often unspoken query was, Why haven't they revolted more and done more to change their circumstances? Students spoke of farmers' consciousnesses "of defeat," "of conservatism," "of damages," and "of anti-ideology." "Consciousness" was loosely attached to nouns, forming phrases such as "master [i.e., master-slave] consciousness" and "insufficient solidarity consciousness." Most pervasive was the talk of farmers' *p'aebae ŭisik* (defeatism), a persistent fear and belief that things will come to naught. One student found this epitomized in farmers' fear of even a phone call from a policeman, and he posed rhetorically, "Isn't it our [students'] function to get rid of defeatism?" Another student explained that this defeatism was the product of political realities in which currying ruling party favor brought real benefits to individuals and villages, including loans and employment opportunities. One student offered this explanation: "Exploited and pushed down for decades, they are overcome by defeatism. . . . Even though the movement has awakened them to injustice, they are still not confident that they can triumph." Another student explained how the movement had transcended this defeatism, liberating farmers from historical experiences that "had enslaved them to the illegality and injustice of remitting tenant rents." They had come to think of Samyang, "which they had breathed like air, as their enemy." Some students attributed farmers' historical passivity to their lack of class consciousness; as one student put it, "History kills it [class consciousness]." Similarly, some students explained that farmers had a "fear of ideology" because of South Korea's "red complex" and because of their wartime experiences. One history major who had been raised in a rural area suggested that because the government got rid of the Left and made people fear ideology, "[farmers] just do what they have to do." These observations recall aspects of the historical sensibility I discussed in chapter 2.

The greatest challenge for students was to reconcile farmers' passivity with their own vision of social transformation and their commitment to farmer subjectivity in movements and history. Many students understood the situation in the following way: farmers are the subjects of history, but history has left them blind to that subjectivity. To create a society in which farmers were subjects, there would need to be education to rescue them from their blindness to this historical subjectivity and farmer-centered movements to transform material conditions. Students and the community of dissent were drawn to flashes of light in history's darkness—interludes of farmers' political action. They were interested not only in political movements but also in much less dramatic oppositional moments—"blind vestiges" untold in history's annals or dissenting consciousness that does not see the historical light because of repressive forces and material conditions. In such an equation, cultural expression (song, dance, oral tradition, etc.) was understood as the repository of such (sub)consciousness. It is not surprising, then, to find that the revival of cultural expression—based on peasant culture—was part of the clearly articulated agenda for nonghwal.

In their quest for farmers' revolutionary spirit, many students looked to farmers' historical subconsciousness. One student who "had learned that everyone has a revolutionary spirit" but had been disheartened after his first nonghwal experience in Kangwŏn Province, was reassured by the activities in Koch'ang: "My disappointment after [nonghwal] last year completely disappeared because I saw farmers' potential revealed through the movement." Another student explained that it was difficult to politicize farmers in Haeri because they had yet to break through Samyang's oppression in order to wake up the subconscious.

The opposition community in general—and student activists in particular—appropriated peasant culture in their oppositional practices. Students asserted that the "community" culture of farmers had been destroyed by "individualistic materialistic culture and administrative force" in the "false name of modernization" (KTNHCW 1987: 131). They called for a revival of "healthy minjung culture" to "realize a national community where humans are liberated" (KTNHCW 1987: 131). They understood the cornerstone of farmers' traditional culture as the integrated nexus of work and play (Choi 1989: 12).

One of nonghwal's paradoxes was that the "subjects" (farmers) turned their heads away from "traditional" culture whereas students maintained it. Students wanted these subjects of cultural production to recapture their own "healthy" culture. As they put it, "The real problem is to draw out their unknown healthfulness through doing minjung culture. . . . It's not showing or teaching them our thing, but showing them their own thing." Students assumed that participation in unified work and play, epitomized historically by *ture* (traditional labor cooperatives), would help farmers "realize their own worth and enhance their consciousness as farmers." In many cases, however, students found their encounters with rural labor and play confusing.

Although students took labor to be the core of farmers' consciousness, it was hard to find labor to be done during nonghwal; when they finally did settle down to work, they found it difficult. One student admitted, "In seminars we frequently hear the words 'labor is the prime mover in human history,' but I still don't really understand. Our goal is to obtain a minjung character. But when a leech attached itself, I flung it off so quickly." Because it rained incessantly during the Koch'ang nonghwal, there was little farm labor to be done. Also, students were confounded that it was usually the richest villagers who offered them sustained work opportunities. This meant that they were helping those who needed it least. The students told me again and again that they wanted to establish a work routine to mimic laboring lives: "If we live loosely [in an undisciplined fashion] then it will seem that we didn't come here to learn, but rather to confirm that we are indeed university students." They cautioned each other to work diligently and to try not to be "caught napping." For one group of students, the chance to clean outhouses was a particularly meaningful experience that they figured "went far to change farmers' understanding of us." Students were adamant that they should perform natural labor: not tasks dreamed up to appease their requests but work that needed to be accomplished. Furthermore, they wanted to be able to locate such labor themselves "with a subject consciousness."

NONGHWAL REFLECTIONS

Nonghwal affected Koch'ang farmers' perspectives on students. The initial resistance to nonghwal, particularly from village leaders, had been considerable. One woman, for example, described the nonghwal students as "all pretty—obviously the sons and daughters of rich people." Although she spoke fondly of the "warm, helpful students in neighboring villages," she complained that those in hers were "a bit cold and they studied so much. . . . They only worked outside for two days." A woman from a village that did not accept a nonghwal team explained that the villagers resented them because they thought that the students had come to demonstrate. Eventually, the tide appraising nonghwal turned. One of the village heads who had opposed nonghwal and ignored the students when they came was later prodded to step down by popular sentiment. Many farmers explained that it was over nonghwal that he had lost his mandate. Some farmers described their already long-standing faith in both oppositional movements and students.

> Long before our movement, I thought that the student movement was absolutely right. University students are the best intellectuals in the country, and they are the people who will make this country prosper. They know everything well, and they reveal what is wrong to the people. . . . Their demonstrations inform us of the wrongdoing of the government and intellectual class. . . . They demonstrate because the government doesn't listen to their demands. They know. [After all] they have all been to foreign countries. Television tells us that those students are red and impure radicals, but I don't believe it because they are all family members of South Korean families. Who among them would want to cooperate with North Korea? The state and the family are one and the same.

But even those farmers who had once thought of students as "dangerous elements threatening national security" came to consider them as family— no different from *nongmin ŭi adŭlttal* (sons and daughters of farmers). Farmers thus came to view the television reporting on the student activists and demonstrations with newfound anger.

Long before the students arrived in Koch'ang in 1987, the matter of the optimal relation of the movement to outside organizers had already become contentious. The nonghwal teams from Koryŏ University (two hundred students) arrived on the scene a month before the farmers traveled to Seoul. Although the students initially aligned themselves with the Relinquish Committee, they later sided with the CFU. Particularly after the farmers returned from Seoul, students' internal dissent over competing farmer alignments with outside forces left them unable to continue their work with the movement. In preparatory trips to the countryside before the formal nonghwal, students sought to identify the "authentic" movement in terms of the criteria of subjectivity introduced above. To determine authenticity, students had to contend with rural stratification beyond the fiction of a homogeneous peasantry. They had to consider, for example, the important distinctions among pure tenants, tenant owners, and prosperous tenants.

These students reached several conclusions after their two exploratory trips in the first and third weeks of June 1987. They decided that nonghwal should find its place in the Koch'ang Tenant Farmers Movement and that it should specifically assist the Relinquish Committee. To build broad support for this "subject organization," they needed to bolster its legitimacy in the community and "give it even more subject consciousness and struggle consciousness." As for the two major external forces (the CFL—represented locally by the Koch'ang Farmers Union—and the CFU), the students suggested that they could serve as a bridge between the two groups. They quickly formed opinions about these organizations, concluding that the CFU appealed to the middle-aged, while the CFL—more progressive in its educational programs—appealed to the younger farmers. The students arranged for their formal nonghwal invitation to be extended by the Relinquish Committee and they decided that in the event of government intervention against the nonghwal, they would respond "in unison" with the Relinquish Committee. Signed by five executive members and seventy villagers, the invitation was a "sincere" request for *nongch'on pongsa hwaltong* (agricultural village service activity) because of the "lack of labor hands." In their own pamphlets, however, the students stated clearly that they would not be "helping" in the movement but supporting the solidarity and organizational strength of the Relinquish Committee (SAAI 1987: 2). They suggested that they could protest at Samyang so as to give farmers courage and to help them "overcome [their] fear of authorities and the police" (SAAI 1987: 3).

The most memorable of nonghwal activities, for both students and farmers, was the festival on the seventh day after the students' arrival. From the outset, students planned the event in order to bring all twelve nonghwal villages together. Some students imagined a festival that would resemble a "traditional" village meeting. At such a festival, farmers and students would forge warm ties. Others planned for a demonstration—a confrontation between the farmers and Samyang. Here they imagined tenant uprisings. Students devoted considerable discussion to deliberating about how such an encounter would turn out. Some envisioned that farmers might become violent and that the accumulated resentment might bubble over. One village team decided that if such a situation arose, they would occupy the Samyang buildings with the farmers. But by the third day of nonghwal, and after six hours of deliberation, all the team leaders agreed that students would not participate in a violent demonstration; they did not want to be held responsible and thus risk continuing student participation in the region. Student plans vacillated among various visions. On the one hand, student-sponsored preparatory activities—from the village discussion sessions to the teaching and planning of the festival itself—were designed to unify the farmers and encourage them in their struggle. On the other hand, students feared a confrontation with Samyang that would be out of their control. One student, for example, in response to a farmer's proposal to demolish a local statue of Kim Sŏng-su, commented, "The farmers showed great development [in protest], but they are not yet enlightened." Later, though, students were self-critical of their very impulse to control the turn of events. They regretted that they had made the signs and coined the slogans for the festival. One student remarked, "It would have been better if farmers had made them with their own hands." Another commented, "Our planning prohibited the self-initiation of farmers." In part, the heterogeneity of age, gender, and social position within and among the villages made it difficult for students to know how to proceed.

The nonghwal teams were divided into committees attending to various subpopulations of the village; this breakdown reminded me of the chapter headings found in traditional anthropological village ethnographies. Students' theoretical assessments as to which villagers were or should become "primary historical movers" or subjects were often challenged by the realities of village life. Students were confronted with competing criteria of legitimacy in the village, including those of formal leadership positions, employment status, class relationships to Samyang, and movement affiliation. Against students' notions of subjectivity or historical legitimacy, no hierarchy made for a perfect fit.

The general custom of nonghwal was to focus on the *ch'ŏngnyŏn* (young and unmarried men). The students' focus on this group was based on several calculations and miscalculations. They thought that married men were consumed with household life and thus unable to engage in the frequent gathering and drinking of the young, unmarried men. They were surprised to find, however, that young unmarried men were still intimately tied to their extended families and to the often rigid requirements of filial duties; this was particularly so because, in many cases, they were the only sons who had agreed (by force or by choice) to remain in the countryside. One team reported that the "problem consciousness" of young men was insufficient—particularly compared with older men—because of a dearth of "organic, active" communication, and that "feudal" (hierarchical) relations with older men had precluded the formation of young men's groups. The students further expected that their proximity in age would help secure positive relations, but instead it was often a source of tension because it served to underscore their different lots in life. Students expected that the young men would be unfettered by a cold war mentality born of Korean

War memories; they instead found that many young rural people were, more than their urban counterparts, still steeped in the physical and social geography of their locale's Korean War experience. Finally, they counted on these younger farmers to be the future of South Korea's agricultural sector. But they were disappointed to discover that because many young men had worked as laborers in the city, it was unlikely or even impossible that they would become "stable" farmers.

In light of these surprises and disappointments, the students who had been assigned to the young men reflected on the importance of interacting with them without being constrained by thinking about their "historical role." In a sense they called for a naturalization of the interactions. Students criticized themselves for having tried to direct conversations to cover particular topics and in so doing precluding freer discussion. Students were frustrated that when they labored alongside the young men, they could not find anything to talk about; there seemed to be no common ground. Having given up on the potential for camaraderie during daytime labor, they pinned their hopes instead on the hours after work. But the evening proved no easier. The men were often exhausted and quickly faded away into private lives beyond the students' reach. Contrary to their expectations, students far outnumbered the young men, making it uncomfortable for the villagers. Many students wanted to arrange informal interaction and to develop friendships. One team, however, reported their success: they had organized a young men's group and "played together [with the farmers] in the water, catching pigs."

Although students proclaimed that the ties with the young farmers should be naturalized, they were by no means ready to relinquish all control. In one reflection session, students decided on this prescription: "Listen to their opinions with a humble attitude and guide them to conclusions." One student reported that "there was one farmer who agreed with us so completely that we stood him up as a leader to actively go forward." One team was particularly content that at the festival (or demonstration) the young men from "their" nonghwal village had been leaders—a "progressive force"—in the chanting of slogans and protesting. They were also pleased that these were the young men who had decided that day on the plan to enter Samyang forcefully—the vanguard of the day's violent activity.

Although the teams assigned to other groups were less burdened with grand expectations, they also had their share of miscalculations and misperceptions. Teams assigned to young teenagers offered, "We should support them in making their opinions scientific and theoretical because they have no individual or group vision of their future." The university students regretted that their own preparation was insufficient because "we don't know what to talk to them about." Across the board, students seem to have been most satisfied with the successes of the children's group. The meetings with children were more frequent and spontaneous than they had even hoped for. Because it was accepted as "natural" for students to play with children, it was quite easy for the students to meet and forge ties with the children's parents and families. They aimed to "grasp reality" through the children. Although there was a women's group, the nonghwal teams all agreed that they should have paid more attention to women. They thought of women as "exploding" under the weight of "double oppression"—landlords and men—and furthermore figured that their spirited participation in the movement had sprung from this oppression. Many groups commented on the ease and enthusiasm with which women learned protest songs.

An important nonghwal issue particularly germane to women and women's labor was the principle to refuse food and drink from villagers, including the *saech'am* (snacks customarily prepared for those who provide labor services). Their logic against eating the food was twofold: to avoid draining limited village resources and to avoid inadvertently creating a hierarchy of hospitality among villagers. But it was nearly impossible to hold to this principle. Students were guests, and furthermore, they had come to provide a service free of charge. It was inconceivable for villagers, especially those inclined to establish rapport with the students, to imagine transgressing this most basic rule of etiquette. Farmers often said, "Food and drink is the only thing we have to give." On the third nonghwal day, one team, already faced with the impracticality of this measure, decided that the issue spoke to a larger matter: they had neither made their original principles clear among themselves nor had they sufficiently communicated them to the villagers. One student who visited a village in another region as part of an initial investigative team was told, "Don't come if you don't plan to receive it [food for labor]." The members of the Seoul National University team decided that they would accept simple things that farmers had made themselves but not purchased goods, such as cola or juice. In Koch'ang, students did informally receive food.

Students also reflected on their own internal organization and interactions. The members of one team thought, for example, that they lacked harmony and direction: "The individual needs to be diminished for successful community life." Another team similarly noted, "The team leader was unable to bring people together, but all the nonghwal team members must be responsible." Several nonghwal teams decided that they had been passive and lacked a "subject-oriented appearance." One team considered this problem to be, in part, the product of excessively maintaining the senior-junior hierarchy among students. In South Korean clubs, such an age hierarchy is firmly upheld, not only by appropriate language usage to reflect status and rank but also through the division of labor and behavior.

Finally, nonghwal teams called for more self-criticism and for greater response to the criticism: "Despite constant reflection, we have seen no change in our actions. We need more criticism of each other—more criticism with love."

Although students did not accomplish their every goal and not all farmer-student interactions were successful, for the most part students endeared themselves to the farmers. There was powerful identification between the farmers' sense that "these students could be my children" and the nonghwal students' feeling that "this could be my homeland." Their identification with each other extended to a particular sense of the nation and of dissent. One village woman told me that she was especially "moved" to learn about an organized group for parents of arrested student activists: "When I heard about that [group], my heart hurt. But I thought the mothers are so smart with such smart children—and I envied them. I thought if all the people in our country were that understanding of each other and united together that well, there wouldn't be incidents like this one [the Samyang tenant struggle]."

In spite of growing student-farmer identification and waning farmer fear of dissent, the gap between farmers and external activists seemed even larger after the September 12 price settlement in Seoul.

SETTLING THE DISSENT

Price settlement did not allay deeper matters of the legitimacy of the Relinquish Committee, the external forces, or the movement itself. At the center of these deliberations were basic concepts of leadership, activism, and settlement. The situation became very divisive shortly after the mid-September dispersal when a quarter-page apology from the Relinquish Committee, signed by Yun, appeared in South Korea's four major newspapers: *Dong-A Daily*, *Chosŏn Daily*, *Chungang Daily*, and *Chŏnbuk Daily*. For some, this apology undermined the legitimacy of the Relinquish Committee. Line by line, the apology denied the historical legitimacy of the entire movement by negating each and every premise of the struggle and by apologizing for having unjustifiably attacked the corporation's good name.

> *Letter of Apology*
> While negotiating a land transaction in the Haeri and Simwŏn districts of Koch'ang County of North Chŏlla Province, even though the land procedures had been carried out in a legal manner and without defect, the resident tenant farmers disseminated lies about the current landlords—the representatives of the Samyang Salt Corporation: Kim Sang-jun, Honorary Chancellor of Koryŏ University and the President of the Korean Red Cross; Kim Sang-hyŏp, Chairman of Samyang Salt Corporation; Kim Sang-don; and Kim Byŏng-hwi. They [the farmers] defamed their reputation and brought

unfair damage to their social prestige. The landlords also incurred massive [financial] losses because of the farmers' long-term, illegal demonstrations and business disruptions at Samyang Corporation and Koryŏ University, neither of which have any relationship to the reclaimed paddy fields.

In this way, the tenant farmers are responsible for legal chaos and for this very unfortunate incident for all strata of our society. For this, we who represent the tenant farmers express our deep apology to Kim Sang-jun, Kim Sang-hyŏp, Kim Sang-don, and Kim Byŏng-hwi, and to all the other members of our society.

September 1987

Representative of the tenant farmers of the reclaimed paddy fields at Ko-ch'ang

[Yun].

It is not entirely appropriate to reckon this apology as Yun's personal betrayal. The eighth and ninth provisions of the final contract that CFU members Cho and Kang had also signed stipulated that an apology to the company would be published in the name of the head of the Relinquish Committee.

Incensed by this widely publicized document, the CFU forces mobilized for an annulment of the contract, a reformulation of the leadership committee, and at least a revision of the terms of the land purchase and the terms of the government loan program for that purchase. Min wanted to offer a "new time frame" or a "correct direction" for the vanguard of the tenant struggle—those people who were "the main force who roll the wagon wheel of history. Male or female, old or young, the tenants—like the sun—radiate light from the center and struggle, putting everything on the line." However, these ongoing campaigns of external activists produced new distances. One student reflected critically on a meeting that he and another student had organized in one of the villages. Although thirty-five people gathered for the meeting in the village hall and many of them showed interest or excitement, the student commented that it was "only those who know something, those not directly related to the profits and losses [of this movement], who spoke up." The more prosperous farmers with government connections and often those higher in the village and social hierarchy participated. Those who were most directly affected by the movement—tenants who stood to lose or gain—left the meeting. Among the meeting's flaws, according to the student, was its public location; a private home would have been much more effective.

The countryside was polarized because some of the CFU affiliates and some of the farmers believed that the company had paid Yun off with an impressive sum of money by the company. This was published in a widely distributed pamphlet against the wishes of some of the members of the non-CFU independent farmers' movement organizations, particularly the independent Koch'ang Farmers Union. Some external activists and farmers feared that it was not just Yun but farmers generally whose integrity had been slandered in the heavy-handed denouncements. Although most farmers acknowledged their debt to outside groups, particularly the CFU and the students, the denouncement canceled the debt because their dignity had been offended. One man who had earlier even contemplated joining the CFU concluded, "If the CFU doesn't publish an apology, then they are really not a group which helps weak people. If they are truly an organization for us, they should fight for weak farmers." A resident of Yun's village elaborated on the ambiguous space between debt to and denunciation of the CFU.

> For farmers to fight like that—in one place—is historically unique. We were really exceptional, but that isn't the "heart of farmers"; it was all because the CFU and other groups helped us, but then the CFU circulated that rumor; of course, the CFU is better than we are, so everybody believed them, but I don't know if it is true or false. I don't know whether they said that based on something or whether they wanted to split the farmers. Yun is just a person who catches fish in the reservoir and sells them himself. I've known him since I was a child; he is not someone whose heart would be "badly eaten."

He repeated many times that the split between farmers was a bad thing but that he still remained grateful for the CFU's help. He explained that although "Min is very smart . . . in terms of character and the things he says, he is really different from us farmers. It is hard for people like us, mere land tillers, to talk to him."

Yun both held fast against the external activists and appropriated aspects of their discourse. Six months after the Seoul movement, he explained his decision to end the Seoul activities in terms of farmer subjectivity: "If at that time we hadn't reached some result, the CFU would have become the subject of the movement." However, his notion of leadership and of the movement was centered on "winning," or accomplishing the task at hand: settling the local land matter. Yun was not ashamed by the accusation that he drank with Samyang officials in Seoul. Such activities, he explained, had been for the sake of negotiation on behalf of the farmers. Nor did he find it incongruous with his notions of the movement to explain that he had— beyond the controversial contract—unwritten agreements with Samyang ensuring that if the appropriate government loans were not issued, the company would arrange a payment program over several years. After several months, those rallying to form a new Relinquish Committee scheduled a large meeting near the reservoir. Although Yun had been asked to come, he refused because he was furious that the meeting had not been discussed with him. His "pride and his sense of subject" kept him away, he explained. One student regarded Yun's absence as an admission of guilt and concluded, "It is wrong to think of him as one of the taejung. He is an enemy." Many onlookers—and organizers in particular—criticized Yun's seemingly self-propelled commitment to the economic struggle and his politically compromising strategies.

In December it was announced that farmers could buy their land with loans at 20 percent down for all land under 2,000 p'yŏng. For the majority of farmers, this was a feasible and reasonable program; for most, it was even more government support than they had counted on. One man claimed that it was at this juncture that the CFU erred in continuing to press for a better arrangement. He explained that if the CFU had at that point agreed on the purchase, the organization could have gone on to the next (organizing) task. Instead, it had become impossible for Min to talk to those who had purchased the land and impossible for them to talk to Min. These strained human relations were traumatic for many farmers, especially for those who had backed the CFU. One man who had decided to purchase his land explained that because he respected Min, he felt ashamed: "Now I can't meet and talk to him because he probably won't understand me and he will probably think I was bought off by Yun and Choi." This farmer explained that Min had partly mistaken Yun; Yun's decision to return to the countryside was not about ideology or politics. Rather, because "Yun and Choi were on the side of the farmers, and knew that they were exhausted, they had wanted to speed things up and return home."

Even the farmers who had taken very definite positions in the course of the Koch'ang Tenant Farmers Movement wavered once they were back in the countryside. One active CFU supporter proclaimed that it was a "shameful thing" that "it had ended up like this." By "this," he seemed to refer to the divisive human relations—particularly embarrassing because of the sacrifices so many outsiders had made. Back in the countryside, "unity" emerged as something worthy of the farmers' highest esteem. Even Yun's obvious local opponents were ambivalent. Cho remarked, "The police and Samyang are one, but Yun holds his distance from both even though he is close to both." He could only condemn him tentatively: "He hates me. So, there is nothing I can do about it. I hate him, I have to hate him." As to the bribe, he wavered: "I have no proof, but it is possible. Perhaps it cannot help but be so."

Students, or at least the most articulate of them, came to support the CFU's policy and platforms. Some farmers resented that the students too had become the voice of the CFU. The students had originally planned fall 1987 and winter 1988 follow-up nonghwal, but they canceled them. It was difficult for students to determine the appropriate course of action for a splintered movement. Many farmers were disappointed that students did not return to the countryside as planned.

One of the results of the internal dissension was that further politicizing activities in this region became—in the short run—more difficult. It is striking that in February 1989, when two hundred thousand farmers gathered in Seoul for unprecedented protests over the U.S. export of foodstuffs, only three farmers from this region were there despite the generally ardent participation of farmers from the Chŏlla provinces. By that time, all the CFU groups in this region had disbanded and only a few activists remained. In spite of its firm commitment to independent local organizing, the Koch'ang Farmers Union had, in the eyes of most farmers, been largely subsumed by the CFU and its vortex of controversy. At one point, rumors even circulated that the local Koch'ang Farmers Union had also been paid off. One of the Koch'ang Farmers Union members echoed Yun's concern that the CFU had become the subject of the movement. What saddened this young, unmarried, and uneducated farmer—who would later become an officer in the Koch'ang Farmers Union—was the CFU's ignorance of the lives of local farmer activists. He explained that because one farmer activist didn't make it to an important meeting, CFU members had spread rumors that it is difficult to meet Koch'ang Farmers Union members: "Intellectuals can't understand; he couldn't come because he was busy working in the fields." He explained that while activists' lives follow the calendar of political events, farmers' lives follow the calendar of work and slack seasons. We were talking after the December 1987 elections, and he commented that elections too were "this way": "Although the important thing is to involve the masses, their [outsiders'] focus is always political issues."

Non-CFU activists resented both the fact and the nature of what some called the "CFU hegemony over the movement." One activist complained about the CFU's constant allusion to its "organizational strength"—the power and authority of the Catholic church—which thereby undermined local initiative and strength. She objected to Min telling the farmers that if things don't work, they would triumph [in Seoul] because of a "hidden card," the Catholic church.

One of the most instructive lessons for me during my fieldwork came about at the restaurant in the Koch'ang bus terminal several months after the Seoul protest. Gathered there were four men—all acquaintances of mine. They were clearly on opposite sides of the political fence. With any of them, I would have probably stayed cautiously clear of any discussion about the other. I would have probably even been hesitant to admit my meeting with the others. Yet here they were, a motley crew—Yun, a Samyang employee, a CFU-affiliated farmer activist, and a policeman—all having coffee together. This is how the dust of conflict sometimes settles, or at least appears to settle, in the countryside, where "eating and living" often transcend ideology.

In the lines of dissent between farmers and outsiders, various outsider activists did not always have a realistic understanding of the fabric of rural life or of the astute politics of farmers. There was increasingly a turn in the community toward the experience of farmers or of the minjung. That is, the farmers movement organizations made attempts to localize their campaigns and to follow farmer self-initiated campaigns. Minjung-as-subject activism, however, often presents a challenge to outside activists' ways of ordering experience. These compromises were difficult because they frequently resulted in less broad-based political action. In this same vein, many in the organizing community and many farmers as well considered the Koch'ang farmers movement a failure. For the organizers, it was a failure because the final settlement was not sufficiently comprehensive or favorable, because activism had stopped in the region, and, most important, because the region had become impossible to organize. For many farmers, however, it was considered a failure because of the divisiveness in the region following the final settlement. Although they were pleased to be landowners, they realized that landownership alone did not solve the fundamental problems of South Korean farmers. Some farmers veered toward more organizerlike structural readings of their history and their world. In the next chapter, I examine the villages—the local context of the movement.

CHAPTER SEVEN

Village Variables, Variable Villages

I have gone out and marked the rents, and we are people too so we can mark the rents differently, and they can be dissatisfied over that, and then they have to go and make the contract at the company, and they can be dissatisfied over that, and having to bow their heads asking for cheaper rents, it's dirty. . . . So they just don't want the tenancy system itself. . . . It has been built up over all these years . . . and they don't want to have to pass this down to their descendants.

SAMYANG LAND MANAGEMENT OFFICE EMPLOYEE

Here I return to the Samyang agricultural estate and tenant villages and locate them in their historical and national contexts. I consider village-level factors, including land patterns, stratification, and the relationship to the company, to explain farmers' participation in the land struggle. I contrast two villages where I resided: one more stratified and with less uniform participation in the movement, the other more egalitarian with more uniform participation. Participation in the movement was invested with distinct social meanings in each village. In Kŭmp'yŏng, the more stratified village, participation was clearly an oppositional activity. In Kungsan, the less stratified village, participation was not considered radical dissent. In drawing this contrast, I consider land tenure distinctions between owners, owner-tenants, tenants, waterway tenants, and double tenants; village and villager relations to the landlord corporation; and the experience of many participants as workers at the Samyang salt fields.

GETTING THERE

The tenant land of Koch'ang's farmers spans two districts: Simwŏn and Haeri. Although both districts have towns that house government offices and periodic markets, the farmers from the Samyang villages generally frequented the market held once every five days at the Haeri township. The seven administrative villages, or twenty "natural villages,"[1] in which Samyang had tenant farmers are located between the Haeri and Simwŏn townships. They follow the curve of the prereclamation horseshoe coastline, winding in and out of the small hills rising from the original shore.

Haeri is twenty kilometers from Koch'ang. There was a direct bus to Koch'ang from Seoul's secondary bus station at Yongsan,[2] which specialized in buses going to smaller cities in the provinces. Even the terminal's graffiti bespoke its social geography: on one of my trips, I discovered "Women! Marry rural men!" spray-painted on a soda machine. Seoul's primary bus terminal, Kangnam, was enormous, modern, and efficient; Yongsan was small, dingy, and crammed with people who appeared out of sorts in the city. Many farmers were self-conscious about this shabbier transportation system: as one farming woman said, "Our bus terminals are [run down] like toilets. . . . It [the underdevelopment of the Chŏlla provinces] started with [President] Park and even in these villages we know about it."

At the time of my fieldwork, the bus fare from Koch'ang to Haeri was ₩340 for a forty-minute trip. These buses, express (more expensive) and regular, were perpetually overcrowded but lively and friendly. At the Haeri township, Samyang farmers waited for the "locals" going to Simwŏn or to Tongho, costing ₩150 and ₩190, respectively. The nonexpress Tongho bus stopped at Kŭmp'yŏng, and the bus connecting Haeri and Simwŏn made a stop at Kungsan. The buses to Simwŏn ran about once an hour, while those to Tongho—farther off the beaten and paved path—ran about once an hour in the morning, late afternoon, and early evening but were sparse in the middle of the day. It was not uncommon for farmers to wait for hours at the Haeri station for a homeward-bound bus.

Haeri was an unimpressive township, with a bus station[3] and a small strip of commercial establishments. Simwŏn, in contrast, the central town in a district with coastal villages made prosperous from seaweed cultivation, was tree-lined and well paved. It was easy to recognize market day, when farmers put on their fancier fare and came back hauling loads, stepping down from buses so crowded one could hardly breathe. During my fieldwork, the local bus company abandoned the practice of employing young helpers who would ride at the rear of the bus to control the rear door and collect fares, adopting instead a system of paying the bus driver at the front. The farmers sorely missed the strong young girls or boys who had helped farmers, burdened with age and packages, off the bus.

KŬMP'YŎNG: THE KNOBBY PATH AND VILLAGE DISCORD

At Kŭmp'yŏng's entrance,[4] there was a small store selling bus tickets, candies, liquor, and a hodgepodge of household items; the remains of what once was a grand mill in the colonial period; and a cement village hall recognizable at a glance as Saemaŭl Movement architecture.[5] It is easy to imagine that this village entrance was once a busy harbor. Now the contour of the former harbor traces the edge of the reclamation paddy. And one could picture the farmers who were squatting on the roadside facing the

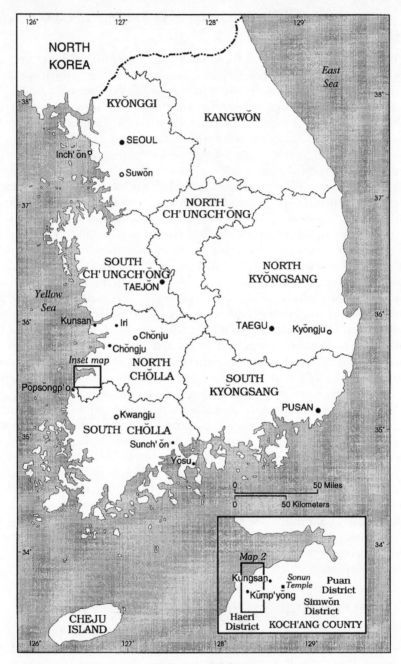

Map 1: South Korea

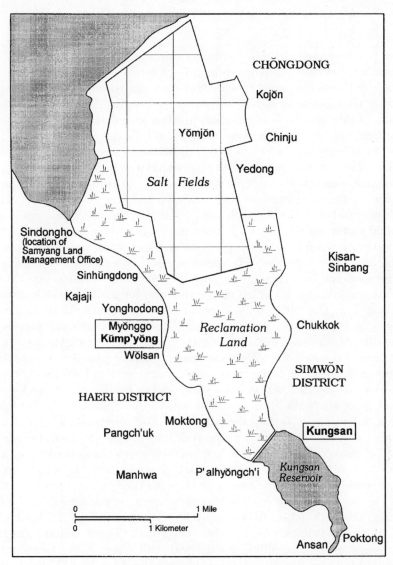

Map 2: Samyang Reclamation Land and the Samyang Villages
(detail from Map 1)

rice paddy, milling about by the boats in another era. Still unpaved in large stretches, the road was large enough for a bus to pass by—as the "direct" buses did[6]—kicking up great clouds of dust and gravel. From the village's rather large entrance with ample room for hanging out, the main village path quickly narrows into a knobby, winding path that is just wide enough for farm machinery to pass comfortably and for a car to cause a stir.

The village geography and basic infrastructure were rich in their references. The unpaved road to the village marked its underdevelopment in a national context and its marginalization as part of Samyang's world. I once asked a group of villagers whether Samyang had ever done anything about the unpaved road. Roaring with laughter, they answered, "Samyang doesn't spend money on this place. . . . They argue over even a single penny." On another occasion a farmer explained the logic of Samyang geography in which only the roads that were somehow tied to the payment of rents were improved, and even then only minimally. The village hall stood on a piece of Samyang land from which the corporation uncharacteristically did not collect rent. The mill and the impressive commemorative stone to the village's most prominent former local landlord (which sits some paces into the village on a grassy, well-maintained clearing inclining slightly away from the road) signaled the village landlords' grander past. The coastal line marked by the edge of the reclamation paddy recalled Kŭmp'yŏng's location on the colonial period grain route and its connection to the Kunsan port, from where the choice grains from North Chŏlla's rice basket made their way to Japan. During the colonial period, the Japanese manager of the local Mokch'ae Estate, a property of the New Development Company, lived in Kŭmp'yŏng. The estate had landholdings as far as the Mujang and Sangha districts, and, as one older farmer remembers, "farmers from all over would come with their rents on their backs or on cow carts."

The shadow of the harbor also recalls not only landlords and their grains, but the humble salt-boiling livelihood of many of the residents prior to reclamation times. One grandmother noted, "There were no yangban here—we were 'boat-riding people' with bad reputations." One farmer pointed out that the village was relatively well-off for Haeri District "with Change descending from Hongsŏng, Cho from Hamyang, and Kim from Kimhae,"[7] but that "we were not like the yangban—the *inmul* [great men] of Kungsan." An old man, however, recalled that, although humble, it was a prosperous livelihood: "Before reclamation the village was much larger than today. . . . With not much paddy or field, we lived by boiling salt, making more money than if we had been farmers. . . . The production was all 'underground' [illegal] because of the government salt monopoly."

The knobby road marked the breaks in village harmony. These village roads were Saemaŭl Movement projects that relied both on semivoluntary labor and on the willingness of those with land abutting the once much narrower path to relinquish their land for the greater village good. A salt field laborer explained, "People didn't want to give up their land. . . . What was the compensation for giving it? . . . The labor required interfered with farm work. . . . The problem with the Saemaŭl Movement was that it went on all too long; year after year there was more compulsory work to do." He also added that the whole problem with President Park was that, like Saemaŭl, he also lasted far too long and administered "more and more for farmers to do." That a knobby road revealed village discord rings true for contrast between Kŭmp'yŏng and Kungsan; in the more uniform Kungsan, the main road was straight and wide.

This village backbone, bent and crippled, wound through the entire base of the village and out the other side to the inland paddy. Farmer-owned paddy was for the most part successfully distributed during the land reform era. From this road, the village climbed upward into a lattice of small paths and crowded houses, looking almost urban in contrast to the less densely populated Kungsan. At one of the bigger intersections was a communal well still used by many village women as a laundry spot. The most impressive farmhouses were those flanking the main road, but they were interspersed with the blind spots of the Saemaŭl Movement: thatched homes in disrepair that peered out from poorly maintained stone walls. For many in the village, times had been hard. In the mid-1980s, the village elders revived an old practice of gathering on the first full moon (taep-orŭm) of the lunar calendar to send away malevolent spirits and beckon fortune for the coming year. Bad luck in the village—several young men "eating pesticides" (a euphemism for suicide)—had prompted the revival of this practice.

Kŭmp'yŏng was thus a patchwork of uneven Saemaŭl developments, which underscored the village's relatively large disparities of wealth. Saemaŭl activities had begun in the village in 1972, stopped temporarily in 1973, and resumed with road construction in 1974. In 1975 and 1976, roofs had been modernized, and from 1976 to 1978, the paths in the rice paddies had been improved. Farmers agreed that Saemaŭl developments in this village were affected not only by the particulars of the village stratification but also by the presence of Samyang. In the case of Saemaŭl planting programs of Green Revolution rice strains, for example, Samyang collected a proportionally larger percentage of the crop. Farmers therefore stopped such production quickly. Typical of most rural villages, the village positions were held by "rich people" who were members of, or sympathetic to, the ruling party. The former village head boasted that in spite of all his efforts for the village through Saemaŭl projects, he had only required villagers to rebuild one of his walls when he donated land for the main path. He bragged that although the ruling party senator built the village a bridge, the opposition party senator had done nothing for the village:

"People with the knife do better for us." He also added, "If I had walked around applauding the [tenant farmers] movement, the village would have been damaged," meaning that had he supported the movement, the village would have lost out on state disbursements. That village heads and other officers were on the ruling party dole was well known; the village rumor mill chased after the route that ruling party bribes traveled. Before the December 1988 election, gossip turned to the uneven dispersal of election payoffs. By that time, the village had already divided clearly along lines that the Koch'ang Tenant Farmers Movement had generated, and it was conspicuous when the disbursements bypassed those who had been active in the protest.

Like contemporary political sympathies, those of the past also resided in village geography. The most vivid signs of this sort were empty ones—places where buildings had been burned down during the Korean War. In Kŭmp'yŏng, the farmhouse of the manager of the Koch'ang Junior High School (Land) Estate, who had owned land in this village and throughout the region, was burned down during the war. The former house of one of the key officials in the villages was also among those burned to the ground. I learned about this hidden geography in hushed tones.

Also political was the village's particular relationship with the company. Kŭmp'yŏng, which sits almost exactly halfway between the salt fields and the offices of Samyang Salt, was well integrated in Samyang's world. Many people in this village had long straddled village and company loyalties. Such divided ties figured in the daily fabric of the Koch'ang movement. Kungsan, more geographically remote from both the salt fields and the land management headquarters, was considerably less divided in this fashion. Whereas in 1987 there were some ten families in Kŭmp'yŏng with very direct links to people with white-collar or semi-white-collar jobs at Samyang, in Kungsan only two families had such direct connections. Also, in Kŭmp'yŏng, eight houses were still owned by Samyang, in contrast to only one house and three house plots in Kungsan. Kungsan farmers had, as they often bragged to me, actively tried to wrestle their house and house plots from Samyang ownership.

One former nonggujang (Samyang assistant in the village) spoke of Kŭmp'yŏng's *chamae kyŏryŏn* (sister relationship) with the corporation.[8] He explained that the corporation was particularly unhappy about Kŭmp'yŏng's active participation in the movement. In addition to Samyang's donation of the land on which the village hall sits, he illustrated the special relationship by remarking on the ₩28,000,000 pump that the company donated for irrigation of the nonreclamation paddy—a helpful addition for the more prosperous villagers with large owner plots. Predictably, it was the poorer villagers who were most active in the movement.

The lineage of Kŭmp'yŏng's nonggujang revealed company-village relations. The selection of village heads was frequently undemocratic. The same person assumed the positions of village head and nonggujang. In Kŭmp'yŏng, the first nonggujang had been the largest local landlord and also a white-collar worker for the corporation. He had breached local ethics by never distributing the requisite *kimi* (food disbursements) during hard times.

Some farmers who had been active in the movement praised one of the former nonggujang, defending him by saying that he had wielded little power. This nonggujang explained that he had been given the position because the nonggujang before him had decided that he was "diligent and trustworthy." One farmer cynically noted that nonggujang are those "with property and a special relationship to Samyang"; he queried, "Can people without money get to do that kind of thing?" The former nonggujang spoke at great length about the difficulties of the delicate position he had held: "[The nonggujang] represents tenants—he is a *simburŭmkkun* [errand runner–worker]; he also farms, determines rents, tells people who have not paid to pay, and communicates directives from the company." He explained that he could not help but be partial to the villagers; Samyang, however, had complained to him when he constantly reported farmers' dissatisfaction over high rents. He also admitted that his relations with fellow villagers were seasonal: "In the fall when I calculated rents there was 'some trouble,' but not much because I tried to make the terms favorable, and during the rest of the year there was 'nothing' [no trouble] at all." He was careful to point out that he had acquired his own relatively extensive property six hundred p'yŏng at a time: "I purchased it with my own skill. It wasn't just that Samyang gave it to me." He went on to say that although he could not participate in the movement openly, "In my heart I was on the side of the farmers." He felt that he could not participate not because of his direct Samyang affiliation but because several of his family members were policemen and employees of the state-run Agricultural Cooperative. His final reflections on the movement revealed his enormous ambivalence about his kinship with Samyang. Reflecting on a terrible accident that had befallen his family just a year earlier, he muttered quietly, "I have a really thankful heart. . . . I have lived in front of the sky without an embarrassing thing, but because of my recent family tragedy I have had to reflect."

In addition to relations with Samyang, Kŭmp'yŏng residents agreed widely that wealth correlated inversely to movement participation. "People who farm small plots shouted loud, while people with larger plots reaped the benefits," said one man who had not participated for reasons of "face," adding that he was thankful for their efforts. This village's central movement participants and CFU members were among the poorest farmers and laborers in the village. Cho, for example, the co-leader of the CFU faction in the movement, was one of this village's poorest household heads; he even bragged that he was among the very few who received welfare payments. At first Cho spoke lightly of the poor–rich gap in the village, saying, "The relations between us aren't so bad." When I met him on his way to Seoul to work as a laborer for the winter months, however, he said, "I would sooner starve to death than work for another man in this village." Similarly, a farmer in another comparably stratified village explained that he only worked for rich local farmers "when they come to me and ask politely."

Educated, wealthier farmers had more to lose in public acts of defiance. A former local landlord's college-educated son regretted that he "could not" participate: "The village needed to participate as a single group, but my [late] father was someone widely known in the area so I am self-conscious of the county, district, and the corporation. . . . I did whatever I could in the village. . . . I really should have gone and made a greeting. . . . There are probably some people in the village [now] who are swearing about me." One former village head and agricultural cooperative head who could not go because of "face" sent his wife and quietly contributed money as well; he added that when there weren't people to recognize him, he did participate. Another farmer declared that the dividing lines in the village and in movement participation were drawn according to levels of education: "The people who graduated from junior high school or high school don't have any intention of doing anything for the village; they don't show any sincere intentions." He further discerned that "no one who graduated from junior high school went to Seoul [to demonstrate] because of their closeness to Samyang employees and because of 'face,' " and he blamed the failures of the movement on this upper stratum's lack of participation. Similarly, one grandmother complained that if the "intelligent men with something worth saying" had gone to Seoul, the settlement price would have been lower. Many farmers explained that because the village head and nonggujang were against it, it was hard to unite the villagers behind the movement.

Over time it became clear that the rewards of the movement, like the movement itself, were stratified. Some poorer farmers wondered about whether they would benefit for having struggled, whereas others maintained that they gained because the village prospered as a whole. One ardent participant was a "double tenant" (the tenant of a tenant to a village cousin) who farmed *hach'ŏndap* (waterway paddy, the land abutting the streams that run from the reservoir to the sea). He was forty-nine and the father of three children who were all working as laborers in Seoul. He had sold the tenant rights for 1,200 p'yŏng of land that he had purchased in 1964 when he met family difficulties in 1972. Both he and his wife participated in the protest despite what were likely to be meager personal rewards, as neither waterway paddy farmers nor double tenants stood to make any gains: "From the time it began we knew there wouldn't be much benefit to us, but if things go well with the village it is also good for me. [After all] you never know when you might become a beggar [and live off the village]." One widowed grandmother, who had sold all her tenant rights in 1980 and 1984 to repay debts and did not participate because she does not farm Samyang land, was similarly pleased that "since the village got the land, I can [if need be] live off the village." One farmer struck an ironic chord when he spoke of his own diligent participation: "People who live well didn't budge, and landless people like us who don't live well really ran [were active]. . . . So the people who live well get to live better and they didn't even buy us one bowl of *makkŏlli* [a cheap, coarse rice liquor] in appreciation." One farmer in his fifties with a considerable amount of tenant, double tenant, and waterway land complained several months after the Seoul demonstration that "these days people who didn't go [to Seoul] talk louder. . . . This is because those who went and those who didn't got the same rewards." As for his own active participation, he explained, "It is our land. How can I be still? But in this village there are those who participate and those who don't. . . . Do persimmons just fall in your mouth if you sit there with your mouth open?" He used this adage to refer to his own participation, but there was an ironic twist because the rewards did fall to those who sat still.

Many of the poorer farmers reflected on the burden of the long-term debt to the government: "Things will be hard for twenty years. It would have been better to not buy it than to just accrue debts." Many went so far as to suggest that poorer farmers would eventually be forced to sell their plots. One middle-aged farmer with both owner and tenant plots whose sibling did white-collar work for the company called the movement "unconscionable" but added that "since it came to be that we could buy it [the land] cheaply, that is a good thing." He added that the real effects of ownership were limited: "It won't have a very big effect. People without money will sell, and people with money will buy." One of the more prosperous farmers who had been active in the movement commented, "The paddies have been made [through the purchase from Samyang] such that they have to be resold. . . . Poor people will be in trouble." This opinion concurred with the perspective of a Samyang management employee who insisted, "If you come here ten years from now you will find that the poor people will live worse. . . . The poor ones are lazy and would have been better off with 2:8 [rent arrangement]." Doubting that the village's collective good was really so good for him, one farmer predicted that rental opportunities for landless farmers would diminish: "When I first went out [to protest] I thought the village would get better, but after thinking about it, I realize it is really unfair to me—only the people with tenant rights will buy it [the land], and then the price will go up and they won't even want to rent it anymore."

The movement did change the village. The village head of fifteen years stepped down in the midst of allegations that he had single-handedly "eaten" campaign money, and because he had resisted the movement entirely. Evidently Cho had spoken to the village head behind the scenes, telling him that the time had come for him to give way to a younger farmer. This signaled a reversal in a village where for ten years none of the monthly or even annual meetings common in many South Korean villages had been held. One farmer active in the movement explained that in Kŭmp'yŏng "if you get a hold of that position [village head] you just [and he parodied the smug gestures of a pompous yangban] say *'ŏhŭm'* [ahem]." He said also that a different farmer who had taken over the village headship for a year some years earlier "ate up all the money and still hasn't coughed it up." Another farmer told me that the village could not unite "because we have been deceived so many times [by the leadership]." The village head who ended up having to step down explained that before the *non sakŏn* (paddy incident)—as the Koch'ang Tenant Farmers Movement was often called—the village had been "pure and kind, but now it is open and democratic." He went so far as to say, "Even during Korean War times people didn't act the way they do now, talking behind my back. . . . The movement people don't like me. . . . If [it gets to the point] where everyone in the village doesn't like me, I will have to move." He concluded that villagers' understandings are "rough and things are all confused."

In the end, he was replaced by a young farmer—only twenty-nine—who had been very active in the movement, but who, on assuming the position, openly declared himself a ruling party supporter and immediately stepped back from movement activities. He explained the turnabout to me as "necessary for an officeholder." By the end of the 1980s, however, the ruling party monopoly on village-level offices had begun to falter in many villages.

KUNGSAN: THE BROKEN BOW AND THE STRAIGHT PATH

Kungsan[9] was popularly called Hwalmae, or Bow, in reference to the bow shape the village had once formed beneath impressive hills, overlooking good rice paddy—the signs of a geomantically auspicious setting. Those lands and about twenty of the village's most prosperous homes were submerged in the reservoir that was constructed to irrigate the Samyang reclamation paddy. Some farmers grinned when they recalled those "tiled" (not thatched) homes, including the most impressive one belonging to the former landlord. Kungsan was one of only three Samyang villages that lost their farmland to the reservoir. After the reclamation, farmers explained that the base of the bow was broken and with it the fortunes of the village turned. In this way, the village became a *p'yenong* (farming failure).[10] With reclamation the village's 107 houses were reduced to only 50 or so, some of which were unoccupied. There was a similar story for Myŏnggo (Kŭmp'yŏng). A farmer told me that the name had meant "singing bird," but that the bird no longer sang after Samyang's arrival.

The path through the village, following the contour of the base of the bow or the banks of the reservoir, was a straightway through which cars could pass comfortably. The village was much closer to a paved throughway than Kŭmp'yŏng was, and its bus stop was just off the paved road. Under a bus station awning put up in the late 1980s, a sign commemorates the 1987 struggle. Just beyond the bus station toward the village was a clearing with a single commemorative stone to one of the more prosperous ancestors of a wealthy but newly settled family. The path then wrapped around a bend and led to the village nestled under the mountains. The village supported a small store, but its wares were minimal, and its location—not combined with the bus stop as in Kûmp'yông—kept it from being as busy as Kŭmp'yŏng's. Although the village store was limited, trucks with eggs, fruits, and vegetables periodically passed through, ringing loudly. In addition to the Haeri-Simwŏn bus that passed in front of Kungsan, villagers could also run from the bus station along a small stretch of the Haeri-Simwŏn highway, or in the paddy adjacent to it, to an intersection where they could pick up the Haeri-Tongho bus. At this intersection there was a more active store where farmers from several villages could congregate for drink and limited food. That store was subsequently torn down to make room for highway expansion at the intersection. Across the street, however, a family moved in from Kungsan and built a house and store on their former fields. Their move coincided with the end of the movement, and as members of one of the Kungsan surname groups who had been aligned against the leadership committee centered in their village, they had perhaps been relieved to leave the village and move to the other side of the reservoir.

Although Kungsan was not a single-surname village, the surnames were limited, making it different from Kŭmp'yŏng, which had many surnames. Single-surname villages are generally understood to be yangban villages. Much of the ethnography of South Korea—particularly that which focuses on kinship systems and practices—documents yangban villages with dominant lineages that make claims to yangban origins. Specifically, this refers to lineages whose forebears passed the state examinations (Janelli and Janelli 1982; Kim T. 1964; Pak and Gamble 1975). The villages I have discussed here are not lineage villages; that is, a majority of the households do not belong to a single lineage (Pak and Gamble 1975: 18).[11] In Kungsan, there was some rivalry among the numerically dominant families. Members of one surname who were relatively prosperous, for example, bought various farm machines hoping to serve the vast majority of the village without machines but found that the those of another surname only patronized the machinery of their own kin.

In the milder months, farmers gathered on the main path, particularly at the intersection where two smaller paths ascended to the village houses. This intersection was also the back of Yun's home and was thus a natural gathering spot for movement talk. Frequently, men squatted in a row alongside houses on the side paths and engaged in lively conversation. The back wall of Yun's house and the lower house walls flanking the inland side of the main road were convenient spots for movement signs—red spray-painted slurs against the company that were always quickly blackened. After the Seoul demonstration it became a backdrop for the signs and slurs of rivalry among movement participants.

The village, smaller, less densely packed, and with fewer walled-in homes, was in every way more open than Kŭmp'yŏng. It was always immediately apparent where people were gathered or who was visiting whom. A quick stop at the first house one encountered after the bus stop—a house that belonged to a descendant of the village Min landlord lineage—and a call across its wide front yard would quickly reveal what was going on in the village. Similarly, evening gatherings seemed to include many more people in more open spaces. One evening a young woman from the CFU staged a *madanggŭk* (yard drama) in front of one of the abandoned houses where I had set up my home.[12] There, in the evening darkness, the farmers enacted the pending August 12, 1987, court trial, with village women strutting as yangban landlords and Yun playing the role of defendant. Although this event was clearly "staged" by an outsider, the spontaneity, the spot, and the script were homespun.

Because the reclamation had so uniformly affected this village, Samyang was prominently inscribed in its past. After the reclamation, tenants of the former landlord Min had all ended up laboring under Samyang. The village, farmers claimed, was some five hundred years old and had over time been dominated by different surnames—Ch'oe, then Chŏng, Na, Yi, Sin, and Min: "Chŏng was very rich, but they married Sin and much of the land went over to them and so Sin became rich. . . . Min married a Sin woman and managed to get the wealth. . . . Min originally held office in Naju; this Min's younger brother, Kyŏng-sik, used his brother's background to make money and then he settled in Kungsan for thirty years until he sold his land to Samyang and left." Villagers do not recall the former landlord, Min, fondly. Even among the wealthy, Min was, one farmer claimed, particularly stingy, for "when King Kojong had a son and taxes were collected for celebrating the birth, Min wouldn't contribute any money." One man explained how farmers came from all four directions to pay rents, and he ridiculed the excesses of the elite: "When grooms and brides passed his

[Min's] home, the groom would get off his horse and the bride off her *kama* [cart] and walk. . . . It was because of yangban like that—discriminating between this and that—that we were invaded by Japan and this country was ruined. That was how the yangban spread their power. . . . People's bones are all just the same. Where is there a yangban or *sangnom* [commoner]?" A former village resident visiting from Seoul offered an ironic anecdote about the former landlord: when Min Kyŏng-sik was still a bachelor, he went to a lineage meeting of the Min family in Seoul and offered to perform in verse. Because he wrote beautifully and was from the family of Queen Min, he was awarded an office in Naju—"Naju about which the Japanese would say, 'Even if we lose Korea, we won't lose Naju' [because it is such precious land]"—where he went on to "exploit Korea's paeksŏng [common people] to make money."

When the so-called Kungsan Reservoir was constructed, there was a trial between Samyang and landlord Min who tried to resist the loss of land that would result from the reclamation project. As one farmer explained, "Of course, since it was a [colonial] government project, Min lost." While the deliberations were still in process, Min died and the reservoir was extended to include more Min land than originally planned. One of the farmers laughed heartily over a story that he heard secondhand from someone who had left the village: a Min-surname high-level officer of the OB Beer corporation (another large South Korean capital corporation) chided his friend Kim Sang-hyŏp, son of Kim Yŏn-su: "Our ancestors sold you land when things were difficult for us." Kim retorted (as if it were a trifling thing), "Take it [the land] then." These simple musings of major capitalists—wordplays over the land and livelihood of hundreds of farmers—had a special irony for the Kungsan farmer who told me this story.

When the Kungsan Reservoir was constructed, Samyang compensated the Kungsan landowners. The late 1980s villagers, however, were largely the descendants of tenant farmers, whose tenant rights had been neither honored nor compensated at that time. In the words of one farmer, "For those who had houses under the reservoir the government made payments, and it also compensated individual owners, most of whom left for Seoul. Although the landlords were able to sell their land, the tenant rights were ruined." This was paralleled more recently when the state built the national highway that passes in front of the village and alongside much of the finest paddy directly below the reservoir. The state compensated the owners of the land it took, but as one farmer noted, "This compensation went to Samyang. If it had been our land we would have gotten it, and that is why we went to Seoul [to protest]."

When Samyang built the reservoir, it also bought all of the houses and house plots in the village. In 1974, the first villager went to the corporation to ask to negotiate the purchase of his house from the company at ₩200 per p'yŏng. He was the descendant of a prosperous smaller landlord whose family's original house and land had been submerged in the reservoir. He had moved into the home immediately after Liberation, purchasing it with rice from the sale of tenant rights to 600 p'yŏng of choice paddy. He reported that it was "in bad repair and about to fall down and that Samyang would be responsible for it if they retained ownership." After purchase he repaired the home. This farmer whose father had been a central activist in the 1955 land struggle was involved in the early stirrings of the movement. In the early 1980s many villagers got together and asked Samyang to sell them their house plots.

Samyang also purchased much of the nonpaddy land that ascended from the houses into the hills when it built the reservoir. These fields for nonrice crops, which were interspersed between the homes and above the village, had been distributed during land reform. Nevertheless, in the late 1980s, several farmers still farmed Samyang-owned fields—land that had originally been house plots and was only later turned into fields. This was also the case for several people who cleared fields for farming in the mountains and for those who farmed plots that farmers had been unable to purchase at the time of land distribution. Kungsan residents made great efforts over the years to purchase this land from Samyang.

Although Kungsan farmers varied in their calculations as to whether they had been better off before or after Samyang, before or after Japanese colonization, or again before or after Liberation,[13] there was a consensus that Samyang's arrival marked a watershed. Speaking about the colonial period, when the land was reclaimed, a farmer said, "It was feudalism then—people who had 'had' and people who didn't 'didn't.' . . . We were against the reservoir, but . . ." As an older man of one of the village's many-generation families put it, "During the colonial period there wasn't as much difference between the rich and the poor [in this village]. . . . It was more severe before that; for peasants, Min was worse than Japanese colonizers, even though we had lost the *kukka* [state]. Through this movement I have come to know the relationship between Samyang and Japan clearly. Koreans or foreigners, people's psychology is all the same; they deprive others if they can." One farmer likened the former Min landlord to a president. Min's rents were not the 5:5 (50% of produce to landlords, 50% to tenants) that farmers recalled from after Liberation, but instead as much as 75 percent of the crop. A sixty-three-year-old farmer explained how much worse Min was: "Until I was fifteen I worked under Min, and it was no different than being a slave, working all day for a bowl of rice."

In the case of Kungsan, farmers were all similarly affected by Samyang. The situation was very different from that in Kŭmp'yŏng. Other villages that lost most of their farmland to the reservoir and villages that were settled entirely on account of the Samyang reclamation project were similarly uniformly affected. In contrast with Kŭmp'yŏng, in these villages the large majority were tenant farmers, nonreclamation land was limited, and the farmers' ties to the corporation were weak. When people in this and other villages remarked that Kungsan had lived well before the reservoir, they meant that those who had ended up leaving the village had done well. Several farmers attested that with the coming of the reservoir the gap between the village rich and poor had narrowed and that this had been particularly apparent during the Korean War "when there were no people's courts in the village, when we lived esteeming one another." [14] One farmer compared Kungsan to Kŭmp'yŏng, saying that although Kŭmp'yŏng farmland increased as a result of reclamation, "they don't really live better, there is just a greater distance between the rich and the poor." At the time when the movement was most divided, one farmer contrasted Kungsan with Sinhŭngdong, a village that was composed entirely of farmers who had immigrated to the region to work for Samyang and was the home of Kang, one of the most ardent CFU supporters: "Our village got 100 percent damages [on account of reclamation]—nothing like Sinhŭngdong [pointing to the irony that its residents had taken a lead in the movement]."

The sense of shared fate in Kungsan stemmed in part from the shared experience of landlessness. Because most farmers were tenants, they were not able to serve as each other's guarantors for securing loans, thus posing real problems for the villagers. The first farmer in the village to purchase a farming machine in 1976 explained it this way: "At that time I had no owned land, only tenant land, but the loan opportunities were all based on having your own land to put up. Because I didn't have any of my own I went to another district to ask a friend to be a land guarantor. . . . I had to beg him again and again, and finally in this fashion I was able to get the machinery. That was when I began thinking that it would be nice if I could get this land, that I would do whatever I had to in order to make it my land." A farming woman put it similarly: "The farmers from this village couldn't put up land to guarantee loans or to get jobs. We had to go to other villages and plead with people with land [to do it for us]—bringing them lots of liquor. Now we can do that for each other in this village—even in that sense alone things have worked out, and we have accomplished a great thing."

In Kungsan the village head and nonggujang positions were assumed by the same person, the younger brother of the most prosperous smaller landlord who had continued to employ mŏsŭm into the 1960s. This farmer also managed the mountain behind the village where there were several graves of Samyang employees, and where local farmers complained that because of Samyang they had not been allowed to bury their own Korean War dead. One of the village's few CFU opposition party supporters noted, "The village head lives only for his own advantage. He looks around, counts [rents], and only acts when there is something in it for him." Others said that the nonggujang did nothing: "He just serves rice to the company employees." Another farmer explained that although they fought with company employees who came out to calculate the rent, they did not fight with the nonggujang since he lived in the village. Seven farmers, however, did report having quarreled with him at some point over the years. In 1984, one of the more active movement participants had a fight with the nonggujang, and when the nonggujang threatened him with not recontracting the farmer's tenant plots, the farmer, angered, called him a "Japanese puppet."

Over and over farmers expressed that Samyang's rent system was anomalous, asserting that nowhere are "there tenants like this," that "nowhere do nonggujang walk up and down the rice fields like this," and so on.[15] When nonggujang came to mark the rents, farmers customarily provided food and drink to bargain for reduced rent costs. Many farmers considered these bribes to be archaic. One grandfather laughed heartily when talking about bribes: "If you bribe them with food or drink they take off exactly the price of the offering from your rents." Another farmer explained that Samyang had learned "the system of counting and assigning rents from the Japanese." Company employees, however, defended the counting system, saying it could not be helped because the production of reclamation land plots was so varied. Above all, for these tenant farmers, these practices signaled a land tenancy situation reminiscent of the colonial period. One farmer said, "In such a country, living in the dream of the Pacific economic age, how can we have these remainders of Japanese imperialism? If that is how it is going to be, why don't we just cut off this land and send it to Japan?"

THE VILLAGES COMPARED

I will now compare these villages in general, the nature of landholdings, and finally their movement participation. This discussion draws on surveys of most of the homes in both villages, 47 in Kungsan (211 residents) and 58 in Kŭmp'yŏng (237 residents).[16]

The average number of people per household in the villages was quite similar: 4.0 for Kŭmp'yŏng and 4.5 for Kungsan. The difference can be attributed to the fact that there were several elderly people living alone or as a couple in Kŭmp'yŏng, whereas in Kungsan—which had received few post-Liberation immigrants—most of the elderly had extended families with whom they could reside. The average age of the head of households was also similar: fifty-five for Kŭmp'yŏng and fifty-three for Kungsan. Kungsan had more children per household (including those not residing in the village) at 4.6 than Kŭmp'yŏng with 4.0.

Kungsan had been somewhat more successful in educating its youth.

Many farmers in Kungsan bragged about these levels, which is understandable considering Kŭmp'yŏng's greater land wealth. The humbler origins of most of Kŭmp'yŏng's residents may account for this disparity. In both villages, sons were educated at least one grade level higher than daughters. And among the sons, one was often more highly educated; in some families it was the oldest son, whereas in families that had only achieved some financial leeway later, it was the youngest son who was so favored. Generally, each village had educated its children through junior high school. Approximately 10 percent in each village had completed only elementary school, and about 25 percent in Kŭmp'yŏng and 32 percent in Kungsan had entered high school. In many cases, students received a high school education while working as laborers for factories in Seoul that offered study programs. I knew of at least sixteen households in Kungsan (34% of households) and fourteen in Kŭmp'yŏng (24% of households) with sons or daughters in factories, most commonly in Seoul and in a few cases in peripheral cities.[17] These figures represent a very conservative estimate; farmers were often hesitant to talk plainly about their laboring sons and daughters as this was not the sort of rural exodus that farmers collectively dreamed of—hoping instead to send their children off for college degrees and white-collar employment. The disparity between the villages, although slight, can at least partially be explained by the fact that more youths in Kŭmp'yŏng labored at the Samyang salt fields. Each village sent a handful of its youth to college—six from Kŭmp'yŏng and five from Kungsan. Again, the education patterns of the heads of households were similar: each village had nineteen household heads with some elementary school education, and each village had one person with middle school or high school experience. The education of many household heads dates back to the colonial period when the educational capital of a middle school education was enormous. Graduation from elementary school alone was highly valued; most of the adults who had attended elementary school in these villages, however, had not been able to graduate.

Although the basic social composition of these villages was similar, there were significant differences in the extent and distribution of landholdings. In the context of South Korea's extraordinarily small plot agriculture, the figures for North Chŏlla Province and Koch'ang County in particular were not at all exceptional; if anything, they were slanted toward slightly larger holdings per household than the national averages. Turning to the two villages in Haeri and Simwŏn districts, however, the plots were somewhat smaller than national averages if the ownership of tenant rights is included under landownership; if, however, the tenant land is excluded, acknowledging that the margin after rent is minimal, the holdings per household in these villages fall incredibly far below national averages (see fig. 3). In Kŭmp'yŏng, if tenant land is included, 66 percent of the farmers were

Figure 3: Size of Owner/Cultivator Plots:
National Average, Koch'ang, Kŭmp'yŏng, and Kungsan (in %)

	<.5 ha	.5-1 ha	1-1.5 ha	1.5-2 ha	2-3 ha	>3 ha
National Average 1987 [1]	27.9	34.6	20.5	8.7	4.9	1.3
Koch'ang 1985 [2]	29	24	18	12	10	3
Kŭmp'yŏng 1988 [3]						
All land	30	33	21	1	5	5
Owned land	69	23	N/A	1	N/A	3
Kungsan 1988 [3]						
All land	28	53	14	2	N/A	N/A
Owned land	88	10	N/A	N/A	N/A	N/A
Extent of costs covered by plot size for 1986 [4]	30	58.6	78.4	90.6		114.2

[1] After Chang 1988: 140.
[2] Koch'ang 1985 Census: 73.
[3] Based on 1988 household surveys in the two villages.
[4] After Yi 1988: 197.

farming under one hectare, compared with 62 percent nationally and 53 percent in Koch'ang. Excluding tenant land, the figures were more dramatic, with 92 percent farming less than one hectare. The average farming land size per household, respectively, was 0.9 hectare (2,820 p'yŏng) including tenant land and 0.6 hectare (1,925 p'yŏng) calculating only owned land. The figures for Kungsan, however, were much more dramatic, indicating both the relative homogeneity in terms of land cultivation and ownership and the village's smaller holdings in contrast with Kŭmp'yŏng. In Kungsan, even if tenant land is included, 81 percent of the village farmed less than a hectare. If tenant land is excluded, Kungsan almost falls off the scale, with 98 percent of its households owning under one hectare of land and 88 percent owning less than 0.5 hectare of land. Kŭmp'yŏng was not so dramatically marginal in terms of the size of its landholdings, but Kungsan farming was by all standards petty farming, averaging 0.7 hectare (2,079 p'yŏng) when tenant land is included and 0.3 hectare (893 p'yŏng) when it is not. It is interesting to note that Kŭmp'yŏng, by national standards but not by Koch'ang standards, had more households with larger holdings, whereas Kungsan was significantly underrepresented at the upper scale of landholdings.

These findings on the extent of landholdings in the villages and calculations concerning the amount of farmland needed to generate sufficient income to maintain a minimum standard of living reveal that it was extraordinarily difficult for the vast majority of households in both villages to maintain this standard (see fig. 3). Nonfarm income, however, including agricultural wage labor, factory wages within the villages, wages from the salt field, animal husbandry, and—for an exceptional few—commercial or white-collar salaries, was not included in these findings. In the case of Kŭmp'yŏng, including tenant land, 84 percent of the households were, in terms of land only, able to cover less than 78.4 percent of costs, with the bottom 30 percent (or 69% if tenant land is not included) maintaining less than 30.4 percent of costs. In Kungsan, 95 percent were able to cover less than 78.4 percent of the costs, with the bottom 28 percent (or 88% if tenant land is not included) covering less than 30.4 percent of costs. Kŭmp'yŏng was thus a more stratified village with greater relative inequality. Its larger landowners stood out clearly not only from most other villagers but also in contrast to Kungsan's largest landowners. Both villages have high percentages of tenant farmers with small plots according to national figures, and this is particularly the case in Kungsan.

Ethnographies of South Korean villages from the 1960s reveal similar patterns in the relationship between land tenure and stratification. Kim Taik-kyoo's 1964 ethnography of a village in which over half the households were of yangban descent and again over half of the village was from a single lineage, reviews the complex interrelations of land, class, kinship, and rural exodus in the post-Liberation and post–land reform South Korean village context. Kim focused on the contrast between the consanguineous and nonconsanguineous groups, corresponding broadly to the upper and lower strata of the village. Although there had been some shifts in the relation between these groups, Kim (1964: 6–7) found that effective vertical relations still existed between the groups that in the past had been largely related as master and slave, or landlord and tenant. He notes that the "most vital problem" in villages is the "mutual aversion between status groups" (Kim 1964: 35). He went so far as to assert that "former landlord-tenant class divisions of pre–land reform days seem to have survived almost intact" (Kim 1964: 39).

In their 1961–1962 ethnography, Ki-hyuk *Pak* and Sidney Gamble (1975: 40) similarly reported that "clan villages fail to adapt to a changing national economy." This study of yangban consciousness and the extent and structure of control of large farms in three plains lineage villages with differing economic profiles offers a fascinating discussion of post-Liberation, post–land reform, and post–Korean War developments. In the South Kyŏngsang Province village, the few sparse large farms (2.9%) belonged to non-lineage outsiders. In the North Chŏlla Province village, a slightly larger number of large farms (8.1%) were entirely owned by the village's dominant lineage, and in the Kyŏnggi Province village described as having no yangban consciousness, there were a significant number of large farms (27%) that were primarily in the hands of former tenants (Pak and Gamble 1975: 179). In the first village only the wealthy maintained their yangban status, in the second the former landlords of the dominant lineage family continued to wield economic and social power, and in the third village—"the most indifferent to social rank"—there was much less lineage control (Pak and Gamble 1975: 168). To an extent we can recognize Kungsan and Kŭmp'yŏng in these patterns: Kŭmp'yŏng recalls Pak and Gamble's second village (which is interestingly a Koch'ang County village), while Kungsan shares features with the Kyŏnggi Province village.[18]

In the Samyang villages, however, the power structure was mediated largely through relations to the corporation. There was a commonsense understanding among farmer organizers that yangban villages were either very easy or very difficult to politicize. Because the lineage organization doubled as an important village hierarchy, if its leaders were disinclined to join, the entire village tended to conform. If, however, the lineage leaders sanctioned farmers' protest activity, the village was quickly swayed. Indeed, in Koch'ang lineage villages the kinship factor worked both ways.

How do Koch'ang tenants stand in a national context? In 1985, after steady increases in the several preceding years, 64.7 percent of farmers nationally were tenants of some kind, including pure tenants (farmers only cultivating tenant land), tenant-owners (farmers cultivating more tenant land than owner land) and owner-tenants (farmers cultivating more owner land than tenant land) (see fig. 4). Nationwide, however, only 2.1 percent of this impressive figure represent pure tenants. For the Samyang villages (and on each count, Kungsan much more dramatically so than Kŭmp'yŏng), the percentages of pure tenants and tenant-owners was much greater; the percentage of pure tenants was fifteen times that of the national average.

The distribution of land types in the villages reveals that tenant land was a much larger portion of Kungsan's land than of Kŭmp'yŏng's (see fig. 5). The major contributor to Kŭmp'yŏng's greater percentage of owner-farmed land was not fields but owner-farmed paddy. In Kŭmp'yŏng, 44 percent of the farmland was owner-farmed land and 56 percent tenant land, whereas in Kungsan, 29 percent was owner-farmed land and 71 percent tenant land. This contrasts with 30.5 percent tenant land for the nation as a whole in 1985. Whether considering tenancy in terms of the

Figure 4: Percentage of Tenants (Pure Tenants and Tenant-Owners):
National Average, Kŭmp'yŏng, and Kungsan (in %)

	Tenant of some kind	Pure tenant	Tenant-owner	Owner only
National Average [1]				
1981	46.4	4.6	41.8	53.6
1983	59.8	2.9	56.9	40.2
1985	64.7	2.1	62.6	35.3
Kŭmp'yŏng [2]	90	21	69	10
	(w/<0.2 ha owner land):	39	51	N/A
Kungsan [2]	96	32	64	4
	(w/<0.2 ha owner land):	65	31	N/A

[1] After Chang 1988: 149.
[2] Based on 1988 household surveys in the two villages.

Figure 5: Total Tenant Land, Owned Land, Water Paddy, and Double Tenant Land and Percentages of Total Land: Kungsan and Kŭmp'yŏng

	Kŭmp'yŏng (%)	Kungsan (%)
Total land cultivated by village in p'yŏng (in ha)	163,586 (54.5 ha)	97,720 (32.5 ha)
Total tenant land in p'yŏng (% of total village land)	66,446 (41)	49,500 (51)
Total owned land in p'yŏng (% of total village land)	73,160 (45)	28,670 (29)
Paddy	48,860 (29)	10,200 (10)
Field	26,300 (16) ·	18,470 (19)
Total waterway plots *(hach'ŏndap)* in p'yŏng (% of total village land)	8,540 (5)	2,350 (2)
Total land cultivated by double tenants in p'yŏng (% of total village land)	19,020 (12)	13,800 (14)

Source: Based on 1988 household surveys in the two villages.

percentage of tenant land or the percentage of tenant farmers, the Samyang villages were quite exceptional.

Notably active in the movement were nonstandard tenants, including tenants of hach'ŏndap (waterway paddy) and *chŏsudap* (reservoir paddy, the land that surfaces when the reservoir drains). These plots cannot be legally owned and thus cannot be legally bought or sold. These plots are made painstakingly but are submerged when the water levels are high. Their cultivation is always a gamble: when they are productive they are enormously so, but in years of heavy rain or floods the entire crop can be ruined. Even more than in the case of reclamation plots, farmers calculated that waterway plots were the free province of the farmer who goes to the trouble to make them—to take the risk. Company employees complained that these plots obstructed the water flow from the reservoir, thus slowing the pace of irrigation for the more standard plots. Although only 8 percent of the Kungsan households had cultivated waterway paddy (total: o.8

hectare), 20 percent of the Kŭmp'yŏng households had this experience (total: 2.8 hectares). Similarly, the Kŭmp'yŏng waterway plots, averaging 711 p'yŏng, were larger than the Kungsan ones, averaging 587 p'yŏng (see fig. 5). Many of the most dramatic statements about the injustices perpetuated by Samyang were made with regard to these waterway and reservoir plots. As one farmer noted, "It doesn't work to take rent from land that was so hard to make." People in Kŭmp'yŏng attributed Cho's leadership to his status as a waterway farmer as well as to his poverty.

Another category of tenants was the *ijung sojak* or *sojak ŭi sojak* (double tenants or the tenants of tenants), those who rented from Samyang tenants and for whom the transfer of land similarly brought no rewards. These farmers were infuriated that when Samyang reduced the rents in 1985 (to 2:8), some tenants did not pass this reduction on to their double tenants. It seems that double tenancy was a relatively recent phenomenon[19] that reflected—like the more general increases in tenancy nationwide—ever-increasing rural exodus and the aging of the rural sector whereby elderly couples or singles were unable to farm their land alone. In each village, there were also isolated examples in which farmers had relinquished their tenant rights to another farmer to whom they were indebted but continued to farm the land as double tenants. In Kungsan thirteen households (27%) had some double tenant paddy, with an average of 1,150 p'yŏng per double tenant household. Seven were double tenants to nonrelatives residing in the village, four to nonrelatives in Seoul, and one to a relative in Seoul. In Kŭmp'yŏng there were eight double tenant households (13%), with an average of 2,113 p'yŏng per household. Two were rented from village nonrelatives, three from village relatives, and three from Seoul relatives. The incomes from double tenancy were supplementary for some farmers, but for others, it was the sole source of revenue. With the purchase of the Samyang land, the double tenant, more than anyone, was reminded that even with Samyang out of the way, farmers' economic problems were hardly solved. Some double tenants feared that double tenancy itself might diminish with increased opportunities for ownership.

MOVEMENT PARTICIPATION COMPARED[20]

Comparison of Kungsan and Kŭmp'yŏng reveals the effects of stratification on the nature and extent of the villages' participation in the movement. In Kungsan, the less stratified village, there were pressures to participate en masse, whereas in Kŭmp'yŏng, many people saved face by not participating. The characteristics that in Kŭmp'yŏng contributed to mobilizing a lower stratum of farmers were less significant in more unified Kungsan where waterway plot or double tenant farmers participated in spite of a lack of direct benefit in order to participate in the collectivity. In Kŭmp'yŏng, they participated in spite of direct benefit to defy the more prosperous farmers.

The unequal distribution of land in Kŭmp'yŏng, with greater inequalities of wealth and relatively large median landholding size, mediated against unified participation. Farmers without tenant landholdings, or those for whom tenant landholdings were but a small part of their total cultivation, were not as concerned with the outcome of the movement. Also, the nature of the motivation to participate varied considerably between long-term tenants (some of whom had farmed plots since reclamation times) and tenants who had purchased the tenant rights only recently. While those who purchased the tenant rights had a strong sense of economic entitlement, long-term tenants calculated their rights in terms of the sheer weight of historical injustices. In Kungsan many more tenants were long-term tillers, whereas in Kŭmp'yŏng many farmers had more recently purchased the tenant rights. In Kungsan many farmers recalled that they themselves or their own ancestors had "made" the paddy. Sales had begun early, in the 1950s, and after a quiet period had become active again in the 1970s. In Kŭmp'yŏng most of the sales were made during the 1970s and only a handful in the 1980s. In discussions with farmers, it was often hard to determine whether they were speaking about the sale of land or tenancy rights because they referred to the price of the tenant rights as the "land price."

Short-term tenants believed that because they had purchased the land, they should rightfully own it. This sentiment was intensified by the escalating prices of the tenant rights over time: from 1.5 times the annual production in the 1960s to 2.5 times the annual production by 1985. One farmer recalled that although tenant rights were bought and sold from the beginning, it was only after the Korean War that a price for tenant rights was more formally "attached to the land" and that since then the prices have been rising steadily. In both villages, farmers explained that they had sold tenant rights because in tough times they needed the cash: "Land is something that is easy to sell according to the flow of the times," or "Land is what you eat off of, and when things get messy, it is what you sell." Some farmers spoke of selling in the turmoil of the immediate aftermath of the Korean War, and others described giving up farming to work at the salt fields. One farmer suggested that "those who wanted to make the arduous efforts to drain the salt" remained, while the others sold out in order to leave or purchase inland paddy. The former nonggujang in Kŭmp'yŏng explained that the practice of the sale of tenant rights began as people left the villages or as "people used their power" (i.e., to coerce others to sell). Movement discourse, however, did not reflect these considerations. Although the movement frequently proclaimed that the rents added up to the equivalent of a land purchase, the farmers did not discuss the fact that they had often purchased tenant rights and that the purchase price had escalated. The sale and purchase of tenant rights took place entirely independently of Samyang: "No one ever got permission. We would just tell them, 'We changed the ownership.' " Company employees complained that because of private arrangements they often did not know who to chase down to collect late rents. In reference to these transactions, one of the high officers in the land management office grumbled, "They talk [in the movement] of 'wanting to overcome the dishonor of being a tenant,' but that is just a pretext. Just look at how few of them have been tenant farmers from generation to generation. . . . Many of them bought the farming rights. . . . Did they farm for Samyang? *They farmed for themselves!"*

The gender composition of village participation varied according to the relationship of the village power elite to the movement. Women participants were more numerous in Kŭmp'yŏng where prominent men resisted the movement. In Kungsan 61 percent of the Seoul participants were men who went without their wives, 16 percent were couples who participated together or in a rotating fashion, and 11 percent were women whose husbands were not involved. Given the unfailing and outspoken role that several woman from Kungsan played in Seoul, I was surprised to discover how relatively small their numbers had been. The gender participation rates for Kŭmp'yŏng were almost completely reversed: 50 percent of the participants were women alone and only 28 percent men alone.

This difference can be understood according to the significance attached to the movement and its activities in the respective villages. Because movement participation in Kungsan was widespread, it was public—the province of men, and especially of powerful men. Also, one of the farmers who was considered to be "behind" the movement was also the most learned man with the most recent history as a substantial landlord. Similarly, although the village head was not an active participant, he did not prevent others from participating; other officeholders, including the Saemaŭl leader, became central figures in the movement. Also, some of the people associated most closely with the movement were known members of the ruling party.

In Kŭmp'yŏng, in contrast, the movement had little to do with village elites; it was the dispossessed who were the core activists. The CFU took root in Kŭmp'yŏng, creating an alternative village hierarchy that operated behind the scenes and in which women played central roles. Although Cho, one of the two most important CFU faction leaders, was from Kŭmp'yŏng, the most important organizer in the village was the wife of one of the poorer households. The central participation of wives also left some room for households—their male representatives—to more easily maintain their ties (kinship or other) with people connected to Samyang or to the government.

In both villages, the participation of farmers who had labored in the salt fields was disproportionately high. Their participation was also noteworthy because they risked being fired from their jobs, and, indeed, a handful were fired because of their movement activities. From the earliest days salt laborers proceeded cautiously; one salt company employee explained how he had surreptitiously met one of the core activists in the middle of the night so as to donate ₩10,000 and sign the petition not to remit rents.

In Kŭmp'yŏng 59 percent of the seventeen households who were laboring at the time or had once labored at the salt fields participated in the movement, while 72 percent of laborers with tenant land participated. These figures were higher than the general participation rate. Of the non-participant laborers, only three were either neutral or unsympathetic to the movement. Although less than 30 percent of the village residents were laborers, 53 percent of the signatures on the 1986 petition not to remit rents from Kŭmp'yŏng were those of laborers. Only 23 percent of the villagers—but 47 percent of the laborers—were signatories. The salt field factor was less significant for Kungsan, both because the village was located considerably farther from the salt fields and because local farmers were much more resistant to laboring at the salt fields. In 1987, many farmers who had quit laboring there explained that they did not have the disposition for it or that they found it too demeaning. Although more people in Kungsan had some experience (largely short-term) at the salt fields (at least—and likely much more—34% of the families), few seemed to have had long-term careers there, and in 1987 only four families (8%) had someone commuting the half-hour walk each way to the salt mines. In Kŭmp'yŏng twelve families (20%) had at least one member commuting the fifteen-minute walk.

In comparing the two villages, it is also helpful to consider those who did not participate. In Kungsan, where the movement was more a unified village concern, the nonparticipants were easy to discern. Of the seven nonparticipating households, one was a prosperous farmer who only farmed his own land, two were double tenants who calculated that they would not benefit if their landlords became owners,[21] one was away at the time, and another was too elderly to participate. Two nonparticipants' reasons were unclear, but both had signed the late 1986 petition not to remit rents.

The thirty households that did not participate in Kŭmp'yŏng were more diverse. Twelve of the thirty appear to have been sympathetic to the movement, according to my discussions with them or to the high incidence of early signers; of these twelve, four had no tenant land, one was a waterway plot farmer, and four had direct familial ties with the corporation. The remaining eighteen nonparticipants, whose views on the movement were either negative or unknown, shared several characteristics: five of them had no Samyang land, one was a double tenant and another a waterway farmer, and eight were directly or indirectly related to the company or to the government.

The size of the landholdings of the nonparticipants reveals that to some extent the participants were correct in their perceptions that the rich people did nothing for the movement and yet disproportionately reaped the benefits. The average size of the tenant holdings of the nonparticipants, 2,012 p'yŏng, was only slightly larger than the village average of 1,748 p'yŏng, but the average of the total landholdings of the nonparticipants, 3,253 p'yŏng, was considerably larger than the village average of 2,079 p'yŏng.

SALT FARMING

With seawater glistening on what resembled a marble floor, the salt fields were an impressive expanse to walk through. The fields were divided and farmed in five-chŏngbo units where from four to five people labored. The salt was raked on this surface, and the water was regulated by water wheels that the workers turned by standing on their spokes. The fields are enormous and raking—like farming—was often solitary labor. The workers were quick to explain that the way they mined the salt with hand-run pumps (and until several years ago, wooden backpacks for carrying the salt) was "just like in photographs from the olden days in China." In 1987 they used carts that they called *kuruma* or *niyak'a* (Japanese words) for transporting the salt.[22] One laborer bemoaned, "People would die with huge black spots on their backs from carrying salt all those years. . . . The only time that work is easy is when you are dead and buried." It is no surprise, one man explained, that these changes in salt farming technology were such a late development because "people in the office make those decisions and they don't know anything about reality." Workers' bodies bore the marks of their daily labor—most noticeably, swollen and reddened arms and legs.

The salt fields seemed to stretch for miles, punctuated only by the narrow row of houses that ran down their middle. Interspersed among the residences were the salt houses where the freshly mined salt was piled in heaps. The homes made up an administrative village, Yŏmjŏn (salt field village). They were small and run-down, and like the houses in nearby villages, they were surrounded with laundry lines, ceramic preservation jars for foodstuffs, and so on. Samyang paid water and electricity, and the house rental prices were nominal. These were the homes of the permanent employees: the managers at the salt farm, many of whom were long-term miners with little education. Several laborers explained that they were no different from the other part-time laborers but that they had somehow garnered the company favor that had won them the positions. If the farmers of Kŭmp'yŏng and Kungsan complained that they were Samyang "boys" or that theirs were "Samyang villages," the salt field village was the quintessential company town. Typically both husband and wife worked in the salt fields, particularly during the labor shortages of the 1980s.

Farmers recalled hard times when salt labor was coveted and management positions required bribes: it was "like pulling a star from the sky." By 1987 labor shortages had entirely altered the situation. Farmers told me how exceptional it had been earlier to receive monetary payments as well as food. Many farmers recalled the bean porridge payments at the salt fields after the Korean War when Samyang was the only place to get food: "We had no choice but to hang our necks on Samyang. [Kim] Yŏn-su had money so he put everything under his name, and we bowed our heads to Samyang and went to work."

One man, who had alternated between salt and rice farming in seven-year stretches, discussed the differences between salt and paddy labor. Salt field work is much easier, he explained, but "since you have to keep time [i.e., report to work at specified times], even if there is nothing to do, your heart isn't at ease. It is like a prison without bars, and people watch you when you leave and you have to bow to them." Farming, he explained, is harder work and the economic rewards fewer, but there is *yudori*,[23] space or free time. I spent many hours with salt laborers who never tired of calculating—often jotting down numbers as they spoke with me—the numerous ways in which they had been cheated. Although the salt industry enjoyed huge profits, their wages and benefits were meager—₩5,000 per day for men and ₩3,800 per day for women. Many of them also noted that because only a few of them were permanent workers—most contracts were renewed each season—the company avoided paying benefits. One of the young laborers whose father had also spent his whole life laboring at the salt fields complained that "the cost of all the annual wages combined is the salt production of only a single day." Salt workers and many farmers alike assumed that for Samyang the tenant rent revenue was actually a negligible sum and merely a support for the real moneymaker—the salt fields. They figured that the tenant rents in kind fed the workers and that the rice harvested from the *chigyŏngdap* (company-owned paddy) that was farmed by hired labor also went directly to feeding the salt employees. One worker told me that at the annual *kosa* (offering services to pray for abundant salt harvest) "the laborers and their supervisors prayed instead that the harvest would be meager." One young laborer refused to collect the free disbursement of salt that the company offered because he found it demeaning. His father chided him, "Even yangban need to eat, don't they?" At the time of the land incident, when Samyang raised their bonus wages, several laborers surmised that they did so "only to stave off unrest."

Although periodic attempts to unionize at the salt fields had met with little success, they had resulted in numerous firings. Among the leadership of the movement, several farmer laborers had formerly been instrumental in organizing a labor union. In the midst of the farmer protest in Seoul, one man recalled those covert activities of 1978: "Now that I think about it, it was a 'temo [demonstration].' " While many laborers spoke of the need for and advantages of labor unions, they also explained that the nature of salt mining precluded them. Because salt mining has no "fixed daily pattern" and is dependent on the timing of the sea and the variable amounts of salt, and because salt needs to be harvested immediately, fixed labor hours were not feasible. Workers also remarked that unions were difficult to organize because "there are always spies among us." There was, therefore, considerable time when the workers sat idle—even the entire day in the case of rain—but they were still, as many laborers complained, required to be at work all day. At the busiest times of the farming season, however, the men were often released for a few hours so that they could tend to their fields. Farmers explained that the company provided this flexibility only because of the labor shortages.

I spoke at length with one man who, after being fired from the salt fields, was spearheading his own campaign against the company. A village renegade, he explained that after having "died and returned to life," he had decided that he would devote his life to salt field labor but that once on the job managers were only suspicious of his positive attitude and diligence. After being fired, "God's voice" convinced him to devote his life to activities on behalf of the laborers: "If I can fight for the rights of 250 laborers, I should do it." Above all, he wanted to eliminate the frequent firing and the constant apologies that workers were forced to write and sign. Samyang's "consciousness," he said, "has not followed the times—they continue to treat the laborers like slaves." He told me that he wanted to write a comic book history of the company to "explain the collaborating and so on . . . to open the eyes of the laborers. It is pitiful that they don't know anything." In light of this sort of awareness, it is not surprising that laborers were strong supporters of the land struggle.

Although these village minutiae—the geography, land use, stratification, and leadership—are critical for explaining local patterns of participation, they are but one of the contexts of this movement. The next chapter situates these villages and the Koch'ang Tenant Farmers Movement in the broader history of the state's intervention in the agricultural sector and of farmer activism over the post-Liberation era.

CHAPTER EIGHT

Farmer Mobilization in Post-Liberation South Korea

The struggle is an unequal one. We should not overestimate or romanticize the capacity of the lifeworld to fight back. The forms of resistance are constrained and continually challenged by new and more effective forms of domination. Still, resistance there is.

MICHAEL BURAWOY (1991: 287)

Most discussions of post–Korean War agriculture neglect farmer consciousness and resistance. This absence is in part due to the optimistic portrayal of agriculture in South Korea, which has been described as "a country where the trickle down [of industrial development to the agricultural sector] did work" (Ban, Moon, and Perkins 1980: 10). The concluding passage of *Rural Development,* the joint effort of the Harvard Institute for International Development and the Korean Development Institute, is revealing: "The specific form of the institutions created is less significant than the fact that in a still poor Asian economy they exist and that they do work" (Ban, Moon, and Perkins 1980: 390).

Writings on farmer consciousness as a historical product rather than an ahistorical cultural characterization have often been pessimistic about actual or potential farmer resistance. Willard D. Keim (1979: 115), for example, writes, "The peasant is a person with few resources, likely to encounter innumerable obstacles to any consistent pattern of behavior that he adopts, so that success in one behavioral area does not easily suggest to him the possibility of change and ensuing success in another behavioral area." Others refer to the conservative force of farmers' memories of far-reaching, widespread suppression, particularly in the immediate post-Liberation and Korean War eras. One contemporary South Korean scholar argues that memories of the suppression of dissent "chill peasant dreams of resistance."

The bitter experience of defeat borne in past attempts to challenge political power has made peasants apolitical. The peasant movements that matured after the Liberation met total defeat in the Taegu Uprising, the Yŏsu Resistance, and the Korean War. Peasants began to show defeatism, political cynicism, apathy, and lack of clarity in their value judgments. They still recall the *bitter experience of [the suppression of] past rebellion and resistance. The painful and vivid memory of the oppression* chills peasant dreams of resistance. Until a new generation replaces the old generation, the experience of defeat will exclude all possibility of resistance. (Ch'oe 1989: 38; emphasis added)

Indeed, the state's immediate post-Liberation political mobilization in the name of anticommunism looms large in farmers' memories, figuring in an anti-ideology or antipolitics stance. Farmers often told me that their lives have nothing to do with *chŏngch'i* (politics) or *sasang* (ideology). For the generation of people who lived through violence and deprivation for the sake of ideology, a seeming apolitical stance can be a very political matter. The ideological stigma attached to rural oppositional participation in the 1960s, 1970s, and even into the 1980s was enormous. This is why farmers worried about the repercussions of political participation, fearing that their children—like the children of Korean War era leftists—would be barred from obtaining a decent education or a good job. Thus individual and collective memories of past resistance and repression continued to be salient over the post-Liberation decades.

Although the power of such experiences cannot be overstated and goes far in explaining *apparent* farmer passivity, there were many active, resisting farmers who were neither apolitical nor acquiescent to the powers that be. Long before the ideological thaw of the late 1980s, farmers' resistance had been mounting. Here I consider the development of farmers' resistance through outright protest activity and daily oppositional practice, and in concert with the vicissitudes of state infrastructural and ideological mobilization. Farmers' resistance has been constrained and perhaps even ironically scripted by these very ideologies and controls. I analyze farmers' quiescence as partly responsive to state repression and ideological control. In recognizing a dialectic between farmers and the state, it is also necessary to consider how periodic state concessions to the rural sector—however small they were—have been made in response to farmers' dissent.

I also consider the national and local heterogeneity of farmers' apperceptions of social justice. Although farmers are keenly aware of the fates of class and regional Others, intrasectoral and regional differentiation have been underrepresented. At the village level, for example, consideration of economic stratification and the distribution of power contributes to an understanding not only of the lived experience of inequality but also of the nature of the local mechanisms of control that operate under the auspices of, and are consciously mobilized by, the state.

Building on chapter 4's discussions of the land reform era—an era of intense state intervention in the agricultural sector and of remarkable farmer struggles—I will review the state infrastructural and ideological mobilization of the agricultural sector and agriculturists through the 1960s, 1970s, and 1980s. I will consider the state's capacity to effect policies and programs that determine farmers' real and relative prosperity, the structure and tactics of the agrobureaucracy, and the ideological control mechanisms that often facilitated farmer internalization of, or at least tacit compliance with, the state's developmentalist rhetoric and rationale. I will then proceed with a corresponding review of farmers' oppositional mobilization and close with current developments.

STATE ECONOMIC RETRENCHMENT AND POLITICAL INTEGRATION: THE 1960S AND 1970S

Beginning in the 1950s and continuing well into the 1960s, industrialization was promoted at the expense of agriculture. The domestic and import policies for agricultural products—particularly the chief staples, rice and barley—were geared to feed the urban laborers cheaply. Domestic prices plummeted because of surplus American grain supports under the PL480 programs; this adversely affected the agricultural sector. This ensured outmigration of the most impoverished farmers to build a labor force and in turn pushed down wages even further. In this way, industrial wages were kept low, allowing industrial capital growth and staving off worker unrest (Lie 1992).

The Park Chung Hee regime (1961–1979) brought some change for the rural sector. With over 55 percent of the population in the countryside in 1960, Park announced that he would develop the agricultural sector, thus appealing to farmers' desperate needs (Pak 1988: 233). In the early 1960s Park used the slogan "Nonggong pyŏngjin" (Agriculture and Industry Advancing Together); this rhetoric, though, was quickly abandoned. Similarly, Park's first Five-Year Economic Plan outlined grand plans for agriculture, but they were never fully implemented.

The year 1961, however, did mark the first time that government purchase prices for agricultural products covered the costs of production. The 1961 Farm Products Price Maintenance Law was established to "maintain proper prices of agricultural products to ensure the stability of agricultural production and the rural economy" (Pak 1988: 240). Although government purchase prices covered production costs for the grain delivery quotas in the early 1960s, they were still considerably lower than market prices (Ban, Moon, and Perkins 1980: 241–242). A fairly good ratio between government purchase prices and market prices continued in 1964 and 1965; from 1965 to 1970 it dipped but still covered production costs.

Park's concern for the rural sector intensified in the 1970s in the wake of an upset in state legitimacy as rural South Korea, particularly the Chŏlla provinces, repealed their support for the ruling party in the 1971 elections. Grain self-sufficiency quickly became a political and economic imperative. In the first half of the decade significant state inputs in agriculture improved the material lives of farmers. The state sponsored economic and extraeconomic programs for increased agricultural productivity and provided the strongest price protection for agricultural products in the postwar period.[1] In 1972 Park organized the Food Production Planning Board to oversee the attainment of grain self-sufficiency.

Toward the end of the decade, however, the state could no longer continue its commitment to a price structure that was truly favorable to agriculture. Neither could it maintain the two-level rice purchase programs begun in 1969 in which the state subsidized both the purchase from farmers and the sale to urbanites to stave off rural and urban unrest. Retrenchment from these programs coincided with record bad harvests and mounting disenchantment with the state-forced planting of high-yield rice varieties. Also, enormous agrobureaucratic infrastructural and considerable ideological penetration—largely organized through the Saemaŭl Movement—intensified throughout the decade. Not surprisingly, as state subsidies of the rural sector came to a halt and ideological control intensified, there were the beginnings of concerted resistance against the state.

Farmers were keenly aware of their relative situation and of their real abilities to cover costs with their incomes. Although many works on Korea have praised South Korean egalitarian growth,[2] such claims are difficult to substantiate for the late 1970s and into the 1980s.[3] In the late 1970s we find growing maldistribution of wealth and a corresponding oppositional consciousness. The Gini Index calculations of household income distribution, for example, demonstrate that while the coefficient decreased significantly in the 1960s (1960: .448; 1965: .344; 1970: .322), it rose in the 1970s (1975: .391; 1980: .389). Relative prosperity ratios between urban and rural household income also explain escalating dissatisfaction in the 1970s. Farm household income as a percentage of urban household income ascended to a high of 138 in 1965, plummeted to 91 in 1970, increased to 118 in 1975 (following the time of greatest state efforts on behalf of the rural sector), and by 1980 dropped to its lowest postwar rate of 84, clearly demonstrating the retrenchment of a true commitment to the agricultural sector and price protection policies (Burmeister 1988: 2; McGinn et al. 1980: 142; Steinberg 1982: 101). The comparison of farmer and laborer incomes in figure 6 similarly indicates that the situation for farmers declined toward 1970, was favorable to them in 1974 and 1975, and again declined from 1976 to 1981. These figures illuminate the significant dip in the early 1970s rural support of the ruling party and Park's early 1970s rural campaigns.

Figures that represent the extent to which farmers were able to cover

Figure 6: Changes in Relative Position of Farmers and Laborers, 1965-1981

		Household normalized income		Household real income		
		Farmer	Laborer	Farmer (A)	Laborer (B)	(A)/(B)
Year	1965	112,201	112,560	447,016	409,309	1.09
	1966	130,176	161,520	464,914	526,124	0.88
	1967	149,470	248,640	493,300	733,451	0.67
	1968	178,959	285,950	527,903	760,532	0.69
	1969	217,874	333,600	561,531	788,652	0.71
	1970	255,804	381,240	580,054	776,456	0.75
	1971	356,382	451,920	715,627	811,346	0.88
	1972	429,394	517,400	761,337	831,833	0.91
	1973	480,711	550,200	780,375	857,009	0.91
	1974	674,451	644,520	835,751	807,669	1.03
	1975	872,933	859,320	872,933	859,320	1.02
	1976	1,156,254	1,151,760	925,744	998,925	0.93
	1977	1,432,809	1,405,080	980,034	1,106,362	0.93
	1978	1,884,200	1,916,280	991,163	1,318,844	0.75
	1979	2,227,483	2,629,556	1,030,288	1,529,701	0.67
	1980	2,693,110	3,205,152	999,299	1,448,329	0.69
	1981	3,687,856	3,817,224	1,005,139	1,398,763	0.72
% Increase	1965-70			5.3	13.7	
	1970-75			8.5	2.0	
	1975-80			2.7	11.0	

Source: After Kim H. 1988: 409.

their costs of living from 1975 to 1985 demonstrate that times grew increasingly difficult. The relationship between farm size and farmer ability to cover household costs indicates a turn to solvency in 1971, followed by faltering figures for the rest of the decade (see fig. 7). This is easily understood by correlating the percentage of the cost of living covered by farming various amounts of land (Hwang Y. 1988: 393; Yi 1988: 197) and the breakdown of the percentage of farmers working different size plots (Chang 1988: 140) (see fig. 8).[4] Corresponding with these trends, farmer debts soared in the 1970s and 1980s. In the 1980s there were drastic increases in the percentages of debt/income (1980: 12.6; 1981: 11.9; 1982: 18.6; 1983: 25.1; 1984: 32.1; 1985: 35.3; 1986: 36.6) (Hwang S. 1988: 447). Additionally, the percent increases in debt were proportionately more dramatic for farmers with less land: 7.7 for 0.5 hectare; 6.4 for 0.5–1 hectare; 5.9 for 1–1.5 hectares; 5.8 for 1.5–2 hectares; and 5.1 for 2 hectares (Hwang S. 1988: 441).[5]

Farmers' relative poverty engendered their perception that there was no future in the rural sector, that day-to-day lifestyle improvements meant

Figure 7: Change Over Time in the Percentage of Household Costs
Covered by Agricultural Income, 1962-1977 (Unit = %)

Year	<0.5 ha	0.5-1.0 ha	1.0-1.5 ha	1.5-2.0 ha	>2.0 ha	Average
1962	66.0	90.9	105.8	106.2	120.8	97.9
1965	58.6	83.8	96.8	103.3	112.5	88.4
1968	57.7	87.8	106.6	117.5	120.2	95.7
1971	69.5	108.6	140.5	139.6	150.1	119.4
1974	78.4	114.8	135.4	159.1	159.3	129.4
1975	73.8	107.8	124.0	138.4	149.0	116.0
1976	73.6	111.3	136.5	142.3	175.9	123.0
1977	50.1	95.5	120.8	134.0	149.0	106.1

Source: After Hwang Y. 1988: 393 (1962-1974); Yi 1988: 197 (1975-1977).

Figure 8: Change Over Time in the Percentage of Household Costs
Covered by Agricultural Income, 1975-1986 (Unit = %)

Year	<0.5 ha	0.5-1.0 ha	1.0-1.5 ha	1.5 - 2.0 ha	> 2.0 ha	Average
1975	73.8	107.8	124.0	138.4	149.0	116.0
1976	73.6	111.3	136.5	142.3	175.9	123.0
1977	50.1	95.5	120.8	134.0	149.0	106.1
1978	54.1	93.7	116.5	120.0	142.7	102.7
1979	45.1	84.3	104.8	115.9	126.3	92.1
1980	39.6	75.0	89.9	101.5	124.4	82.1
	(28.4)[i]	(34.7)	(20.7)	(8.8)	(6.4)	
1981	41.9	84.7	105.7	114.8	130.7	92.5
1982	45.1	84.9	100.0	114.8	130.5	93.0
1983	44.8	69.4	90.2	94.9	110.7	82.2
	(28.6)	(35.9)	(19.6)	(8.0)	(5.3)	
1984	45.1	68.5	93.3	105.2	124.2	86.6
1985	35.6	59.8	82.9	103.1	115.2	78.9
	(27.7)	(35.6)	(20.2)	(8.3)	(5.7)	
1986	30.4	58.6	74.8	90.6	114.2	72.1
	(28.3)	(34.8)	(20.3)	(8.4)	(5.9)	

Source: After Yi 1988: 197.
[i] Numbers in parentheses refer to the percentage of farming households in this category.

little for the long run. Villagers, moreover, have been well aware of the urban snobbery toward ch'onnom (country bumpkins or hicks) (Cho 1981: 22–23). Mick Moore (1984: 595) explains that the rapid exodus of village youth in the 1980s promoted the fear that "the village is no longer reproducing itself as a social unit." Indeed, it became difficult over the years for young rural men to marry—a vivid sign of the problem of reproduction in villages. In activist education campaigns for farming women in Koch'ang, it was very effective to begin explanations of the Korean political economy by querying, "Why is it that your sons cannot get married?"[6] In late 1980s demonstrations against U.S. import liberalization, farmers' banners chided the United States: "Export women, not agricultural products." In the countryside, acts of farmer suicide—which were often committed through the ingestion of farm chemicals—were understood to be reflections of the bleak prospects for agricultural villages, if not acts of outright protest.

The state-initiated Saemaŭl Movement began in the 1970s. Although it implemented economic and technological development programs, the "movement" functioned as a massive state indoctrination campaign.[7] Its activities were focused on aesthetic and practical material improvements in villages. Of primary concern was the public appearance of villages from afar: thatched roofs were abolished and the walls encircling houses improved, particularly in villages visible from the highway. Also included were the enlargement of village roads, the improvement of house drains and village wells, and the construction of village halls. The programs also affected agricultural lands, including the rearrangement of paddy, and the repair of bridge posts, reservoirs, and waterways. Village improvements made in the name of the Saemaŭl Movement were in fact mostly assumed by the farmers themselves.[8] Also noteworthy was the uneven distribution of Saemaŭl money and services. Thus some farmers came to resent the program.

The rhetoric of the Saemaŭl Movement centered on the idea that individual effort and sacrifice would solve the economic problems of the rural sector. Farmers were understood to embody cultural practices and ideologies ill-suited to healthy national development. A survey of urban South Koreans in 1967 demonstrated that poverty was largely attributed to "a lack of effort and ability on the part of the poor people." Such "individualistic" explanations of poverty were highest among upper-class respondents (82.6%) and significantly less pervasive among lower-class respondents (68%) (Hong 1982: 70). Vincent Brandt and Man-gap Lee (1981: 135) argue that although the rural development of the 1970s "ha[d] actually taken place through structural reforms in the provision of services to farmers and improved access to expanding markets," the efforts of the decade were couched in terms of the community development of self-help and cooperation. By the late 1970s, Park's Saemaŭl Movement and its threefold call to action—diligence, cooperation, and self-help—had become a model for the nation as village writ large and thus a call to sacrifice for the state.

The quotidian effects and sensibilities of the structure and disciplinary tactics of the Saemaŭl Movement were reminiscent of the colonial period. The colonial period Nongch'on Chinhŭng Undong (Agricultural Village Development Movement) sought to mitigate "ideological pollution" or national and class consciousness; work hours and intensity were extended, and austerity was promoted (Han 1989: 115–116). The roots of Saemaŭl campaign slogans can be found in the colonial period call for the *kongdong-ch'e yuje ŭi puhwal* (rebirth of community legacy) (Han 1989: 117).[9]

If Saemaŭl rhetoric was about individual reform and community cooperation, many of the program's initiatives set out to control villages through intensified intervention. For example, the movement contributed to increasing infrastructural incorporation of villages such that the units of bureaucratic control became smaller and smaller. In one county in South Chŏlla Province, for example, the 1965 the population was 141,845 with 104 *haengjŏng purak* (administrative villages vs. *chayŏn purak*, or natural villages), but by 1987 the number of administrative villages had increased two and a half times, to 263, although the population had almost halved to 72,023 (Kim T. 1989: 78). The control of the selection of village heads was another conduit of state control. Generally the village head or the Saemaŭl leader led the fifteen-member village-level development committee, and the remaining members were the heads of other village-level groups (Han 1989: 132). Beginning with President Rhee's 1949 Regional Self-Government Law (Chibang Chach'ibŏp) villagers elected village heads through 1958, at which time the law was reformed so that village heads were selected by district heads. After the 1960 Student Revolution, the election process was reinstated, but in 1961 President Park revived an appointment system (Kim T. 1989: 80–81). Into the 1980s the state exercised control through village heads. The story of a village head appointment in a North Kyŏngsang Province village is revealing. In this village with thirty households of the same Kim lineage and thirty-eight households with other surnames, local officials consistently chose members of the dominant Kim lineage as village head. In a late 1980s election, however, because a Kim of the same lineage was running for local office as an opposition party candidate, government officials appointed a non-Kim. As soon as the election was over, however, they reinstated a Kim (Kim T. 1989: 92).

Village-level Saemaŭl leadership was also chosen among local elites. The majority of these leaders were appointed by the village head, powerful local men, and county or district heads; the rest were elected by the members of a village development committee, self-appointed, or named by village residents (Han 1989: 132). From 1970 to 1979, for example, less than 45 percent of the Saemaŭl village-level leaders were selected by an all-village election. Elected or appointed, these local officeholders were controlled from above. All officeholders, including Saemaŭl leaders, were required to take the civil service oath of office: they swore to be sincere, dutiful, and obedient and not to participate in any dissenting activity (Kim T. 1989: 90). The Saemaŭl leaders were trained at specially designated institutes all over South Korea. By 1974, the government reported that three and a half million people had received this leadership training (Brandt and Lee 1981: 69).

Obedient villages, like individuals, had much to gain by supporting the ruling party and the Saemaŭl campaigns. As a result, a hierarchical reward system developed, based largely on grassroots support for the ruling party and its programs. Larry L. Burmeister (1988: 46) notes, "Rural areas became the bastions of government party support due to the efficacy with which scarce resources could be channeled into the countryside at election time. Government largesse in times of political crises (e.g., the need for electoral legitimation) assumes added importance when there are few other organized channels of interest articulation available." The Saemaŭl Movement mobilized compliance through unevenly distributed bribes to various members of the village elite, including the village head and the Saemaŭl leaders. "Carrot and stick" disciplinary tactics pitted villagers and villages against each other. Programs discriminated among villages and between more and less prosperous farmers within villages. These inequities, however, have often been occluded by the overall downward trend of the sector. In each village, the Saemaŭl campaigns granted leadership roles to many villagers, who consequently attained personal prestige and economic as well as extraeconomic side benefits. Beginning in 1973, outstanding local leaders were awarded prizes at televised events (Brandt and Lee 1981: 69–70).

As the Saemaŭl campaigns became stratified between and within villages, they generated farmer resentment and resistance. Reports testify that some of the poorest farmers—tenant farmers and wage-labor agriculturists—resisted the Saemaŭl Movement's forced voluntary labor donations because they competed with work hours for which they could be compensated. Indeed, this was the case in the Koch'ang villages. No Kŭm-no, a farmer activist and writer, articulated this disenchantment. In his South Chŏlla Hamp'yŏng County village, farmers were required to contribute a prescribed amount of money or twenty-five days of labor to build the village hall. What happened was that the wealthier and more powerful farmers contributed amounts they determined by themselves; this infuriated the poorer villagers, since they had no say in the amount of their labor contributions (No 1986: 141). As a result of withholding money and resisting labor contributions, the poorest and richest farmers tended to contribute less labor than others (Brandt and Lee 1981: 92). Brandt and Lee (1981: 120, 129) found that Saemaŭl campaigns were less successful in villages with a higher percentage of poor families and most effective in those with "relative equality of land distribution." Saemaŭl programs were also successful in villages with coordinated leadership, such as the members of a single lineage, which mediated against the mobilization of class differences.

Villages competed with each other for limited state resources. In 1973, a system was initiated in which the villages were classified according to their degree of self-reliance: *kich'o* (basic), *chajo* (self-helping), or *charip* (independent). Here again the rhetoric of self-reliance reveals the state's interest in rural development with minimal state inputs (Brandt and Lee 1981: 71). In the initial stages at least, the state contributed more to the well-motivated villages. Farmers were savvy about these reward structures, and No (1986: 139) explains that the members of his village assumed that if they did not participate their village would be hated by the authorities. No (1986: 89) recalls that on the day "when the lights came on" in his village—when electricity was installed—a ruling party senator bragged to the villagers and told them that by the end of the 1970s they would all have a car and that if they have the "back," or favor from support of the ruling party, many things would be achieved. Richard Wade (1983: 18) documents the same tactics in the structure of the irrigation association: for example, cash prizes were awarded to those villages that paid their taxes most promptly. Similarly, village leaders assumed that they had to mobilize their village successfully to accrue benefits. In this way, farmers learned the importance of village compliance with state directives and support for the ruling party. Indeed, all the way up the ladder of the agrobureaucracy, officials had to report on the successful implementation of programs to ensure their own position and well-being. The entire structure was oriented toward giving orders to inferiors and reporting to superiors, thus relying on the "coordination of efforts by a large number of government agencies in order to get quick results" (Brandt and Lee 1981: 95; see also Moore 1984: 590). Officers went to extremes to cajole compliance with state directives.

In 1971 the state initiated the planting of a high-yield strain of rice called *t'ongilbyŏ* (rice grain). In keeping with many of the infrastructural and ideological traits of the Saemaŭl Movement, the program was executed in an undemocratic manner and did not benefit the farmers in the long run. Burmeister (1988: 58) explains that the t'ongilbyŏ planting program was an "economic and political penetration scheme launched from above." His study of the Green Revolution highlights the state-centered character of Korean agricultural "development" (Burmeister 1988: 59). While the initial t'ongilbyŏ yields represented significant improvements, the program's drawbacks became increasingly clear to farmers: the t'ongilbyŏ variety required more farmer input, particularly fertilizers; Koreans did not like the taste of the rice; and, finally, the t'ongilbyŏ was extremely sensitive to cold and thus not well suited to South Korea's climate and rice-growing calendar. To compensate for its sensitivity to the cold, farmers resorted to planting later, but in so doing they were not able to double crop with barley. Burmeister (1988: 58) explains that the "*t'ongilbyŏ* route to rice self-sufficiency led to decreased aggregate food self-sufficiency due to interference with previous cropping system patterns." Furthermore, research on the *Japonica* rice varieties, better suited to the Korean taste and climate, came to a halt during this period (Burmeister 1988: 65). In most cases farmers sustained monetary losses for having planted t'ongilbyŏ varieties because the market prices for them were 10 to 15 percent lower than those for standard strains in the early 1970s and 17 percent lower in 1976–1984; for farmers to accrue benefits, the t'ongilbyŏ yield needed to be 15 to 25 percent greater than standard strains, but for 1978–1983 one statistical base indicated a margin of only 9.4 percent (Burmeister 1988: 57–61). The t'ongilbyŏ planting program was most widespread in 1977, 1978, and 1979 (54, 85, and 61 percent, respectively, of the total paddy planted) (Burmeister 1988). This combined with weak harvests in the late 1970s and a particularly devastating crop in 1980, with yields not even two-thirds of those of the previous year, to produce high levels of farmer discontent. The state responded to farmer resistance to t'ongilbyŏ planting in 1980 by relaxing its controls on planting, although it still aimed for levels of 50 percent. By 1984, however, farmers were given full freedom in rice selection (Brandt and Lee 1981: 63).

A SLOW ASCENT: FARMERS' MOVEMENTS IN THE 1960S AND 1970S

The 1950s and 1960s can be characterized by steady and well-entrenched *yŏch'on-yado* (rural support of the ruling party and urban support of the oppositional party) and meager farmer mobilization. Some farmer activists refer to this era as the *tanjŏlgi* (break period)—a quiet stretch between periods of active resistance.

The 1960s combined sparse farmer activism with hints of the intensive state agrobureaucratic and repressive intervention that would later follow. By the 1970s, however, farmer activism was burgeoning. In the early stages, farmers' organizations were largely church organizations dependent on foreign capital and devoted to service rather than outright activism. Waning state support, increased ideological manipulation, and the escalation of repressive measures combined under the Yusin regime (1972–1979) to escalate farmers' dissatisfaction. Also, farmers' consciousness of the escalating economic inequalities spurred action. Farmers' movements of the 1970s converged on two broad issues: the failure of state economic programs, including waning rice supports, and price determinations that disadvantaged nongrain goods; and the "undemocratic" nature of state intervention—the exclusion of farmers from the institutions and directives that affected their well-being. In addition to the declining prosperity of the agricultural sector, farmers were also polarized by the real gaps between development programs' winners and losers. Furthermore, the labor movement also stimulated rural activism.

The escalation of farmer activism through the 1970s can be examined through shifts and turns of the Catholic Farmers Union, the leading farmers' activist organization. The CFU originated in the Agricultural Village Young Men's Division (JAC) established under the Catholic Young Men's Labor Committee in 1964. In 1966 the JAC became a freestanding committee with headquarters in Kumi in North Kyŏngsang Province where they opened a night school, chicken and pig farms, and a cooperative estate. The JAC set out to educate people "to change their environments themselves" through the "Christian spirit" (Yi 1986: 91). These early 1960s efforts of the Catholic church mirror aspects of the state approach to the rural sector and farmer well-being in which individual effort and sacrifice were heralded as the keys to improved distribution. In 1970, the JAC joined the International Federation of Catholic Farmers, an organization geared to a scientific approach to agricultural problems. In 1971, the JAC was reorganized and announced its commitment to a more protest-oriented approach to agricultural problems, in which they would take up farmers' rights and social justice and champion "Christianity's function to respond to social demands" (Yi 1986: 91).

In 1972, the JAC was reorganized as the Catholic Farmers Union, a self-conscious farmers' movement organization. Their first sustained activism—relief efforts in over forty villages in response to extensive flooding of the Southern Han River—was jointly undertaken in 1973 with the Agricultural Problem Research Center at Kŏn'guk University. These relief activities led to the founding in 1974 of the German-funded Christian Academy, where CFU leaders joined with Kŏn'guk University specialists to educate farmers to produce a core of farmer activists.

The Christian Academy set out to "stimulate farmers' movements" in order to "overcome the economic, social, political, and cultural isolation of farmers in the attainment of a healthy democratic society" (Yi 1986: 93). The headquarters were set up in Suwŏn City outside of Seoul, and a three-stage educational program was established. At each stage, farmers who demonstrated promise for further study and movement leadership were encouraged to continue to the next level of training. The participants were considerably more prosperous than most farmers, and the vast majority were men. From 1975 to 1979, over nine hundred farmers received the five-day basic education, and from among them over three hundred were selected to receive the second-level training sessions that began from six months to a year later (No 1987: 148). Fifty people were then selected to receive the extensive final training from 1977 to 1979. The first-level education program, a five-day stay, introduced farmers to the basics of agricultural economics and led them in discussions of the Korean cultural and rural social organizational barriers to rural activism and oppositional consciousness. The second-level training, a four-day program, employed a critical case study approach to various regional agricultural problems and the related farmer protest activities. The final training was a twenty-one-day program designed to train activist leaders for movement organizations and particular campaigns in their communities. Before the third-level training, the farmers met with activists/scholar mentors for a year, reviewing analytical texts on the agricultural situation in South Korea. The proliferation of farmers' movement organizations, most notably county-level branches of the CFU, and numerous movements in the late 1970s cannot be considered independent of the Christian Academy training. Indeed, the majority of key regional activists had received the three-stage training, and early incidents mostly occurred where activists and organizations were in place.

The earliest 1970s farmers' movement, the so-called Koguma Sakŏn (Sweet Potato Incident), protested state *nonghyŏp* (Agricultural Cooperatives), government price-setting policies, and agricultural directives. Beginning in November 1976, the Sweet Potato Incident was the call of some seven thousand sweet potato producers in South Chŏlla's Hamp'yŏng County for repairs for damages. (Hamp'yŏng County had long been a leading region in farmer activism.) After three years of struggle the movement was victorious. The record of activism became a forum for discussing the limitations and problems of CFU-directed movements. From its 1976 beginning through April 1978, the farmers fought directly with the agricultural cooperatives, but these local protests met with little success. It was only following an eight-day hunger strike staged one year later, in April 1979, at a Catholic church in South Chŏlla's Kwangju County that the government finally compensated the farmers. Of the seventy hunger strikers, however, only four were from the region in question and only one was a sweet potato producer. Instead, the strikers were primarily CFU members from many regions, students from Kwangju, and people fighting for democracy. Although the incident has been memorialized as an early and effective antistate farmers' movement, many activists recalled that the material and human resources behind the movement were largely external. It was also criticized on the grounds that although the problem and the settlement were related to the agricultural cooperatives, they had little to do with broader state issues (No 1987: 339–340). Activists would later reflect on the isolation of 1970s movements from a broader political agenda, the undemocratic structure of their organizations, and the absence of self-initiated farmer activity. Also pinpointed was their consideration of farmers as an undifferentiated mass, which led to the privileging of the more prosperous farmers and their concerns. Similar complaints were lodged in the Koch'ang case.

By the end of the 1970s, a nationwide task force for farmers' movements determined that farmers needed to address problems with the agricultural cooperative system, the rice price setting, the tax system, the land system, and the solidarity of farmers' movement organizations. The Christian Farmers League set out to augment as well as challenge CFU activities. The CFL, a loose federation, distinguished itself from the more centralized and hierarchical CFU, which reflected the structure of the Catholic church. Not surprisingly, there was competition for membership and farmers' movement hegemony between the two organizations.[10]

If the end of the decade was marked at once by the systematization of and reflection on farmers' activism, it also brought a state crackdown on such activism. The Christian Academy program came to a dramatic halt in March 1979 when seven of the academy's instructors were arrested for violation of the Anti-Communist Law in what was clearly a government attempt to stigmatize burgeoning oppositional activity in the countryside. No Kŭm-no wrote about the so-called Christian Academy Incident in *Ttang ŭi adŭl* (Son of the Earth), a two-volume account of daily life and his own activism in his South Chŏlla village. When the educators were arrested in Seoul, authorities came to No's faraway South Chŏlla home and held him for three days, demanding that he concur that those arrested had tried to indoctrinate him with Communist teachings.[11] The government's attempt to suppress the Christian Academy attests to the state's heightened fear of the political threat of rural movement activity. Although the incident made organizing difficult in many rural areas (No 1987: 160), it communicated to farmer and nonfarmer activists that farmers' movements could not be wrested from broader political issues—such as the infringement of human rights and the excesses of the authoritarian state—and it thus provided a powerful argument for a more far-reaching agenda for farmers' movements. Indeed, 1980s activism grew in new and expanded directions.

CHALLENGES FROM WITHIN: FARMERS' MOVEMENTS IN THE 1980S

As the 1960s and 1970s began with social and political realignments, so did the 1980s, with elections in the wake of President Chun's violent suppression of the Kwangju Uprising. In the early 1980s, rural support of the ruling party reached new lows. Dissenting organizations and activities increased in all sectors, which in turn generated intensive state repression. The Saemaŭl Movement campaigns waned, however, and the state began to make concessions to farmers' demands.

This escalation of farmer dissent was a response to several factors: decreasing terms of trade for the agricultural sector; market liberalization's drastic effects on farmers, particularly nongrain producers; the unpopularity of the Chun regime; and widespread antigovernment protest activity. In light of meager returns and lack of government willingness to support or protect the sector economically, farmers were less and less willing to follow the government directives as to what to plant, what labor to provide, or in which activities to engage. Additionally, trade liberalization and inequities in the 1980s health insurance and tax programs contributed further to farmers' mobilization. By the late 1980s, in addition to increases in the frequency of farmer activism, there were qualitative changes in the structure and content of movement organizations and their agenda.

In the 1980 Democracy Spring (the short period following the assassination of President Park and preceding Chun Doo Hwan's ascent to the presidency) several county-level farmer organizations were formed—the start of the organizational changes that were eventually realized later in the decade. Although weak in comparison to the branches of the CFU and the CFL, they represented locally based organizations that could become the cell units of a national oppositional structure independent of the foreign-capital, church-based, activist-centered groups. In 1981 there was even a failed attempt to make a national farmers' group, the Han'guk Nongminhoe (Korean Farmers Association). Chun's military regime continued to silence protest activity in the aftermath of the brutal suppression of the Kwangju Uprising. Farmers, like many other Koreans, experienced the Chun regime as a reign of terror and violence. In spite of enormous initial energy, farmers' movements in fact made little headway at this juncture.

By the end of the decade, however, these earlier efforts culminated in a widespread summons for "unification of farmers' movements," both in terms of organizational structure and activist agenda. Such a unification signaled a broadening of the political agenda in which farmers' movements would join with other activist groups to make collective demands. For instance, calls for unification at the national level went hand in hand with an agenda to localize farmers' movements. County-level groups were to be farmer based and democratic; they privileged the agenda of the poorer farmers.

Many of the pathbreaking organizational changes occurred in the already very active Muan and Hamp'yŏng counties of South Chŏlla. In those regions, 1984 was an important turning point when the CFU and the CFL joined for a nondenominational political struggle, the Hamp'yŏng-Muan Nongmin Taehoe. Although this open political struggle at a local marketplace was suppressed by one thousand civil servants and six hundred police, it had raised dozens of human rights and political issues, including Chun's visit to Japan and farmer debt. In Hamp'yŏng this demonstration was followed in 1985 by the creation of a county-level independent organization, which effectively disbanded the local Catholic and Christian groups (No 1989: 344). At that time this was still the only county-level independent organization, while the CFU and the CFL had organizations in some fifty counties. After 1985, however, farmers' movement groups were increasingly organized at the county level and integrated independent of the religious organizations; by the end of 1985, there were eight county-level organizations (No 1989: 344–345).

In 1985 farmer demonstrations over beef imports marked a turning point. Farmers publicly slaughtered cattle to protest the import-related price drops of beef that had coincided with their compliance with government directives to raise cattle to supplement their incomes. Many officials and farmers alike were surprised at these violent and public outbursts. Struggles over the low cattle prices in 1985 in Hamp'yŏng represented a convergence of farmer issues, including the antidemocratic, forced nature of agricultural village development programs, farmer debt, and global power alignments as they were manifested in South Korea's vulnerability to U.S. pressures for import liberalization. In Hamp'yŏng County, another major issue was the relatively greater hardship created by falling cattle prices for less prosperous farmers.[12]

In the late 1980s the farmers' movements increasingly focused their attention on the state. The struggles were not simply economic ones that could be settled either locally or by strictly addressing state economic policies.[13] As it became clear that compliance with state directives was often detrimental to farmer well-being, many farmers concluded that the state lacked a commitment to the rural sector.

As the 1980s progressed, farmers called for price supports that would cover production costs. This reflects both increasing rural poverty and farmers' escalating confidence in demanding a minimum standard of living. In 1986 there were mounting demonstrations by the various vegetable producers, particularly of onions and garlic, who demanded government support to ensure sale prices that would cover production costs. Continuing in 1987 and 1988, some eighty local struggles took place against the import of agricultural goods (No 1989: 334). The state became implicated not only because of its continued neglect of the agricultural sector but also because of its repressive measures. By 1987 the public discourse against the violence of the state in the student and laborer torture incidents of 1986 and 1987 and the increasing public awareness of the Kwangju Uprising during and after the 1987 election led farmers to decry the local bureaucratic and police intervention in their daily lives and in their protest activities. Underground movies depicting the Kwangju Uprising and the June and August 1987 protests became a standard component of farmers' movement education programs. And the politically and economically marginalized Chŏlla provinces continued to be at the forefront of the politicization of economic struggle.

The year 1987 proved a watershed in farmer activism and marked a dramatic turn away from an activist-centered movement (No 1989: 347). As the Koch'ang Tenant Farmers Movement demonstrates, farmer activism was itself on trial. Dozens of county-level organizations were formed in 1986 and 1987 (No 1989: 345–346). In February 1987, the efforts of the early 1980s were realized in the formation of the Chŏn'guk Nongmin Hyŏphoe (National Farmers Association), which served as a loose federation of independent county-level organizations. The National Farmers Association was determined to solve the land problems, organize training for farmers, organize farmers in support of national unification, block reactionary farmers' groups while drawing out their less reactionary members, and reorganize agricultural cooperatives under their auspices (No 1989: 350). In addition to the escalation of the county-level organizing, grassroots-initiated protest activity also began in 1987. The South Chŏlla–centered water tax refusal movement, for example, was organized by farmers with no particular group affiliation and drew unprecedented numbers of farmers (No 1989: 346). In 1988, 7,000 gathered in Naju in South Chŏlla Province to protest the water tax (No 1989: 334).

In 1988 farmer dissent reached new heights as thousands of farmers gathered to protest in Seoul. In January, over 4,000 gathered in front of government offices in Kwach'ŏn to protest beef imports. In April, various farmers' movement organizations joined with increasingly popular producer groups for a rally against the import of American agricultural goods; held at Kŏn'guk University, the demonstration proceeded to the city streets where it was violently suppressed, as were all urban demonstrations at that time. In May, 30,000 had assembled at various points on the outskirts of Seoul in preparation for a large protest against imports, but police were mobilized all over the city and resorted to blocking the highway to prevent farmers from making their way to Seoul. In spite of these obstacles, however, an impressive 5,000 gathered. In a July demonstration, farmers even tried to enter the Senate.

In 1988 it was, above all, farmer health insurance that focused farmer attention against the state. It became clear that this was an inversely graduated tax in which farmers bore the heaviest burdens, paying much more than even the wage-earning civil servants residing in the same villages. Even conservative farmers, who were reconciled to a diminishing agricultural sector, were furious at this blatant maldistribution of resources detrimental to poorer farmers. For many, this was the final straw in an already growing sense of the relative impoverishment of the rural sector. The program was announced in January, and by February 2,000 farmers in Hamp'yŏng had returned their cards, refusing to pay (only 20% of the residents had paid) (No 1989: 316). By late February an independent group had formed in Hamp'yŏng to protest the health insurance policies. They insisted that the rate was too high and that the insurance workers despised farmers. In March 10,000 farmers gathered at a large demonstration in Hamp'yŏng; they were met with police suppression and arrests, which farmers then vehemently protested.

The Koch'ang Tenant Farmers Movement fell at a critical juncture in the 1980s development of farmer dissent. By 1988, in a refigured climate of protest, monthlong demonstrations in Seoul were no longer so exceptional as they had been in summer 1987. Farmers had become a regular part of Seoul's political landscape. In particular, farmer protest against the import of agricultural goods coincided with the escalation of anti-Americanism toward the end of the decade.

Also in flux toward the end of the decade was the ideological tenor of farmers' movements. In addition to political escalation, domains that had been beyond discourse in the cold war years entered speech and action. Beginning in the middle of the decade, land issues burgeoned in a way that would have been ideologically untenable earlier. Indeed, this was the context of the Koch'ang Tenant Farmers Movement. The Koch'ang movement touched on farmer issues that although not directly pitted against the state, exposed many controversial national historical issues. In the aftermath, a series of incidents erupted involving long-term tenancy to corporations and the state. In Kangwŏn Province, farmers protested at the provincial offices for the return of 15,000 p'yŏng taken by the American military government. In April 1988, over one hundred of these farmers demonstrated in front of the Korean Broadcasting Service and the National Assembly to win ownership of their waterway plots. In fall 1988, farmers from P'yŏngt'aek in Kyŏnggi Province staged a monthlong sit-in to get their land from Sejong University, which had purchased what was originally government-sponsored reclamation land. Such incidents were particularly symbolic because they referred back to the land reform measures and thus to the policies of the U.S. military government and the Rhee period.

By the late 1980s, however, most land struggles did not have such deep roots. They instead took up the problems of widespread tenancy as a result of land speculation and absentee ownership. There is disagreement as to whether post-Liberation retenantization was the result of flaws in the land reform itself or of post–land reform agricultural policies. Samyang tenancy was thus atypical in the late 1980s. Nationally, tenant land, at 4 percent of total land, was at an all-time low. It had hovered between 15 and 17 percent from 1964 to 1977, after which it rose sharply to 22.3 percent in 1981, 26.8 percent in 1983, and 30.5 percent in 1985. The figures for tenant farmers (farmers with at least some tenant land) follow a similar curve, with an all-time low in 1957 at 11.9 percent, hovering between 26 and 30 percent from 1960 to 1975, and increasing dramatically in 1977 to 36 percent, in 1981 to 46.4 percent, in 1983 to 59.8 percent, and in 1985 to 64.7 percent.[14]

This late 1970s and 1980s retenantization did not reflect the reinstatement of semifeudal land relations but rather the increased drain of young men from the countryside to labor in the cities, leaving only women and older people who could not farm even their small plots alone. In the late 1980s, 78.9 percent of landlords gave age as the reason they rented their land to tenants (Chang 1988: 161). Two-thirds of the nonresident landlords were people who had owned the land since they were in the village, but these figures decreased in farming areas closer to cities where more land was purchased for speculation (Chang 1988: 160–161). Most were thus not financially reliant on rent extraction but maintained the plots for their symbolic value as "homelands" or purchased them for their speculative potential. The 1984 average landlord plot size was 863 p'yŏng, well under 0.5 hectare, and the average annual rent of ₩250,000 amounted to less than one month of an urban salary (Chang 1988: 161). Small plot landlords and even absentee landlords did not become the objects of farmer protest. Again, Samyang was not a typical landlord in the 1980s. Although the movement rhetoric often referred to increasing rates of tenancy in the 1980s, the tenancy in the Samyang case was not the sort that was on the rise.

Most of the 1980s land-related struggles, as in the Samyang case, protested vestiges of land reform injustices—that is, land that was somehow excluded—or state-landlord situations. In September 1988, the National No-Compensation Land Relinquishment Committee was formed; this national land organization represented the unification of the interests of the CFU, the CFL, and the National Farmers Association. A 1986 survey indicated that 19.3 percent of farmers felt that the state should ensure equal distribution of land, and 53.8 percent felt that the state should put an upper limit on the amount of ownership. In turn, 31.1 percent of these farmers believed that reforms should be achieved through *hyŏksinjŏk kaehyŏk* (radical reform), while 55.3 percent advocated *chŏmjinjŏk kaehyŏk* (gradual reform) (Ch'oe 1989: 59–60).

ESCALATING FARMER MOBILIZATION AND STATE RESPONSE: INTO THE 1990S

As farmers' opposition against the state became more political and vehement, the state made economic and political concessions to the rural sector. Candidates for the December 1987 direct presidential election addressed farmers' issues, particularly the soaring debt levels and absentee landownership. "Land to the farmers"—recalling post-Liberation farmers' slogans—was the political slogan of both the ruling and the opposition parties. Concerning farmer debts, the ruling party suggested a policy for the development of agricultural income, and the opposition parties offered their solutions as well: Kim Dae Jung called for a debt settlement law to wipe off all debts within a year, Kim Young Sam argued for a seven-year repayment program with a five-year grace period, and Kim Chong P'il backed a ten-year repayment and ten-year grace period (No 1989: 325). Also in 1988 the government responded to escalating water tax struggles with its decision to halve the water tax rates across the board and gave in to the pressures for agricultural cooperative democratization. In 1983 one million people signed a petition calling for the direct election of the local agricultural cooperative president. As a result of such activism, direct election of the cooperative heads was finally reinstated in September 1988, for the first time since 1961.

Positive state response to rural activism and the relaxation of cold war tactics, as well as the decreased rural responsiveness to such tactics, eliminated the once-powerful stigma of rural organizing. This change challenged the legitimacy of the state political mobilization of compliance for benefits. The tables were turned in the late 1980s when farmer activists

told farmers that officials and police would fear a well-organized oppositional village and that the bureaucracy would favor such villages over those
that strictly supported the ruling party. In the case of the Koch'ang villages,
the police and state officials came to fear those villages most closely affiliated with the CFU. Against all odds and local precedent, there were even
cases in which farmers' movement activists became village heads and ran
for public office.

In keeping with this strengthening of activism were organizational developments. The efforts begun by the 1987 formation of the National Farmers
Association—an organization whose goal was to unify farmers' movement
associations and support the autonomy of county-level associations—intensified with the 1990 formation of the National League of Farmers Associations (Chŏnnong, Chŏn'guk Nongminhoe Ch'ong Yŏnmaeng). Chŏnnong
was established by dismantling the two existing national-level groups: the
aforementioned National Farmers Association and the National Farmers
Movement Federation (Chŏn'guk Nongmin Undong Yŏnhap), a federation formed in 1988 that included the national religious organizations
(CNCYCW 1990: 2). This organization set out to become a single organizational matrix that could at once represent all farmers in the national arena
and ensure the local autonomy of county-level activist organizations. Committed to *chajujŏk taejung chojik* (autonomous mass organization), Chŏnnong aimed to move away from activisms in which "farmers are merely
objects to be led" (CNCYCW 1990: 1). They set out to overcome organizational impediments to successful farmer activism, including the dearth of
local leaders, "authoritarian" organizational practices, and the financial de-
pendence of local units; their internal and activist agenda converged on
the call for "democratization" (CNCYCW 1990: 5). Chŏnnong set out to
continue not only the spirit and doctrine of 1980s farmers movements but
also the "historical tradition" of the immediate post-Liberation National
League of Farmers Unions (also known as Chŏnnong) (CNCYCW 1990:
3). With Chŏnnong spearheading activities and the vitality of increasing
membership and county-level organization, farmer activism achieved new
visibility and broad social significance.[15]

In addition to this continued integration and localization of farmer activism, the mounting concern in the late 1980s and early 1990s over the
Uruguay Round (concluded in 1994) further coalesced farmer political
consciousness and organizational awareness. In this regard the comments
of Chŏnnong provincial activists at a public forum, "The Current Situation
of Farmers' Movements and Organizational Challenges," are revealing.
P'yo Man-su noted that in the face of the "import problem," optimism
is impossible. He continued, however, that these understandings do not
always translate into activism; they can instead engender profound resignation and pessimism (Chŏnnong 2 1990: 12). In a similar vein, Ch'oe Chin-

guk remarked that the import issues present a stark reality and deeply implicate the United States (Chŏnnong 2 1990: 13). Pak Pong-jun added that farmers increasingly sensed that they must solve their own problems and that they could be a powerful social force if they united effectively (Chŏnnong 2 1990: 13). He maintained that the farmers' fundamental ideas about activism were profoundly affected by the 1987 labor struggles, particularly the return visits of laborers for the August *ch'usŏk* (harvest festival) in the wake of these struggles. Laborers came home boasting "We ourselves fought and were given raises, and it is because of our struggle that the Labor Laws were reformed" (Chŏnnong 2 1990: 12). He also noted that after June 1987, farmers' democratization consciousness reached new heights as political rhetoric and the mass media disseminated and focused on the "democratization of everything" (Chŏnnong 2 1990: 12).

The confidence in dissent and the mandate for democracy coincided with the impending Uruguay Round negotiations in 1993, when there were high-profile protests throughout the country: in some regions, farmers refused to sell their rice to the government at the state-set prices and blocked the agricultural cooperative offices with sacks of rice (*Daily Report*, December 1, 1993, 29); in others, they staged funerals—clad in mourning clothes made from rice sacks—to symbolize the death of Korean farmers (*Daily Report*, December 7, 1993, 25). Demonstrations in Seoul in December 1993 gathered as many as thirty thousand protesters.

Just as the minjung movements in other sectors are widely understood to have waned in the 1990s, farmer activism coalesced around the GATT negotiations when it became clear that the South Korean rice market would be opened. Not only did farmer activism reach new heights—organizationally and in terms of the numbers of farmers who participated—but the closed rice market was mobilized as a symbol of national identity and well-being. A newspaper editorial championed farmers as it chided the United States.

> Watching over the rice negotiations, our people are upset over the excessive pressure from the United States. . . . We believe that Americans are fully aware of the deep and long history of the love and affection that the ROK people have for rice. Our people's love for rice is the same whether one is a farmer or not. Therefore, Americans are well aware of the fact that for our people, rice is tantamount to life itself. . . . Military security is important for our people, but safeguarding our rice is just as important. (*Daily Report*, December 7, 1993, 25)

Although most South Koreans understood the inevitability of opening the rice market, they registered overwhelming opposition to it (*Daily Report*, December 7, 1993, 26). To many it augured the beginning of a virtual demise of agriculture, as production costs in South Korea are over three times greater than in the United States (*Daily Report,* December 7, 1993, 28; December 8, 1993, 26). In addition to concerns for the farm sector, polls revealed other more general anxieties, including food security, the unsuitability of foreign rice for Korean consumption, the environment, and suspicions that foreign rice is contaminated (*Daily Report,* December 8, 1993, 26). A Chŏnnong newspaper editorial even suggested the significance of the rice market for unification: "One of the biggest reasons that the Chŏnnong is advocating 'unified agriculture' is that in a unified fatherland the security of our food supply is crucial and also because we believe that autonomous unification will only be possible when we are self-sufficient in our basic food supply" (Kim T. 1993: 1). After the opening of the rice market had been declared officially, the president and many government bureaucrats and elected officials presented formal apologies in an effort to reassure the public. President Kim Young-sam said, "We have exerted every possible means and method to save our rice, the flesh and blood of our nation" (*Daily Report,* December 9, 1993, 29).[16]

Examining farmer mobilization in post-Liberation South Korea, it is clear that the state and oppositional mobilization of farmers must be understood in concert. The time line drawn here posits that the late 1940s were a time of extensive rural activism. Although silenced, those years deeply affected farmer consciousness. The 1950s—the Korean War era—were subsumed in the war and the urban industrial focus of its aftermath. Although a decade of neither significant farmer activism nor intensive agrobureaucratic or repressive intervention, the 1960s brought both rudimentary state and oppositional infrastructures. These developments were intensified in the 1970s, and in the late 1970s there was a convergence of state political mobilization, waning state economic support, increasing political mobilization, and burgeoning farmer activism. Finally, in the 1980s, the frequency and political character of farmers' movements escalated, representing qualitative changes in both the structure and content of movement organizations and their agenda. By the end of the decade, the agenda of farmers' struggles was integrated into broader social struggles against the authoritarian regime. Additionally, the farmers movements' internal struggles mirrored redefinitions that were taking place in the community of dissent.

In the final years of the 1980s and in the 1990s, farmers protesting in Seoul had symbolic valence beyond their numbers. Late twentieth-century trade negotiations have propelled the rural sector and the fate of its various farm products into national and international arenas. Globally unsurpassed rapid rural exodus rates have fashioned Seoul into an overpopulated city with vast numbers of first-generation urbanites not far removed from their rural roots. The images of farmers protesting in Seoul—some who look not unlike city youth and others who bring to mind the grandfathers and grandmothers of rural pasts—are variously signified. For some, these images recall "brilliant" legacies of resistance in Korea on the eve of, during, and in the immediate years following the Japanese colonial period; for others, they signal South Korea's global vulnerability or the "backwardness of the past." Regardless of the vicissitudes and variety of their urban images today, in the sweep of post-Liberation South Korean history, farmers emerge not as passive objects but as subjects who have been simultaneously structured by and resisted ideological, political, and economic realities.

CHAPTER NINE

Conclusion:
Post-1987 Epics of Dissent

I want to draw minjung holding flowers.
KIM CHŎNG-HŎN (1993: 13), CONTEMPORARY SOUTH KOREAN ARTIST

For participants in the Koch'ang Tenant Farmers Movement and in 1980s dissent more broadly, minjung emerged as a way of thinking about the past and imagining the future. It figured as an epic of struggle that reflected South Korea's postcolonialism and national division. The minjung imaginary was a configuration of the narratives and practices of dissent that coalesced in a particular historical moment, an era distinguished by the culture and politics of military authoritarianism.

From the vantage point of the mid-1990s, the 1980s has become for many a distant past. This era has receded into "history" because of local and transnational social and political transformations. In South Korea, 1980s social movements culminated in *munmin chŏngbu* (civilian rule). This national transformation occurred in the relaxation of cold war politics precipitated by the Soviet breakup and German unification. In South Korea, the demise of the cold war challenged the long-standing military authoritarian rhetoric and control. Likewise, socialism's devalued currency unsettled the rationales and visions of dissent.

Both transformations, however, were incomplete. Into the 1990s, the Koreas remain one of the last flash points of the cold war. The machinations over North Korean nuclear power plants in 1994 resuscitated old rhetorics at home and abroad, notably in the United States. Furthermore, many South Koreans have not been convinced by the promise of civilian rule and the proclamation of a "New Korea." And many dissidents have resisted easy embrace of consumer capitalism.

In the 1990s the movements of dispossessed people in South Korea have not waned. Agricultural policies consolidated under the GATT agreement threatened the rural sector even more radically than during past authoritarian regimes. With the grim realities of the post–Uruguay Round era, many farmers have little hope of surviving. Given falling rural land prices, many farmers would not be able to pay their debts even if they sold their land. Thus many farmers cannot contemplate leaving the countryside for urban employment (Kim H. 1994: 35).[1] Furthermore, farmer activism has achieved new levels of organization, autonomy, and participation. This escalation of farmers' activism has been evident both in the struggles against the Uruguay Round and in the advances of *nongminhoe* (farmers [activist] committees).

In spite of this widespread activism, minjung epics and cultures of dissent have waned. The celebrated minjung activism of the 1980s—of farmers, laborers, and urban poor—has seemingly fallen outside the purview of public discourse. Farmers' movements have become less and less easily subsumed in middle-class imaginaries, epics, or organizations of struggle. It has become clear that 1990s activism cannot be easily subsumed under a singular aesthetic or narrative of dissent. With civilian rule the objects of dissent are more dispersed and the narratives and organization of the dissent are more fragmented. In the 1990s, a discourse of simin (civil) movements has become central to the public discourse of dissent.

The wane of encompassing epics of dissent and the continuity of "minjung" activisms are revealed in a vignette in an editorial in a progressive weekly. Kim Chong-ch'ŏl (1994: 112) went to see an *undongkwŏn yŏn'gŭk* (activist play) called "The Dawn of Labor" (Nodong ŭi saebyŏk) at which a woman seated behind him told him, "Nowadays, it is really rare to find a college student who thinks to come to this sort of play. Today's guests are mostly people from labor unions. Throughout the 1980s, progressive theater troops performed at the labor unions, so the laborers didn't feel the need to come, but now they come." As the activism of farmers and laborers slips beyond the 1980s minjung imaginary and outside 1980s movement structures, it becomes invisible because it does not conform to the watersheds as they are drawn by urban intellectuals.

In the same way that contemporary farmer activism is a blind spot to much of 1990s discourses of dissent, dimensions of past activism have also been occluded in 1990s discourses and memory. As the excesses and extremes of the minjung era are tallied, 1980s activism is wrested from its historical conditions of production and its own dialogue with the past. In a retrospective gaze, minjung is homogenized against what was in fact a vast array of competing practices and discourses. The occlusions of discourses of dissent have their own social life, which fashions current and future activisms. In the same way that the 1980s activism explored here through the Koch'ang Tenant Farmers Movement was articulated through particular historical aesthetics, 1990s activism fashioned itself through the public discourses on and the memory of the 1980s.

In this chapter I take up the changed discursive climate of 1990s activism and the relation to social movement programs and practices. The discursive shifts will be examined through the changing aesthetics of minjung art and the articulation of simin movements and of the *sinsedae* (new generation). The interstices between these discourses and the case of farmers' activism will be examined through 1990s shifts in the rhetoric and practice of nonghwal and through more recent meetings with Koch'ang activists in 1993.

GETTING DOWN TO EARTH, IN ART AND ACTIVISM

The 1993 art exhibit of the recent works of Kim Chŏng-hŏn, "The Path of Land, The Path of Earth" (Ttang ŭi kil, hŭk ŭi kil), self-consciously called for a post-1987 art. His artistic innovations ran parallel with the transformations of social movement discourse and nonghwal that I discuss below. His innovations are germane to this book because they turn on the representation of land and farmers. Kim, renowned for a distinguished career in the minjung art movement in the 1970s and 1980s, asks, "What would a national art for the 1990s look like?" He answers with an artistic tribute to soil. He suggests ways to move beyond minjung protest art with its agents of struggle and its historical epics. He explains that despite his lack of personal inclination, he too "ran" (participated in social activism) under the banner of "min" (the Chinese character for "people" used in both minjung and minjok). He goes so far as to say, "Having passed the last years in a household under the *tollim* [name] [2] of 'min,' I have left no paintings that are really any good" (1993: 13). Kim is tired of portraying peasant struggle: "I want to draw minjung holding flowers (1993: 13)."

The exhibit's rural scapes assert that "land" (*ttang*) and "earth" (*hŭk*) must be united: "This exhibit is about my dream of a world that unites land and earth" (Kim C. H. 1993: 13). Although the 1980s "focused on land as a political symbol—the era demanded that—now the focus needs to be on the life that comes from the earth and its harmonious existence with the earth" (Kim C. H. 1993: 13). This shift from land to earth means many things to Kim. Land is a capitalist category; earth is a "much more embracing, philosophical, primitive concept." Land is a "historical category," and its ownership is at the heart of historical struggles throughout the world. "Isn't it because of its ownership category that all the divisions, wars, and bloodshed have come to be? . . . It is land that determines the style of humans' lives. Even so, humans try to control the land. It is precisely this land that humans live on, trying to control and exploit it." Earth, in contrast, has no landlords: "It is the stage on which all living things are created." Finally, it is to earth that humans and human desire—"even the desire to paint"—return (1993: 16).

In the spirit of the earth, Kim (1993: 14) is determined to pay attention to the little, trifling things, to pay his respects to its "living force." Tucked in the corners and shadows of all of his paintings are farm implements, eating utensils, and weeds. "Together with the Land I" (Ttang kwa tŏburŏ I) is a collage of roughly sketched farming utensils, a brimming bowl of rice, and an irregular patch of earth in which a single weed is growing. In "Together with the Earth I" (Hŭk kwa tŏburŏ I) an elderly farming woman, earthworms, mollusks, farming utensils, butterflies, a small tree, a crow, a bird's nest filled with eggs, a snake, a cabbage, and a weed are all sketched into a plot of red earth. In "Let's have a cup of makkŏlli [crude rice liquor] and then get back to work" (Makkŏlli hansabal masigo hapsida) a smiling farming man leaning on his hoe extends a wooden bowl of makkŏlli to a smiling farming woman with a small farming utensil in her hand; they are painted in earth colors and drawn as if they were molded from the land that recedes behind each of them, fading off to a vanishing point. The background is deep green; between the two is the silhouette of a tree sketched in black, and in the bottom corners are two small green weeds. In "The Plaque of Hwangt'ohyŏn" (Hwangt'ohyŏn ŭi hŭkt'ap) we find a somewhat different expression of Kim's new aesthetic: here he has raised a commemorative plaque from nothing but, and commemorating nothing but, the earth itself. This piece stands out in contrast to decades of art that portrayed minjung subjects of struggle and the oppressive state.

Kim Chi-ha, an important dissident literary figure of the 1970s and one of the architects of the 1980s minjung imaginary, composed the introductory essay to this catalog. He praised Kim Chŏng-hŏn's work for inaugurating the union between the "life [living things] cultural movements" and the environmental movement. The poet augured that these movements will unite the *chumin* (residents) of every region to know "the value of their traditional life" and to protect "our communal minjung culture" (Kim Chi-ha 1993: 5). He explained that these movements give hope to fulfilling the project of (national) unification (1993: 5).

In the shift from "the revolutionary peasant of minjung past" to artist Kim's "minjung holding flowers" is a transformation in the epics of activism and cultural identity. None of the farmers in Kim's exhibit actually holds flowers, but in one painting, *Walking in the Open Land* (Tŭllyŏk ŭl kŏrŭmyŏ) (fig. 9), a farmer with his hands relaxed behind his back ambles down a narrow path between rice fields. Small white flowers bloom in the tufts of grass to the side of the path.

Kim's depictions of the tools of farmers' toil, the rice bowls at the end of a laboring day, and the unspoiled landscape are compelling for their

Figure 9. Painting by Kim Chŏng-hŏn, "Tŭllyŏk ŭl kŏrŭmyŏ" [Walking in the Open Land]

everydayness. On the eve of nationwide farmer struggles against the GATT negotiations and in the midst of soaring *land* [*not* soil/earth/dirt] prices that have effectively polarized the classes in urban areas, however, his cry sounds a bit romantic. The discontinuities he draws seem to proclaim a new dawn in the stuff of old imaginaries. I notice this particularly in Kim's romance with farmers sketched from the soil. Pre-1987 minjung epics were also about peasant culture and communalism, indigenous socialisms, and local solutions.

In spite of these blind spots, Kim Chŏng-hŏn's work and reflections capture elements of both on-the-ground social transformations and the various public discourses that grapple with that transformation. In the same way that Kim has decided to paint against the land, many social commentaries on 1990s activisms are posed against the past. They reveal a widespread social fatigue and even disgust with that culture of dissent. Many people distance themselves not only from the military authoritarian culture of the recent past but also from the righteousness and drama of dissent—from the totalizing projects of both the Left and the Right. Recalling the 1980s, what comes to people's minds are the infringements on personal life imposed by both military authoritarian rule *and* the culture of dissent. People remember: *when* urban spaces were consumed by the violence of demonstrations and their suppression; *when* the government demanded sacrifice and restraint in the name of political stability and economic development; and *when* the moral prerogatives of the Left made those with progressive inclinations feel guilty that they could not do more. These 1990s reflections explore the culture of 1980s dissent not as an autonomous realm but as reflections of the political and social character of their times. The 1990s, in contrast, are marked by widespread embourgeoisement. The celebration of consumer capitalism is epitomized by increasingly visible upper-class enclaves in Kangnam, the area south of Seoul's Han River; and by the extension of personal and political freedoms.

The contrast of these decades can be gleaned through the articulation of simin movements as compared with minjung movements and a sinsedae that distinguishes the culture and orientation of 1990s youth from that of the 1980s undongkwŏn.[3]

DRAWING A LINE: THE "NEW GENERATION" AND "CIVIL MOVEMENTS"

Many South Koreans observe that the 1990s *hakpŏn* (those who entered college in the 1990s) are different from the 1980s hakpŏn.[4] The South Korean anthropologist Cho Haejoang (1994*a*: 143) reports 1990s hakpŏn's resistance and discomfort with 1980s students: as one student told her, he feels closer to his teachers who came of age in the 1970s than to his seniors from the 1980s. Cho (1994*a*: 146) explains that 1980s students arrived at college campuses that were completely enveloped in the atmosphere and activities of the student movement. Even if not all students were *undongga* (committed activists), the vast majority shared the movement perspective and "carried the weight of the country on their backs." Students of the 1980s, Cho continues, saw the prohibition of campus newspapers, stood by as friends were taken off to be tortured, and experienced the sudden disappearance and even the suicides of classmates. Students came to feel that "the only way to live with a conscience is to be a *t'usa* [fighter]." In the innermost recesses of their hearts, the non-t'usa lived with the sense that they were sinners and were reviled by activist classmates (1994*a:* 147). It is this extreme righteousness that the "new generation" rejects.

Kim Chi-ha (1991: 5) also spoke out against this generation in response to a sudden succession of student activist suicides.[5] He charged that this generation of students—dressed in military fatigues and conducting militarylike meetings and demonstrations—glorified death and celebrated the disappearing ghost of militarism. After his criticism appeared in 1991, Kim was immediately dismissed from a number of dissident literary and activist organizations, in some of which he had even played a founding role. By the middle 1990s, however, we can see that Kim foretold new forms and aesthetics of activism.

Although sympathetic to the new generation's revulsion against the 1980s, Cho Haejoang is also sympathetic to the generation produced by the 1980s and praises their remarkable historical role: "Especially if you think of their parents' [the Korean War generation] enormous allergy for social movements, this generation is the one that promoted historical progress" (1994*a:* 146). She also laments the historical circumstances that produced their culture of dissent: the culture and educational system of military authoritarianism (1994*a:* 147). Their military-style education taught this generation to find the *right* answers and ironically imparted to them the military temperament that would later allow them to combat fearlessly and righteously these very institutions of oppression (1994*a:* 145, 147). With a clear enemy to *t'ado* (overthrow)—the military authoritarian regime—these students put their lives on the line. Cho (1994*a:* 149–150) laments that it was the 1980s movements' single-minded obsessions, exclusions, and righteous self-sacrifice that produced a 1990s "movement void": "[These movements] turned away from or even oppressed those contradictions that emerged from people's daily lives—so instead of readying people for the next era of social movements, they've silenced them." The new generation "has come to even hate the term 'social movement'" (Cho 1994*a:* 151).

In a 1994 editorial for the progressive weekly *Han'gyŏre 21,* "The New Generation and the Waterways of History," Kim Chong-ch'ŏl (1994: 112) writes about a young woman who told him, "These days it is really hard to do *tongari* [club] activities. When the new university students join the ideological circles [clubs] if anything seems even a bit above them or uninteresting, they immediately leave—it is really hard to sustain organizations. You can't get them to read ideological books, or fortify them with ideological arms." Kim (1994: 112) notes that in "our country and the world over" phrases like "history progresses" or "the history of humanity is a history of class struggle" have become the maxims of another age.

Students today arrive at campuses that are no longer the playing fields of the police. The campuses once again "belong to the students," who whir in consumer capitalism and employment preparation (Cho 1994a: 147). The posters of the Korean University Student Association Federation (Hanch'ongnyŏn, Han'guk Taehak Ch'ong Haksaenghoe Yŏnhap) that were once at the heart of campus life have become "part of the campus scenery" (Cho 1994a: 152). Cho describes this generation's "lighter feeling." Although many people have charged that this generation is more individualistic and even selfish, Cho (1994a: 152–153) argues that like their activist predecessors, they too are resisting. They ask "Why," not about military authoritarianism, but about "me" and they assert, "I don't want to do [this or] that." I think that Cho meant to say that their individualistic orientation itself is a resistance against the cultural and political matrix that fashioned their predecessors: military authoritarian schooling and childhood. Raised under "another order," they know little of the freedom or autonomy they would like to achieve. Their enemy, Cho (1994b: 200) declares, "is within themselves": "There is a huge distance between what they want to become, and what they are able to become."

Paek Uk-in, a prolific social commentator, extends Cho's analysis of university student generations to the broader social and cultural generational divide across the late 1980s watershed. He argues that South Korea has moved from the "age of politics" that peaked in the 1980s to "the age of culture." In a pithy shorthand, Paek (1993a: 28) notes, "This is no longer an age in which Im Su-gyŏng could become a heroine." Im, a college student movement activist who defied the National Security Law and traveled to North Korea in 1989 to participate in an international youth congress, was immediately imprisoned upon her return. Paek's (1993a: 28) "age of politics" was epitomized in the culture and lifestyle of the undongkwŏn, which ran on prohibition, restraint, and discipline. Society was restrained by ideology (1993a: 38) and governed by "[the] comparatively narrow frame of our kungmin's [state people] consciousness and lifestyle" (1993a: 25–26) and "ideals of discipline, frugality, industry, and unconditional obedience" (1993a: 42).

Paek (1993a: 26) points out that in the age of culture, youth has emerged as the "new generation," in contrast to their predecessors who were named for politics (e.g., the "4-1-9 generation"). The new generation instead distinguishes itself by its consumption and style—"leisure, sex, and beauty" (Paek 1993a: 38). Liberated from the homogenizing effects of totalitarian politics and revolutionary responses, the new generation reflects the "accelerated nuclear fission into various groups differentiated by ways of life, thought, and consciousness" (Paek 1993a: 25–26). Paek is less concerned than Cho about the lasting effects of military authoritarianism on this generation: "People are thinking now is the time to renounce ideologies which restrain you and to follow your desires" (1993a: 38). Paek's 1987 watershed is thus a constellation of clear dyadic transformations in step with Cho's characterizations: politics to culture, production to consumption/lifestyle, laborers to middle class, restraint to indulgence, homogeneity to diversity.

The articulations of simin undong (civil movements) rely on the same watersheds that are proclaimed for the new generation. As the students are fashioned in relation to undongkwŏn, citizens' movements are a complex response to, but not a full-fledged rejection of, minjung movements. In the first issue of the English-language journal of the Citizens' Coalition for Economic Justice (Kyŏngsillyŏn, Kyŏngje Chŏngŭi Silch'ŏn Simin Yŏnhap), the organization that is most widely considered to represent simin undong, a short interview declares a new era of social activism. Cho Woo-Hyun, the chairman of the organization's Policy Research Committee, is described this way: "He views civil activities from a pure perspective *without* ideology and has an interest only in living with ordinary citizens through grassroots civic movements." The text elaborates,

> Professor Cho *didn't* make his start as a labor activist. He *wasn't* even concerned about the labor issue at first. Rather, he majored in Labor Economics *by chance,* and the American traditional methodology he studied in the U.S. led him to analyze the Korean labor situation. Considering his age when he came to take practical interest in laborers, the word of a forerunner [*sic*] may *not* be proper in describing him. Nevertheless, he will not fall behind any forerunners with respect towards love of laborers. (Citizens' Coalition for Economic Justice 1994: 19; emphasis mine)

Although this description is a seemingly unremarkable portrait, the implicit markers distinguish civil from minjung movements. Cho's perspective is "pure" and "without ideology." Never self-fashioned as an "activist" or "forerunner," he is instead an "ordinary citizen" driven in a "new direction" by the "Laborers' Great Struggle of 1987–1988" (1994: 19). Minjung movements are by implication ideological, instrumental, tainted, and activist-centered.

The implicit criticisms of Cho, Paek, and the Kyŏngsillyŏn vita above call for a new sort of activism—what they call "new social movements," referring to many of the ideas and scholars discussed in chapter 1. Paek (1993a: 25–25, 45–49) predicts that production-based movements will not be able to sustain themselves as the paradigm shifts from production to consumption, and that movements will become fragmented to reflect the splintering interests of consumer and cultural identities.

Most articulators of simin movements, however, do not entirely dismiss minjung activism. This is not surprising because so many of them were active during the minjung era. Paek (1993*b*: 237–238), for example, chastises simin movements for ignoring minjung interests: "Simin movement organizations need to recognize humbly the limitations of the movement line that advocates operating within the system. Even if we sufficiently recognize the importance of simin movements' efforts to extend the space of *simin sahoe* [civil society] and to work within the system on policy formation, their long-term development will be thwarted because they exclude the interests of the minjung." He (1993*b*: 237–238) concedes that minjung movements need to take up the new spaces of protest, of daily life: "Minjung movements need to embrace . . . those spaces employed by the simin movement organizations and the regional movements that have drawn the attention and support of the taejung." Paek imagines that simin and minjung movements can coexist, learning from and even incorporating each other's interests and tactics.

In spite of her trenchant critique of the excesses of 1980s social activism, Cho Haejoang also champions a coexistence that she elaborates through the personal transformation of minjung activists into the 1990s.

> Our history will certainly begin anew if they [1980s activists] can continue to lead social movements, while becoming more introspective about their lives, recapturing their lost youths, repairing some of the chronic practices born in the elitism of their [historical] era's mission, and learning to love themselves a bit more. In this way, those who [in the 1980s] lived feeling inferior because they couldn't become fighters and who have a sharp historical consciousness can become an enormous latent citizen force. If social movements are lifelong ventures, then this generation now in their 30s must prepare themselves to lead society. (1994*a*: 155)

For 1980s activists, Cho encourages a more civil activism; for the "new generation," she counsels the need to escape the uniformity and groupism of their generation. They should search for a desirable society in—and fashion it through—their daily lives (1994*b*: 203).

Chŏng T'ae-sŏk also calls for coordinated simin-minjung movement efforts. He explains that before 1987, minjung and simin movements were indistinguishable because of their shared enemy: the military authoritarian regime. Although it has disappeared, he still argues for unity because of the ongoing national division that transcends class (Chŏng 1993: 199) and because if simin is to mean those people who have the right to legal freedoms and equality, then "we can say that minjung are simin" (Chŏng 1993: 204).

Ko Sŏng-guk, an activist-writer for a national policy research center, claims that the distinctions between minjung and simin movements are narrowly figured according to class. Simin movements charge that minjung movements are class based, and minjung movements respond that simin movements are only about the middle class. Minjung movements argue that South Korea is a class society and that the middle-class simin movements should also take up minjung interests (Ko 1993: 235), whereas simin movements reject the class epic of the minjung movements—"minjung as the great subjects of struggle" against the "ruling classes" (1993: 236). Ko (1993: 251) calls instead for kungmin or taejung movements that would transcend class-based distinctions. He uses "kungmin" to refer to the citizens of a modern state without the middle-class, urban connotations of "simin." Taejung, like minjung, refers to the masses in a grassroots sense but is less tainted by the ideological or activist underpinnings of minjung.

Not all 1990s activists, however, are ready to relinquish minjung terminologies or programs. In *Iron* (Theory), a journal that maintains the 1980s radical line, Kim Se-gyun (1993: 117) argues that simin is an "antiminjung" bourgeois social category. He advocates the struggle for a minjung society *outside* of the system (1993: 117) and he criticizes the distinction that simin movement activists make between "production" and "daily life" (1993: 120–121). Daily life, he maintains, has been and continues to be central to minjung movements (1993: 120–121). As for the contemporary crisis of minjung movements, he makes a distinction between movements in which minjung participate and those with revolutionary platforms. He asserts that the former—minjung movements at the "taejung movement level"—are not in danger, but that those at the "political movement level" are faltering (1993: 131). The task now, he insists, is to resist all impulses to join forces with the simin or new social movements (1993: 136).

Together these activists are responding—almost alarmingly—to the discursive shift that has rapidly repositioned minjung movements and a minjung imaginary to the margins. Excepting Kim Se-gyun, they all project a uniform culture of dissent across the 1987 divide when movements were united against the authoritarian state. This reckoning retrospectively records dissent from the bird's-eye view of the authoritarian state. For farmers' movements, these divides are certainly untidy. Lives spill over the divide, across these sea changes. I will now discuss nonghwal practices and discourses over this divide as a window on transformations "in the field."

THE NEW NONGHWAL?

Students' sense of nonghwal has shifted in accordance with their sense of changes in the student population and of the increasing autonomy of farmer activism. Much of this was not new to 1990s nonghwal; the contours of a dialogue with the past have in fact been continuous.

Let me begin with an anecdote from my 1993 return visit to Koch'ang.

I attended a planning session with college students and farmers for the upcoming summer nonghwal. I accompanied several farmers from Kŭmp'yŏng to the meeting, which was held some distance away at a deserted school. I found that the mood and sensibility of dissent that I have sketched in this book had changed. The charged atmosphere of the earlier covert nonghwal was gone. Students' romanticism of farmers had waned, as had farmers' idealization or fear of activist students. I was also struck by the more relaxed and less politically charged exchanges between students and farmers. Both groups seemed less susceptible to the stock characterizations of epic narratives, such as the student North Korean sympathizer, the selfless student revolutionary, the peasant revolutionary, the Communist peasant, and so on. Addressing the farmers and students, one nonghwal leader noted, "Nowadays many farmers quip that the students sent to their villages don't seem like undongkwŏn students. They don't seem sufficiently moral or upright. These days when farmers want to criticize nonghwal students this is what they say." Farmers and students alike roared with laughter, recognizing the remarkable change in political tides. But several years ago, undongkwŏn was a code word for North Korean–sympathizing revolutionary student activists, just the sort most farmers avoided. Here undongkwŏn had become a standard for students to live up to. The laughter also reflected the topsy-turvy circumstances in which farmers had become the primary activists and the arbiters of dissent. Farmers did not mince words: they were doing the educating. One farmer activist instructed the crowd: "The best way to create members for nongminhoe [farmers committees] is to be an exemplary farmer with extensive technical knowledge. For example, if you know a lot about greenhouses, after delivering lots of technical advice, with lots of nitty-gritty detail, you can suddenly add, 'By the way I'm a member'—that is how to instantly convert farmers." For the students' benefit, he added, "Don't think that it is only members [of nongminhoe] who have a ttŭt [a clear purpose]. In fact, that isn't the case at all. Rather it is often the nonmembers who have more ttŭt." Cho from Kŭmp'yŏng yelled out, "Yeah, in our village people aren't active, but it doesn't mean they don't have ttŭt at all. You shouldn't think that farmers don't know anything—they know a lot."

After these presentations the crowd splintered into village groups in which the student leaders of the upcoming nonghwal teams met with farmers from their assigned villages. Because the university department that would head for Kŭmp'yŏng was unrepresented that day, two students from other departments joined the farmers. By then tipsy from makkŏlli, Cho busily lectured the students about this and that, but they took little note. He seemed hardly to notice, but one farmer was quietly disappointed.

The farmer was Im, whom I knew well and at whose house I was staying. Earlier that morning he had wavered as to whether or not to attend, and early in the previous evening he had told a neighbor that he would not go. Im's wife had been perturbed at the neighbor for pressuring him to give up a day's work at such a busy time of the season. Although Im had supported the Koch'ang struggle, it was really his wife who had been the household's activist. Shy and sparing with words, Im had stood by quietly at most of the meetings in those days. Later in the evening prior to the nonghwal gathering, a young couple from a neighboring village dropped by to discuss the meeting. They were college graduates who had settled in a neighboring village to farm and to organize. Their visit reminded me of the exhilarating visits of activists who had brought news and excitement when I lived in Kŭmp'yŏng. Im's wife, who had earlier seemed miffed that her husband might attend the meeting the next day, perked up and scrambled to put out drinks and edibles. After the young couple left, we chatted briefly about them. Im and his wife worried that their inexperience with farming and inability to sustain hard labor—the husband was pale and thin, the wife about to have her first baby—would make it difficult for them to survive in the countryside. The young couple had rented a small plot and were trying to make a go of it as tenant farmers. I was surprised that they were renting a room in what had been during the Koch'ang struggle one of the most conservative villages—a small village far off the main path where almost everyone was related. They had moved there because that was where they had found a room. I learned that several activist couples who had settled in neighboring regions when I was living in Koch'ang had all left. Some left for other struggles; others gave up activism altogether. On the day of the meeting, Im and his wife were up early for field work, and by midmorning they had slaughtered a pig and were eating it with some neighbors. It was not clear when the young couple would arrive to fetch us, and Im again wavered as to whether or not to attend. His teenage daughter teased him, "Are you planning to go looking like that?" He washed up a bit and put on a fresh undershirt and long-sleeved shirt, and we all eventually set off with the young couple.

Im's disappointment about the absence of students was not surprising since his resolve to attend the meeting seemed to have gone unappreciated. After the village-level meetings the entire group reconvened for public introductions of a paired student and farmer from each village. Many of the introductions were humorous—especially when female students were paired with farming men—and at many points the crowd burst into laughter. Im, however, had by then drifted to the sidelines. So had another Kŭmp'yŏng farmer whom I was surprised to see at this gathering. He was one of the wealthiest and most educated men in the village and had taken no part in the Koch'ang struggle. After the introductions many students and farmers gathered for a pick-up game of softball, but many of the Kŭmp'yŏng farmers soon fell away from the activity. I joined the female students who had gathered with representatives from the local women's associations in a corner of the school grounds. The farming woman who led the meeting had just come from church—it was Sunday—and she complained about the many raucous and drunk farmers gathered there. When we returned to the village, Im's wife asked Im about the students who would come to the nonghwal that year and he muttered that the Kŭmp'yŏng students had not come—that it was something about their being busy studying for exams.

In contrast to Im's heavy mood, I was mostly impressed with the meeting's lightheartedness. There were no police or local officials lurking about and no fear of the sort that would have enveloped such a gathering only five or six years earlier. There was considerable talk about the mounting trade pressures from the United States—at many mentions of *migungnom* (a derogatory term for Americans), glances and smiles shifted in my direction—but it was not shrouded in the historical epics and drama of more minjung times. Nonetheless, it was clear that nonghwal was to abet farmer activism.

Student publications from the nonghwal organizations at Yonsei and Koryŏ universities and a 1993 nonghwal guidebook published by the Korean University Student Association Federation reveal the changing discourses and aesthetics of nonghwal for the new generation. In keeping with the Koch'ang anecdotes above, the new nonghwal was built on refashioned images of both students and farmers. Nonetheless, in these writings there are many features of earlier nonghwal that challenge the facile ways in which the 1980s–1990s divide is drawn.

Publications of the 1990s distinguish their nonghwal from the old and different nonghwal of their 1980s *sŏnbae* (seniors). One 1987 hakpŏn student who had come back to finish up college after his military service described "what comes to mind about the nonghwal of the past," including "the sound of seniors' scoldings," "dozens of rules and regulations," and "surveillance" (ANH 1993: 2). He wrote, "These are the things that occur to me long before anything about the importance of farmer and student solidarity" (ANH 1993: 2). He continued that nonghwal need not be the stuff of such painful memories but "enjoyable labor," "encouraging each other," and "fortifying our love for each other" (ANH 1993: 2). Furthermore, he cautioned that if the nonghwal labor is too difficult, students won't learn the "joy of labor" (ANH 1993: 2). As for the rules—dozens of which came to mind—"they should be applied on a premise of love and encouragement rather than of exclusion and rebuke" (ANH 1993: 2). Finally he declared, "Let's be proud of our members and pass these warm summer [nonghwal] days even more warmly" (ANH 1993: 2). A 1994 pamphlet noted, "When we hear about sŏnbae's nonghwal we think that times have changed, but that nonetheless we also do a great job at nonghwal"

(MKCH 1994: 12). Elaborating on images from the old nonghwal, they mentioned "not sleeping so as to labor harder," "not spilling a single grain of rice," "being encircled by the local police, village leaders, and even the county head," and "having to set up tents outside of the village and sneak in secretly to work" (MKCH 1994: 12).

The old nonghwal was also imagined according to what students assumed were very recent changes in villages. Many of these changes, including rural prosperity and farmers' awakened consciousness, shocked the students. A 1994 nonghwal pamphlet offered "the details of one student's nonghwal account" in order to consider how to "get beyond" the "old nonghwal thesis" (MKCH 1994: 7). One student reflected that with all of the recent economic problems with the agricultural sector, he had expected to find farmers "living even harder" but was surprised to see how well they lived—"drinking OB beer, serving coffee, and educating their children in the city" (MKCH 1994: 8). He conceded that although farmers were "somewhat excluded culturally," overall their lives were not so different from his own (MKCH 1994: 8). The students were thus cautioned that when preparing for nonghwal it is a mistake to imagine "your grandmothers' and grandfathers' era" (MKCH 1994: 9). They were told not to anticipate *toenjang* (a soup made from fermented soybeans that is considered a humble fare) in the fields but "*paekpan* (rice with many side dishes, considered an urban fare) taken out from restaurants and bread and beers at snack time in the fields" (MKCH 1994: 9). The pamphlet went on to explain that these culinary transformations were not signs of wealth but evidence that farm labor was in short supply in the countryside and that restaurant takeout was actually cheaper (MKCH 1994: 11). Furthermore, it stressed that villages are still marginal in their city-centered society (MKCH 1994: 11).

In the same way that the students cautioned against images of downtrodden farmers that they assumed were at the heart of their seniors' nonghwal, they also warned against romanticizing farmers' "community." Solidarity with farmers, they described, is extremely difficult to achieve if students maintain unrealistic images of them: "We have to get beyond the idea that farmers are only about groups . . . or that it is only about dark and hopeless existence. . . . From this nonghwal forward, let's think about the reality of their cultural life." They gave the example that it is unreasonable to visit the villages expecting women to be singing traditional *minyo* (folk songs) when it is pop music that they really enjoy (MKCH 1994: 44).

As for farmers' consciousness, the student from the "personal account" above wrote, "Farmers know exactly what they are faced with [agricultural policy, GATT, etc.]. . . . I didn't conscientize them. Instead it was me who went there and learned" (MKCH 1994: 8). One of the new nonghwal's slogans similarly proclaimed, "Let's move beyond the old '*minjung yŏndae* [solidarity]'." As one student put it, "Nonghwal isn't about imparting one or another political ideology, or about a struggle to conscientize or organize farmers. It is about university students being reborn as organic intellectuals through a new experience" (MKCH 1994: 8).

Some reflections, however, highlighted their debt to the old nonghwal. A senior in 1994 wrote, "Before farmers didn't welcome nonghwal, but thanks to the struggle of those before us, they do now" (MKCH 1994: 3). Students also reflected that the unpalatable rules and restraints of past nonghwal were in step with their times. They were times of "violent politics" and "direct suppression" when "just to form a farmers' committee (nongminhoe) was to be treated like a ppalgaengi (red)": "Our seniors fought together with farmers just to be able to establish these committees. They had to appear very upright, and it was of necessity that they reflected on and were criticized for their mistakes" (MKCH 1994: 12).

Students articulated concrete perspectives and programs in accordance with their understanding of changed circumstances. At the heart of the self-proclaimed "new nonghwal" was a refashioned vision of "student and farmer solidarity." The solidarity was to be less total, less romantic, and more mutually instrumental. They acknowledged the fundamental divides between farmers and students but explained that their brief interactions are mutually serviceable for strengthening both student and farmer activist groups. This instrumental approach acknowledged that students' village presence can promote the farmers committees but entertained little romance of "conscientizing" farmers. In this sense they imagined a transformed minjung. As for fortifying the student groups, the new nonghwal was less convinced that the experience of farm labor or the exposure to the lives of South Korea's dispossessed alone would enhance their organization or activities. Rather, they argued that nonghwal offers students the chance to get away together and to strengthen friendship and solidarity. Here nonghwal is rendered more like a summer camp. "You should be able to feel the hand of the student committee [haksaenghoe] in the rich human relations" (HTCHY 1993: 3).

In their discussions of student and farmer solidarity, students began with reappraisals of the minjung: "First let's throw out the question, is it only the fighting minjung who are the minjung?" (MKCK 1994: 9). The minjung conjures images of "striking laborers" and "dying farmers," "but in fact the concept of minjung refers to all of us who in the course of living encounter contradictions. . . . Isn't the fact that it is poor people who come to mind when we think of minjung a sign of our elitism? . . . Aren't all of our parents who struggle so hard to pay our school fees minjung? Or the people who clean and manage [the campus] for us—aren't they minjung? . . . Before we leave for nonghwal we have to think of ourselves as minjung" (MKCH 1994: 9). Earlier nonghwal students were similarly committed to becoming minjung, but in their reckonings it was the *struggle* against the contradictions that was defining.

Nevertheless, even though the students declared everyone minjung, they wrote of farmer suffering and of the real differences between students and farmers, not unlike their 1980s sŏnbae: "Even if we talk about solidarity, the positions are different. Farmers experience the contradictions directly. They are its subjects. Students experience them [the contradictions] only indirectly and go to many efforts to solve them. . . . The reality is that it is difficult for students to be the direct subjects of agricultural policy" (MKCH 1994: 11). And students still wrote about farmer suffering and hardship.

The solidarity of the new generation was to be less political: "Extend the attention you have given and your attachment to your own [new generation] lives . . . to your minjung siblings" (MKCH 1994: 13). "[Nonghwal] isn't necessarily about anything political. You can talk to farmers about each and every aspect of life, and you can point out contradictions. . . . Go ahead and show them your personal style. Build even greater trust with farmers. . . . Let's show them [farmers] the kindness of the new generation" (MKCH 1994: 13). Similarly they warned against unnecessary "goal consciousness," which inhibited student–farmer relations: "Don't overdo it with the political talk" (MKCH 1994: 39). This instrumental solidarity was fashioned according to nonghwal's real benefits for farmer and student organizing. Students wrote that nonghwal is not about "service" but that it could be used to extend their experience beyond the campus (MKCH 1994: 10). Through nonghwal, student groups would also become more *taejungjŏk* (popular) (MKCH 1994: 11). Although hopeful about nonghwal's potential for student organizing, students cautioned that it shouldn't be too purposive: " 'Let's strengthen the student committee' can't become our slogan" (MKCH 1994: 12).

Nongminhoe, students imagined, are strengthened when they "leave a good impression" (MKCH 1994: 11). In this spirit the students cautioned that in the villages they must be constantly mindful of what might seem trifling details—that "even when taking a rest you must take note of who is around you" (MKCH 1994: 11). One pamphlet said that "nonghwal shouldn't be an activist space in which students are the proxy for farmers but . . . an activist space for autonomous farmers committees" (HTCY 1993: 4). In a similar vein, a farmer's detailed account of nonghwal in 1991 reminded students that because they do not understand the "reality" of farming villages, they have a narrow sense of the impact of their visits: "It isn't that any single person decided to join the farmers committee because of the students, but their visit still strengthened the farmers committee" (Kim S. 1991: 146).

In keeping with this softened student-farmer solidarity, there were new ideas about a more egalitarian and democratic nonghwal organization. *Kyuyul* (rules), a long discussion argued, should be about "attitudes or perspectives of life" rather than constraint, interference, or control (MKCH 1994: 33). Rules are to be deliberated and decided on together "with love" (MKCH 1994: 33): "Why doesn't the [Nonghwal] Preparation Committee after the first day of nonghwal meet with the trustworthy nonghwal members and together debate and decide on the rules? You can call the rules a 'lesson of love' and hang them where you are staying" (MKCH 1994: 34). Sŏnbae were instructed not to intimidate their *hubae* (juniors): "When you are together with the farmers you must draw out the juniors to speak" (MKCH 1994: 39). The new nonghwal was also supposed to be more fun. Students were reminded that it isn't just the farmers who need special activities. They recommended games for a healthy "group life" (MKCH 1994: 41).

Unimaginable in 1980s nonghwal maxims were the many calls for student-student friendship—quite different from 1980s "comrades in struggle": "Ten days is a really long time for getting to know each other. . . . You can't always be put together or made-up for ten days" (MKCH 1994: 41). One pamphlet made the following appeal:

All of you near to me, my *tongji* [friends] . . . if you have a friend for whom you still have a bit of a prickly feeling somewhere in your heart, then work with them during nonghwal. Just as you will have a valuable experience [through nonghwal], how about taking an interest in what that friend is feeling, in what [nonghwal] has awakened in them? During these ten days together, let's strengthen our relationships. (ANH 1993: 1)

Calling for more fun, friendship, and less romanticism of farmers' hardship, the new nonghwal downplayed the importance of students' farm labor. If nonghwal was narrowly focused on participation in farm labor, as they imagined it had been in the past, it would be a paltry affair: "Students would say, 'Me too, I did labor'—and farmers would reflect, 'There wasn't much work for students to do' " (MKCH 1994: 11). Rhetorically, they asked, "If you go to nonghwal how would you feel about just laboring and getting evaluated?" and urged, "Let's not make it 'Nonghwal! memories of tedious labor' " (MKCH 1994: 41). Students were also warned not to overwork because "there is much more to nonghwal than labor" (MKCH 1994: 32). Yet 1990s nonghwal notes still waxed enthusiastic on field work: "It is wonderful for farmers to know that their experience of pain [through labor] is not unrelated to your existence. . . . Getting to know people through labor is different from relating to a friend—but what an experience to be praised for your labor!" (HTCY 1993: 1).

As we have seen, many aspects of 1980s nonghwal and minjung sensibilities have been disrupted. Farmer and student solidarity is to be forged not on the basis of unified engagements with the past and shared social visions but on an understanding of mutual reinforcement. Nonghwal is not to be modeled after images of a communitarian rural village but fashioned in accordance with the vicissitudes of 1990s youth culture. Nonghwal is not to be the drab labor of personal sacrifice and restraint or the training ground for broad-based social dissent, but a colorful space where farmers might listen to pop songs and students can play games. Nonetheless, although students no longer consider farmers to be organic revolutionaries or duped masses, farmers are still symbols of hard labor and relative dispossession. What has changed, however, is the realization that students do not have the rights to or the responsibilities for farmers' struggles. These distinctions run parallel with the distinctions between minjung and simin movements. In the same way that the simin concept defines a fragmented space for middle-class dissent that is not articulated in a national imaginary such as minjung, the new nonghwal self-consciously delimits its own autonomy from farmers or epics about them. Nevertheless, it is not entirely divorced from the legacy of minjung representations. Similarly, the minjung-simin distinctions are never fully drawn. These various declarations of the new era are distinctions both drawn against and in part delineated by the older discourses and dialogues.

KOCH'ANG ACTIVISTS INTO THE 1990S

Let me walk across the 1980s–1990s watershed through a brief revisit in 1993 to the modest network and remote landscape of the movement I examined from 1987 to 1988. I was struck by the messiness of this case— that the facts seemed both to endorse and to defy easy periodization. Revisits are encounters with a constellation of barometers; one measures change across the biographies or the landscapes one knows best. These meetings, however, were in no way singularly emblematic of the times. That none of these farmers were active in movements focused on the impending GATT negotiations in no way negates the escalating struggles of this era or reveals a particular local trend.

After decades of full-time activism, one of the central "external activists" from the CFU, Pae, had taken a high position in a new company committed to manufacturing food products from only homegrown (South Korean) grains. As he handed me his name card and fax number, he laughed at the seeming incongruity of his new status—the activist gone corporate. He had since split up with his wife—"I liberated her"—and he reflected that his years of activism, the spiral of his dissent, had diminished her confidence and autonomy. Remembering that his wife had been an ardent supporter of the activities in Koch'ang and an activist leader in her own right, I paused at this news and its obvious resonance with the response of the second wave of U.S. feminism to the gender inequalities in the civil rights and New Left movements. Since I had last seen him, Pae had arranged for his aging mother to return to South Korea from Chicago where she and many of his relatives had been living for decades. He escorted me to a mountainous Buddhist retreat, which he had built with funds from a wealthy local physician whom he met when he was recovering from a near-fatal car crash. That day he introduced me to two visitors—both men who had passed much of the 1970s and 1980s in prison—who were there to rest and reflect. At this retreat nestled in beautiful hills at some distance from the nearest city, Pae looks forward to quieter times in which 1980s activists can gather for reflection, meditation, and the achievement of personal as well as political goals. Although he was, as I had fondly remembered him, spirited and energetic, these new guises—the corporate position and the religious retreat—bespoke new activisms and new sensibilities.

Cha, who some years earlier had briefly attended a regional university and had begun his activist career with the tenant movement, was now a newlywed farmer. During 1987 and 1988, he had been constantly frightened by the admonitions of the elders of his conservative kinship village and by the threats from local authorities. In 1993 we met at a cramped and busy lunch place in downtown Seoul where he unabashedly raised his voice about the ongoing political and economic injustices in South Korea, complaining that the so-called civilian government wasn't at all civil. I found his brazen tone and newfound confidence unbelievable. In the interim years he had become very active in the county farmers' committee. He had also worked on and off as a factory laborer in Seoul and had become involved in a national organization devoted to the "marriage problem" of rural men. His new wife, a university graduate, Seoulite, and former student activist, had agreed—against the demographic grain—to settle in his village where his family "modernized" their farmhouse for her auspicious arrival. Although this marriage reminded me of those that some female student activists made in the 1980s, this case seemed different. There was no formal resolve about politicizing the village or strengthening the local farmers' committee. In a different vein, in keeping with the lifestyle orientation of simin movements and the "individualistic" flavor of the sinsedae, Cha talked at great length about the sort of marriage and family he wanted to have. Defying all cultural norms, especially in a conservative kinship village, he and his wife are determined to have only one child, girl or boy.

Furthermore, he has already decided to send the child into the nearby hills alone to teach her or him self-reliance. He will never, he explained, indulge his child as he had been indulged as the youngest son and the one designated to stay back in the countryside to care for his parents.[6] He wants a free-spirited, independent child and that sort of marriage as well. This domestic vision, like his forthright political denunciations, would have been unthinkable several years earlier. Indeed, the entire constellation—his marriage to a former student activist, his confident political proclamations, and his vision for the next generation—revealed social and personal transformations entirely at odds with the moment in which I had come to know Cha.

Song had been one of the most ardent activists. One of the poorest farmers in his village, he bragged at length about his self-sacrificing activities in the movement and about his current experiments with organic farming. He explained that he continues to relinquish profits for social struggle—this time for environmental activism. He chuckled about the ironic fortune of the Chŏlla provinces: although the northwestern coast was impoverished because it missed out on state development programs, it was spared the environmental destruction of the rest of South Korea: "How lucky we are to have been excluded." Song repeated stories that he had told me many times before about his natural intelligence and his youthful cunning. With a different birth, he went on, he would be the equal of any elite today. He then launched into stories about his recent negotiations with professors and middle-class people in Seoul over his state-of-the-art organic farming. Remembering Song's irreverent manner and his ardent participation in demonstrations all over Seoul during the Samyang protests, it was interesting to see that he had settled into new dissent as he cultivated his garden.

Finally, I met Oh, an English major, who after graduation settled in a rural village with her boyfriend for farming and farmer organizing. Her boyfriend, an activist from the early 1980s who had served a prison term for antigovernment activities, grew tired of the slow-paced rewards of rural activism. The couple decided to return to Seoul despite the derision of local activists who condemned them for deserting the cause and making it impossible to organize that village in future years. The costs of personal decisions like this one recall the 1990s image of 1980s dissent—its rules, lack of charity, and hard edges. I was with Oh at a Seoul café in 1988, when she briefly left the table to join activists sitting nearby. It was painful even for me to overhear them denounce her "selfish" departure from the countryside. Back in Seoul, her boyfriend returned to organizing workers in small-sized firms, which had been overlooked in the 1987 labor struggles. She began teaching English and organizing at a neighborhood night school (*yahak*) for workers of all ages. By 1993, the couple had married, purchased a small apartment in a working-class neighborhood in Seoul, and given birth to a daughter. Her husband, who had never finished college after his imprisonment, was taking classes to finish up his degree. He planned to graduate and obtain a teacher's certificate so that he could someday earn a regular salary and continue political activities on the side. Oh entrusted her daughter to her mother—visiting only on Thursdays and picking her up for the weekends—and continued to teach at the night school. The students included the wives of laborers, laborers, and some middle-class housewives eager to learn English at no charge. By 1993, the 1980s divides between working and middle classes had blurred somewhat and it had become harder for Oh to recognize the minjung in this crowd.[7] Many people at that time had noticed that the cafés in working-class neighborhoods were no longer so different from those in rich enclaves and that laboring women had acquired the consumption tastes of the middle class.[8]

Oh worries about where she is going with these activities. She frets that teaching English is becoming not the means to other political discussions and activism but simply the end in itself. She mused that perhaps she is merely imparting bourgeois cultural capital. She is also concerned about her own forfeited postgraduate studies. She thinks about studying abroad, but her family responsibilities and financial situation seem to preclude this. She is debating which credentials or "employable skills" might best carry her into the future. Their adjustment to the new era is neither the culture of the new generation, nor of simin movements, nor the old epics and activisms.

In these brief encounters with Pae, Cha, Song, and Oh, there are glimpses of new spaces and aesthetics of dissent but also of old imaginaries. In keeping with the waning of the minjung imaginary, Pae has turned his attention to the external activists themselves—a community in transition. For Oh, the raison d'être of a night school has become much less clear. Farmers Song and Cha articulate their own activism on new fronts: organic farming, family structure, and child-rearing practices. Dissent of the 1980s maps an era against which aspects of the present are reckoned, such as the personal costs of 1980s activism for Pae and the long-term effects of personal sacrifice for Oh. The brief vignettes explored here suggest the sorts of discursive articulations that will fashion generational "positions" of dissent.[9]

EPOCHS AND EPICS

I have briefly explored the transformed discursive contexts of dissent. The historicization of the 1980s—the marking of an epoch—inscribes the epics of today's dissent. These are not, however, complete or total; the epochs are variously rendered and porous, and the epics are heterogeneous, emergent, and dialogic. People meander past the divides, fashioning their lives and activisms in the shifting milieu. No doubt the decade will settle variously across diverse cohorts and be fashioned anew at the hands of multiple interests, and in the play of memory and the imaginary. It is such plays of memory, the imaginary, and interests that this book has traversed.

I began this book's discussion of the Koch'ang Tenant Farmers Movement by attempting to set it discursively in an epic—of minjung—that was pervasive at a particular historical moment. I took up minjung as a dialogue with the past that contextualized the politics and practices of dissent. Through this ethnography of a social movement, I have tried to show that movements are best examined as processes that emerge in the cultural idioms, historical aesthetics, and material reality of particular historical moments. As I suggested in chapter 1, this ethnography is—finally—not a documentary of the movement but an attempt to sketch its discursive, idiomatic, and temporal contours. The story is unruly, as I warned it would be. I hope, however, that it reveals something about the making of dissent and the fashioning of social activists. Throughout the book, I have tried to suggest that dissent is always an engagement with the past. The past echoes in the epics of dissent; and from these epics new epochs emerge.

APPENDIX 1

CHRONOLOGY

1894	Tonghak Peasant Revolution.
1910–1945	Japanese colonial period.
1924	First Samyang agricultural estate, Changang, in Chŏlla Province.
1931–1933	Samyang reclamation project in Sŏnbul District, Hamp'yŏng County, South Chŏlla Province.
1936	Haeri reclamation project begun; finished in 1938.
1946	Samyang receives permission to make salt fields at the Haeri Agricultural Estate. Construction begun in 1947, completed in 1949.
1949	Kim Yŏn-su appears before the Committee to Punish Anti-National Violations.
	Land Reform Act promulgated; finalized in 1950.
June 25, 1950	Korean War begins; continues to 1953.
October 1, 1951	10-1 Incident at the Haeri Agricultural Estate.
1955	Land struggle at the Haeri Agricultural Estate.
May 1980	Kwangju Uprising.
May 13, 1987	First trial of tenants who did not pay their rents in Chŏngŭp, North Chŏlla Province.
June 10, 1987	Democratization Revolt in Seoul.
June 23, 1987	Yun, head of the Relinquish Committee, gives an address at a rally in Chŏnju, North Chŏlla Province.
June 29, 1987	Roh Tae Woo announces democratic reforms, including an open election for the presidency.
August 12, 1987	Last trial of tenants who did not pay rents in Chŏngŭp, North Chŏlla Province.

August 12, 1987	Midnight, farmers enter the Samyang headquarters in Seoul.
August 13, 1987	Farmers meet the press and the landlords.
	First negotiation session.
August 15, 1987	First article on the farmers' struggle appears in *Dong-A Daily;* farmers begin to protest against the newspaper for distortion of facts.
	Song-and-dance protests begin.
	Yun visits Seoul National University to ask students for side-line support.
August 16, 1987	Taehangno Incident begins.
	Second negotiation session.
August 19, 1987	Protest at *Dong-A Daily* headquarters.
August 20, 1987	Samyang guard hits farmer.
August 21, 1987	Second article appears in *Dong-A Daily.*
	Third negotiation session.
August 23, 1987	Fourth negotiation session.
August 24, 1987	Attempted Murder Incident.
August 25, 1987	3:00 P.M., the company gates are opened.
August 26, 1987	Fifth negotiation session.
August 27, 1987	Farmers hold prayer service for wounded students.
	Sixth negotiation session.
August 31, 1987	General assembly of farmers, straw vote taken on land price.
September 1, 1987	Reenactment of the Attempted Murder Incident.
September 2, 1987	Farmer contingent occupies the office of Kim Sang-hyŏp, president emeritus of Koryŏ University.
September 5, 1987	Seventh negotiation session.
September 6, 1987	Eighth negotiation session.
September 7, 1987	Formal split of the farmers at a general assembly at the Samyang headquarters.
	Contingent of farmers dig up grave of Kim Sŏng-su in Seoul.
September 11, 1989	Farmers sign a purchase contract.

APPENDIX 2

THE COLONIAL PERIOD NORTH CHŎLLA PROVINCE, PEASANT PROTEST, AND SAMYANG

Colonial period North Chŏlla Province stands out for its high levels of Japanese landownership, tenancy, contractualization, and peasant dissent.

With its good farmland, particularly rice paddy, North Chŏlla was the object of Japanese interest; the Japanese Oriental Development Company sponsored more immigration to North Chŏlla than to any other province (Pak 1985: 99). By 1938, 20 percent of the Oriental Development Company's land was concentrated in North Chŏlla. In 1918, Japanese landlords held 5.4 percent of land nationwide, but in North Chŏlla they controlled 21 percent (Pak 1985: 99).

In the early 1930s the percentage of tenant farmers in North Chŏlla was the highest in the country (Pak 1985: 92–94). In 1943, the percentage of owner-cultivators—nonlandlords who owned more than 90 percent of the land they worked—was 5.1 percent, lowest among all the provinces (national average: 17.6%). Part-owners—farmers who owned 50 to 90 percent of the land they worked—also constituted the lowest percentage in North Chŏlla, at 10.1 percent (national average: 15.9%). Tenants, full tenants, and those owning 10 to 50 percent of the land they worked also made up the highest percentage at 81.1 percent (national average: 65%) (Cumings 1981: 283).

Also high in North Chŏlla were the levels of landlord-tenant written contracts (74% compared to 27% nationwide), which made tenants vulnerable to landlord exploitation (Pak 1985: 95–98). As large estates and the Oriental Development Company claimed much of the farmland, word-of-mouth tenant arrangements became contractualized. Pak (1985: 106) argues that high rates of contractual tenancy made it easier to shift the sojakkwŏn (tenant rights) from one peasant to another: "Traditionally existing tenant rights were completely denied by written contracts, leaving tenants powerless if the landlord canceled these rights." By the 1930s, tenants' demands for lower rent were secondary to protests against the transfer of tenant rights (*sojakkwŏn idong*); at that time 82 percent of disputes nationwide concerned such transfers (Pak 1985: 106).

The nature of the rental agreements affected peasant well-being as well. In North Chŏlla Province most rents were fixed; that is, the amount to be remitted was set (Pak 1985: 95). There were three systems of rent remittance: *t'ajopŏp*, in which farmers remitted a portion of the harvest, usually 50 percent; *chŏngjopŏp*, in which farmers remitted a fixed rent; and *chibohopŏp*, in which farmers remitted a fixed percentage of their crop, the extent of which was determined before harvest. In Haeri, Samyang began with t'ajopŏp and over time shifted to chibohopŏp. Pak (1985: 96–98) argues that with chibohopŏp landlords were able to manipulate the rates to their advantage. In the early 1930s in North Chŏlla, 6 percent of arrangements were t'ajopŏp, 45 percent chŏngjopŏp, and 40 percent chibohopŏp.

In North Chŏlla, tenant disputes were most active in those counties with many large Japanese landlords, including Kimje, Chŏnju, Chŏngŭp, and Iksan (Pak 1985: 109). In addition to protesting the transfer of rents, tenants also rose up against the marŭm (landlord stewards), who were typically paid a certain percentage of rents and thus shared an interest in landlord profits (Pak 1985: 106). North Chŏlla tenants also protested against the institutions of the colonial state. Police stations and estate offices were attacked as organs representing the colonial government (Pak 1985: 108). Pak (1985: 101) argues that in colonial North Chŏlla "class and national problems converged" and peasant movements were both antilandlord and anti-Japanese. More than in any other region, the province's peasant movements "most clearly demonstrate the character and limits of peasant movements of that time" (Pak 1985: 92).

In spite of such conditions, peasant protest organizations in North Chŏlla were relatively scarce (Pak 1985: 113). In 1933, for example, although there were 1,301 peasant movement units nationwide (93,079 peasants), in North Chŏlla Province there were only nine movement units (1,542 peasants) (Pak 1985: 113). Outside instigators, particularly those who had studied abroad in Japan or had participated in independence movements in Manchuria, worked largely in Seoul and in the northern provinces (Pak 1985: 114). Pak (1985: 114) suggests that because of the high tenancy rates, there were fewer middle-class farmers who could play central roles in peasant movements and organizations. In addition, Japanese landlords with large holdings were skillful at thwarting peasant dissent, and the control mechanisms of the agricultural estate mediated against organized activity; prevalent instead was spontaneous action independent of organizations, which Pak calls "proto-organization activity" (Pak 1985: 114). Bruce Cumings (1981: 284–286) similarly points out that "landlord authority in regions of high tenancy can constitute a simple but formidable structure of restraint, especially when buttressed by mobile national policing apparatuses," and that "radicalism is inversely related to tenancy." In his analysis of peasant activism after liberation, Cumings (1981: 280) argues that North Chŏlla was among the less active provinces because of the intensity of state controls: "The committees in North Chôlla, a province well-laced with roads and railroads, were easily deposed" (Cumings 1981: 281).

In these contexts, what sort of colonial landlords were the Koch'ang Kims? Kim Yong-sŏp (1987), the foremost scholar of the Korean landlord-tenant system, completed a study of the early holdings of the Koch'ang Kims which reveals the character of these landlords.[1] Kim analyzed the rent records of Kim Sŏng-su's adopted father, Kim Ki-jun, from 1918 to 1924. Kim Sŏng-su's land included plots in Koch'ang County. In 1924, the end of the period Kim Yong-Sŏp surveyed, the Kim family had organized its first nongjang—the Changsŏng Estate. He maintains that the shift to the nongjang system, which spurred increases in rice production, was indicative of the Kims' collaboration with the Japanese.

Kim Yong-sŏp (1978: 114) sums up the management techniques of the farmer estates as follows: (1) increasing the percentage of those paying fixed rent, (2) making farmers pay land and water tax, (3) effecting a quick turnover of farming rights, and (4) decreasing the percentage payments to the managers and changing them frequently. The estate structure intensified the early management techniques that the Kims had employed (Kim 1978: 89). From 1918 to 1924, in what Kim calls "the greatest violence committed by landlords," farming rights were transferred in 58.84 percent of the cases. Fixed rents were established in 30.16 percent of the cases, percentage rents in 69.84 percent of the cases. Kim (1978: 96) argues that because fixed rents were more advantageous for landlords, over time they increased this form of rental arrangement.

APPENDIX 3

REGIONAL PARTICIPATION IN THE MOVEMENT

Here I will review how several parameters correlated with participation in the movement across the entire region.[1] I will refer to two figures: figure C-1 provides a list of the natural villages according to their administrative village and district, indicating the proportion of tenant households in each village; figure C-2 lists the villages in descending order of the percentage of the village population that signed the 1986 agreement not to remit rents to Samyang.[2]

Taken together, figures C-1 and C-2 demonstrate that the percentage of tenant households/total households is positively correlated with the intensity of participation (see fig. C-2, column 8). Also correlated in this fashion is the percentage of paddy/total land (see fig. C-2, column 9). The figures, however, reveal a number of discrepancies. Several factors explain them, including the village's relationship to the leadership of the movement; the village's relationship to the corporation (including proximity); and the village's settlement pattern. Below are notes on some of the villages that begin to explain the discrepancies in figure C-2, as well as offer additional information on the participation of various villages.

Poktong was a predominately single-surname kinship village in which the tenant farmers were united in their participation. At the Tongho gathering (see chap. 6), for example, the entire village participated. Nineteen Koryŏ University students settled in one village home for nonghwal.

In **Chukkok** approximately 20 percent of households were pure tenants. They hosted a very large and successful nonghwal in which seventy students stayed in the village hall.

Figure C-1: Tenant Household/Total Household in Samyang Tenant Villages

	Tenant household (n=)	Total household (n=)	%
Haeri-myŏn			
Kŭmp'yŏng-ri [1]			
Myŏnggo [2]	65	80	81
Yonghodong	17	36	47
Moktong	20	25	80
Wŏlsan	20	23	93
Tongho-ri			
Sindongho	30	60	50
Sinhŭngdong	14	16	87
Kajaji	25	30	83
Ansan-ri			
Poktong	13	21	61
Ansan	60	60	100
P'alhyŏngch'i	15	20	75
Pangch'uk-ri			
Pangch'uk	N/A	N/A	N/A
Manhwa	N/A	N/A	N/A
Simwŏn-myŏn			
Kungsan-ri	52	60	86
Chusan-ri			
Chukkok	100	120	83
Kisan-Sinbang	28	32	87
Kojŏn-ri			
Chinju	37	42	88
Yedong	7	17	41
Yŏmjŏn	N/A	N/A	N/A
Kojŏn	77	90	85
Mandŏl-ri			
Chŏngdong	65	75	86

Source: Based on 1988 household surveys for Kŭmp'yŏng and Kungsan and on interviews and written materials for the other villages.

[1] Administrative village.

[2] Natural village.

Figure C-2: Regional Movement Participation

	1 Haeri (H) or Simwŏn (S)	2 % signatures/ total household	3 % signatures/ tenant household	4 (n=)	5 % participation/ total household	6 % participation/ tenant household	7 (n=)	8 % tenant households / total household	9 % paddy/total land [2]
Poktong	H	56	84	11	57	92	12	61	62
Kungsan	S	48	51	27	85	85	41	86	95
Chukkok	S	46	56	56	41	50	50	83	N/A
Moktong	H	44	55	11	36	50	9	80	80
Chinju	S	40	45	17	N/A	N/A	N/A	88	60
P'alhyŏngch'i	H	35	35	7	nearly all tenant households	nearly all tenant households	75	76	N/A
Pangch'uk [1]	H	35	85	13			N/A	N/A	N/A
Myŏnggo	H	18	22	15	46	59	26	81	66
Kojŏn	S	17	17	16	0	0	0	85	30
Tongho [1]	H	12	10	11	N/A	N/A	N/A	65	7
Yonghodong	H	8	17	3	30	64	11	47	50
Yŏmjŏn	S	0	0	0	0	0	0	N/A	95
Ansan	H	0	0	0	0	0	0	100	76
Wŏlsan	H	0	0	0	8	10	2	86	70
Kisan-Sinbang	S	0	0	0	50	57	16	87	40
Yedong	S	0	0	0	very few	very few	very few	14	60
Chŏngdong	S	0	0	0	0	0	0	86	15

Source: Based on 1988 household surveys for Kŭmp'yŏng and Kungsan and on interviews and written materials for the other villages.

[1] The figures for these administrative villages are not broken down into their natural villages.

[2] Paddy (*non*) refers to land on which rice is cultivated.

The people I spoke with characterized **Moktong** as one of the poorer of the Samyang villages. It was a multisurname village from which many people had departed to Seoul in recent years. Few families had been able to educate their children beyond middle school. Eight of the villagers were pure tenants with plots under one hectare. A nonghwal team stayed in one of the village's deserted homes.

The numbers for the natural village **Pangch'uk** are somewhat uncertain because it was hard to gather whether they also referred to the administrative village's (also called Pangch'uk) second natural village, Manhwa. Tucked in the hills, Pangch'uk was more secluded than most of the other Samyang villages and there were many elderly residents. This village also hosted a successful nonghwal. No one in the village worked for Samyang and the plots were generally small, averaging 700 p'yŏng. It appeared that most of the tenants stayed in Seoul for the duration of the protest; even the wife of the village head joined for a period. Many of the farmers in this village were dissatisfied with the terms of the settlement.

The signatures for the natural village **Kojŏn** might have also included some from Yedong, another of the administrative village's (also called Kojŏn) natural villages. The small percentage of tenant land/total land in part explains the lack of participation; it is, however, also important to note that their tenant plots were made only in the late 1960s when Samyang converted some salt field land into paddy. The paddy tenant rights were, I learned, distributed to those who had helped in the senatorial campaign of one of the members of the Samyang Kim family. Most of those people had immediately sold their tenant rights. The village's paddy, farthest from the reservoir and nearest to the sea, continued to be difficult to irrigate. The village head explained the lack of participation: "It would have been sinful for us to participate because it had only been a short while since the land had become paddy." He explained that historically the reclamation had been detrimental for the village because it had ruined thriving salt production at the time.

The figures for **Tongho** would have been easier to interpret had they been broken down according to the natural villages comprising this administrative village: Kajaji, Sinhŭngdong, and Sindongho. Most of the signatures were in fact from Kajaji and Sinhŭngdong, thus representing larger percentages of those villages than the figures reveal. A number of the key CFU members were from these two villages. Both of these villages were Samyang settlement villages, made up of immigrants who came to the region to work on the reclamation project and to farm the new paddy. They were thus multisurname villages in which the members shared similar life trajectories and economic levels. One of Kajaji's most active movement participants said, "This isn't really a village—it is just a place to which people fled and depended on Samyang. . . . There are no rich people here."

Many people characterized Kajaji as the poorest of the Samyang villages, in which few people continued their schooling beyond middle school. Interestingly, the village was the home of one of the few Christian churches in the region. Many Kajaji villagers had worked as laborers for Samyang, particularly in the carrying and lifting section of the salt fields where there had been considerable efforts at unionizing. Sinhŭngdong held out longest of all the villages in each of the rent boycotts, and its residents were the last to be able to purchase their land because they were required to settle their debts (from the boycotts) before purchase. In the end, they secured special loans in addition to the general purchase loans in order to be able to afford the purchase.

Yonghodong was a multisurname village that had dwindled in size considerably since the 1960s. The village had only one Samyang laborer. The village was relatively poor. Of the 11 household representatives in Seoul, 6 were women. There had been no nonghwal. The village head also participated in the movement.

Ansan was one of the wealthiest villages in the region. Its members joined neither as signers nor as participants in Seoul. The average landholdings were about 4,000 p'yŏng; a large percentage of the youth completed high school and some even went on to college. None of the villagers worked at the salt fields. Much of the tenant land of this village was reservoir plots, and because the purchase of such plots was impossible there was little incentive to participate.

Wŏlsan was unique for its high percentage of owner paddy land. A largely single-surname village, it was economically quite homogeneous. The village's most ardent participant was a member of another surname, and it is interesting that he departed for Seoul shortly after the protest there. The village youth were pressured not to participate because of the many white-collar workers who commuted to the company from the village. The nonggujang, not a member of the dominant surname, explained the lack of participation in this way: "In our hearts we supported the movement, but we didn't let people know. . . . We didn't understand the 'no-compensation' claim—we have a conscience—one can't just take others' land." There was no nonghwal in this village and thus no participation in the Tongho festival.

It is possible that no signatures are listed for **Kisan-Sinbang** because they were included under Chukkok. The village head was a key leader in the movement. Also active was an Agricultural Cooperative employee.

Yedong was located at the edge of the salt fields. A kinship village with many elderly couples and deserted homes, it had depopulated very rapidly over the 1980s. The tenant plots were small, and a number of its residents labored for Samyang.

NOTES

CHAPTER ONE

1. I generally use "farmer" for agriculturists, or in Korean, *nongmin*. I employ "peasant" when it is clear that "nongmin" is meant to refer to premodern agriculturists.

2. See also Johannes Fabian's (1979) guest-edited volume of *Social Research*, "Beyond Charisma: Religious Movements as Discourse." Drawing on Foucault, he writes of "an interpretive approach to movements as historical phenomena, one, however, that does not reduce them to causes and forces which always would have to 'predate' (logically if not chronologically) prophetic vision" (1979: 28).

3. See Apter and Sawa 1984 for a fascinating ethnography of social struggle in contemporary Japan.

4. In a similar vein, the anthropologist George E. Marcus offers "juxtaposition" to both renew and negate the once long-standing, and now forgotten, anthropological mainstay—comparison. He argues that the juxtaposition of "incommensurables" serves to "deterritorialize culture in ethnographic writing" (Marcus 1994: 566).

5. I have introduced the Korean word here to signal its reference to those who studied in Japan during the colonial period—both those who were leaders in oppositional movements inside and outside of Korea and those who settled comfortably into the life of a privileged native elite, able to circulate in the metropole (see Wales and Kim 1941: 89–98). Among yuhaksaeng in the 1980s, there was a similar split between those receiving training to become the engineers of the state and those who considered themselves to be dissidents. I do not, however, mean to suggest that this dichotomy necessarily prefigured a clear division of practice on their return to South Korea.

6. In 1464 the Wŏn'gak Temple was constructed at the site, and three years later a pagoda, the thirty-story stone Wŏn'gaksa Sipsamch'ŭng Sŏkt'ap, was erected.

In 1618, Kwanghae Kun had the temple destroyed but left the pagoda standing, and in 1900, Sir John MacLeavy Brown, the head of Korean Customs who was residing in Korea, designed the park (Clark and Clark 1969: 180).

7. North Chŏlla's capital city Chŏnju, for example, is known as a conservative city; the Yi clan of Chŏnju was the ruling family of the premodern period, the Chosŏn Dynasty (1392–1910). Through the 1970s, this dynasty was referred to as the Yi, or Yi-Chosŏn, but in this book I use Chosŏn in concurrence with those who suggest that the use of Yi or Yi-Chosŏn replicates the Japanese colonial perspective in which the period was characterized by the hegemony of a single family line.

8. The decision of one of the group's participants to take a position at a major university in Seoul dismayed the other members; it smacked of a desertion of their commitment to strengthening cultural life in South Korea's periphery.

9. The importance of assistants in the field remains neglected. Roger Sanjek (1990: 407) suggests that "there needs to be written a 'Secret History of Assistants.' " Gerald D. Berreman (1972) discusses the effects of his assistants' class, ethnic, and religious affiliations on his fieldwork, which were brought home to him as the course of his fieldwork shifted with the arrival of a new assistant. Margery Wolf (1992) explores the way in which her assistant's personal passions and interests guided the attentions of her own field research and analysis in her multigenre text, A Thrice-Told Tale.

10. Roger Sanjek's (1990) edited volume Fieldnotes provides fascinating glimpses into an unexplored dimension of anthropology: the construction of field notes in the doing and writing of ethnography.

11. Above all, it was the entry of the South Korean middle class into the struggles that both the domestic and foreign press acclaimed as their hallmark. The sight of middle-class housewives and office workers protesting on the streets challenged media and popular stereotypes of demonstrators as student radicals and revolutionaries under North Korean Communist sway.

12. The Kwangju Uprising refers to the state suppression of a popular uprising against the military takeover by Chun Doo Hwan in 1980. The hangjaeng (uprising) is by now the most common reference to the events in Kwangju, but it has also been underplayed as a sat'ae (incident) and sometimes called a haksal (massacre). Officially silenced by the state, it became a powerful symbol of the crimes of the South Korean state against its people. Throughout the 1980s, underground publications, videos, and whispered dialogues documented the severity of the Kwangju massacre that had been officially reported as merely the necessary suppression of the radical activities of a cadre of criminals against the state. Although the state officially recognized less than 50 deceased, unofficial estimates escalated over time to over 2,000. By 1987, the state could no longer dismiss the Kwangju events and publicly addressed the atrocities in 1988. By the end of the decade, former president Chun was tried for these activities, and the uprising and its suppression were widely publicized. Additionally, the role of the U.S. military, under whose command the South Korean Army officially stood, was increasingly the focus of anti-American sentiment. Kwangju, in South Chŏlla Province, is the nearest large city for Koch'ang residents and throughout my fieldwork there were hushed stories of locals who had been there either as citizens or as army and police officials.

13. Koji technically refers to the rice or money received up front before doing

the farm labor; in this case it is also used to refer to the person who performs this labor. It is understood to be an arrangement for poor farmers who need a cash or rice advance.

14. During the time of my fieldwork, the exchange rate for the South Korean wŏn fluctuated between $1 = ₩700 and $1 = ₩750.

15. Interestingly, when the movie based on this serial novel premiered in fall 1994, right-wing groups threatened to bomb the theaters (Sterngold 1994: 3). Although by 1994 such materials—historical and fictional—were less subject to censorship, stirrings over the nuclear plants in North Korea and the death of Kim Il Sung initiated a backlash of cold war politics.

CHAPTER TWO

1. Tonghak appears in the literature as alternatively a *nan* (confusion), a hangjaeng (uprising), and a *hyŏngmyŏng* (revolution).

2. This sense of legacy subverts more standard Confucian notions in which state bureaucrats and gentleman scholars are the most prideworthy ancestors.

3. Arjun Appadurai (1993: 413) writes in this vein of "pariah patriots, rogue nationalists" or of the "poor cousins in the story of nationalist struggle"—defeated nationalist projects. He also notes that the "nationalist genie" is diasporic, which has certainly been the case for Korea such that much nationalist struggle took place outside its territorial borders. On Korean diasporic nationalism, see, for example, Abelmann and Lie 1995.

4. C. A. Bayley criticizes a similar tension in subaltern studies between "political autonomy" and "moral community." He points out the conflict between the "autonomous subject actor" and the "moral community" of "folk religious values" or the "peasant commune" (Bayley 1988: 113). Suggesting that in history the "political autonomy of the subaltern is constantly subverted" and that "elite politics, institutions and economic and social distinctions among the peasants play a central role in limiting and forming subaltern action," he objects to the gloss of the "moral community." He asserts that if either the political autonomy or the moral community is privileged, "total history" or "rounded history" is not possible (Bayley 1988: 114–115). See Abelmann 1993 for further discussion of minjung and subaltern studies.

5. Ranajit Guha (1987: 7) similarly offers that Indian historiography focuses on the failure of anticolonial struggles. In the Korean context, this point is particularly salient: "It is the study of this *historic failure of the nation to come to its own*, a failure due to the inadequacy of the bourgeoisie as well as of the working class to lead it into a decisive victory over colonialism and a bourgeois-democratic revolution of either the classic nineteenth-century type under the hegemony of the bourgeoisie or a more modern type under the hegemony of workers and peasants, that is, a 'new democracy'—*it is the study of the failure which constitutes the central problematic of the historiography of colonial India.*" Because Korea's liberation was imposed and because there are two Korean states that claim to be the legitimate offspring of colonial struggles, many historians endeavor to explain or explain away "failure."

6. We can find parallels in the Indian subaltern studies project. Ranajit Guha,

one of the school's central figures, identifies the "politics of the people" as an "autonomous domain" emerging from a divergent cultural community at the source of a people's politics. Guha (1987: 3) explains that in colonial historiography, the people are excluded as a "diversion from a supposedly 'real' political process" and that they are treated only as followers or converted—the objects of elite politics. Instead, in an alternative historiography, the "masses mobilized by the elite to fight for their own objectives managed to break away from their control and put the characteristic imprint of popular politics on campaigns initiated by the upper classes" (Guha 1987: 6).

7. Guerrilla forces organized to drive out the Japanese (Eckert et al. 1990: 221).

8. In the aftermath of German unification and the collapse of Soviet communism, Korean unification has been entirely resignified as a practical matter to be considered and debated rather than an axiomatic nationalist agenda (Grinker 1995). In the concluding chapter, I will discuss the implications of the post-Soviet order for South Korea.

9. In this vein, I take inspiration from Victor Turner's (1974: 102) discussion of Mexico's Hidalgo Insurrection in which he distinguishes between "symbolic deposits in social time" and of those in "actual historical time." See Kim S. 1989 for a fascinating analysis of South Korean "mythical pasts" as they are evoked in Cheju Island shamanism.

10. "Yangban" refers to a premodern ruling estate, often landowning, comprised of bureaucrats with official rank. More generally, it distinguishes lineages that hailed from such ancestry. Its contemporary usage refers formally to family heritage and more loosely to those of "good breeding."

11. There has been considerable debate regarding the origins of the Tonghak Revolution, especially concerning its relation to the earlier Tonghak religion. Founded by Ch'oe Che-u, the Tonghak religion flourished in the 1860s primarily among the peasantry. Its millenarian creed championed the cause of the common people against a corrupt government. The various perspectives on the origins seem to span between the idea that the Tonghak Revolution succeeded the Tonghak religion as a radical peasant leadership propelled by a "blind crowd" and the notion that the peasant mass propelled the movement beyond its programs and leadership.

12. In a personal communication, a historical properties officer in the Ministry of Cultural Affairs indicated that the state had consciously decided to downplay the social reformist aspect of the Tonghak Revolution in its commemorative activities, choosing instead to champion it exclusively as an independence struggle against Japan.

13. As it often does, "grandfather" refers here to an elder.

14. Controversy exists as to whether Tonghak slogans about land were in fact a call to distribute land to its cultivators. There is considerable debate about Confucian legacies of land distribution principles. For example, the often-discussed Chinese well-field system is, according to Wm. Theodore de Bary (1985: 32), "one of the most talked about institutions in Neo-Confucian literature" whose " 'utility' may from the beginning have been more symbolic and pedagogical than practical."

15. Kaehwap'a advocated that Korea "engage in foreign trade and initiate a process of enlightenment reform" (Lee 1984: 267).

16. This is a political organization of intellectuals who had been exposed to Western liberalism and "battled to secure the nation's independence and the rights of the people" (Lee 1984: 302).

17. This refers to the faction of King Kojong's father, Hŭngsŏn Taewŏn'gun, who instituted broad-based social reforms beginning with Kojong's reign in 1864 (Lee 1984: 261).

18. Lee Ki-baik (1984: 290) characterizes these efforts as "the reform movement of the old Progressive Party in a new manifestation."

19. "Sangmin" refers to commoners, as a premodern status distinction (vs. yangban). "Sangnom" is a crude, somewhat derogatory reference to commoners (vs. sangmin).

20. Laurel Kendall points out that this dialogue can be seen as a discussion among the ghosts of those who met with untimely and miserable deaths—miserable for never achieving their desired independent *and* unified Korean peninsula. See Kendall 1985: chap. 7 for a discussion of unrequited ghosts.

21. Suh Nam-dong (1981*b*: 68) summarizes the lineage of Kim Chi-ha's aforementioned protagonist Chang as follows: "Three generations were killed during the Tonghak upheaval and only a son by a prostitute survived, but was killed during the liberation movement in the Japanese period; a son of his, again born of a prostitute, survived. He was later killed, allegedly as a Communist during the Korean War. And again a son born of a prostitute survived. This one is Chang Il-dam." Chang, a radical activist and Jesus-like figure, has thus inherited a collective experience of oppression, and the illegitimate child has in turn fostered a covert tradition.

22. In rural areas, it is not uncommon to find such private centers established by well-educated local elites with interests in regional history and ethnology or folklore.

23. I am unsure of the history of this term. This history would likely reveal, in the now-ubiquitous words of Eric Hobsbawm and Terrence Ranger (1983), the "invention of tradition." Although "han" is not employed frequently in the collective historical sense evoked here, it is widely used by women in a more personal sense to indicate their hardships. In *The Life and Hard Times of a Korean Shaman*, Laurel Kendall (1988: 56) considers a moment during the Korean War when the shaman decides that it is better to make a dangerous escape than to die with *wŏnhan* ("the resentment and spite carried by a restless and consequently malevolent ghost"), saying, "But if we were killed trying to escape, at least we wouldn't die burdened with regrets for our passivity." I am fascinated by the association of passivity and wŏnhan such that the resolution of han or wŏnhan is activism.

CHAPTER THREE

1. 10-ri = 4 kilometers. "Three thousand ri" is symbolic because it refers to the expanse of a unified Korea, north and south.

2. Historically, Samyang Inc. was the landlord, but in June 1956, Samyang Salt split from Samyang Inc., and in 1987 it managed the tenant and salt fields. Samyang Inc. complained that the tenant farmers had come to the wrong headquarters. The Samyang Salt headquarters is housed in two small rooms in Seoul; the func-

tional headquarters is the land management office in the Tongho village in Haeri District, Koch'ang County.

3. This chapter is based on several sources. I was residing with the protesters at the Samyang headquarters for most of the month. In mid-August I took a short trip down to the villages to get a sense of life among those who had decided not to participate in the Seoul protests. I was very fortunate to have access to minute-by-minute notes taken by one of the nonfarmer activists. These notes, written in a tiny hand in pencil in the quadrants of a regular-sized piece of paper folded in four, are a record of the minutiae of the month. They were considered at the time a precious record of the goings-on of the movement; during the confusion of the Attempted Murder Incident (discussed later in this chapter) I was entrusted with them for safekeeping. In this chapter and in chapter 5, I have also made use of tapes of the negotiation sessions with the company that I was able to copy.

4. The concept of *simin* (literally, citizen) had a distinctly urban flavor: middle-class urban residents were simin while farmers were nongmin (agricultural people). I discuss the changing contours of simin in the Conclusion.

5. At the first trial in Chŏngŭp on May 13, 1987, seventy farmers managed to gather, although local officials and policemen had been stationed in each village to prevent farmers from leaving. The court cases coincided almost exactly with nationwide June democratization activities. On June 23, for example, Yun, the head of the Samyangsa Sojak Yangdo Ch'ujin Wiwŏnhoe (Samyang Tenant Relinquish Committee) gave an address at a general rally in Chŏnju, passing out 6,000 pamphlets. The number of farmer observers increased with each successive trial. The idea of going to Seoul was first proposed during the informal discussions after the July 2 trial.

6. See Kim K. 1994 for a description of a 1985 student protest.

7. This term could also be translated as "outside influences." In its positive sense, the term referred to outside support. In the negative sense in which some employed it, the term implied outside powers to be reckoned with, or, alternatively, instigators who had somehow led the farmers astray. I also employ the "outside organizer" and "outside activist" to refer to "oebuseryŏk."

8. Kim Sang-jun, Kim Sang-don, Kim Sang-hyŏp, and Kim Byŏng-hwi.

9. Korean is written as a combination of han'gŭl (an indigenous phonetic alphabet) and Chinese characters. Because Chinese characters are considered foreign by many, much of contemporary Korean prose is written in han'gŭl. The official policy on Korean orthography has changed significantly over the years. Different eras of students have been variously educated in Chinese characters.

10. It is widely considered that around one-fourth of the South Korean population is Christian. The rates in urban areas, particularly among the middle classes and women in Seoul, are considerably higher. Some South Korean Christians are fundamentalist in orientation and observe a multitude of prohibitions, among them, smoking and drinking. See Clark 1986 and Cox 1995.

11. In the villages, the tenant farmers would often show me these products to stress Samyang's ubiquity and the absurdity of their consumer loyalty.

12. The proximate causes of the marginalization of the Chŏllas is the economic underdevelopment of the southwestern coastal areas throughout the Park period and the remarkable exclusion of Chŏlla peoples from elite political, bureaucratic,

and military posts. This came to a head in 1980 in the Kwangju Uprising. Historically, some people account for the regionalism by looking at the geographic contours of the pre-Silla period unification of the three kingdoms. The farmers I spoke with, however, agreed that the regionalism that had figured so prominently in the 1988 presidential elections was a post-Liberation phenomenon engendered by sustained underdevelopment of the provinces. Chŏlla peoples continue to experience discrimination in hiring, housing, and marriage (see Kim S. 1988).

13. The experience of a university professor who relocated from North Chŏlla to Seoul in the early 1990s reveals the province's particular character. A scholar of peasant society and history, he had come to realize just how tailored his own research interests and class syllabi had been to North Chŏlla's public culture and student composition. In Seoul, students and colleagues showed little interest in, or affinity for, farmers.

14. In the 1980s, only 5.8 percent of South Korea's population lived in North Chŏlla, but 11 percent of the country's cultivated land was in this province. And while only 20.8 percent of South Korea's population resided in agricultural villages (Koo 1987a: 97), the figure in North Chŏlla in 1984 was 60.5 percent. Furthermore, 70 percent of the cultivated land produced rice, which was the highest percentage in the nation. O Kŏn (1985: 118) suggests that North Chŏlla is "affected more by state purchase prices than any other province."

15. The leadership committee of the Relinquish Committee consisted of the early initiators of the movement and of leaders from the better-represented villages. In many cases, these village representatives were farmers who held village leadership positions. The leadership committee, however, was flexible, and over time other farmers joined them in this circle.

16. South Korea sent troops to Vietnam from October 1965 to March 1973. The Defense Ministry reported 312,853 troops sent, 4,678 killed, 5,000 wounded, and 41,000 enemy deaths at the hands of South Korean troops (Han 1978: 893; Sterngold 1992: 6). The story of South Korean troops in Vietnam has been neither well documented in historical accounts nor openly discussed in South Korea (Suk and Morrison 1987).

17. In accordance with the dictates of patrilineal kinship ideology there is still a considerable stigma attached to nonkin adoption in South Korea (Janelli and Janelli 1982: 53–57).

18. On December 31, 1986, the Land Leasing Protection Law (T'oji Imdaech'a Pohobŏp) had been proposed for promulgation on October 1, 1987. It was postponed, however, because of opposition from farmers' organizations. The opposition contended that the proposed law would favor nonresident landowners. An editorial in the Korea Student Christian Federation journal called for abolishing the proposed law because it violated the teachings of the Bible: "Biblically speaking, land is owned by God who gave it to farmers. God gave it to the farmers to let people 'live and prosper on the land.' " The editorial continued that the proposed law violated principles of social justice and that it was a violation of the 1949 Land Reform Law, which upheld the principle that cultivators should own the land they worked (HKHCY 1987: 58–59).

19. A federation of various social movements or organizations that was formed in 1987 to unify the opposition.

20. The mockery of officialdom is a standard feature of Korean popular folk theater, song, and dance.

21. The details of this address will be taken up in chapter 5.

22. Korean speech is distinguished according to both the social distance between the speakers—including age, kinship relations, and social status—and the conversation's level of formality.

23. The newspaper was founded immediately following the March First Movement. The Japanese permitted its start as part of their so-called Cultural Politics, ostensibly a loosening of control.

24. Over the course of the month the farmers printed four such reports that they tried to distribute widely in Seoul. These were homespun, quickly produced, simple pamphlets that they distributed to onlookers at the headquarters and through the various movement channels in Seoul.

25. This refers to the company's claim that the land did not yet produce rice at the time of the land reform. See chapter 4.

26. This refers to farmers' claim that some farmland was turned into salt fields so as to avoid land distribution. See chapter 4.

27. Older men from the villages and young organizers who were studying the instruments played the music. In the villages few young people take interest in the instruments.

28. It is impossible to make a clear distinction between organizers and farmers because most of the farmers' association members were farmers themselves. It is relevant, however, to distinguish between Koch'ang farmers and farmers who were not from the Samyang villages.

29. Historical discussions of the CFU can be found in chapter 8. Chapter 6 focuses on the relationship between farmers and organizers.

30. For many farmers, it was not simple to locate their laboring children, many of whom had no phones or certain addresses. I accompanied one woman who had her daughter's address written on a tattered piece of paper; she had moved, and we followed clue after clue to find her, but with no success.

31. The issues around Chŏlla identification would, in the months to follow, become a nationwide discussion as the opposition party split in two: Kim Dae Jung from the Chŏlla provinces formed one party and Kim Young Sam from the Kyŏngsang provinces took up the other. The ruling party candidate, Roh Tae Woo, was also regionally identified with the Kyŏngsang provinces.

32. These notions reflect hierarchies of the dominant ideology of the premodern Chosŏn Dynasty. There are also rich popular culture repositories that subvert these codes. I was struck, for example, by the words of a cab driver in Kwangju, the capital of South Chŏlla Province, who called not for a time when his children could be educated but for a time when without education his children could prosper. His comments, of course, also reflected the political winds of the late 1980s.

33. The *Farmer Song* had become a way of pulling everyone together, and for a few moments after the last verse the crowd could focus on a discussion, a plan of action, or instructions. When attention waned, farmers and organizers alike would call for song.

34. Jean-Paul Sartre makes a similar point: "For it is necessary to reverse the common opinion and acknowledge that it is not the harshness of a situation or the

sufferings it imposes that lead people to conceive of another state of affairs in which things would be better for everybody. It is on the day that we are able to conceive of another state of affairs, that a new light is cast on our trouble and our suffering and we *decide* that they are unbearable" (Bourdieu 1977: 74).

35. Roh Tae Woo, presidential candidate for the ruling party in the 1987 election, entered the race with the catchphrases "ordinary people" and "Trust me." Roh, who had played a pivotal role in establishing former President Chun's military rule, promised democratization in response to the popular movements of June 1987. "Ordinary people" was employed by Roh to project a new and softer personal image.

CHAPTER FOUR

1. "Feudalism" is employed to criticize contemporary vestiges of premodern social forms and relations. Susan Shin reminds us that "Korea never knew political feudalism," but that "the personal subordination of cultivator to landowner in the early Yi Dynasty strongly resembles that of a peasant to his lord in a truly feudal society" (1975: 50; see also Grajdanzev 1944: 117). The prominent South Korean historian Sin Yong-ha, for example, refers to "feudal" rents for Korea because "coupled with the aspect of non-economic coercion, its structure and nature would readily lend itself to classification as feudalistic" (Sin 1978: 26). "Feudal" is popularly used to describe antiquated or anachronistic behaviors and institutions, while "semifeudal" (*pan-ponggŏnjŏk*) is used by highly educated South Koreans to refer to the continued hegemony of traditional elites and stratification systems.

2. See Appendix 2 for a general discussion of the colonial period North Chŏlla Province.

3. Samsusa means literally the "three-water company." Purportedly the company name was changed in 1931. The shared first syllable in Samyangsa, "three" refers to the expression "ch'ŏn chi in samchae" (heaven, earth, people—three talents). Water was abandoned as it was inauspicious—companies aim to accumulate, but water washes things away—and was replaced with "yang" for "grow and nurture," which was appropriate for a foodstuffs industry (SY60 1985: 83).

4. The term "nonggujang," which is unlikely to have survived into the 1980s elsewhere in South Korea, derives from colonial period divisions of the land into *nong-gu* (literally farm(land) sections), with corresponding *jang* (heads) for each section. Hoon K. Lee (1936: 157) points out that the marŭm or *saŭm* were called *nonggam* (supervisor of farming).

5. The use of this language seems to imply that Samyang promised eventual landownership to the tenants.

6. There are parallels with the Tonghak Peasant Revolution historiography discussed in chapter 2.

7. In chronologies in both the fiftieth- and sixtieth-anniversary volumes it is recorded that the construction was completed in 1938 when the Haeri Land Office was constructed.

8. Eckert (1986: 538–539) suggests that Kim Yŏn-su, like many of Korea's early capitalists, was as "landlord and bourgeois at one and the same time . . . able to

remain one of the country's biggest landlords right on to 1945 . . . largely because he was able to draw on Japanese financial resources rather than on his own."

9. This explanation was perhaps adopted from movement rhetoric.

10. Some farmers said that in the early days Samyang's rents were 3:7 (³⁄₁₀ to the landlord, ⁷⁄₁₀ to the farmer), while other farmers said it was 5:5 (½ to each). Most farmers agreed that for some time—they varied as to the date of the transition; some put it at the Korean War (1950) and others at Liberation (1945)—the rent collection system had been *mutkalim,* which refers technically to a 50–50 division of *mut* (gatherings of rice stalk after harvest). One farmer complained that the company always took the best mut. Another farmer recalled that rents had changed from a 5:5 mutkalim to 3:1 (⅓ landlord, ⅔ tenant) in 1945 in accordance with a military government directive and finally to 3:7 (³⁄₁₀ landlord, ⁷⁄₁₀ tenant). During the court trials farmers testified that although 3:7 in theory, in practice they often took 5:5 (CR August 1987). Many farmers explained that with each progressively more favorable rent agreement, farmers assumed more of the costs such that "they put more and more of a burden upon us." Samyang's 3:7 arrangement until 1985 was by all calculations certainly in the lower 30 percent of rent costs nationwide. The post-1985 2:8 arrangement was easily in the lowest 20 percent, and by one 1986 calculation it was in the lowest 1.6 percent of rents (Chang 1988: 169).

11. A newspaper editorial letter in *Haebang Ilbo* (Liberation Daily) reveals the heterogeneous membership of the December 8, 1945, 600-person inaugural meeting of Chŏnnong:

> I wish that more of the representatives were farmers. When I looked around, everyone looked like an "interi" [intellectual]. . . . They wore western clothes and shaved their faces; there were no differences among them. Perhaps they took their "A-frames" from their backs, left their carts in storage, and changed into different clothes to come to the conference. But I wished there were more farmers. . . . Local representatives! In the future, send more farmers! Among the ten people you send, perhaps one intelligentsia would be enough. (Lee 1977: 135)

12. From Yi Mok-u's "Taegu sip-il p'oktong sakŏn" (The Taegu October 1st Riot Incident) in *Sedae,* October 1965, 230–231 (Scalapino and Lee 1972: 262).

13. Chang Sang-hwan (1988: 138) argues that the land reform was a turning point away from a colonial semifeudal society to neocolonial bureaucratic monopoly capitalism. Moreover, he contends that the land reform effectively weakened the rapidly growing alliance of farmers and workers after 1945, thwarting a more progressive "historical development." Chang argues that the "subject" of the movement was neither landlords nor farmers, but rather the combined interests of the U.S. military and South Korean governments (1988: 133).

14. Ban, Moon, and Perkins (1980: 287) calculate that by 1965 only 16 percent of the total cultivated land was still tenant land, of which half should have been distributed; the other half was accounted for by the exemptions including, for example, clan land, land of educational institutions, and reclaimed land. The matter of these exemptions—both the efficiency and the legitimacy of their promulgation—was central in the Koch'ang Tenant Farmers Movement. Consideration of the efficacy of the land reform depends on the feasibility of land purchase at that time and, in turn, on the ability of new owner-farmers to sustain a livelihood. Chang Sang-hwan (1988: 135) calculates conservatively that only 10 percent of tenant

land was resold before farmers completed their payments, while Chang Su-hyŏn reports that, according to some district employees, about two-thirds of the land was sold before the payments were completed.

15. The South Korean land reform did not lead to any substantial change in the size of farming units (Koh 1962: 434; Lee 1979: 494). From 1953 to 1961, agricultural output grew 3.6 percent yearly, not a significant increase over the 2.9 percent annual growth during the colonial period. Rice output growth was even less impressive at 2.7 percent yearly from 1957 to 1969, contrasting with higher 3.9 percent annual rates during the 1930s. Ban, Moon, and Perkins (1980: 297) conclude that the "direct impact of land reform on productivity was probably neither strongly positive nor strongly negative." Koh Yeong Kyeong (1962) goes even further in his claim that land reform "was one of the major causes for the devastation of Korea's farm economy." Chapter 8 returns to South Korea's post-Liberation farm economy.

16. See Brandt (1971: 55) for discussion of a similar incident.

17. Even today some fields are salty. Not only is productivity lower on salty fields, but the work required for farming is much greater because in order to get rid of the salt, farmers repeatedly flood and drain the paddy. The facility of this work depends on the proximity of the field to the waterways. However, once the reclamation paddy or so-called *haedap* (sea paddy) is finished, it is more productive than *yuktap* (land paddy) and is easier to irrigate and farm.

18. The Korean phrase used here, "when it became Liberation," is noteworthy because of the passive voice, which emphasizes that the Liberation came to be, rather than having been achieved.

19. This is corroborated by urban perspectives on rural areas as places where the unenterprising are left behind.

20. *Hwarang* is a word for the young, male Buddhist military trainees of the Silla Period (A.D. 668–934) known for their mastery of military, Buddhist, and secular arts.

21. I met Pak Yun-do in Seoul many months after the conclusion of the struggle. I had asked to meet with executives from Samyang Salt, and Vice President Kim Sŏn-hwi appeared with Pak, explaining that he would be able to answer my questions. Over the course of the interview, though, Kim Sŏn-hwi began to speak for himself. When I explained that I had met with little luck in attempts to talk with the management of Samyang Salt in Haeri, Kim apologized profusely, saying over and over that they would gladly answer any queries I had.

22. One of the provisions of the land reform law was a ceiling of three hectares for individual owners.

23. According to the terms of their histories cited above, this date is incorrect; 1936 is recorded as the start of the project.

CHAPTER FIVE

1. I take nationalisms to be arguments about political legitimacy in the name of a culturally constructed group (Anderson 1983; Gellner 1983). Richard Fox (1990: 2–4), preferring "nationalist ideologies" to nationalisms, considers them "produc-

tion[s] of conceptions of peoplehood" and examines how "national cultures emerge from nationalist ideologies."

2. I concur with Brackette Williams's (1990: 128) characterization of traditions as "competing sources of criteria around which persons with different claims to these selected features can construct the coordinates to their struggle to control the total system of meanings or to defend themselves against others who would do so."

3. South Korea's post-Liberation era reveals remarkably intensive and rapid state-controlled industrial growth and the emergence of large-scale corporations, chaebŏl (conglomerates). Forty-three chaebŏl controlled 49.4 percent of the GNP, and the top five among them 39.9 percent (Im 1991: 54). The extent of state economic intervention has been widely documented (Amsden 1989; Woo 1991). State and management control of labor with authoritarian institutions and ideologies sustained the low wages that facilitated successful export-oriented growth (Lie 1992).

Nonetheless, over the 1980s and into the 1990s chaebŏl have become more autonomous from the state (Kim E. 1988; Yoon 1989) and a capitalist class of owners and high-level managers have become more visible in the South Korean political and cultural landscape. Chaebŏl have become increasingly able to manipulate state institutions and directives, and the values and lifestyles of capitalists have become more visible in particular neighborhoods and even apartment complexes in Seoul's urban landscape (Koo 1987a), as has their cultural control via educational and media institutions (Hong 1985: 109).

4. Scholars diverge in their discussion of the reasons for this lack of legitimacy. Competing considerations include Confucian disdain for commercial activity and a related discomfort with money and conspicuous consumption; illicit business practices; and the elitism or classism of the class (Hong 1985). Hagen Koo (1987b:389) argues that the bourgeoisie have been unable to achieve ideological and social hegemony because the state's protection of capital against labor has tainted them and has "had a detrimental effect on the legitimacy of capital accumulation itself." Eun Mee *Kim* (1988: 117) contrasts the 1960s, in which the "illicit accumulation of wealth" (criminal economic activity, favoritism, etc.) was at issue, with the 1980s and 1990s, in which the chaebŏl were charged with responsibility for inequities of the distribution of wealth.

5. A growing literature traces the Confucianization of Korea—most intensively over the Chosŏn Dynasty—as a social and cultural revolution that challenged "indigenous" social structure and beliefs (Deuchler 1977, 1992; Haboush 1991; Janelli and Janelli 1982). In this narrative the "elements of the lower class" can figure as a cultural repository of such indigenous legacies. There is no consensus, however, that legacies of village egalitarianism necessarily mediate against the culture of capitalism or capitalists.

6. It would be an overstatement to suggest that this discussion has dominated the discourse of political legitimacy in South Korea. Quite apart from these cultural formations, there have been long-standing arguments that geopolitical and economic realities preclude democracy. For example, the state has defended authoritarianism in the face of the Communist threat. This logic suggested that if domestic moorings are loosened, a North Korean invasion will ensue. Additionally, evolu-

tionary conceptions of economic and political development have suggested that full-blown democracy is a luxury reserved for the "more developed" countries and economies.

7. Park (1970: 53) goes on at some length, making the point that fundamental social structural aspects of the Chosŏn Dynasty are in fact continuous with the preceding Koryŏ period: "The Yi Kingdom differed little from its predecessor in its basic characteristics as a centralized and autocratic society supported by a hereditary ruling class of royal relatives and court scholars."

8. Here Park (1970: 92) considers, for example, *hyangyak*, "agreements reached among the villages and within counties for their independent and autonomous government," and kye, cooperative lending groups, which he praises for their local cooperation but charges were still "bound together by antiquated loyalties and sympathies." Yunshik *Chang* (1991: 124) also discusses the democratic, egalitarian hyangyak: although "the hyangyak movement began as an attempt by the government to indoctrinate peasants with Confucian teaching," it echoed what "had long been the rules of interpersonal relations among peasants."

9. Kim, scapegoated for the 1980 civilian uprising in Kwangju against the military takeover by Chun Doo Hwan (president, 1980–1988), was later imprisoned and sentenced to death. After considerable international outcry, however, Kim was exiled abroad. He returned to South Korea and ran for the presidency in 1988; due to a regional gridlock between the two primary opposition parties, the ruling party candidate, Roh Tae Woo, who had served under Chun, was victorious. In 1992, Kim again made an unsuccessful bid for the presidency, after which he formally retired from electoral politics.

10. In the 1970s and 1980s isolated cases of protest suicides were broadly reported by the South Korean media and were widely understood as symbolic acts of protest.

11. Here, one thousand ri refers not to a specific distance but more generally to a great distance.

12. Such patriarchal rhetoric is widespread in South Korean companies, particularly for female factory labor (Janelli 1993; Kim C. 1992; Kim S. 1990).

13. This refers to the South Korean popular response against Japanese textbooks' treatment of Korea in general and of Japanese colonialism in particular.

14. Examining the day-to-day workings of the movement and listening particularly to the tapes of the closed sessions between the farmers and landlords, I realized that my own memory had exaggerated the role of the "external forces" in the division of the movement. The tendency of many other onlookers, however, was to underestimate their contribution in this regard.

15. Such a desecration is enormous in light of the Korean ideology and practice of ancestor worship. See Janelli and Janelli 1982.

CHAPTER SIX

1. It was very difficult to arrange for this interview. He was perplexed as to how I had found him and was tight-lipped for the first hour of our conversation. He warmed up, though, as the discussion allowed him to boast of his insider knowledge of, and keen insight into, the Koch'ang Tenant Farmers Movement.

2. This CFU representative documented his involvement in a twenty-odd page narrative for circulation among a small number of movement participants.

3. "Nonghwal" is shorthand for *nongch'on hwaltong* (agricultural village action). The interviews I draw from in this section were conducted in cafés and lunch spots in the vicinity of Seoul's Koryŏ University.

4. It was the national security law that allowed indiscriminate and tyrannical state actions in the name of national security and anticommunism.

5. The university school year begins in the spring.

6. In South Korean school and work settings, people are very clearly identified by their cohort group and identify those above them as *sŏnbae* (seniors) and those below them as *hubae* (juniors).

7. Spring 1984 was a major turning point in the student movement history as campus autonomy measures prevented the police from entering college campuses (see Dong 1987).

CHAPTER SEVEN

1. *Chayŏn purak* (natural villages) refer to hamlets that have a village identity and often a village head but are administratively subsumed under a larger village structure.

2. In the early 1990s, the station was moved and greatly improved. Today it is no longer a poor cousin of the Kangnam Bus Terminal, the city's main station.

3. Shortly after the end of my fieldwork the bus station was transferred to a larger and slightly more impressive building.

4. It is actually a subvillage of Kŭmp'yŏng, a natural village called Myŏnggo, that I discuss here. As Kŭmp'yŏng's centrally located and largest subvillage, it was usually referred to as Kŭmp'yŏng.

5. This campaign, its programs and ideological character, will be discussed in chapter 8.

6. The buses that go past most of the villages, heading straight for Tongho.

7. The reference to surnames and their place of origin—to lineages—is often a mark of status.

8. This phrase usually refers to special relationships between universities or towns in South Korea and another country.

9. This name is comprised of the Chinese characters for "bow" and "mountain."

10. To suggest that the fortune of the village turned with the reformation of the land is an example of a geomantic calculation.

11. In Korea women join their husbands' patrilineages through marriage and formally retain their maiden names. In these villages, households were typically referred to according to the native village or town of the mother. (My house was called the *miguktaek*[American house].) Alternatively, houses are referred to as "the home of the mother of 'so-and-so,' " typically the youngest child.

12. The house, formally owned by one of the neighbors, had for some time been a gathering spot for the drinking occasions of village bachelors.

13. Liberation is a marker around which South Koreans contrast pre- and post-Liberation days. As Laurel Kendall (1988: 46) writes of Liberation Day, "[It] has

become historical shorthand for the complex events and powerful emotions that marked Korea's emergence from colonial rule."

14. It is typical, however, for farmers to assert that although their region was horribly stricken during the Korean War, their own village was peaceful. In spite of claims about village equality, even after the Korean War and as late as 1961 there were still farmers in this village working as mŏsŭm (hired hands employed by other farmers in the village). They were paid from 3 to 4 kama of rice or, for a special mŏsŭm, from 8 to 9 kama in *pyŏttan* [stalk] per year, and although only the man himself was in residence, the employer provided clothing and other incidentals for the rest of his family.

15. Until 1985, Samyang's rent was calculated by a percentage of the crop according to estimates of the crop size before harvest. The rent was figured by looking at one *toe,* that is, a single p'yŏng on each unit of 60 p'yŏng (called a *paemi* or a *panggu* in this region). This technique contrasts with percent rent that is figured as a percentage of the crop after harvest; both of these are "percentage" calculations as opposed to "fixed" rent calculations whereby the amount to be remitted is fixed regardless of the vagaries of the yearly crop. Percentage systems diminish farmers' risks in the case of a bad farming year, but they also diminish opportunities for profit in good times.

16. The general statistics that I received at the respective Simwŏn and Haeri District offices indicated 57 homes and 259 residents for Kungsan and 62 homes and 333 residents for Kŭmp'yŏng. The Kŭmp'yŏng statistics are from February 15, 1986. I was told in 1987 that the Kungsan statistics were "recent," but they were undated.

17. One father of three laboring daughters who had not heard from one of them in over a year explained, "She probably hasn't contacted me because she is afraid that we will ask her for money." He continued, "After key money [deposit], room money, food money, clothes money, and makeup money, she probably doesn't have anything left." Kendall points out that factory girls' contributions to rural household economies is a difficult interview subject because farmers are reluctant to report their daughters' contributions (pers. comm.).

18. Clark Sorensen (1988) observes that the historical weight of land tenure stratification combines with contemporary shifts of population and land purchase to effect greater stratification at the village level. He argues (1988: 224) that in the village he studied class differences were exaggerated with migration and the sale of lands between 1977 and 1983. He explains (1988: 225) that this realignment does not reflect a diminishing middle class of farmers, but rather the gap between landowning farmers and nonowners.

19. Some farmers suggested that the practice had begun only in the last five or ten years.

20. See Appendix 3 for a discussion of the movement participation across all of the Samyang villages.

21. One of these farmers, however, was an original signer of the late 1986 petition that villagers quietly stamped to announce their resolve not to remit the rents. With constant surveillance by police and local authorities in these villages that had no contemporary experience with sustained protest or affiliation with oppositional organizations, we can imagine that signing must have been dramatic and that farm-

ers must have worried about the repercussions of their actions. In Kungsan, the men of twenty-seven households and six women—who could represent either other households or double representation from one household—signed, totaling about half of the households. Considering that the movement began in Kungsan with Yun, it is not surprising to find this high percentage of signatories. These figures were the second highest after Poktong, another village that had lost its land in the reservoir, and were followed closely by those of Chukkok, a village where some of the key leadership members resided (see Appendix 3, fig. C-2).

22. In these villages many work-related words continued to be spoken in Japanese. *Niyak'a* is a Korean pronunciation of the Japanese word *niyaka*.

23. This is another instance of the Korean pronunciation of a Japanese word, *yutori*, employed in a discussion of labor.

CHAPTER EIGHT

1. Eddy Lee (1979: 503) contends, however, that the grain support programs were more beneficial to rich farmers because of the relatively higher proportion of rice in their production.

2. There are, however, serious problems with the state-generated statistical base according to which distributive equality has often been calculated. McGinn et al. (1980: 141) point out that "Korea's data problems are those common to countries that have made less statistical effort than Korea has: coverage exclusions, definitional inconsistencies and ambiguities, probable response biases." They fail to take into account incomes over $5,000 (Mason et al. 1980: 410, 482). Eddy Lee (1979: 494) suggests that the figures are always conservative because the Survey of Farm Household Economy conducted by the Ministry of Agriculture and Fisheries since 1963 has not included the 5 percent of farmers who farm less than 0.5 hectare and the landless and farmer laborers. Similarly, Moo Ki *Bai* (1978: 88) asserts, "The Farm Household Economy Survey is not very suitable to the purpose of analyzing income distribution in rural areas or among rural families, and contains an upward bias, too." Additionally, Han Do Hyun (1989: 144) also warns that it is easy to overestimate income increases in the 1970s because the statistics are skewed by the real increases of prosperous farmers.

3. Although published in 1980, Ban et al.'s optimistic study of the agricultural sector relies on statistics ending in 1975. The conclusions were calculated for what was a brief period (the first half of the 1970s) of the retrenchment of state neglect of agriculture and were thus overly optimistic.

3. Figures 7 and 8 are not corrected for nonfarmland income, most notably, wage labor and animal husbandry.

5. Over the years income maldistribution has been exacerbated by inequalities of taxation because the poor have been subject to proportionately greater state extraction. In 1970, the bottom 10 percent of income earners paid 13 percent of their income in taxes, and by 1980 this figure had more than doubled to 28 percent (Koo 1984: 1,035). This came to a head with the late 1980s escalation of farmer dissatisfaction with the water tax and the blatant inequalities in health insurance rates. Over time indirect taxation constituted an increasing portion of the total

tax, from 53.5 percent in 1965 to 61.8 percent in 1975 and 63.3 percent in 1980, representing thus a heavier burden for poorer people (Koo 1984: 1034–1035).

6. The failing economy of the sector is revealed by the older village bachelors who have stayed in the countryside to help their aging parents. One hears often of farmers who went to the city to marry but whose wives left them when they returned to the countryside to farm.

7. In this vein, Mick Moore (1984: 580; see also Han 1989: 148) argues that "the process of politicizing the farm sector, of which Saemaŭl was a part, now poses a threat to the political stability of Korea which cannot easily be managed."

8. Brandt and Lee (1981: 60) calculate for 1974, for example, that while government inputs were 60 million, farmer inputs, inclusive of their labor, were 204 million. From 1971 to 1974, only 22 percent of the inputs were state expenditures, and in 1976 this figure had fallen to 16 percent (Brandt and Lee 1981: 73). Similarly, Han (1989: 141) calculates state inputs from 1971 to 1978 at 28 percent.

9. Han suggests that this call was a measure to strengthen landlord control over tenants and to further integrate landlords in a system of intensive state exploitation. There are also American roots to "community development" efforts, beginning with a 1955 South Korea–U.S. initiative and the June 1956 South Korea–U.S. Cooperative Economic Committee (Hanmi Hyŏptong Kyŏngje Wiwŏnhoe). Community development was placed under the Ministry of Reconstruction in 1958, transferred to the Office of Rural Development in 1962, and in 1970—in conjunction with the Saemaŭl Movement—placed under the Ministry of Home Affairs, which controlled local administration and the police (Han 1989: 118).

10. By the end of the 1980s, however, pressure mounted for the unification of farmers' movements.

11. The trial of the arrested Christian Academy educators began in August 1979 under Park's Yusin regime and led to public discussion of the torture committed against those arrested. The arrested activists formally declared that they had been coerced with torture to admit to Communist sympathies.

12. When poorer farmers—often young unmarried men—borrowed state money, it was conditional on the purchase of calves; in 1984, when the prices began to fall, the farmers tried to sell the cows and were told they would have to repay the loans if they did so. In 1985 cows purchased in 1982 for ₩1,000,000 to ₩1,200,000 were selling for ₩600,000, with estimated losses of ₩400,000 to ₩600,000 per cow. In 1988 the farmers demonstrated, demanding ₩1,000,000 in reparations per household (No 1989: 326–328). Many bachelor farmers reported such stories as their motivation for becoming activists.

13. Pak Chin-do (1988: 243) lists thirteen farmer grievances against the state in the 1980s, among them: (1) although the state forced farmers to plant barley with the promise that they would purchase it, they did not; (2) the state told farmers to raise cows and then imported beef; (3) the state told them to engage in sericulture, which led to debt; (4) the water cooperatives and paddy arrangement programs were corrupt; and (5) the state advised farmers to raise chestnuts and the price plummeted.

14. Less than 10 percent of the tenant farmers represented by these statistics were pure tenant farmers. In 1985, for example, as few as 2.1 percent were pure

tenants, and among tenant owners roughly two-thirds were farmers with more owned land than tenant land (Chang 1988: 149).

15. As of February 1994, Chŏnnong registered approximately 100,000 members in 90 county-level organizations (*Daily Report*, February 2, 1994, 21).

16. The final settlement provided a gradual opening with a ten-year grace period: "minimum market access of 1 percent to 2 percent of 1986–1988 domestic consumption in the first five years from 1995 and 2 percent to 4 percent in the rest of five years" (*Daily Report*, December 14, 1993, 34).

CHAPTER NINE

1. The diminishing rural sector has taken on a particular cultural or symbolic significance. In the 1993–1994 GATT struggle, farmers became national symbols. When the president apologized to the entire "kungmin [state/nation people]" for having betrayed them by signing the GATT agreement, it was less the real lives and livelihoods of rural people and more the significance of homegrown rice considered uniquely suited to Korean tastes and bodily composition that seemed to be at issue. In 1994 it was not the rural vote—which the ruling party had nurtured for decades—that governed this matter, but rather a symbolic geopolitical-cultural struggle.

2. Kim's use of "household" and "name" suggests a metaphorical family/lineage of activism over the last decades. This usage also implicates the patriarchal Korean family. "Tollim" refers to a Chinese character that is passed down in the patrilineage from generation to generation in family members' first names.

3. "Undongkwŏn" refers literally to those on the "side" or in the "field" of activism; as such it is a less specific term than "undongga," which implies a committed activist.

4. Over the last few years, graduate students from South Korea in the United States have been interested in distinguishing the cultural and political differences of the various hakpŏn. One recent Korean American immigrant who frequently returns to Seoul told me, "In [South] Korea each year is like a decade."

5. These suicides occurred in response to the brutal suppression by police of students' commemorative activities for Kang Kyŏng-dae, a student killed by the combat police.

6. According to Korean patrilineal logic, the oldest son would be designated to tend the farm and care for the parents. With rapid rural exodus, however, these responsibilities often fall to the youngest son, left in the countryside after his older brothers have all left for the city.

7. Paek Uk-in argues that laborers have transmogrified from "laborers to simin," from "producers to *saenghwalja* (those who live)" (1993*a:* 45), and that they have become middle class or middle class-like (1993*a:* 29). This point is echoed by Hwang Chu-sŏk (1994: 78), who writes about the shift of labor movements from *saengjon* (survival) movements from the 1970s to the mid-1980s to *saenghwal* (lifestyle) movements in the late 1980s and into the 1990s: "In the times when survival was at issue, violent movements with molotov cocktails and the like were appro-

priate, but when it is a society where quality of life is the concern, the tactics and strategies have to change, and the subjects can't but be different."

8. See Janelli and Janelli 1993: 200–201 for a fascinating discussion of white-collar workers' diminished sympathy for blue-collar workers in the aftermath of the successes of the labor struggle.

9. In her analysis of generational cohorts of women in China, Lisa Rofel (1994: 248) writes, "I have argued that there is no one fixed space from which all Chinese women speak in a sovereign voice. . . . Chinese women stand in a variety of generational and class positions which have been discursively articulated in history."

APPENDIX TWO

1. Published in 1978, "The Landlord System of the Late Yi Dynasty and Japanese Colonial Period—Case Study 4: Landlord Management and Capital Conversion in the Kobu Kim Family," infuriated the Kim family. Kim Yong-sŏp had seen the materials on which he based this writing already thirty years earlier, but he had worried about the landlord's response. He finally wrote the article in the 1970s because he thought he was going to die.

APPENDIX THREE

1. Although identifiable as a region because of the villages' shared relationships to Samyang, this identification for the most part only acquired real social significance because of the movement.

2. When farmers quietly stamped their signatures in 1986, there was considerable fear about the repercussions of their action.

BIBLIOGRAPHY

Abelmann, Nancy. 1993. "*Minjung* Theory and Practice." In Harumi Befu, ed., *Cultural Nationalism in East Asia: Representation and Identity*, 139–166. Berkeley: Institute of East Asian Studies.

Abelmann, Nancy, and John Lie. 1995. *Blue Dreams: Korean Americans and the Los Angeles Riots.* Cambridge, Mass.: Harvard University Press.

"Aegukchŏk nongch'on hwaltong ŭl wihae uri irŏk'e hapsida" (For a Patriotic Nonghwal Let's Do It Like This). 1993. Yonsei University. Cited as ANH.

Alonso, Ana Maria. 1988. "The Effects of Truth: Re-Presentations of the Past and the Imagining of Community." *Journal of Historical Sociology* 1:33–57.

Alvarez, Sonia E., and Arturo Escobar. 1992. "Conclusion: Theoretical and Political Horizons of Change in Contemporary Latin American Social Movements." In Escobar and Alvarez, eds., *The Making of Social Movements in Latin America: Identity, Strategy, and Democracy*, 317–329. Boulder, Colo.: Westview Press.

Amsden, Alice. 1989. *Asia's New Giant: South Korea and Late Industrialization.* New York: Oxford University Press.

An Pyŏng-ok. 1987. "Tonghak nongmin chŏnjaeng yŏn'gu hyŏnhwang kwa munjejŏm" (Investigation on the Issue of the Tonghak Farmers' War). *Yŏksa Munje Yŏn'guso hoebo* (Historical Issues Research Bulletin) 5:10–12.

Anderson, Benedict. 1983. *Imagined Communities: Reflections on the Origin and Spread of Nationalism.* London: Verso.

ANH. See "Aegukchŏk nongch'on hwaltong ŭl wihae uri irŏk'e hapsida."

Appadurai, Arjun. 1993. "Patriotism and Its Futures." *Public Culture* 5: 411–429.

Apter, David E., and Nagayo Sawa. 1984. *Against the State: Politics and Social Protest in Japan.* Cambridge, Mass.: Harvard University Press.

Bai, Moo Ki. 1978. "Examining Adelman's View on Relative Income Equity in Korea: With Focus on Her Studies Outlined in the World Bank Report." *Social Science Journal* (Korean Social Science Research Council) 5: 85–99.

Ban, Sung Hwan, Pal Yong Moon, and Dwight H. Perkins. 1980. *Studies in the Modernization of the Republic of Korea, 1945–1975: Rural Development.* Cambridge, Mass.: Harvard University Press.

Barry, Randall K. 1991. "'Korean' in ALA-LC [American Library Association and the Library of Congress] Romanization Tables: Transliteraton Schemes for Non-Roman Scripts." Washington, D.C.: Library of Congress.

Baudrillard, Jean. 1983. *In the Shadow of the Silent Majorities.* Trans. Paul Foss, John Johnston, and Paul Patton. New York: Semiotexte.

Bayley, C. A. 1988. "Rallying Round the Subaltern." *Journal of Peasant Studies* 16: 110–120.

Berger, John. 1982. "Stories." In Berger and Jean Mohr, *Another Way of Telling,* 279–289. New York: Pantheon Books.

Berreman, Gerald D. 1972. "Prologue." In *Behind Many Masks: Ethnography and Impression Management in a Himalayan Village,* xvii–lvii. Berkeley, Los Angeles, and London: University of California Press.

Bourdieu, Pierre. 1977. *Outline of a Theory of Practice.* Trans. Richard Nice. New York: Cambridge University Press.

———. 1990. "Social Space and Symbolic Power." In Bourdieu, *In Other Words: Essays Towards a Reflective Sociology,* 123–139. Stanford, Calif.: Stanford University Press.

Brandt, Vincent. 1971. *A Korean Village: Between Farm and Sea.* Cambridge, Mass.: Harvard University Press.

Brandt, Vincent, and Man-gap Lee. 1981. "Community Development in the Republic of Korea." In Ronald Dore and Zoe Mars, eds., *Community Development: Comparative Case Studies in India, the Republic of Korea, Mexico and Tanzania,* 49–136. London: UNESCO.

Burawoy, Michael, et al. 1991. *Ethnography Unbound: Power and Resistance in the Modern Metropolis.* Berkeley, Los Angeles, and Oxford: University of California Press.

Burmeister, Larry L. 1988. *Research, Realpolitik, and Development in Korea: The State and the Green Revolution.* Boulder, Colo.: Westview Press.

Ch'oe Mun-sŏng. 1989. "Nongmin e taehan chŏngch'ijŏk chibae kujo" (The Political Control Structure of Farmers). In Han'guk Nong-Ŏch'on Sahoe Yŏn'guso, ed., *Han'guk nongŏp nongmin munje yŏn'gu,* 2:15–68.

Chang Sang-hwan. 1988. "Hyŏnhaeng t'oji munje ŭi sŏnggyŏk kwa haegyŏl panghyang" (The Character and Solution Course of the Contemporary Land Problem). In Han'guk Nong-Ŏch'on Sahoe Yŏn'guso, ed., *Han'guk nongŏp nongmin munje yŏn'gu,* 1:109–191.

Chang, Yunshik. 1991. "The Personalist Ethic and the Market in Korea." *Comparative Studies in Society and History* 33: 106–129.

Cho Chŏng-nae. 1987. *Han'gil Sarangbang.* Lecture and discussion, Seoul.

———. 1986. *T'aebaek sanmaek* (The Taebaek Mountain Range). 10 vols. Seoul: Han'gilsa.

Cho Haejoang. 1981. "A Study of Changing Rural Communities in Korea." *Korea Journal* 21: 18–25.

———. 1994a. "90 nyŏndae sahoe undong e taehayŏ" (Concerning Social Movements in the 1990s). In Cho Haejoang, ed., *Kŭl ilki wa sam ilki* (Reading Sentences and Reading Life), 3:141–177. Seoul: Tto Hana ŭi Munhwa.

———— 1994*b*. "'Pan-munhwa' undong kwa 'sinsedae'" ('Counterculture' Movements and the 'New Generation'). In Cho Haejoang, ed., *Kŭl ilki wa sam ilki* (Reading Sentences and Reading Life), 3:179–203. Seoul: Tto Hana ŭi Munhwa.

Choi, Chungmoo. 1989. "Shamanism and the Making of the Revolutionary Ideology in Contemporary Korea." SSRC Conference, Thailand. Unpublished manuscript.

Chŏng Ch'ang-nyŏl, Kang Man-gil, and Kim Chin-gyun. 1987. "Han'guk minjungsa sagŏn chŭngŏn kirok" (The Record of the Testimonies of the Han'guk minjungsa Incident). 1987. *Yŏksa pip'yŏng* 1: 343–377.

Chŏng Ho-ung. 1994. "*T'oji*, saeroun sosŏl ŭi t'ansaeng" (*T'oji*, and the Birth of a New Novel). *Kil* 59: 206–212.

Chŏng Kyŏng-mo. 1984. *Tchijŏjin sanha* (Torn Rivers and Mountains). Seoul: n.p.

Chŏng T'ae-sŏk. 1993. "Han'guk simin sahoe wa minjujuŭi ŭi chŏnmang" (The Prospects for Korean Civil Society and Democracy). In Haksul Tanch'e Hyŏbŭihoe, ed., *Han'guk minjujuŭi ŭi hyŏnjaejŏk kwaje: Chedo, kaehyŏk mit sahoe undong* (The Current Process of Korean Democracy: System, Reform, and Social Movements), 177–211. Seoul: Ch'angjak kwa Pip'yŏngsa.

Chŏn'guk Nongminhoe Ch'ong Yŏnmaeng Chunbi Wiwŏnhoe (National League of Farmers Association Preparation Committee) 1990. "*Chŏnnong" kyŏlsŏng kwa nongmin undong ŭi panghyang* (The Founding of "Chŏnnong" and the Direction of Farmers' Movements). Seoul: National League of Farmers Association Preparation Committee Policy Office. Cited as CNCYCW.

Chŏngŭp Court Record. May–August 1987. Cited as CR.

Chŏnnong 2. See "Chwadam: Nongmin undong ŭi hyŏnsangt'ae wa chojikchŏk kwaje."

Christian Institute for the Study of Justice and Development. 1988. *Lost Victory: An Overview of the Korean People's Struggle for Democracy in 1987.* Seoul: Minjungsa.

"Chwadam: Nongmin undong ŭi hyŏnsangt'ae wa chojikchŏk kwaje" (Round Table: The Current Situation of Farmers' Movements and Organizational Challenges). 1990. *Chŏnnong* 2 (May): 9–27. Cited as Chŏnnong 2.

Citizens' Coalition for Economic Justice. 1994. "Person in CCEJ." *Civil Society* 1: 19.

Clark, Allen D., and Donald Clark. 1969. *Seoul, Past and Present: A Guide to Yi T'aejo's Capital.* Hollym Corporation.

Clark, Donald N. 1986. *Christianity in Modern Korea.* New York: Asia Society.

Clifford, James, and George E. Marcus, eds. 1986. *Writing Culture: The Poetics and Politics of Ethnography.* Berkeley, Los Angeles, and London: University of California Press.

CNCYCW. See Chŏn'guk Nongminhoe Ch'ong Yŏnmaeng Chunbi Wiwŏnhoe.

Commission of Theological Concerns of the Christian Conference of Asia, ed. 1981. *Minjung Theology.* London: Zed Press.

Cox, Harvey. 1995. "Shamans and Entrepreneurs: Primal Spirituality on the Pacific Rim." In Cox, *Fire from Heaven: The Rise of Pentecostal Spirituality and the Reshaping of Religion in the Twenty-first Century,* 213–241. New York: Addison-Wesley.

CR. See Chŏngŭp Court Record.

Cumings, Bruce. 1981. *The Origins of the Korean War: Liberation and the Emergence of Separate Regimes.* Princeton: Princeton University Press.

Daniel, E. Valentine. 1984. *Fluid Signs: Being a Person the Tamil Way.* Berkeley, Los Angeles, and London: University of California Press.

de Bary, Wm. Theodore. 1985. Introduction. In Wm. Theodore de Bary and Ja-Hyun Kim Haboush, eds., *The Rise of Neo-Confucianism in Korea,* 1–58. New York: Columbia University Press.

Deuchler, Martina. 1977. "The Tradition: Women During the Yi Dynasty." In Sandra Mattielli, ed., *Virtues in Conflict: Tradition and the Korean Woman Today,* 1–47. Seoul: Samhwa.

———. 1992. *The Confucian Transformation of Korea: A Study of Society and Ideology.* Cambridge, Mass.: Council on East Asian Studies, Harvard University.

Dong, Wonmo. 1987. "University Students in South Korean Politics: Patterns of Radicalization in the 1980s." *Journal of International Affairs* 40: 233–255.

Eckert, Carter. 1986. "The Colonial Origins of Korean Capitalism: The Koch'ang Kims and the Kyŏngsŏng Spinning and Weaving Company, 1876–1945." Ph.D. dissertation, University of Washington.

———. 1990. "The South Korean Bourgeoisie: A Class in Search of Hegemony." *Journal of Korean Studies* 7: 115–148.

Eckert, Carter, Ki-baik Lee, Young Ick Lew, Michael Robinson, and Edward W. Wagner. 1990. *Korea Old and New: A History.* Seoul: Ilchogak.

Epstein, Barbara. 1990. "Rethinking Social Movement Theory." *Socialist Review* 20: 35–65.

Escobar, Arturo. 1992a. "Culture, Economics, and Politics in Latin American Social Movements Theory and Research." In Escobar and Alvarez, eds., *The Making of Social Movements in Latin America: Identity, Strategy, and Democracy,* 62–88. Boulder, Colo.: Westview Press.

———. 1992b. "Imagining a Post-Development Era? Critical Thought, Development and Social Movements." *Social Text* 10: 20–56.

Escobar, Arturo, and Sonia E. Alvarez, eds. 1992a. *The Making of Social Movements in Latin America: Identity, Strategy, and Democracy.* Boulder, Colo.: Westview Press.

Escobar, Arturo, and Sonia E. Alvarez. 1992b. "Introduction: Theory and Protest in Latin America Today." In Escobar and Alvarez, eds., *The Making of Social Movements in Latin America: Identity, Strategy, and Democracy,* 1–15. Boulder, Colo.: Westview Press.

Fabian, Johannes. 1979. "The Anthropology of Religious Movements: From Explanation to Interpretation." *Social Research* 46: 4–35.

Fischer, Michael. 1986. "Ethnicity and the Post-Modern Arts of Memory." In James Clifford and George E. Marcus, eds., *Writing Culture,* 194–233. Berkeley, Los Angeles, and London: University of California Press.

Foucault, Michel. 1972. *The Archaeology of Knowledge and the Discourse on Language.* New York: Pantheon.

———. 1975. "Film and Popular Memory." *Radical Philosophy* 11: 24–29.

———. 1982. "The Subject and Power." In Hubert L. Dreyfus and Paul Rabinow, eds., *Michel Foucault: Beyond Structuralism and Hermeneutics,* 208–228. Chicago: University of Chicago Press.

Fox, Richard G. 1990. Introduction. In Fox, ed., *Nationalist Ideologies and the Production of National Cultures,* 1–14. Washington, D.C.: American Anthropological Association.

Gayn, Mark. 1981. *Japan Diary*. Rutland, Vt.: Charles E. Tuttle.

Gellner, Ernest. 1983. *Nations and Nationalism*. Oxford: Basil Blackwell.

Gragert, Edwin Harold. 1982. "Landownership Change in Korea under Japanese Rule, 1900–1935." Ph.D. dissertation, Columbia University.

Grajdanzev, Andrew J. 1944. *Modern Korea*. New York: John Day.

Gramsci, Antonio. 1971. *Selections from the Prison Notebooks of Antonio Gramsci*. Ed. and trans. Quintin Hoare and Geoffrey Nowell Smith. New York: International Publishers.

Grinker, Roy Richard. 1995. "The 'Real Enemy' of the Nation: Exhibiting North Korea at the Demilitarization Zone." *Museum Anthropology* 19(3).

Guha, Ranajit. 1987. "Some Aspects of the Historiography of Colonial India." In Guha, *Subaltern Studies: Writings on South Asian History and Society*, 1–8. Delhi: Oxford University Press.

Haboush, JaHyun. 1991. "Confucianization of Korean Society." In Gilbert Rozman, ed., *The East Asian Region: Confucian Heritage and Its Modern Adaptation*, 84–110. Princeton: Princeton University Press.

Hall, Stuart. 1985. "Signification, Representation, Ideology: Althusser and the Post-Structuralist Debates." *Critical Studies in Mass Communication* 12: 91–114.

———. 1988. *The Hard Road to Renewal*. London: Verso.

Halliday, Jon, and Bruce Cumings. 1988. *Korea: The Unknown War*. New York: Pantheon Books.

Hamkke hanŭn nongmin. 1989. "Hwangt'ohyŏn esŏ kŭmnaru kkaji" (From Hwangt'ohyŏn to kŭmnaru). (June): 77–81.

Han Do Hyun. 1989. "Kukka kwŏllyŏk ŭi nongmin t'ongje wa tongwŏn chŏngch'aek—Saemaŭl Undong ŭl chungsim ŭro" (State Power and the Policies of Farmer Control and Mobilization—Focusing on the Saemaŭl Movement). In Han'guk Nong-Ŏch'on Sahoe Yon'guso, ed., *Han'guk nongŏp nongmin munje yŏn'-guso*, 2:113–152.

Han, Sungjoo. 1978. "South Korea's Participation in the Vietnam Conflict: An Analysis of the U.S.–Korean Alliance." *Orbis* 21: 893–912.

Han'guk Kidok Haksaenghoe Ch'ong Yŏnmaeng (Korean Student Christian Federation). 1987. "Imdaech'a pŏp ŭi munjejŏm kwa sŏnggyŏk" (The Problems and Character of the Land Leasing Law). *Han'guk nongŏp kwa nongmin undong* (Korean Agriculture and Farmers' Movements). Cited as HKHCY.

Han'guk Kidok Haksaenghoe Yŏnmaeng (Korean Christian Student League). 1985. "Nongch'on hwaltong annaesŏ" (A Guide to *Nonghwal*). Cited as HKHY.

Han'guk Minjungsa Yŏn'guhoe (Research Group on Korean People's History). 1986. *Han'guk minjungsa* (The History of the Korean *Minjung*). Vol. 2. Seoul: P'ulpit. Cited as HMY.

Han'guk Nong-Ŏch'on Sahoe Yŏn'guso (Research Institute on the Society of Korean Farming and Fishing Villages). 1988. *Han'guk nongŏp nongmin munje yŏn'gu* (Research on Problems of Korean Agriculture and Farmers). Vol. 1. Seoul: Yŏn'-gusa.

———. 1989. *Han'guk nongŏp nongmin munje yŏn'gu*. (Research on Problems of Korean Agriculture and Farmers). Vol. 2. Seoul: Yŏn'gusa.

Han'guk Taehak Ch'ong Haksaenghoe Yŏnhap, Nong-hak Yŏndae Saŏpkuk. "93

Yŏrŭm nonghwal t'oron cheansŏ" (Discussion Proposals for 1993 Summer *Nonghwal*). 1–17. Cited as HTCHY.

HKHCY. See Han'guk Kidok Haksaenghoe Ch'ong Yŏnmaeng.

HKHY. Han'guk Kidok Haksaenghoe Yŏnmaeng.

HMY. See Han'guk Minjungsa Yŏn'guhoe.

Hobsbawm, Eric, and Terrence Ranger, eds. 1983. *The Invention of Tradition.* Cambridge: Cambridge University Press.

Hong, Doo-Seung. 1982. "Social Class and Perceptions of Life Chances." In Yunshik Chang, Tai-Hwan Kwon, and Peter J. Donaldson, eds., *Society in Transition, with Special Reference to Korea,* 67–78. Seoul: Seoul National University Press.

Hong Tŏng-nyul. 1985. "Han'guk chabon'ga kyegŭp ŭi sŏnggyŏk." In Kim Chingyun, ed., *Han'guk sahoe ŭi kyegŭp yŏn'gu,* 1:81–110. Seoul: Hanul.

HTCHY. See Han'guk Taehak Ch'ong Haksaenghoe Yŏnhap.

Hwang Chu-sŏk. 1994. "Tongne an e kukka ka itta" (The State Is in the Neighborhood). In Tto Hana ŭi Munhwa, ed., *Nae ka salgo sip'ŭn sesang: Sahoe undong kwa na* (The World I Want to Live In: Social Movements and Me), 70–87. Seoul: Tto Hana ŭi Munhwa.

Hwang Su-ch'ŏl. 1988. "Nongga puch'ae ŭi silt'ae wa nujŏk wŏnin" (The Current Situation and Causes of Accumulation of Farmer Household Debt). In Han'guk Nong-Ŏch'on Sahoe Yŏn'guso, ed., *Han'guk nongŏp nongmin munje yŏn'gu,* 1:431–466.

Hwang Yŏn-su. 1988. "*Tokchŏm chabon kwa nongsanmul kagyŏk munje*" (Monopoly Capitalism and the Agricultural Product Price Problem). In Han'guk Nong-Ŏch'on Sahoe Yŏn'guso, ed., *Han'guk nongŏp nongmin munje yŏn'gu,* 1:367–404.

Im Myŏng-jin. 1985. "'Non iyagi'" wa namŭn iyagi" (Things Left to Talk about *Non iyagi*). *Nammin* 1:190–208.

Im Yŏng-il. 1991. "Han'guk sahoe ŭi kibon kujo." (The Basic Structure of Korean Society). In Han'guk Sanŏp Sahoe Yŏn'guhoe, ed., *Han'guk sahoe wa chibae ideollogi,* 39–65. Seoul: Noktu.

Janelli, Roger, and Dawnhee Yim Janelli. 1982. *Ancestor Worship and Korean Society.* Stanford, Calif.: Stanford University Press.

Janelli, Roger, with Dawnhee Yim Janelli. 1993. *Making Capitalism: The Social and Cultural Construction of a South Korean Conglomerate.* Stanford, Calif.: Stanford University Press.

Kang Man-gil. 1985. "Sosŏl *T'oji* wa Han'guk kŭndaesa." (The Novel *T'oji* and Modern Korean History). In Kang, *Han'guk minjok undongsaron* (The Theory of the History of Korean National Movements), 325–341. Seoul: Han'gilsa.

Keim, Willard D. 1979. *The Korean Peasant at the Crossroads: A Study in Attitudes.* Bellingham: Western Washington University Center for East Asian Studies.

Kendall, Laurel. 1985. *Shamans, Housewives, and Other Restless Spirits: Women in Korean Ritual Life.* Honolulu: University of Hawaii Press.

———. 1988. *The Life and Hard Times of a Korean Shaman: Of Tales and the Telling of Tales.* Honolulu: University of Hawaii Press.

Kim Chi-ha. 1977. "A Declaration of Conscience." *Bulletin of Concerned Asian Scholars* 9: 8–15.

———. 1991. "Chŏlmŭn pottŭl! yŏksa esŏ muŏt ŭl paeunŭn'ga?" (Young Friends! What Are You Learning from History?). *Chosŏn Ilbo,* 5 May, 5.

————. 1993. "Ttang ŭn kŏruk hada" (Land Is Sacred). In Kim Chŏng-hŏn, ed., *Ttang ŭi kil, hŭk ŭi kil* (The Path of Land, the Path of Earth), 4–5. Seoul: Tosŏch'ulp'an Hakkoje.

Kim Chong-ch'ŏl. 1994. "Sinsedae wa yŏksa ŭi mulkil" (The New Generation and the Waterways of History). *Han'gyŏre 21*, 3 March, 112.

Kim Chong-gyu. 1988. *Han'guk kŭn-hyŏndaesa ŭi ideollogi* (Modern Korean Society's Ideology). Seoul: Nonjang.

Kim Chŏng-hŏn. 1993. "Ttang kwa hŭk ŭl kŭrimyŏnsŏ" (While Drawing Land and Earth) In Kim, *Ttang ŭi kil, hŭk ŭi kil* (The Path of Land, the Path of Earth), 12–16. Seoul: Tosŏch'ulp'an Hakkoje.

Kim, Choong Soon. 1992. *The Culture of Korean Industry: An Ethnography of Poongsan Corporation.* Tucson: University of Arizona Press.

Kim Dae Jung. 1987. *Prison Writings.* Berkeley, Los Angeles, and London: University of California Press.

Kim, Eun Mee. 1988. "From Dominance to Symbiosis: State and *Chaebol* in Korea." *Pacific Focus* 3: 105–121.

Kim, Kwang-ok. 1994. "Rituals of Resistance: The Manipulations of Shamanism in Contemporary Korea." In Charles F. Keyes, Laurel Kendall, and Helen Hardacre, eds., *Asian Visions of Authority: Religion and the Modern States of East and Southeast Asia*, 195–219. Honolulu: University of Hawaii Press.

Kim Hong-sang. 1988. "Nongch'on kongŏphwa chŏngch'aek ŭi ponjil kwa munjejŏm" (The Nature and Difficulties of the Industrialization Policy in Agricultural Villages). In Han'guk Nong-Ŏch'on Sahoe Yŏn'guso, ed., *Han'guk nongŏp nongmin munje yŏn'gu*, 1:405–427.

Kim Hun. 1994. "Ppyŏ ppajin 20-nyŏn, pit i 6-ch'ŏnman" (Twenty Years of Backbreaking Labor, debts ₩60,000,000). *Sisa Journal* (10 November): 34–35.

Kim Sang-hyŏng, ed. 1971. *Sudang Kim Yŏn-su.* Seoul: Kinyŏm Saŏphoe.

Kim Se-gyun. 1993. "Minjung undong ŭi hyŏnjejŏk wich'i wa chŏnmang" (The Contemporary Position and Prospects for *Minjung* Movements). *Iron* (Theory) 7: 102–139.

Kim, Seong Nae. 1989. "Lamentations of the Dead: The Historical Imagery of Violence on Cheju Island, South Korea." *Journal of Ritual Studies* 3: 251–285.

Kim, Seung-Kuk. 1988. "The Formation of Civil Society and the Rise of Regionalism in Korea." *Korea Journal* 28: 24–34.

Kim, Seung Kyung. 1990. "Capitalism, Patriarchy, and Autonomy: Women Factory Workers in the Korean Economic Miracle." Ph.D. dissertation, CUNY Graduate Center.

Kim Sun-mi. 1991. "P'och'ŏn-gun nongminhoe ŭi yŏrŭm 'nongch'on hwaltong' " (The "Summer Nonghwal" of the P'och'ŏn County Farmers Committee). *Chŏnnong* 3: 137–148.

Kim Tae-hwŏn. 1993. "Uri modu him ŭl moŭl ttae" (The Time Has Come for All of Us to Gather Our Strength). *Chŏn'guk nongmin sinmun* (National Farmers Newspaper), 1 September, 1.

Kim T'ae-il. 1989. "Han'guk nongch'on burak ŭi chibae kujo: Kukka 'kkŭnap'ul' chojik ŭi chibae" (The Structure of Rule of Korean Agricultural Villages: Rule by State "*kkŭnap'ul*" Organizations). In Han'guk Nong-Ŏch'on Sahoe Yŏn'guso, ed., *Han'guk nongŏp nongmin munje yŏn'gu*, 2:60–112.

Kim T'aek-kyu. 1964. *The Cultural Structure of a Consanguineous Village: A Survey on the Mode of the Life of Hahoe-dong, a Yangban Village* (Tongjok purak ŭi saenghwal kujo yôn'gu). Seoul: Ch'onggu.

Kim, Uchang. 1989. "The Agony of Cultural Construction: The State and Culture in Korea." Draft for a workshop, "State and Society in Contemporary Korea." Harvard University.

Kim, Yong-bock. 1981. "Messiah and *Minjung*: Discerning Messianic Politics Over Against Political Messianism." In Commission of Theological Concerns of the Christian Conference of Asia, ed., *Minjung Theology*, 183–194. London: Zed Press.

Kim Yong-sŏp. 1978. "Hanmal-ilcheha ŭi chijuje—sarye 4: Kobu Kimssiga ŭi chiju kyŏngyŏng kwa chabon chŏnhwan" (The Landlord System of the Late Yi Dynasty and Japanese Colonial Period—Case Study 4: Landlord Management and Capital Conversion in the Kobu Kim Family). *Han'guksa yŏn'gu* 19: 65–135.

Ko Sŏng-guk. 1993. "Han'guk sahoe kaehyŏk kwa sahoe undong ŭi kwaje" (Korean Social Reform and the Task of Social Movements). In Haksul Tanch'e Hyŏb-ŭihoe, ed., *Han'guk sahoe undong ŭi hyŏksin ŭl wihayŏ* (For the Reform of Social Movements), 227–249. Seoul: Paeksan Sŏdang.

Koh, Yeong Kyeong. 1962. "Land Reform and Agricultural Structure." *Korean Affairs* 1: 428–439.

Koo, Hagen. 1984. "The Political Economy of Income Distribution in South Korea: The Impact of the State's Industrialization Policies." *World Development* 12: 1029–1037.

———. 1987a. "The Emerging Class Order and Social Conflict in South Korea." *Pacific Focus* 2: 95–112.

———. 1987b. "Dependency Issues, Class Inequality, and Social Conflict in Korean Development." In Kyong-dong Kim, ed., *Dependency Issues in Korean Development*, 375–397. Seoul: Seoul National University Press.

Koryŭ Taehakkyo Nonch'on Hwaltong Chunbi Wiwŏnhoe. 1987. "87 nyŏn nong-ch'on hwaltong charyojip" (1987 Agricultural Action Resource Collection), 1–164. Cited as KTNHCW.

KTNHCW. See Koryŏ Taehakkyo Nongch'on Hwaltong Chunbi Wiwŏnhoe.

Lee, Chong Sik. 1977. *Materials on Korean Communism, 1945–1947*. Honolulu: Center for Korean Studies.

Lee, Eddy. 1979. "Egalitarian Peasant Farming and Rural Development: The Case of South Korea." *World Development* 7: 493–517.

Lee, Hoon K. 1936. *Land Utilization and Rural Economy in Korea*. Chicago: University of Chicago Press.

Lee Ki-baik, ed. 1984. *A New History of Korea*. Trans. Edward W. Wagner. Cambridge, Mass.: Harvard University Press.

Lie, John. 1992. "The Political Economy of South Korean Development." *International Sociology* 7: 285–300.

Marcus, George E. 1994. "What Comes (Just) After 'Post'? The Case of Ethnography." In Norman Denzin and Yvonna Lincoln, eds., *Handbook of Qualitative Research*, 563–574. London: Sage.

Mason, Edward S., Mahn Je Kim, Dwight H. Perkins, Kwang Suk Kim, and David

Cole, eds. 1980. *The Economic and Social Modernization of the Republic of Korea, Studies in the Modernization of the Republic of Korea: 1945–1975.* Cambridge, Mass.: Harvard University Press.

McGinn, Noel F., Donald R. Snodgrass, Yong Bong Kim, Shin-Bok Kim, and Young Kim. 1980. *Education and Development in Korea, Studies in the Modernization of the Republic of Korea: 1945–1975.* Cambridge, Mass.: Harvard University Press.

Melucci, Alberto. 1985. "The Symbolic Challenge of Contemporary Movements." *Social Research* 52: 789–816.

———. 1988. "Social Movements and the Democratization of Everyday Life." In John Deane, ed., *Civil Society and the State: New European Perspectives,* 245–260. London: Verso.

Minjok Kodae Ch'ong Haksaenghoe. "1994 Nonghwal charyojip" (94 Nonghwal Resource Collection). Cited as MKCH.

Mitchell, C. Clyde. 1952. "Land Reform in Asia, A Case Study." *Planning Pamphlets* 78: 1–34.

Mitchell, Timothy. 1988. *Colonizing Egypt.* Cambridge: Cambridge University Press.

MKCH. See Minjok Kodae Ch'ong Haksaenghoe.

Moon, Okpyo. 1990. "Urban Middle-Class Wives in Contemporary Korea: Their Roles, Responsibilities, and Dilemma." *Korea Journal* 30: 30–44.

Moore, Mick. 1984. "Mobilization and Disillusion in Rural Korea: The Saemaŭl Movement in Retrospect." *Pacific Affairs* 57: 577–598.

Mouffe, Chantal. 1988. "Hegemony and New Political Subjects: Toward a New Concept of Democracy." In Cary Nelson and Larry Grossberg, eds., *Marxism and the Interpretation of Culture,* 89–104. Urbana: University of Illinois Press.

Mun'gwadae nonghwal 2-ch'a tapsa pogosŏ (Second Agricultural Action Investigation Report of the College of Arts). 1987. Koryŏ University, June. Cited as SAAI.

Myers, Ramon H., and Yamada Saburō. 1984. "Agricultural Development in the Empire." In Myers and Saburō, eds., *The Japanese Colonial Empire, 1895–1945.* Princeton: Princeton University Press.

Nash, June. 1979. *We Eat the Mines and the Mines Eat Us: Dependency and Exploitation in Bolivian Tin Mines.* New York: New York University Press.

Nelson, Laura. 1994. "Gender, Nation, and the Politics of Consumption in South Korea." Conference on "Women in South Korea," University of British Columbia. Unpublished manuscript.

No Kŭm-no. 1986. *Ttang ŭi adŭl: Ŏnŭ nongmin undongga ŭi ssŭgi* (Son of the Earth: The Writings of One Farmer Activist). Vol. 1. Seoul: Tolbegae.

———. 1987. *Ttang ŭi adŭl: Ŏnŭ nongmin undongga ŭi ssŭgi* (Son of the Earth: The Diary of One Farmer Activist). Vol. 2. Seoul: Tolbegae.

———. 1989. "Hyŏndan'gye nongmin hyŏnsil kwa nongmin undong ŭi kwaje wa Panghyang" (The Reality of Farmers and the Process and Direction of Farmers' Movements at This Point in Time). In Han'guk Nong-Ŏch'on Sahoe Yŏn'guso, ed., *Han'guk nongŏp nongmin munje yŏn'gu,* 2:289–368.

Nora, Pierre. 1989. "Between Memory and History: Les Lieux de Mémoire." *Representations* 26: 7–25.

O Kŏn. 1985. "Chŏnbuk nongmin undong ŭi hyŏnhwang kwa kwaje" (The Current Situation and Processes of Farmers' Movements in North Chŏlla). *Nammin* 1:117–128.

Ogle, George E. 1990. *South Korea's Dissent within the Economic Miracle.* London: Zed Press.

Osgood, Cornelius. 1951. *The Koreans and Their Culture.* New York: Ronald Press.

Paek Uk-in. 1993*a.* "Taejung ŭi sam kwa han'guk sahoe pyŏnhwa ŭi yoch'e" (Transformations in the Life of the Masses and Korean Society). In Nara Chŏngch'aek Yŏn'guhoe, ed., *Han'guk sahoe undong ŭi hyŏksin ŭl wihayŏ* (For the Reform of Social Movements), 17–49. Seoul: Paeksan Sŏdang.

———. 1993*b.* "Siminjŏk kaehyŏk undong e taehan pip'anjŏk p'yongka: (A Critical Evaluation of Civil Reformist Movements). In Haksul Tanch'e Hyŏbŭihoe ed., *Han'guk minjujuŭi ŭi hyŏnjaejŏk kwaje: Chedo, kaehyŏk mit sahoe undong* (The Current Process of Korean Democracy: System, Reform, and Social Movements), 212–239. Seoul: Ch'angjak kwa Pip'yŏngsa.

Pak Chin-do. 1988. "*8.15 ihu han'guk nongŏp chŏngch'aek ŭi chŏn'gae kwajŏng*" (The Process of Development of Post 8.15 [1945] Korean Agricultural Policy). In Han'guk Nong-Ŏch'on Sahoe Yŏn'guso, ed., *Han'guk nongŏp nongmin munje yŏn'gu,* 1: 221–248.

Pak, Ki-hyuk and Sidney P. Gamble. 1975. *The Changing Korean Village.* Seoul: Shin-Hung Press.

Pak Kyŏng-ni. 1988. *T'oji* (Land). 9 vols. Seoul: Chisik Sanŏpsa.

Pak Myŏng-gyu. 1985. "Ilcheha chŏnbuk nongmin undong" (Colonial Period North Chŏlla Peasant Movements). In *Nammin* 1: 91–127.

Park Chung Hee. 1970. *Our Nation's Path: Ideology of Social Reconstruction.* Seoul: Hollym Corporation.

Plotke, David. 1990. "What's So New About New Social Movements?" *Socialist Review* 20: 81–102.

Popular Memory Group. 1982. "Popular Memory: Theory, Politics, Method." In Richard Johnson, Gregor McLennan, Bill Schwarz, and David Sutton, eds., *Making Histories: Studies in History-writing and Politics,* 205–252. London: Centre for Contemporary Cultural Studies.

Price, Richard. 1983. *First Time: The Historical Vision of an Afro-American People.* Baltimore: Johns Hopkins University Press.

Rofel, Lisa. 1994. "Liberation Nostalgia and a Yearning for Modernity." In Christina K. Gilmartin, Gail Hershatter, Lisa Rofel, and Tyrene White, eds., *Engendering China, Women, Culture and the State.* Cambridge: Harvard University Press.

Rorty, Richard. 1991. "The Professor and the Prophet." *Transition* 52: 70–78.

Rosaldo, Renato. 1980. *Ilongot Headhunting, 1883–1974: A Study in Society and History.* Stanford, Calif.: Stanford University Press.

———. 1989. *Culture and Truth: The Remaking of Social Analysis.* Boston: Beacon Press.

SAAI. See Mun'gwadae nonghwal 2-ch'a tapsa pogosŏ.

Sahlins, Marshall. 1985. *Islands of History.* Chicago: University of Chicago Press.

Samyang osimnyŏn (Samyang, Fifty Years). 1974. Seoul: CH Samyangsa. Cited as SY50.

Samyang Yŏmŏpsa. 1987. "*Samyangsa sojaktap yangdo ch'ujin undong e kwanhan chilŭi e taehan hoesin*" (The Response to Questions Concerning the Samyang Tenant Relinquish Committee). Seoul: n.p., 1–7. Cited as SYY.

Samyang yuksimnyŏn (Samyang, Sixty Years). 1985. Seoul: CH Samyangsa. Cited as SY60.

Sanjek, Roger. 1990. *Fieldnotes: The Making of Anthropology.* Ithaca: Cornell University Press.

Scalapino, Robert A., and Chong-Sik Lee. 1972. *Communism in Korea, Part I: The Movement.* Berkeley, Los Angeles, and London: University of California Press.

Scott, James C. 1985. *Weapons of the Weak: Everyday Forms of Peasant Resistance.* New Haven: Yale University Press.

Seremetakis, Nadia. 1991. *The Last Word: Women, Death, and Divination in Inner Mani.* Chicago: University of Chicago Press.

Shim Hun. 1986. *Sangnoksu.* Seoul: Pŏmjosa.

Shin, Gi-Wook. n.d. *Social Change and Peasant Protest in Modern Korea.* Seattle: University of Washington Press. Forthcoming.

Shin, Susan S. 1975. "Some Aspects of Landlord-Tenant Relations in the Yi Dynasty." *Occasional Papers on Korea* 3: 49–77.

———. 1978. "Economic Development and Social Mobility in Pre-Modern Korea: 1600–1860" (re: Kim Yong-sop's 1970 *Studies in the Agrarian History of the Later Chosŏn Period). Journal of Peasant Studies* 7: 187–197.

Sin, Yong-ha. 1978. "Landlordism in the Late Yi Dynasty." *Korea Journal* 1: 25–32, 2: 23–29.

Sorensen, Clark W. 1988. *Over the Mountains Are Mountains.* Seattle: University of Washington Press.

Starn, Orin. 1992. "'I Dreamed of Foxes and Hawks': Reflections on Peasant Protest, New Social Movements, and the *Rondas Campesinas* of Northern Peru." In Arturo Escobar and Sonia E. Alvarez, eds., *The Making of Social Movements in Latin America: Identity, Strategy, and Democracy,* 89–111. Boulder, Colo.: Westview Press.

Steinberg, David I. 1982. "Development Lessons from the Korean Experience—A Review Article." *Journal of Asian Studies* 42: 91–104.

Sterngold, James. 1992. "South Korea's Vietnam Veterans Begin to Be Heard." *New York Times,* 10 May, 6.

———. 1994. "New South Korean Movie Exposes Fears of North." *New York Times,* 17 September, 3.

Suh, Kwang-sun David. 1981. "A Biographical Sketch of an Asian Theological Consultation." In Commission of Theological Concerns of the Christian Conference of Asia, ed., *Minjung Theology,* 15–37. London: Zed Press.

Suh, Nam-dong. 1981a. "Historical References for a Theology of *Minjung.*" In Commission of Theological Concerns of the Christian Conference of Asia, ed., *Minjung Theology,* 155–182. London: Zed Press.

———. 1981b. "Towards a Theology of *Han.*" In Commission of Theological Concerns of the Christian Conference of Asia, ed., *Minjung Theology,* 55–72. London: Zed Press.

Suh, Sang-chul. 1978. *Growth and Structural Changes in the Korean Economy, 1910–1940.* Cambridge, Mass.: Harvard University Council on East Asian Studies.

Suk, Chin-Ha, and James L. Morrison. 1987. "South Korea's Participation in the Vietnam War: A Historiographical Essay." *Korea Observer* 18: 270–316.

SY50. See Samyang osimnyŏn.

SY60. See Samyang yuksimnyŏn.

SYY. See Samyang yŏmŏpsa.

Taehaksaeng Nongch'on Hwaltong (University Students Agricultural Action). 1986. *80-nyŏndae minjung ŭi sam kwa t'ujaeng yŏksa* (The History of the Fights and Struggle of the People in the 1980s), 406–427. Seoul: Pip'yŏngsa. Cited as TNH.

Taussig, Michael. 1989. "Terror as Usual: Walter Benjamin's Theory of History as a State of Siege." *Social Text: Theory/Culture/Ideology* 23: 3–20.

TNH. See Taehaksaeng Nongch'on Hwaltong.

Touraine, Alain. 1981. *The Voice and the Eye: An Analysis of Social Movements.* Cambridge: Cambridge University Press.

———. 1988. *The Return of the Actor.* Minneapolis: University of Minnesota Press.

Turner, Victor. 1974. "Hidalgo: History as Social Drama." In Turner, *Dramas, Fields and Metaphors: Symbolic Action in Human Society,* 98–155. Ithaca: Cornell University Press.

Visweswaren, Kamala. 1994. "Betrayal: An Analysis in Three Acts." In Inderpal Grewal and Caren Kaplan, eds., *Scattered Hegemonies,* 90–109. Minneapolis: University of Minnesota Press.

Wade, Richard. 1982. *Irrigation and Agricultural Politics in South Korea.* Boulder, Colo.: Westview Press.

———. 1983. "South Korea's Agricultural Development: The Myth of the Passive State." *Pacific Viewpoint* 24: 11–28.

Wales, Nym, and Kim San. 1941. *Song of Ariran: A Korean Communist in the Chinese Revolution.* San Francisco: Ramparts Press.

West, James, and Edward J. Baker. 1988. "The 1987 Constitutional Reforms in South Korea: Electoral Processes and Judicial Independence." *Harvard Law School Studies in East Asian Law, Korea* 2: 135–177.

Williams, Brackette F. 1990. "Nationalism, Traditionalism, and the Problem of Cultural Inauthenticity." In Richard G. Fox, ed., *Nationalist Ideologies and the Production of National Cultures,* 112–129. Washington, D.C.: American Anthropological Association.

Williams, Raymond. 1976. *Keywords.* New York: Oxford University Press.

———. 1977. *Marxism and Literature.* London: Oxford University Press.

Wolf, Margery. 1992. *A Thrice-Told Tale: Feminism, Postmodernism and Ethnographic Responsibility.* Stanford, Calif.: Stanford University Press.

Woo, Jung-en. 1991. *Race to the Swift: State and Finance in Korean Industrialization.* New York: Columbia University Press.

Yi U-jae. 1986. *Han'guk nongmin undongsa* (The History of Korean Farmers' Movements). Seoul: Hanul.

———. 1989. "8.15 chikhu nongmin undong yŏn'gu" (Research on Farmers' Movements Immediately after 8.15 1945). In *Han'guk nongmin munje yŏn'gu* (Research on Problems of Korean Agriculture and Farmers), 2:189–288. Seoul: Yŏn'gusa.

Yi Yŏng-gi. 1988. "Nongminch'ŭng punhae ŭi tonghyang kwa kyech'ŭng kusŏng" (The Disintegration of Farmer Classes and Their Class Composition). In Han'-guk Nong-Ŏch'on Sahoe Yŏn'guso, ed., *Han'guk nongŏp nongmin munje yŏn'gu,* 1:193–217.

Yoon, Jeong-Ro. 1989. "The State and Private Capital in Korea: The Political Economy of the Semiconductor Industry, 1965–1987." Ph.D. dissertation, Harvard University.

INDEX